ALSO BY MICHAEL W. HUDSON

Merchants of Misery:
How Corporate America Profits from Poverty
(editor)

The Monster

The Monster

How a Gang of Predatory Lenders

and Wall Street Bankers

Fleeced America—

and Spawned a Global Crisis

Michael W. Hudson

Times Books

Henry Holt and Company

New York

Times Books
Henry Holt and Company, LLC
Publishers since 1866
175 Fifth Avenue
New York, New York 10010

Henry Holt® is a registered trademark of Henry Holt and Company, LLC.

Library of Congress Cataloging-in-Publication Data

Hudson, Michael W.
    The monster : how a gang of predatory lenders and Wall Street bankers fleeced
America—and spawned a global crisis / Michael W. Hudson.—1st ed.
        p. cm.
    Includes bibliographical references and index.
    ISBN 978-0-8050-9046-8
    1. Subprime mortgage loans—United States.   2. Mortgage-backed securities—
United States.   3. Investment banking—Corrupt practices—United States.
4. Financial crises—United States.   5. Global Financial Crisis, 2008–2009.
I. Title.
    HG2040.5.U5H843 2010
    332.63'2440973—dc22   2010003223

First Edition 2010
Designed by Meryl Sussman Levavi

Printed in the United States of America
1   3   5   7   9   10   8   6   4   2

To anyone who's ever been broke,
busted, ripped off, cleaned out,
or drowning in debt

"Stuff happens."
        —ROLAND ARNALL, 1939–2008

Contents

The Monster

Introduction:
Bait and Switch

A few weeks after he started working at Ameriquest Mortgage, Mark Glover looked up from his cubicle and saw a coworker do something odd. The guy stood at his desk on the twenty-third floor of downtown Los Angeles's Union Bank Building. He placed two sheets of paper against the window. Then he used the light streaming through the window to trace something from one piece of paper to another. Somebody's signature.

Glover was new to the mortgage business. He was twenty-nine and hadn't held a steady job in years. But he wasn't stupid. He knew about financial sleight of hand—at that time, he had a check-fraud charge hanging over his head in the L.A. courthouse a few blocks away. Watching his coworker, Glover's first thought was: How can I get away with that? As a loan officer at Ameriquest, Glover worked on commission. He knew the only way to earn the six-figure income Ameriquest had promised him was to come up with tricks for pushing deals through the mortgage-financing pipeline that began with Ameriquest and extended through Wall Street's most respected investment houses.

Glover and the other twentysomethings who filled the sales force at the downtown L.A. branch worked the phones hour after hour, calling strangers and trying to talk them into refinancing their homes with high-priced "subprime" mortgages. It was 2003, subprime was on the rise, and Ameriquest was leading the way. The company's owner, Roland Arnall, had in many ways been the founding father of subprime, the business of lending money to home owners with modest incomes or blemished credit histories. He had pioneered this risky segment of the mortgage market amid the wreckage of the savings and loan disaster and helped transform his company's headquarters, Orange County, California, into the capital of the subprime industry. Now, with the housing market booming and Wall Street clamoring to invest in subprime, Ameriquest was growing with startling velocity.

Up and down the line, from loan officers to regional managers and vice presidents, Ameriquest's employees scrambled at the end of each month to push through as many loans as possible, to pad their monthly production numbers, boost their commissions, and meet Roland Arnall's expectations. Arnall was a man "obsessed with loan volume," former aides recalled, a mortgage entrepreneur who believed "volume solved all problems." Whenever an underling suggested a goal for loan production over a particular time span, Arnall's favorite reply was: "We can do twice that." Close to midnight Pacific time on the last business day of each month, the phone would ring at Arnall's home in Los Angeles's exclusive Holmby Hills neighborhood, a $30 million estate that once had been home to Sonny and Cher. On the other end of the telephone line, a vice president in Orange County would report the month's production numbers for his lending empire. Even as the totals grew to $3 billion or $6 billion or $7 billion a month—figures never before imagined in the subprime business— Arnall wasn't satisfied. He wanted more. "He would just try to make you stretch beyond what you thought possible," one former Ameriquest executive recalled. "Whatever you did, no matter how good you did, it wasn't good enough."

Inside Glover's branch, loan officers kept up with the demand to produce by guzzling Red Bull energy drinks, a favorite caffeine pick-me-up for hardworking salesmen throughout the mortgage industry. Government investigators would later joke that they could gauge how dirty a home-loan location was by the number of empty Red Bull cans in the Dumpster out back. Some of the crew in the L.A. branch, Glover said, also relied on cocaine to keep themselves going, snorting lines in washrooms and, on occasion, in their cubicles.

The wayward behavior didn't stop with drugs. Glover learned that his colleague's art work wasn't a matter of saving a borrower the hassle of coming in to supply a missed signature. The guy was forging borrowers' signatures on government-required disclosure forms, the ones that were supposed to help consumers understand how much cash they'd be getting out of the loan and how much they'd be paying in interest and fees. Ameriquest's deals were so overpriced and loaded with nasty surprises that getting customers to sign often required an elaborate web of psychological ploys, outright lies, and falsified papers. "Every closing that we had really was a bait and switch," a loan officer who worked for Ameriquest in Tampa, Florida, recalled. "'Cause you could never get them to the table if you were honest." At company-wide gatherings, Ameriquest's managers and sales reps loosened up with free alcohol and swapped tips for fooling borrowers and cooking up phony paperwork. What if a customer insisted he wanted a fixed-rate loan, but you could make more money by selling him an adjustable-rate one? No problem. Many Ameriquest salespeople learned to position a few fixed-rate loan documents at the top of the stack of paperwork to be signed by the borrower. They buried the real documents—the ones indicating the loan had an adjustable rate that would rocket upward in two or three years—near the bottom of the pile. Then, after the borrower had flipped from signature line to signature line, scribbling his consent across the entire stack, and gone home, it was easy enough to peel the fixed-rate documents off the top and throw them in the trash.

At the downtown L.A. branch, some of Glover's coworkers had a flair for creative documentation. They used scissors, tape, Wite-Out, and a photocopier to fabricate W-2s, the tax forms that indicate how much a wage earner makes each year. It was easy: Paste the name of a low-earning borrower onto a W-2 belonging to a higher-earning borrower and, like magic, a bad loan prospect suddenly looked much better. Workers in the branch equipped the office's break room with all the tools they needed to manufacture and manipulate official documents. They dubbed it the "Art Department."

At first, Glover thought the branch might be a rogue office struggling to keep up with the goals set by Ameriquest's headquarters. He discovered that wasn't the case when he transferred to the company's

Santa Monica branch. A few of his new colleagues invited him on a field trip to Staples, where everyone chipped in their own money to buy a state-of-the-art scanner-printer, a trusty piece of equipment that would allow them to do a better job of creating phony paperwork and trapping American home owners in a cycle of crushing debt.

* * *

Carolyn Pittman was an easy target. She'd dropped out of high school to go to work, and had never learned to read or write very well. She worked for decades as a nursing assistant. Her husband, Charlie, was a longshoreman. In 1993 she and Charlie borrowed $58,850 to buy a one-story, concrete block house on Irex Street in a working-class neighborhood of Atlantic Beach, a community of thirteen thousand near Jacksonville, Florida. Their mortgage was government-insured by the Federal Housing Administration, so they got a good deal on the loan. They paid about $500 a month on the FHA loan, including the money to cover their home insurance and property taxes.

Even after Charlie died in 1998, Pittman kept up with her house payments. But things were tough for her. Financial matters weren't something she knew much about. Charlie had always handled what little money they had. Her health wasn't good either. She had a heart attack in 2001, and was back and forth to hospitals with congestive heart failure and kidney problems.

Like many older black women who owned their homes but had modest incomes, Pittman was deluged almost every day, by mail and by phone, with sales pitches offering money to fix up her house or pay off her bills. A few months after her heart attack, a salesman from Ameriquest Mortgage's Coral Springs office caught her on the phone and assured her he could ease her worries. He said Ameriquest would help her out by lowering her interest rate and her monthly payments.

She signed the papers in August 2001. Only later did she discover that the loan wasn't what she'd been promised. Her interest rate jumped from a fixed 8.43 percent on the FHA loan to a variable rate that started at nearly 11 percent and could climb much higher. The loan was also packed with more than $7,000 in up-front fees, roughly 10 percent of the loan amount.

Pittman's mortgage payment climbed to $644 a month. Even worse, the new mortgage didn't include an escrow for real-estate taxes and insurance. Most mortgage agreements require home owners to pay a bit extra—often about $100 to $300 a month—which is set aside in an escrow account to cover these expenses. But many subprime lenders obscured the true costs of their loans by excluding the escrow from their deals, which made the monthly payments appear lower. Many borrowers didn't learn they had been tricked until they got a big bill for unpaid taxes or insurance a year down the road.

That was just the start of Pittman's mortgage problems. Her new mortgage was a matter of public record, and by taking out a loan from Ameriquest, she'd signaled to other subprime lenders that she was vulnerable—that she was financially unsophisticated and was struggling to pay an unaffordable loan. In 2003, she heard from one of Ameriquest's competitors, Long Beach Mortgage Company.

Pittman had no idea that Long Beach and Ameriquest shared the same corporate DNA. Roland Arnall's first subprime lender had been Long Beach Savings and Loan, a company he had morphed into Long Beach Mortgage. He had sold off most of Long Beach Mortgage in 1997, but hung on to a portion of the company that he rechristened Ameriquest. Though Long Beach and Ameriquest were no longer connected, both were still staffed with employees who had learned the business under Arnall.

A salesman from Long Beach Mortgage, Pittman said, told her that he could help her solve the problems created by her Ameriquest loan. Once again, she signed the papers. The new loan from Long Beach cost her thousands in up-front fees and boosted her mortgage payments to $672 a month.

Ameriquest reclaimed her as a customer less than a year later. A salesman from Ameriquest's Jacksonville branch got her on the phone in the spring of 2004. He promised, once again, that refinancing would lower her interest rate and her monthly payments. Pittman wasn't sure what to do. She knew she'd been burned before, but she desperately wanted to find a way to pay off the Long Beach loan and regain her financial bearings. She was still pondering whether to take the loan when two Ameriquest representatives appeared at the house on Irex Street. They brought a stack of documents with them. They told her, she later recalled, that it was preliminary paperwork, simply to get the process started. She could make up her mind later. The men said, "sign here," "sign here," "sign here," as they flipped through the stack. Pittman didn't understand these were final loan papers and her signatures were binding her to Ameriquest. "They just said sign some papers and we'll help you," she recalled.

To push the deal through and make it look better to investors on Wall Street, consumer attorneys later alleged, someone at Ameriquest falsified Pittman's income on the mortgage application. At best, she had an income of $1,600 a month—roughly $1,000 from Social Security and, when he could afford to pay, another $600 a month in rent from her son. Ameriquest's paperwork claimed she brought in more than twice that much—$3,700 a month.

The new deal left her with a house payment of $1,069 a month—nearly all of her monthly income and twice what she'd been paying on the FHA loan before Ameriquest and Long Beach hustled her through the series of refinancings. She was shocked when she realized she was required to pay more than $1,000 a month on her mortgage. "That broke my heart," she said.

For Ameriquest, the fact that Pittman couldn't afford the payments was of little consequence. Her loan was quickly pooled, with more than fifteen thousand other Ameriquest loans from around the country, into a $2.4 billion "mortgage-backed securities" deal known as Ameriquest Mortgage Securities, Inc. Mortgage Pass-Through Certificates 2004-R7. The deal had been put together by a trio of the world's largest investment banks: UBS, JPMorgan, and Citigroup. These banks oversaw the accounting wizardry that transformed Pittman's mortgage and thousands of other subprime loans into investments sought after by some of the world's biggest investors. Slices of 2004-R7 got snapped up by giants such as the insurer MassMutual and Legg Mason, a mutual fund manager with clients in more than seventy-five countries. Also among the buyers was the investment bank Morgan Stanley, which purchased some of the securities and placed them in its Limited Duration Investment Fund, mixing them with investments in General Mills, FedEx, JC Penney, Harley-Davidson, and other household names.

It was the new way of Wall Street. The loan on Carolyn Pittman's one-story house in Atlantic Beach was now part of the great global mortgage machine. It helped swell the portfolios of big-time speculators and middle-class investors looking to build a nest egg for retirement. And, in doing so, it helped fuel the mortgage empire that in 2004 produced $1.3 billion in profits for Roland Arnall.

* * *

In the first years of the twenty-first century, Ameriquest Mortgage unleashed an army of salespeople on America. They numbered in the thousands. They were young, hungry, and relentless in their drive to sell loans and earn big commissions. One Ameriquest manager summed things up in an e-mail to his sales force: "We are all here to make as much fucking money as possible. Bottom line. Nothing else matters." Home owners like Carolyn Pittman were caught up in Ameriquest's push to become the nation's biggest subprime lender.

The pressure to produce an ever-growing volume of loans came from the top. Executives at Ameriquest's home office in Orange County leaned on the regional and area managers; the regional and area managers leaned on the branch managers. And the branch managers leaned on the salesmen who worked the phones and hunted for borrowers willing to sign on to Ameriquest loans. Men usually ran things, and a frat-house mentality ruled, with plenty of partying and testosterone-fueled swagger. "It was like college, but with lots of money and power," Travis Paules, a former Ameriquest executive, said. Paules liked to hire strippers to reward his sales reps for working well after midnight to get loan deals processed during the end-of-the-month rush. At Ameriquest branches around the nation, loan officers worked ten- and twelve-hour days punctuated by "Power Hours"—do-or-die telemarketing sessions aimed at sniffing out borrowers and separating the real salesmen from the washouts. At the branch where Mark Bomchill worked in suburban Minneapolis, management expected Bomchill and other loan officers to make one hundred to two hundred sales calls a day. One manager, Bomchill said, prowled the aisles between desks like "a little Hitler," hounding salesmen to make more calls and sell more loans and bragging he hired and fired people so fast that one peon would be cleaning out his desk as his replacement came through the door. As with Mark Glover in Los Angeles, experience in the mortgage business wasn't a prerequisite for getting hired. Former employees said the company preferred to hire younger, inexperienced workers because it was easier to train them to do things the Ameriquest way. A former loan officer who worked for Ameriquest in Michigan described the company's business model this way: "People entrusting their entire home and everything they've worked for in their life to people who have just walked in off the street and don't know anything about mortgages and are trying to do anything they can to take advantage of them."

Ameriquest was not alone. Other companies, eager to get a piece of the market for high-profit loans, copied its methods, setting up shop in Orange County and helping to transform the county into the Silicon Valley of subprime lending. With big investors willing to pay top dollar for assets backed by this new breed of mortgages, the push to make more and more loans reached a frenzy among the county's subprime loan shops. "The atmosphere was like this giant cocaine party you see on TV," said Sylvia Vega-Sutfin, who worked as an account executive at BNC Mortgage, a fast-growing operation headquartered in Orange County just down the Costa Mesa Freeway from Ameriquest's headquarters. "It was like this giant rush of urgency." One manager told Vega-Sutfin and her coworkers that there was no turning back; he had no choice but to push for mind-blowing production numbers. "I have to close thirty loans a month," he said, "because that's what my family's lifestyle demands."

Michelle Seymour, one of Vega-Sutfin's colleagues, spotted her first suspect loan days after she began working as a mortgage underwriter at BNC's Sacramento branch in early 2005. The documents in the file indicated the borrower was making a six-figure salary coordinating dances at a Mexican restaurant. All the numbers on the borrower's W-2 tax form ended in zeros—an unlikely happenstance—and the Social Security and tax bite didn't match the borrower's income. When

Seymour complained to a manager, she said, he was blasé, telling her, "It takes a lot to have a loan declined."

BNC was no fly-by-night operation. It was owned by one of Wall Street's most storied investment banks, Lehman Brothers. The bank had made a big bet on housing and mortgages, styling itself as a player in commercial real estate and, especially, subprime lending. "In the mortgage business, we used to say, 'All roads lead to Lehman,'" one industry veteran recalled. Lehman had bought a stake in BNC in 2000 and had taken full ownership in 2004, figuring it could earn even more money in the subprime business by cutting out the middleman. Wall Street bankers and investors flocked to the loans produced by BNC, Ameriquest, and other subprime operators; the steep fees and interest rates extracted from borrowers allowed the bankers to charge fat commissions for packaging the securities and provided generous yields for investors who purchased them. Up front fees on subprime loans totaled thousands of dollars. Interest rates often started out deceptively low—perhaps at 7 or 8 percent—but they almost always adjusted upward, rising to 10 percent, 12 percent, and beyond. When their rates spiked, borrowers' monthly payments increased, too, often climbing by hundreds of dollars. Borrowers who tried to escape overpriced loans by refinancing into another mortgage usually found themselves paying thousands of dollars more in backend fees— "prepayment penalties" that punished them for paying off their loans early. Millions of these loans—tied to modest homes in places like Atlantic Beach, Florida; Saginaw, Michigan; and East San Jose, California—helped generate great fortunes for financiers and investors. They also helped lay America's economy low and sparked a worldwide financial crisis.

The subprime market did not cause the U.S. and global financial meltdowns by itself. Other varieties of home loans and a host of arcane financial innovations—such as collateralized debt obligations and credit default swaps—also came into play. Nevertheless, subprime played a central role in the debacle. It served as an early proving ground for financial engineers who sold investors and regulators alike on the idea that it was possible, through accounting alchemy, to turn risky assets into "Triple-A-rated" securities that were nearly as safe as government bonds. In turn, financial wizards making bets with CDOs and credit default swaps used subprime mortgages as the raw material for their speculations. Subprime, as one market watcher said, was "the leading edge of a financial hurricane."

* * *

This book tells the story of the rise and fall of subprime by chronicling the rise and fall of two corporate empires: Ameriquest and Lehman Brothers. It is a story about the melding of two financial cultures separated by a continent: Orange County and Wall Street.

Ameriquest and its strongest competitors in subprime had their roots in Orange County, a sunny land of beauty and wealth that has a history as a breeding ground for white-collar crime: boiler rooms, S&L frauds, real-estate swindles. That history made it an ideal setting for launching the subprime industry, which grew in large measure thanks to bait-and-switch salesmanship and garden-variety deception. By the height of the nation's mortgage boom, Orange County was home to four of the nation's six biggest subprime lenders. Together, these four lenders—Ameriquest, Option One, Fremont Investment & Loan, and New Century—accounted for nearly a third of the subprime market. Other subprime shops, too, sprung up throughout the county, many of them started by former employees of Ameriquest and its corporate forebears, Long Beach Savings and Long Beach Mortgage.

Lehman Brothers was, of course, one of the most important institutions on Wall Street, a firm with a rich history dating to before the Civil War. Under its pugnacious CEO, Richard Fuld, Lehman helped bankroll many of the nation's shadiest subprime lenders, including Ameriquest. "Lehman never saw a subprime lender they didn't like," one consumer lawyer who fought the industry's abuses said. Lehman and other Wall Street powers provided the financial backing and sheen of respectability that transformed subprime from a tiny corner of the mortgage market into an economic behemoth capable of triggering the worst economic crisis since the Great Depression.

A long list of mortgage entrepreneurs and Wall Street bankers cultivated the tactics that fueled subprime's growth and its collapse, and a succession of politicians and regulators looked the other way as abuses flourished and the nation lurched toward disaster: Angelo Mozilo and Countrywide Financial; Bear Stearns, Washington Mutual, Wells Fargo; Alan Greenspan and the Federal Reserve; and many more. Still, no Wall Street firm did more than Lehman to create the subprime monster. And no figure or institution did more to bring subprime's abuses to life across the nation than Roland Arnall and Ameriquest.

Among his employees, subprime's founding father was feared and admired. He was a figure of rumor and speculation, a mysterious billionaire with a rags-to-riches backstory, a hardscrabble street vendor who reinvented himself as a big-time real-estate developer, a corporate titan, a friend to many of the nation's most powerful elected leaders. He was a man driven, according to some who knew him, by a desire to conquer and dominate. "Roland could be the biggest bastard in the world and the most charming guy in the world," said one executive who worked for Arnall in subprime's early days. "And it could be minutes apart." He displayed his charm to people who had the power to help him or hurt him. He cultivated friendships with politicians as well as civil rights advocates and antipoverty crusaders who might be hostile to the unconventional loans his companies sold in minority and working-class neighborhoods. Many people who knew him saw him as a visionary, a humanitarian, a friend to the needy. "Roland was one of the most generous people I have ever met," a former business partner said. He also left behind, as another former associate put it, "a trail of bodies"—a succession of employees, friends, relatives, and business partners who said he had betrayed them. In summing up his own split with Arnall, his best friend and longtime business partner said, "I was screwed." Another former colleague, a man who helped Arnall give birth to the modern subprime mortgage industry, said: "Deep down inside he was a good man. But he had an evil side. When he pulled that out, it was bad. He could be extremely cruel." When they parted ways, he said, Arnall hadn't paid him all the money he was owed. But, he noted, Arnall hadn't cheated him as badly as he could have. "He fucked me. But within reason."

Roland Arnall built a company that became a household name, but shunned the limelight for himself. The business partner who said

Arnall had "screwed" him recalled that Arnall fancied himself a puppet master who manipulated great wealth and controlled a network of confederates to perform his bidding. Another former business associate, an underling who admired him, explained that Arnall worked to ingratiate himself to fair-lending activists for a simple reason: "You can take that straight out of *The Godfather*: 'Keep your enemies close.'"

1. Godfather

In his early years as a businessman, Roland Arnall didn't give much thought to the home-loan business. He was a real-estate developer. He preferred big deals that measured in the tens of millions: shopping centers, apartment complexes, commercial loans. As the owner of a savings and loan in the 1980s, he channeled his institution's deposits into his own real-estate projects and loans to fellow developers. By the middle of the decade, however, Arnall could no longer insulate his Los Angeles County–based operation, Long Beach Savings and Loan, from the fallout of the S&L debacle. As bad loans on shopping malls and high-rises pushed many S&Ls into insolvency, regulators began placing limits on how much money the institutions could risk on large commercial investments. The regulators pushed Arnall to diversify Long Beach's holdings.

Arnall complained that the bureaucrats didn't understand how things worked in the real world. "He hated the regulators," one former aide recalled. "He couldn't understand their constant meddling in his affairs." Arnall knew, though, that he needed to get them off his back. He hired an employment consultant to find someone to start a home-mortgage division at Long Beach Savings. The headhunter got in touch with Mark Schuerman, a banking consultant in Orange County. Schuerman had a long résumé in the lending business. His father had run a small consumer-finance company in Indiana. In the 1970s,

Schuerman himself had worked for Advance Mortgage, Citibank's mortgage banking division.

Over lunch, Arnall asked Schuerman if he would be willing to run a residential mortgage operation for Long Beach Savings, making first mortgages to borrowers with good credit. Arnall said all the right things: he would leave Schuerman alone to run his own shop. Schuerman could have an open checkbook to spend whatever it took to make the business take off. Schuerman could have a five-year contract and a piece of the action; if the mortgage division did well, Schuerman would do well, too. Schuerman liked Arnall. He was smart, engaging, persuasive. But one thing worried Schuerman: Arnall's zeal for growth. Arnall seemed a bit like a child, unable to understand that some things take time. "How soon can we get to a billion dollars a month?" Arnall prodded. Schuerman was taken aback. Citibank, the nation's biggest mortgage lender, was doing barely $1.1 billion a month in home-loan volume. To think that a start-up lender could quickly get to that level was foolhardy, Schuerman thought. He could see that, if he went to work for Long Beach, Arnall was going to "have a foot up my ass every day."

Soon after, Schuerman phoned Arnall to tell him he was interested in the job, but he couldn't expand the new division as fast as Arnall wanted and still do things right. "I don't work miracles. I do loans. We can grow it, but we've got to have a foundation." Schuerman wasn't going to risk his reputation by pushing growth too far, too fast. In the mortgage business, he knew, this would be a recipe for disaster. Lenders that lowered their standards in an effort to grow quickly often ended up with sizeable losses from loan delinquencies and fore-closures.

Arnall backed off. Of course, he said, he wanted to build a solid base before ratcheting up loan volume. He invited Schuerman to meet again, and they worked out a deal. As they made plans to get started, Arnall readily agreed to Schuerman's proposal that they base the home-loan division in Orange County rather than Long Beach. The location Schuerman picked, Town and Country Road in the city of Orange, was just off the Orange Crush, the interchange that brought together the Santa Ana, Garden Grove, and Orange freeways, not far from John Wayne Airport. It was a short commute for Schuerman from his home in Riverside County, avoiding the traffic snarls for which Los Angeles was famous. It was a good place to locate the new division, too, because the nearby Orange County towns of Garden Grove and Anaheim, as well as neighboring Riverside County, were relatively low-cost places to live—making it easy to recruit mortgage talent, particularly the office support staffers necessary to start up the business.

In September 1986, Schuerman began work at Long Beach Savings. He was excited about the challenge, but he and Arnall soon realized their timing was off. By the summer of 1987, it was becoming clear that it was a bad time to be offering conventional "A-credit" mortgage loans. There were too many big, established players in the market, and price wars had driven profit margins into the ground. Long Beach's home-loan division struggled to stay above water.

Schuerman met Arnall for lunch at Arnall's members-only dining establishment in Los Angeles, the Regency Club, in the summer of 1987. They agreed something had to change. Schuerman suggested they convert the mortgage division into a consumer lender focused on second mortgages to people with modest incomes or weak credit histories. Arnall was surprised to learn that Schuerman had some experience selling second mortgages from his time working at Citibank. But he loved the idea. As always, he wanted to move fast. How soon, he wanted to know, could they open fifty branch offices?

* * *

When it came to building his businesses, Roland Arnall was always in a hurry. He had gotten his start as an entrepreneur as a teenaged immigrant, selling eggs door-to-door in his adopted hometown of Los Angeles. How Southern California came to be his home was a story of war, survival, and exodus. He was the son of Eastern European Jews—his mother, a nurse, was Czech and his father, a tailor, was Romanian, from Transylvania. The couple had moved to Paris in the late 1920s. As precondition to marriage, she had insisted he get rid of his Austrian-Hungarian accent. It was a difficult task, but he managed it. His father's success in shedding his accent "saved our lives," the son later recalled, because it allowed the family to avoid scrutiny during World War II.

Roland was born in Paris on March 29, 1939. With the German invasion, the Arnalls fled the capital and took refuge in a village in southern France, Pont-les-Bains. Like many French Jews during the war, the Arnalls avoided detection by the Nazis and their collaborators by hiding their identities and living as Catholics. One story had Roland becoming an altar boy, or at least dressing as one. Roland didn't learn he was Jewish until after the end of the war, when he was eight or nine years old. His mother told him she wanted him to learn Hebrew and explained why. Most of his relations, he learned, had died in the Holocaust. "The next day," he recalled, "I had my first major fight at school. The boys accused me of having killed Christ."

He was twelve when his family moved to Montreal in the early 1950s. The Arnalls tried to enter the United States but couldn't get visas. After five years in Canada, they tried again, choosing California as their destination. "My father returned from a family visit to Beverly Hills. He said he had found the place to live. A place where there were no poor people," Arnall said more than a half century later.

After the family settled in Los Angeles, Roland began his business selling eggs door-to-door. Then he enlisted his younger brother, Claude, and switched to peddling flowers on street corners. Soon, he expanded, hiring employees to do the selling for him and buying a truck to keep his vendors supplied. Arnall used the profits from his flower business to buy his first home. Then he sold the house and funneled those profits into buying investment property. By his late twenties, he'd established himself as a real-estate developer, a young man with a distinct accent, oversized dark-rimmed glasses, and an air of earnestness. He soon discovered that, in Los Angeles, real estate and politics were inseparable. If you wanted to get something done—win a zoning variance, speed up permits, snag a piece of land with untapped potential—you needed friends in positions of power.

Arnall made it his mission to cultivate ties with local politicians. One of them was Art Snyder, a former Los Angeles City Council staffer who had been elected to a council seat in 1967. Snyder was part Irish and part German, a red-haired, red-faced political scrapper whose blue-collar demeanor helped him win a surprising number of votes in the Latino precincts of his east side district. In the decades to come, Snyder would become known as one of the city's slickest operators, with government ethics watchdogs accusing him of hiding cash he had pocketed from a city contractor and later, as a lobbyist, of creating an elaborate money-laundering system to conceal the source of local campaign donations. Snyder's relationship with Arnall produced an early controversy in the politician's life, as well as a taste of unflattering publicity for the young developer. In 1968, Snyder began pushing a $6 million housing project proposed by Arnall and his development firm, REA Companies. (REA stood for "Roland E. Arnall.") Arnall wanted to build five hundred homes on land he had bought from the city. Snyder said the project would provide much-needed low-cost housing.

Arnall was the only bidder on the tract. He paid $75,000 for thirty acres. To some, it smelled like a sweetheart deal. Opponents of the project suggested Snyder backed it because Arnall had contributed $1,000 to his campaign. Anthony Rios, a community activist who'd built Latino political clout in Los Angeles, feared the project wouldn't help low-income people at all, but instead squeeze them out of the area by pushing up rents. Rios said he had learned Arnall was negotiating with Prudential Insurance Company to finance the project, and Prudential had been secretly promised a zoning change that would make the land more lucrative. As the debate flared, a council member opposed to the deal shouted, in Hollywood style, "You don't want the truth!"

Arnall's financing and the zoning change fell through, and, after putting down a $7,500 deposit, he stiffed the city for the rest of what he owed on the raw land. When city officials pointed out his delinquency, he explained that he had always intended to pay; he'd simply "goofed" and misread the due date for the outstanding balance on the purchase price. He wrote a check for what he owed.

Six months later, though, Snyder went back to the city council and reopened the controversy. He asked the city to take the land back. Now that his construction plans had run aground, Arnall had creditors breathing down his neck. The land was useless to him and he needed the money. Council members bickered anew over this latest wrinkle. Then they rejected Snyder's plea to bail Arnall out.

* * *

The failed housing venture didn't slow Arnall down. Real estate, he knew, is a gambler's game. The best players understand that reversals of fortune are a fact of life for any developer, and the best way to weather such misadventures is to play with other people's money. "Real-estate development is a function of the availability of money. And the availability of money is a function of the stupidity of lenders," one builder in Atlanta, Georgia, told Martin Mayer, the dean of American business writers, in the late 1970s. Developers are always hungry for more financing and bigger deals; pulling back after a stumble is rarely an option. "If there's money available, they'll build and develop whether there's a need for it or not," a former Arnall business associate said. Maintaining an illusion of success and clout is crucial to keeping the money flowing and enduring the ups and downs.

Throughout the '70s, Arnall lived a double life. He ate in the best restaurants, lived in Los Angeles's prosperous Hancock Park neighborhood, courted the city's power brokers. He spread money among many of California's top Democrats. He was friendly with the city's trailblazing African-American mayor, Tom Bradley. He supported Governor Edmund G. "Jerry" Brown Jr.'s reelection with a $25,000 loan. All the while, Arnall was fighting to stay afloat, flirting with bankruptcy and borrowing money to keep his business solvent. For a time, Arnall teamed with Beverly Hills Bancorp, with the bank providing the financing and Arnall scouting for the land and putting the deals together. In 1974, the bank filed for bankruptcy, under pressure from federal securities cops and investors who claimed it had defaulted on obligations. Arnall and REA Companies weren't part of the investigation, but the bank's fall left him without a reliable funding partner. He came close to losing everything. He recovered, as he often did, by coaxing more loans out of friends and associates. One friend who provided last-ditch loans recalled that Arnall nearly went under three or four times in those years.

As the decade came to a close, Arnall decided to change his fortunes. He filed an application to open an S&L, Long Beach Savings and Loan. At the dawn of the Reagan era, it was relatively easy to open an S&L, or "thrift" as they were often called. S&Ls had their origins as building and loan societies founded to help average folks achieve the dream of home ownership. For much of their history, they distinguished themselves from banks by accepting savings deposits and providing home mortgages but not offering checking accounts or making business loans. In theory, at least, they were supposed to be the kind of community-based and community-minded institutions immortalized by Jimmy Stewart's role as George Bailey, president of the Bailey Building and Loan, in *It's a Wonderful Life*.

The seeds of the destruction of the old building and loan model had been planted in the 1960s. Congress had tried to limit the interest rates that thrifts charged home owners in a roundabout manner, by limiting how much interest they paid to their depositors. If S&Ls didn't have to pay high rates to their depositors, the thinking went, they wouldn't charge high rates to their borrowers. By the late '70s, painfully steep inflation had outstripped what S&Ls could pay depositors, and 85 percent of S&Ls were losing money. The Carter administration and the Democratic Congress decided to save the industry by throwing out the rule book. This meant not just phasing out the limits on the interest rates that institutions could pay their depositors, but also eliminating a wide variety of other regulations that had governed the industry. State governments also got into the deregulatory spirit, competing with one another in offering the lowest barriers to entry for founding S&Ls as well as the most lenient oversight once institutions were established. This shredding of financial regulation gained speed after Ronald Reagan took office in 1981. When he signed an S&L deregulation bill into law in the White House Rose Garden in 1982, Reagan quipped, "All in all, I think we hit the jackpot."

The new rules allowed S&Ls to invest heavily in shopping malls, high-rises, and other speculative projects and to bankroll real-estate deals that did not require down payments from the borrowers. The rules also made it possible for a single investor to own an S&L. What's more, budding S&L impresarios didn't need to pony up much money as start-up capital; instead, they could list "non-cash" assets as evidence that they had the capital cushion to operate in a stable manner. This allowed entrepreneurs to use undeveloped land to capitalize new thrifts. Lots of developers joined Arnall in the rush into the thrift business, especially in California, where lax regulations made it ridiculously easy to obtain an S&L charter. Consultants and law firms made money by offering seminars on how to open a savings and loan, including one titled, "Why Does It Seem Everyone Is Buying or Starting a California S&L?" The new breed of S&L proprietors plowed money into all manner of investments: junk bonds, hotels, mushroom ranches, windmill farms, tanning beds, Arabian horses.

Long Beach Savings took chances, bankrolling Arnall's real-estate deals, including strip malls and larger shopping centers. Arnall even tried to put together a chain of car washes, but got out of car-wash franchising after realizing it was rife with corruption; as a cash-only business, it was easy for on-site managers to skim away most of the profits. A car-wash operator shocked one of Arnall's aides, Bob Labrador, by unlocking the trunk of his Cadillac and revealing boxes piled high with loose cash. Arnall had no interest in putting himself in a position that allowed others to filch profits from him.

Long Beach's biggest business was making large commercial loans to other entrepreneurs. Commercial real-estate loans are usually riskier than single-family home loans. Arnall, though, had an advantage over most existing S&L operators. Those companies were financial institutions trying to make it big in what, to them, was a new endeavor, commercial real estate. Long Beach Savings, on the other hand, was more like a development company masquerading as an S&L. Commercial real estate was the world Arnall knew. He loved to drive around L.A. in his Jaguar and point out the various projects he'd built or refurbished. With a few exceptions, Long Beach Savings did a good job of picking the projects it agreed to finance. Arnall and his staff agonized over which loans to make in the thrift's early years.

Sometimes, Arnall used his S&L's commercial lending program to get control of other developers' projects. He'd identify a project that needed an infusion of credit, for expansion or to fix cash-flow problems. He'd come in as a money partner, forming a joint loan venture. If he saw an opening—such as a cost overrun—he'd put the screws to his partner and take over the project for himself. Tom Tarter, a Southern California banker who got to know Arnall in the early '80s, learned about Arnall's modus operandi through contacts in the L.A. business community, including one friend who had received such treatment. Arnall's strategy was confirmed by Bob Labrador, an executive at Long Beach around that time. "It wasn't done in a very overt way—you wouldn't know it unless you were a fly on a wall," Labrador recalled. "I learned over time how he operated. . . . He wasn't like a vicious shark about it. He just continually worked it to his advantage, until he had the upper hand."

A lawsuit filed in the 1980s in Los Angeles Superior Court claimed Arnall took his hard-nosed approach toward business associates even further. Six of Arnall's partners in an investment deal charged that he had stolen money from them through "intentional fraud." Arnall had formed Victory Square Ltd., to buy a multitenant office building in Los Angeles. The aggrieved partners asserted that Arnall and another investor played a financial shell game that spirited away $165,000 belonging to the partnership. Arnall's collaborator, the suit alleged, purchased the property from its owner in early 1982, then sold it at a quick markup to Victory Square, violating his fiduciary duty to the other partners. In court papers, Arnall's attorneys said the allegations were baseless. A judge or jury didn't get a chance to decide who was in the right; the case was settled on confidential terms in 1987. However it ended, the charges were an early example of what would become a pattern in Arnall's business career: a deal was struck, Arnall profited, and the other people involved came forward to claim that Arnall and his allies had used shifty tactics to squeeze them out of money.

* * *

For generations, mortgages had been a plain vanilla business. People took out mortgages to purchase homes, borrowing at fixed interest rates over a fixed numbers of years. They looked forward to the day when they had paid off their mortgages and owned their homes free and clear. Some families held mortgage-burning parties after they'd made the final payment on their house notes. The idea of borrowing against the family homestead—taking cash out with a second mortgage—was considered vaguely disreputable, an act of desperation or irresponsibility. "The second mortgage category . . . suffered from a pretty bad reputation," one credit marketing executive recalled. "It generally tended to be a credit facility of last resort, and was done by people in dire straits."

During the Reagan years, the financial industry set out to change that mind-set and remake the mortgage industry in the bargain. Banks and S&Ls inundated American home owners with junk mail and print advertisements. "Don't sit on your equity," one ad said. "Turn it into cash with our home equity loan." Another ad depicted a couple, beaming in front of their home. The caption: "We just discovered $50,000 hidden in our house!" Marketing executives at Citicorp and its competitors worked to obscure the stigma carried by second mortgages. Home owners were encouraged to use the extra cash to cover their children's college tuition or take their dream vacations. "Calling it a 'second mortgage,' that's like hocking your house," a former Citicorp executive recalled. "But call it 'equity access,' and that sounds more innocent."

Citicorp and other banks generally marketed these home-equity products to white, middle-class home owners with good credit histories. Black and Latino home owners tended to get snubbed, regardless of their incomes or credit records. There were few bank branches located in minority neighborhoods, and for several decades entire neighborhoods had been deemed too risky for lending, a practice known as "redlining." This legacy of discrimination meant that blacks and Latinos often had trouble finding banks willing to lend them money.

That vacuum was filled by the forerunners of subprime, a collection of downscale consumer-finance companies and "hard-money" mortgage lenders that were happy to troll for customers with weak credit or humble incomes. The companies loaned money at steep prices to home owners who had few other options. The hard-money shops were the ultimate lenders of last resort. To them, one thing mattered: How much equity had the borrower built up in the property? Credit history and income didn't much matter. As long as there was a cushion of equity, the lender would make the loan, secure that if the borrower fell behind, it could foreclose, resell the property, and make a profit—or at least break even. Even in a period of high interest rates—mortgage rates soared well above 10 percent at the start of the '80s, and clung just below 10 percent as the decade ended—hard-money lenders' prices were eye-popping. It wasn't unusual for them to charge 20 up-front points in fees and costs on top of 20 percent interest; mortgage industry hands joked that these were 20/20 mortgages, "perfect vision loans."

One of the most insatiable of the hard money sharks, Virginia-based Landbank Equity Corporation, promoted its loans through the persona of "Miss Cash." "When banks say 'No,' Miss Cash says 'Yes.'" That "yes" came with a steep price. Landbank charged an average of 29 percent in origination and processing fees. Two sisters from Salem, Virginia, paid $3,750 in up-front charges to borrow $7,500. The tactics used by Landbank and similar hard-money lenders went a long way toward explaining why, over the course of the '80s, foreclosure rates tripled nationwide.

Consumer-finance companies weren't quite as pricey as hard-money lenders. A home loan at one of the national consumer-finance chains, such as Household Finance, ITT Financial, or Transamerica Financial, might carry 10 up-front points on top of interest rates of 15 to 18 percent. Such price tags allowed the lenders to say, with a straight face, that they were doing customers a favor: they were providing a lower-cost alternative to the hard-money crowd.

Consumer-finance companies had traditionally focused on making small personal loans. By the '80s they had moved into the home-equity market, often using small loans to fish for borrowers who could be cajoled into taking out larger loans using their homes as collateral. A customer might come into a storefront office and borrow $300 to cover some medical bills. Or she might buy a washing machine on credit from a retailer, which then sold the loan contract to the consumer-finance company. Either way, the finance company peppered these new customers with offers for more money. The idea was to convert short-term borrowers into lifetime customers—to keep people continually in debt by getting them to take out a new loan before they had paid off the balance on the old one. After rolling over customers' small-scale loans a few times, the finance company often talked them into transferring the escalating debt into a new mortgage against their homes. One industry analyst dubbed this process "moving up the food chain." Consumer lawyers who spent their days suing the companies had another name for this process of serial refinancings packed with high up-front fees: "loan flipping."

Consumer-finance companies and hard-money lenders could do much as they pleased, because, by the early '80s, state and federal lawmakers had thrown out the restrictions on the kinds of loans mortgage lenders could offer and the prices they could charge. This deregulation had been propelled, in part, by the big banks' campaign to make home-equity lending respectable. "Borrowers at finance companies are now learning that 'deregulation' really means the door is open for abuse," the majority leader of the Wisconsin state senate told the *Wall Street Journal* in 1985. Many consumer-finance companies became sink-or-swim pressure cookers for employees. Senior managers were constantly on the phone, berating branch managers: Where's your volume? Why are your collections down? An executive at ITT Financial liked to rank the branches he oversaw by production of new loans. The manager of the top branch for the month won accolades and a bonus. The manager of the lowest-producing was required to keep a lump of rubber dog shit on his desk for the next month, to remind him of his poor performance. The only way to get the offending dollop off his desk was to sell more loans.

Doing whatever it took to book loans became part of the culture at some finance companies. The nation's biggest consumer-finance operations—ITT, Household, and Transamerica—set aside millions to settle class-action lawsuits accusing them of cheating borrowers. In Arizona, a judge scolded Transamerica for trying to throw a seventy-seven-year-old widow out of the home her late husband had helped her build forty-two years before. Lennie Williams, a retired house cleaner, was getting by on $438 a month. Her mind was failing her, and she got snookered into signing up for a mortgage that obligated her to pay Transamerica $499 a month. The loan carried 8 points in up-front charges and an interest rate of nearly 18 percent. The mortgage salesman who put together the deal later testified he didn't think

Williams understood the loan, but he had said as little as possible about the details because he didn't want to lose the sale.

"I didn't want to bring up the fact that we could foreclose on your home. People don't want to hear this," he explained. "When you close a loan, you try to get through with it. You say everything you have to say and no more."

∗   ∗   ∗

Mark Schuerman was aware of the unsavory practices of the hard-money lenders and consumer-finance companies as he steered Roland Arnall's S&L into the low-end mortgage business in the last months of 1987. He knew the pitfalls and temptations of the game. He wanted, he said, to create an organization in which employees didn't feel pressured to cut corners to meet unreasonable sales goals.

Schuerman was an easygoing man with a dry wit. He wasn't the kind of executive who managed by yelling and belittling. "To me, it's fun and challenging to get people to do what you want and feel good about it," he told a reporter during his days at Long Beach. "In fact, it's the only way I know for a guy like me—who doesn't have any musical talent—to get a chance to lead an orchestra."

To build his staff, he hired a couple of fellow Midwesterners, Bob Dubrish and Pat Rank, as his top aides. Both were experienced consumer-finance hands. They'd worked together at ITT Financial. Dubrish had played tight end in the University of Illinois's powerhouse football program. He was tall, likeable, and soft-spoken, a savvy manager and a good salesman. Rank was tall, hardworking, and sharp-tongued. Rank, Schuerman learned, said what he thought, and he was usually right.

Schuerman and his lieutenants decided the best way to put together a staff for Arnall's new enterprise was to raid established consumer-finance companies. They targeted Transamerica, knowing its branch managers weren't paid well and got a lot of abuse from higher-ups. Long Beach identified a group of branch managers who were willing to make the jump. They agreed to resign from Transamerica en masse. Arnall decided to celebrate. He threw a dinner for the new hires a night or so before the date appointed for the defections. After he got some drinks into them, Arnall circled the room, asking what each hireling's goal would be for loan volume in his new post at Long Beach. The liquor had loosened their tongues, and several offered optimistic figures for what they could produce. Each time somebody gave a number, though, Arnall scoffed. "We can do twice that," he said.

On the agreed-upon day, only one of the bunch quit to join Long Beach. The others changed their minds. Perhaps, Schuerman thought, Transamerica had caught wind of the jailbreak and persuaded them to stay by offering raises and promotions. Or maybe there was another reason: Arnall had scared them away. They were used to the pressure to produce, but they'd never encountered anything like Roland Arnall's hunger for loan volume.

No matter. Long Beach kept working to tempt folks to leave. Eventually the bank hired perhaps fifty employees away from Transamerica. The math was simple. Branch managers at Transamerica were making $35,000 to $40,000 a year. Long Beach could pay them more than that to start and, given its bonus structure, could give them a chance to eventually triple what they'd been making at their old jobs. Long Beach was so successful in its recruiting incursions that Transamerica's lawyers began to send threatening letters.

* * *

The second-mortgage business took off. It performed so well that the S&L ran out of cash to bankroll its home loans. The nest egg created by customers' savings deposits simply wasn't big enough. There was only one thing to do: go to Wall Street.

The solution to Long Beach's problem was an investment banking innovation called "securitization." Mortgages could be pooled together, and then bonds, known as "mortgage-backed securities," would be sold to investors. The income stream from borrowers' monthly payments underpinned the bonds. Investors paid cash up front to purchase the securities, which gave them the right to get back the money they had put up as well as healthy interest payments.

For mortgage lenders, securitization provided a means for turning long-term mortgages into quick profits. Instead of having to wait around for home owners to make their mortgage payments month by month, year by year, lenders could immediately turn the loans into cash by selling the loans for use in securities deals. The rapid turnaround allowed lenders without much capital of their own to make more loans and dramatically increase their volume of lending. Before securitization, lenders had either held on to their loans, collecting the payments until the home owners owned their houses free and clear, or sold them one by one or in groups on the "secondary market" to investors, who took over the right to collect on the loans. This tended to limit the ability of lenders to increase their loan volume. They either had to entice customers to deposit savings in the bank to bankroll loans, or they had to go through the paperwork-heavy process of selling loans on the secondary market.

The attraction for investors was twofold. First, pooling thousands of loans into a mortgage-backed securities deal provided a cushion against the impact of borrower defaults. If some borrowers didn't pay, the income stream from other loans in the pool would cover the losses from the loans that had gone bad. Second, securitization decreased information costs for investors. By pooling mortgages and having ratings agencies affix a grade to the securities, investors could get a prediction of expected returns without having to investigate whether each borrower or each lender was on the up-and-up.

Mortgage-backed securities had first emerged in the 1970s, under the aegis of Ginnie Mae and Fannie Mae, two government-sponsored enterprises created to increase home ownership. Then Salomon Brothers, the Wall Street firm immortalized in Michael Lewis's *Liar's Poker*, got into the act. It created the first private mortgage-backed securities deal in 1977, helping Bank of America pool together a portion of its home mortgages. In 1978, Salomon opened Wall Street's first mortgage securities department. In 1983, Salomon invented a new kind of mortgage-backed security that not only bundled together mortgages but also sliced and diced them into "tranches" (French for "slice") that carried varying levels of risk. The riskier the slice, the greater return investors could expect, to compensate them for the greater chance of borrower defaults and other factors that might prevent them from getting repaid with interest. Tranches allowed investors to calibrate the level of risk and reward they wanted.

By the late '80s, a growing number of Wall Street firms were securitizing conventional mortgages—those taken out as first mortgages by borrowers with good credit. There was also a small market for securities based on second mortgages, which generally went to borrowers who were considered higher risks—the kind of loans that Long Beach Savings had begun making after the conventional mortgage business had proven to be a disappointment.

Long Beach did a small securitization with Drexel Burnham Lambert, the hard-charging investment bank best known as home base for junk-bond king Michael Milken, but then moved its business to Greenwich Capital, an investment bank that had established a Wall Street beachhead in a leafy Connecticut suburb a train ride north of Manhattan. Greenwich pooled Long Beach's newly minted second mortgages into a series of deals that helped the S&L keep its residential mortgage volume on an upward arc.

Despite its burgeoning home-loan business, Long Beach was getting heat from regulators. Its assets included hundreds of millions in raw land and commercial real estate, the kinds of investments that were causing big problems at other S&Ls. Long Beach's second-mortgage business wasn't yet big enough to balance its mix of assets. To keep the feds happy, Long Beach needed *more* home mortgages. It achieved this by approaching another S&L, Orange County's Guardian Savings and Loan, and suggesting a trade: some of Long Beach's commercial loans in exchange for some of the residential mortgages that Guardian had originated.

At year's end, 1987, Schuerman, Rank, and Dubrish headed over to Huntington Beach to take a look at the home loans that Guardian was offering to swap.

2. Golden State

G uardian Savings and Loan was owned by Russ and Becky Jedinak. By vocation, Russ was a salesman, not a banker. He had started his career as a pharmaceutical rep for American Home Products, climbing to national sales manager by the age of twenty-three. He soon shifted to real estate and began building homes and other projects around Orange County. He was tall and handsome and competed in marathons. He married and divorced four times. He flew his own four-seater jet. He lived in the Bahamas and sailed his yacht through the Panama Canal. His fifth wife, Becky, became his bookkeeper and business partner. Becky was the hands-on manager: tough, beautiful, vigilant over every detail. She kept Guardian running, with an eye on the bottom line. He dreamed the dreams and made the deals. "He wanted to be the biggest, richest person in the world," one former business associate said. "Russ was classic frat boy; teeth, grins, and handshakes," another recalled. "After that you ended up talking to Becky, who was very attractive but had the warmth of a porcupine." She liked to say, "I worry about the pennies, and the dollars take care of themselves."

Like Roland Arnall, the Jedinaks started their S&L in the early '80s in order to finance real-estate development plans. That changed when they hired Jude Lopez, an experienced hand in the Southern California lending business. Lopez suggested they get into hard money, making first mortgages that refinanced borrowers' existing home loans. But

Lopez had a caution: they should expect to foreclose on a significant number of borrowers, and end up with a large portfolio of "real estate owned" properties—homes the S&L would itself own once the borrowers could no longer keep up with their payments. "You're going to end up with forty REO properties on your books," Lopez told Russ Jedinak. "These people have a habit of not paying their bills. You're basically making a loan based on the value of the property alone."

Russ knew real estate, so he asked: What would the LTVs be? LTV stood for "loan-to-value" ratio. If you had a $65,000 mortgage on a $100,000 home, the LTV would be 65 percent.

Lopez assured Russ they would never lend more than 70 percent of a home's value, and the average would be closer to 65 percent. Russ could live with that. If a borrower defaulted, there would be enough equity in the home for Guardian to claw back its money. Soon Russ was living by this maxim: "If they have a house, if the owner has a pulse, we'll give them a loan."

Guardian sniffed out borrowers through independent brokers, who made the first contact with home owners, put together their loan applications, and steered them to the S&L. Some brokers were so pleased with the generous fees they collected on the deals that they dropped other lenders and funneled all of their clients to Guardian. Lopez personally approved each loan. He made sure the appraisals were accurate and the LTVs were low. After the mortgages were made, Guardian maintained a tough collections policy: if the borrower fell one month behind on payments, the lender filed for foreclosure. "You have to be aggressive—put the hammer down early," Lopez said. "In this kind of business, if you get three months behind it's difficult to catch up." One mortgage broker recalled: "Russ had no problem taking back the property. He was quite okay with that." In its first full year, Guardian's mortgage-lending program foreclosed on twenty-four properties. The S&L was able to sell the bunch for a $400,000 profit, Lopez said.

One day in 1987, Guardian got a visit from Wall Street. Russ had bought an apartment complex in Galveston, Texas, and arranged with Michael Milken's firm, Drexel Burnham Lambert, to sell some bonds backed by the property. Drexel specialized in "junk" bonds, unpredictable investments in which there was a high chance that the issuer would default. Investors expected higher interest to compensate them for taking on that additional risk. When Drexel bankers came to Orange County to discuss the apartment deal, Russ Jedinak introduced them to Lopez, who showed them the home loans Guardian was making. The bankers, always on the lookout for ways to put their creative financing skills to use, told Jedinak and Lopez they could put together a mortgage-backed bond deal with Guardian's high-interest loans.

* * *

Mark Schuerman and the other Long Beachers began sifting through loan files at Guardian's headquarters in December 1987, looking for home-loan deals they'd be willing to take as part of the residential-mortgages-for-commercial-mortgages swap they'd arranged with Guardian. After they'd looked at perhaps a hundred files, something began to dawn on them: these were really good loans, with lots of profit built into the fees and interest rates and, through the magic of securitization, an efficient way of extracting that profit.

It was a lightbulb moment. "This is it," Schuerman thought. Booking first mortgages instead of second mortgages was an important part of the equation. First mortgages required little more time or cost to originate, but they produced much bigger loan volumes. Why make $30,000 or $40,000 loans when you could be making loans for $200,000? Guardian targeted home owners who had fixed-rate, finance-company loans with interest rates of 14 to 18 percent, and put them in adjustable-rate mortgages with an initial six-month teaser of 11.5 percent. Those loans could earn 5 or 6 percentage points over Treasury securities, the standard measuring stick for most investments. Investors who bought bonds backed by Guardian's loans were willing to take 1.5 points over Treasuries. And Guardian could take the rest, 4 or 5 points per loan. Schuerman could see that a well-run lender could make three or four times the profits on these sorts of first mortgages than it could on second mortgages.

"That's a lot of money, man," Schuerman recalled. "You do a one-hundred-million-dollar deal, you make five million dollars." Plus, the millions rolled in year after year, as borrowers continued to make payments on their mortgages. Russ Jedinak had stumbled onto something new, a melding of creative home lending and Wall Street financing, the essence of the subprime mortgage business. "He's the guy that started the business," Schuerman said. "He's a footnote, but he's the guy."

It was such a good idea that Long Beach Savings did what any self-respecting competitor would do: it stole the idea for itself. Schuerman, Rank, and Dubrish let Arnall know they had uncovered a new business model. "Great," Arnall said. "Start tomorrow."

Arnall wasn't a deep thinker. Schuerman was convinced Arnall never read a single piece of paper given to him. He acted from his gut. The result, in terms of dollars and cents, was a history of magnificent blunders and magnificent triumphs. Trusting Schuerman and the other Long Beachers to move into first mortgages was one of his brilliant calls. From this moment, Arnall was set on the path to build an empire. If Russ Jedinak thought big, Arnall thought bigger, and he had the brains and guile to make his aspirations a reality.

In those days, nobody used the term "subprime." Long Beach called its loans "B-firsts." This made it clear they were first mortgages and distinguished them from "A-loans," which were for borrowers with good credit. B-firsts were expensive, but they were cheaper than the loans peddled by hard-money lenders. Schuerman and his team saw the loans as the equivalent of a "fixer-upper": home owners who'd hit a financial bump could pay off their bills, improve their credit record, and then, after a couple of years, refinance into a cheaper loan. "These were good people who for some reason in their lives had had one or two bad falls," Bob Labrador, the former Long Beach executive, recalled. "They had real jobs and you could document their income. . . . Mark felt he did a service to deserving people."

* * *

Arnall mostly left Schuerman, Dubrish, and Rank alone to run the mortgage operations. He worked in Los Angeles while Schuerman oversaw things down in Orange County. Still, managers and workers in the mortgage unit felt Arnall's impatience, the boss's hunger to grow. "He never cared how you got the volume and where it came from and what you had to do to get it," Dennis Rivelli, a former Long Beach manager, recalled. "He could care less. Just pump it out and move on."

Rank ran the quality-control side of the business. He instituted checks and balances to ensure bad loans didn't get through. Borrowers' incomes had to be verified and property appraisals had to be accurate. Long Beach had a crack staff of review appraisers who rechecked appraisals as the loans came in the door. Arnall didn't see the point. "I don't think we need all these appraisers," he told Schuerman.

The internal quality-control watchdogs were caught between Arnall at the top and the sales force below. The salespeople were men and women who'd mostly learned the loan business at Transamerica and other rough-and-ready consumer-finance shops. The watchdogs fought a constant battle to maintain standards, to rein in the aggressive instincts of the salespeople who made money by booking as many loans as possible. "You tell a consumer finance kind of group to get volume, they'll get volume," Schuerman recalled. The key was to encourage the salespeople to produce, but not to cut corners by falsifying loan paperwork or putting borrowers into loans they couldn't afford. "I don't care about volume," Rank told Rivelli. "I can sleep at night if I can say I funded loans that made sense."

Each month, as the numbers grew bigger, Arnall threw a celebration to mark the new record. Then he'd tell Schuerman and the rest that the record was now their floor; they had to beat it the next month. Arnall never asked Schuerman to do anything that was wrong. But Arnall, Schuerman decided, didn't understand the "consumer finance code," the idea that you had to calibrate your loan originations by taking market conditions and loan performance into account. There were periods when it made sense to "throw out the rule book," loosening lending guidelines and pumping up the volume. But you had to be prepared to dial things back, get more conservative, and cut back on volume, as market conditions declined or loan defaults started ticking upward.

✳ ✳ ✳

Even if it could never meet Arnall's uncompromising expectations, the mortgage unit did post some impressive numbers, hitting $90 million a month in mortgage volume within its first three years of making B-firsts. Long Beach was especially good at wooing the mortgage brokers who brought in the loans. It courted brokers with golf outings and coached them on the new push for B-loans. Brokers were used to the dowdy A-loans market, a cookie cutter business where the prices were uniform and borrowers either qualified or didn't. B-loans were more labor-intensive because the borrowers' credit histories tended to be messier. Long Beach promised brokers they could make higher fees and, once they got the hang of it, turn the deals around quickly. "We made those promises," Labrador said. "We lived up to those promises. The brokers fell in love with us."

Long Beach had another asset in its campaign to woo brokers: a platoon of women who worked as wholesale loan reps. They were smart, they worked hard, and they were, by all accounts, beautiful—so gorgeous they became known as "The Killer B's," a squad of knockouts who flirted and cajoled, persuading goo-goo-eyed male brokers to put their clients into one of the various "B-loan" programs that Long Beach offered for credit-challenged home owners. Long Beachers bragged their company had "good prices, good programs, and beautiful women." "They could get into the door. Every male broker wanted to talk to them," said James Gartland, who worked as a mortgage broker in Orange County in the late '80s. "At the same time, they were disarming enough to talk to women."

The women and men on Long Beach's sales staff dressed well, partied hard, and drove expensive cars. They were the vanguard of a new mortgage industry. The business was, at that moment, being transformed from a slow-moving world of bean counters and sober middle managers who got paid to tell borrowers "no" as often as they said "yes" to a domain of salesmen and deal makers. It was not a coincidence that the new mortgage culture grew up in Orange County, a land where "cowboy capitalists" and get-rich-quick schemers had long held sway.

* * *

In the early hours of January 16, 1987, Duayne "Doc" Christensen died in a one-car crash on Orange County's Corona del Mar Freeway. His Jaguar veered off the highway and slammed into an eight-foot-wide bridge pylon. Family, friends, and famous well-wishers packed Christensen's memorial service. Robert Goulet sang Christensen's favorite song, "Send in the Clowns." Televangelist Robert Schuller, who'd built Orange County's acclaimed Crystal Cathedral, paid his respects. A pastor from Schuller's ministry asked the mourners to withhold judgment of the deceased: "Forgive him for not being as much as we wanted him to be."

Christensen's death laid bare what authorities called one of the most audacious insider bank fraud schemes in memory. Christensen and a companion, Janet Faye McKinzie, siphoned some $40 million out of his S&L, Santa Ana's North America Savings and Loan, through a series of elaborate ruses involving faked documents and shell companies.

Christensen's death may not have been an accident. Regulators were preparing for a government takeover of his S&L, an event he certainly knew would lead to the exposure of his crimes. Police found no skid marks indicating he had braked, and the angle of the crash suggested the car had been steered into the abutment rather than simply running off the road. Some who knew Christensen, though, suspected he'd faked his death and was sitting in the sun sipping drinks on some tropical isle.

A few months after Christensen slammed his car into the highway wall, an enterprising writer for *Forbes* magazine traveled to Southern California and reported that the "American Riviera" of coastal Orange County had surpassed Florida and the New York–New Jersey megalopolis as home to the nation's largest collection of boiler rooms. Beehives of telephone salesmen worked out of office buildings in Newport Beach and around John Wayne Airport, cold-calling unsuspecting marks and persuading them to fork over money for illusory investments. At least one hundred boiler rooms in the county flogged gold, platinum, and other precious metals. Others peddled coins, gems, oil partnerships, and artichoke ranches.

Boiler-room telephone operations got their name because, in their early years, they saved on rent and hid from authorities by tucking themselves in basements and boiler rooms. The designation stuck because the idea of heat is central to boiler-room culture—a telephone operation was said to run at "full burn" when every phone station was manned by a salesman, and they generated "heat" when the salesmen were doing their jobs with urgency, working the phones and riffing effectively on their scripted sales pitch. "It's a numbers game," one longtime boiler-room salesman explained. "Make enough calls, and you sooner or later get the deals." It was the same spirit that a generation later would infuse the mortgage boiler rooms run by Orange County's subprime lenders.

In the spring of 1987, five dozen local and federal cops raided three closely tied boiler rooms in Orange County that authorities alleged were selling bogus investments in gold and other precious metals under the names World Equity Mint, Associated Miners Group, and Liberty Mint and Mint Management. An informant identified in court papers only as "George Washington" said the companies pulled in up to one hundred thousand dollars a week. Half went to operating expenses, the informant said, and the rest went to supporting the owner's extravagant lifestyle as well as to building the stash "he hides in anticipation of police investigation."

As Ronald Reagan's second term neared its end, Orange County had established itself as a hotbed not only for boiler rooms and S&L shell games, but for real-estate swindles and mail fraud as well. U.S. postal inspectors called the county "the fraud capital of the world." Near the height of the S&L crisis, *Orange County Register* columnist Jonathan Lansner observed that his newspaper was publishing articles about local business fraud "at a pace of just under one a day." "Some days," he said, "it seems that more Orange County business deals are discussed in court rooms than in board rooms." One local private detective who specialized in investigating shady real-estate contracts told *Forbes*: "I've worked cases where the lender loaned money to people who didn't exist, who bought houses from people who didn't exist, whose documents were notarized by people who didn't exist. In one case there were only two true facts: There was a house and a savings account. The savings account had 40 signers and only one was a real person."

* * *

It wasn't hard to understand why Orange County had become fertile ground for boiler rooms and other white-collar misconduct. Long before TV shows such as *The OC* and *The Real Housewives of Orange County* introduced Middle America to the region's exotic mélange of beaches, mega-malls, and bustling plastic surgery practices, Orange County embodied the high life. It was sunny and manicured—scrubbed clean of the kind of gray film that covers many urban areas in the Midwest and Northeast. "You don't hear much about unusual concentrations of fraud in Green Bay or Buffalo," *Wall Street Journal* writer Hal Lancaster noted in an essay on the county's mixture of glitz and snake oil. "Con men hate snow." Besides, if you've had some legal scrapes back east, it's easier to begin anew in a fast-growing place where many people are strangers to each other and, in absence of a tradition of "old money," nobody asks where your wealth comes from, no matter how much you flaunt it. Lancaster visited Newport Beach's swanky Fashion Island Shopping Center in the late '80s, eyeballing the seaside community's "tanned and elegant ladies" as they stepped out of their Mercedes-Benzes and BMWs and inspected the designer offerings at Neiman Marcus and Bullocks Wilshire. "In the squat office buildings that ring Fashion Island," he noted, "the odds are good that someone is getting fleeced. Law-enforcement authorities say that at any given time, a host of fraudulent telemarketing operations mingle with the many legitimate businesses here." As one postal inspector told Lancaster: "They seem to like these industrial parks. We call them fraud farms."

People with an expansive definition of free enterprise found a welcoming home in Orange County. The county had grown from barely 130,000 souls at the start of World War II to a population of more than two million in the '80s. It was, as one scholar put it, "a modern-day version of the California gold rush—making Orange County the new frontier West of the second half of the twentieth century." The rush was led by a tight group of ranchers-turned-developers, real-estate speculators, and prosperity-gospel evangelists who championed individual uplift and disdained government interference in the marketplace. Given the county's history and culture, it's no wonder that more than a few locals came to the conclusion that a bit of entrepreneurial derring-do wasn't a bad thing. "Many of these people got too much power and money too soon," one Newport Beach psychotherapist told *Forbes*. "Their moral and ethical codes haven't caught up."

That was a description that could certainly fit Doc Christensen. The son of Seventh-Day Adventists, Christensen considered a career as a minister, but instead became a dentist. After a while, his interest in dentistry waned; he spent much of his time thinking up ways to make money. He began to offer investing seminars to physicians. He opened a mortgage company, and soon he was the target of lawsuits accusing him of mortgage fraud. That didn't prevent him from getting a license to operate an S&L, however. He had pulled together a few million dollars to capitalize the venture and brought in an experienced banker to serve as the front man. That was enough to satisfy the regulators, who issued Christensen a license to open North America Savings in 1982.

He met Janet McKinzie a year later. Both of their marriages were rocky. He was wealthy, educated, and handsome, a fit six-footer "with a lopsided grin that made him look much younger than his fifty-three years." She was thirty-three, slender, with "almost white, baby fine hair." She had grown up in poverty and was determined never to be poor again. She was a hard-driving real-estate agent who was so high strung, one friend recalled, that she carried a big jar of Excedrin, popping the pain reliever constantly. Christensen tried to help her relax by prescribing her a hodgepodge of powerful antianxiety drugs, including Xanax, Halcion, and lithium.

Christensen hired McKinzie as a "consultant," and over the next four years the two turned the S&L into their personal cash box. McKinzie flew back and forth between Southern and Northern California on a Lear jet paid for by North America Savings. She spent money with lavish obsession, blowing $750,000 on shopping sprees at the Neiman Marcus in Newport Beach. Her $165,000 Rolls-Royce Corniche sported the personalized license plate "XTACI."

Christensen and McKinzie milked the S&L by plowing its money into a variety of deals in which they had hidden interests, in one instance, authorities alleged, designating McKinzie's hair dresser as the president of one of the front companies they controlled. In another instance, North America Savings paid less than $4 million for a condo project in Lake Tahoe, Nevada, then sold it back and forth between the S&L and front companies to artificially inflate its value to $40 million.

Not long before his car wreck, Christensen took out a $10 million insurance policy and made McKinzie the beneficiary. It was little comfort for McKinzie. With Christensen dead, she was left to take the rap. When her case came to trial, the best her attorney, Richard "Racehorse" Haynes, could do for a defense was to claim she was too strung out on prescription drugs to pull off such an elaborate swindle. Haynes said Christensen used the pills to control McKinzie, turning her into a "washed-out zombie." This defense was undermined by evidence that McKinzie had orchestrated a cover-up. She ended one note coaching a business associate how to lie to investigators with the instruction, "P.S. Please destroy after reading." A judge sentenced her to twenty years in prison. She was one of more than a thousand S&L insiders nationwide convicted of felonies.

In the midst of the S&L crisis, U.S. attorney general Richard Thornburgh wondered whether the debacle might be "the biggest white-collar crime swindle in the history of our nation." Thornburgh, who had gained a reputation as a corporate crime fighter when he was a prosecutor in Pittsburgh, had been appointed to run the Justice Department to help improve the image of the scandal-prone Reagan administration. He stayed on under the new president, George H. W. Bush, and vowed to punish the executives whose crimes had helped destroy the S&L industry. Thornburgh focused a large part of his agency's investigative muscle on the seven-county region of Southern

California dominated by Orange and Los Angeles counties. During a congressional hearing, he explained that no less than 76 percent of the 21,714 allegations of insider abuse at S&Ls that had been reported to his department came from the region. In Orange County alone, twenty-seven S&Ls failed, at a cost of more than $10 billion to taxpayers, more than twice the amount that had been set aside in the insurance fund that was supposed to cover S&L failures across the entire United States, and a lopsided share, for a single county, of the $124 billion that American taxpayers eventually shelled out to clean up the S&L mess nationwide.

One street corner in Irvine, in the heart of Orange County, accounted for $8.4 billion of the losses. Charles Keating's Lincoln Savings and Loan and Charles Knapp's American Savings and Loan were headquartered across the street from each other at Von Karman Avenue and Michelson Drive. Lincoln's failure cost taxpayers $2.66 billion. The collapse of American Savings cost $5.75 billion, more than any other thrift failure.

Both Keating and Knapp went to jail for S&L-related felonies, but it was Keating who, with a little help from Wall Street, became the poster boy for S&L criminality. Keating had been a champion swimmer and navy fighter pilot. As a lawyer and businessman in Cincinnati, he had won fame as an antiporn crusader. He charged that communists were using smut and immorality to undermine America. In one of his many public appearances, he told an auditorium of high school girls the story of a young mother who was hit by a car while she pushed a baby carriage across the street. The woman, Keating explained, had been wearing Bermuda shorts, and the driver had been distracted by her bare legs. He implored the girls to sign a pledge not to wear Bermuda shorts.

President Reagan considered appointing Keating as his ambassador to the Bahamas, but the nomination was sidetracked when it came out that the Securities and Exchange Commission had slapped Keating with an injunction in 1979 for using his position at an Ohio bank to arrange for millions of dollars in sweetheart loans to insiders and cronies. Securities cops alleged that one of the insiders was Keating himself. The government charged, too, that Keating and others had used "fraud and deceit" to sell dicey securities to investors. He settled the charges by agreeing not to violate securities laws again.

He moved his base to Arizona, where he took over a failing home-building concern, American Continental Corporation, or ACC. He had bigger ambitions and wanted to buy an S&L to support them, but he didn't have the necessary cash. He turned to junk-bond king Michael Milken, who had set up a West Coast outpost of the Wall Street investment house Drexel Burnham Lambert. Milken arranged the financing for Keating's $51 million purchase of Orange County–based Lincoln Savings and Loan. Keating didn't have to put up any of his own money.

Just as Keating needed Milken, Milken needed Keating. Milken had created a huge market for junk—risky bonds issued by financially weak companies that want to borrow money—by selling investors on the idea that they weren't as chancy as the name implied. Milken was looking for places where he could off-load the worst junk and "restructure" bonds on the verge of default, obscuring their true default rates and artificially inflating their values. Lincoln Savings, federal regulators charged, would become one of a dozen "captive" S&Ls, a daisy chain of thrifts willing to issue and buy Milken's junk bonds and swap them back and forth among themselves. The S&Ls, the regulators alleged, let Milken buy junk bonds in their names; at the end of each day they were informed which junk bonds they had purchased. He was, financial writer Ben Stein would say, "sucking the blood of captive S&Ls like a vampire."

After Keating took control of Lincoln in early 1984, he suspended the thrift's home-loan program and began plowing its funds into multimillion-dollar commercial projects, along with nearly $3 billion of Milken's junk bonds. Lincoln employed many of the fast-and-loose practices Keating had been accused of in Cincinnati on a wider scale in Orange County. Auditors found the S&L had recorded millions in sham profits on real-estate deals that were little more than accounting gimmickry.

As financial pressures and regulatory battles mounted, Keating kept Lincoln alive by selling "subordinated debentures"—$250 million in junk bonds issued by ACC, the S&L's parent company. The bond investors, twenty-three thousand in all, weren't sophisticated. Most were elderly. Many were longtime Lincoln customers who'd come into branch offices around Orange County to roll over certificates of deposit that were expiring. CDs were safe and government-insured; the junk bonds were backed only by the faith and credit of ACC. Later, Keating admitted to one federal regulator that ACC and Lincoln were continuing to sell junk bonds and present themselves as secure and sound at a time when Lincoln was staring down a $2 billion loss.

Much like the young salesmen who would peddle mortgages for Orange County's subprime lenders two decades later, Lincoln's junk-bond salesmen were egged on by managers who promised perks and bonuses and demanded they sell with single-minded tenacity. At one meeting of Lincoln sales staffers, a top executive dressed up as a cowboy and gave his young charges this advice: "When you get a customer, be sure to sell them a bond. If they say no, offer them a bond. And if they still are not interested, try to sell them a bond." Inside Lincoln's branches, workers wore T-shirts that read "Bondzai" and "Bond for Glory." Salesmen told customers the bonds were "comparable to a CD." If customers asked if they were buying a "junk bond," the salesmen replied that the term was misleading. What they were really getting were "young bonds." A memo written in Phoenix by ACC executives ended with this admonition: "And always remember the weak, meek and ignorant are always good targets."

Many lost their life savings when Lincoln went under in 1989. They were people like Anthony Elliott, an eighty-nine-year-old widower from Burbank. He lost perhaps $200,000. On Thanksgiving Day 1990, he sat down and typed a suicide note: "There is nothing left for me of things that used to be. My government is supposed to serve and protect, but who? Those who can gather the most savings from retired people." Three days later, a Sunday, he climbed into his bathtub and slit his wrists and forearms with a straight razor. He was dead when his part-time housekeeper found him the next day.

As the scheme began to unravel, Keating fended off regulators by doing what he'd always done: threatening his enemies and calling on his friends. He intimidated the regulators by filing lawsuits accusing them of "a pattern of harassment and misrepresentation." He hired private detectives to snoop on William K. Black, the litigation director for the Federal Home Loan Bank Board. At one point, Keating's lawyers claimed he was a victim of a secret homosexual conspiracy hatched in federal thrift regulators' San Francisco offices.

Keating traded on the clout of five U.S. senators who'd shared roughly $1.3 million in campaign contributions from him. Among them was a newly elected senator from Arizona, John McCain. As former navy fliers, Keating and McCain had become close, with Keating treating McCain and his family to free plane rides and vacations at Keating's hideaway in the Bahamas. The senators, who would become known as the "Keating Five," championed Keating's cause with the regulators who were trying to slow him down.

Keating also enlisted the help of Alan Greenspan, onetime chairman of President Ford's Council of Economic Advisers. Greenspan was now working as a private consultant. As a young economist, he had been a disciple of Ayn Rand, the charismatic proselytizer of free market beliefs. In 1963, he had written an essay for Rand's journal arguing, "it is precisely the 'greed' of the businessman . . . which is the excelled protector of the consumer." Regulation of business practices, Greenspan said, was unnecessary. "What collectivists refuse to recognize is that it is in the self-interest of every businessman to have a reputation for honest dealings and a quality product." He said a company couldn't afford to risk the years it had spent building up its reputation "by letting down its standards for one moment or for one inferior product; nor would it be tempted by any potential 'quick killing.'" If Keating needed someone to help him get the regulators off his back, Greenspan was his man.

As Keating's hired gun, Greenspan wrote a letter to regulators pronouncing Lincoln's management as "seasoned and expert" and concluding that the S&L was "a financially strong institution that presents no foreseeable risk" to the Federal Deposit Insurance Fund. By the time Greenspan's miscalculations were exposed he was already serving as chairman of the Federal Reserve, the government entity chiefly responsible for overseeing the banking system. "When I first met the people from Lincoln, they struck me as reasonable, sensible people who knew what they were doing," Greenspan told the *New York Times*. "I don't want to say I am distressed, but the truth is I really am. I am thoroughly surprised by what has happened to Lincoln." It would not be the last time Greenspan was forced to admit a mistake in judgment.

* * *

Roland Arnall's Long Beach Savings avoided the fate of Lincoln Savings and other S&Ls in large part because of the profits it was posting from its subprime mortgages during the late '80s and early '90s. As its subprime unit cranked up, Long Beach's profits exploded, growing from $2.8 million in 1988 to $14.1 million in 1989. Regulators might not have liked Arnall's big real-estate deals or Long Beach's brand of risky home loans, but they couldn't argue the thrift wasn't serving the mission of S&Ls—to make home loans—or that it didn't have the money to shield it from losses in commercial real estate. Long Beach was successful because, at the behest of regulators, it was doing the opposite of what Alan Greenspan—and other fans of deregulation—had recommended for S&Ls. Greenspan had advised that S&Ls should diversify their risks by increasing their investments in quick-buck commercial real-estate deals and reduce their dependence on long-term home loans. Long Beach was moving away from commercial investments and focusing itself, more and more, on residential lending.

Long Beach also survived because Arnall was, by nature, a suspicious man. He hated the idea of anyone getting the best of him in a business deal. That's why, unlike other S&L operators, he resisted the blandishments of Michael Milken. Milken had tried to make a move on Long Beach, to get the thrift to join Lincoln Savings and the other captive S&Ls that helped keep his junk bond scheme flying. Bob Labrador, Long Beach's treasurer in those days, heard Milken speak in the mid-1980s at a dinner in Los Angeles for banking professionals. Labrador was persuaded by Milken's argument that markets were undervaluing his junk bonds, creating an opening for investors who were savvy enough to snap up the cheap assets. The S&Ls that were doing well investing in Milken's junk included Beverly Hills' Columbia Savings and Loan. With Milken's help, the S&L gobbled up more than $4 billion in junk bonds and became, on paper, the nation's most profitable S&L.

Labrador could see the riches Columbia was producing through the fortunes of a friend who happened to be Columbia's vice president of finance. Labrador's pal drove around in a new Mercedes. Sometimes he and Labrador vacationed at Utah's Deer Valley Resort, in condos owned by Columbia. Columbia's conspicuous success helped sway Labrador to the idea that Long Beach should consider investing in junk bonds, too. "I thought they were a way I could make a name for myself. I could be a hero," Labrador recalled wryly.

Arnall considered the idea. But he decided to steer away from Milken and his investments. He never said why—he often kept his reasons to himself. Looking back, Labrador wondered if it was a takes-one-to-know-one shrewdness: "He may have seen himself in Milken: *He's just like me; he's going to sell everybody on this and when it blows up, he's gone.*" Labrador thought it was a bit like Arnall's decision not to get into franchising car washes. Arnall never wanted to put himself in a spot where a business partner was in control. He wanted to be the one with the upper hand.

3. Purge

In the summer of 1990, Greenwich Capital put together a $70 million mortgage-backed securities deal for Roland Arnall's S&L. It was the first time Long Beach had "publicly placed" securities backed by subprime mortgages, meaning that the transaction was filed with the Securities and Exchange Commission and Greenwich was able to peddle the assets to a wider array of investors than would have been possible under a "privately placed" deal. With Greenwich securitizing many of Long Beach's loans, the S&L didn't have to worry as much about drawing in customer deposits to fund its mortgage operations. Gaining access to the nation's capital markets changed the tenor and scale of Long Beach's business. "It was a significant transitional moment," Bob Labrador, Long Beach's treasurer, said. "You had to keep pumping out more and more loans to feed the Wall Street machine."

Arnall maintained a hectic pace as his empire grew. He lived on the phone, making deals, seeking inside information, and trying to shake loose more money from financial backers. In the '80s, he had one of the earliest car phones installed in his Jaguar, running up bills of $10,000 to $15,000 a month as he cruised around Southern California. He eventually stopped driving himself and hired a chauffeur. One story had it that he was forced to stop driving after he'd rung up too many tickets for running red lights while gabbing on the phone and for double-parking because he didn't want to waste valuable time searching for a space.

He expected his subordinates to match his pace and his drive. Sometimes he exercised his authority by yelling and blustering. More often he used the silent treatment. When a trusted adviser fell out of favor, Arnall began to refer to him as "what's his name." Arnall believed he was simply enforcing accountability within his organization. "He was demanding. But if you did what you said you were going to do, your life was fine," one longtime employee recalled. Some thought his management style was dictatorial. "With Roland, it was always a search for the guilty," a former Long Beach manager said. Once, a young switchboard operator who didn't realize that it was the boss calling in made a faux pas. Arnall was impatient to be connected to an assistant immediately, and he let the young phone operator know it. "All I can say is just *chill*," the operator replied. The young man was gone the next day. In another episode, Arnall was giving a tour of his headquarters to a group of financial backers, a task he enjoyed. As he was extolling the virtues of his S&L, a fax machine screeched and spewed out an offensive, hand-drawn cartoon: a crude, larger-than-life rendering of a penis. Arnall was livid. He promised heads would roll, demanding that his aides hunt down and punish the prankster. The matter was dropped, a former Long Beach executive said, when it was established that the fax had come from the offices of one of Long Beach's biggest-producing mortgage brokers.

Arnall kept his top executives in their places by withholding their year-end bonuses until well into the next year, sometimes for months. That extra period allowed more opportunities for mistakes or missed loan-production goals, which he could use as an excuse for shaving a bit off their checks. "He would say: If it hadn't been for that thing in May, it would have been bigger," a former employee recalled. He also kept them on their toes by assaulting them with a succession of proposals for improving the S&L's efficiency and profits. He might have read something in a business management book, or met someone on a plane or at a party who might be, as a former employee put it, "in the ladies' undergarment business." The new idea or new business contact would become Arnall's latest preoccupation. He might hire his golden boy to come work at Long Beach, or decide that someone already working for him was an undervalued talent. This favored employee would enjoy a honeymoon in which he or she could do no wrong. "He was an idol worshipper," one former business associate noted. But almost as quickly as Arnall could fall in love with an employee, he could fall out of love, too. The once-invaluable employee would be demoted to "what's-his-name" status.

One senior manager thought the way to stay in Arnall's good graces was to cut corners to get the job done. "The only way you could survive and excel was to cheat," the former executive said. "Those who cheated were rewarded. Those who did the right thing were treated as second class." One area in which Long Beach cheated was in feeding inaccurate information to federal regulators. The regulators required Long Beach to submit a detailed business plan. The S&L had to project its loan volume and then hew to its projections—with the trend lines neither too far below projections nor too far above. But the subprime lending program was doing well enough by the early '90s that loan volume was growing faster than expected. Long Beach fudged its books, shoving loans it had made in one month into the next to hide the true level of growth. According to the former executive, Arnall was aware this was being done.

* * *

Russ and Becky Jedinak weren't as adept as Roland Arnall when it came to escaping the S&L industry's problems. After making money for years, their S&L, Guardian, had fallen on hard times, losing almost $5 million over 1989 and 1990, in part because regulators had forced them to change the thrift's accounting practices to set aside more cash for covering bad loans.

At the same time, Guardian was drawing attention for the kinds of loans it was making to vulnerable home owners. "What we're seeing is people with little expectation of being able to repay a loan are being lent money—especially elderly black people," the litigation director for Bet Tzedek Legal Services, a law clinic for the impoverished and unlucky, told the *Orange County Register*. Eventually, as California's real-estate market fell in the early 1990s, some pools of Guardian's adjustable-rate loans would suffer delinquency rates of 23 to 51 percent.

Examiners with the federal Office of Thrift Supervision concluded

that Guardian had gouged and misled its borrowers. Top Guardian officers also approved loans with false or unverified documentation,
according to the OTS. The agency also charged that the S&L had misled
the government, trying to hide its dicey practices by removing or "losing" boxes of records. "Guardian has . . . violated laws and regulations"
and "is vulnerable to acts of fraud," the agency said. One case cited by
the OTS involved Odessa Howell, a seventy-five-year-old widow who
was battling cancer. She signed for two loans from Guardian totaling
more than $300,000. She was supposed to get some money to pay for
home improvements, but a large slice of the loan proceeds was diverted
into fees and other charges, including more than $100,000 that went
into a mortgage broker's pocket. Howell said she didn't have "the faint-
est idea" what happened to the cash. The OTS noted the deal was put
together with falsified paperwork that bestowed the elderly borrower
with a make-believe job at a make-believe company. "The stated source
of repayment for the loans was based upon a financial statement for a
business that neither exists nor with which Ms. Howell is affiliated."

Russ Jedinak countered that the government was flat-out wrong.
"The fact is we've never had any financial losses due to fraud, or financial losses due to the funding of our single-family home loans," he
said. But the government had a stranglehold on Guardian. In early
1991, Russ agreed to resign as chairman, and Becky agreed to resign
as senior executive vice president. Russ, the S&L said, would "pursue
other interests." Russ's defenders thought he mainly had erred by
antagonizing regulators rather than trying to smooth things over with
them. "He's a high-powered salesman," Jude Lopez, the Jedinaks' former aide, said. "He doesn't understand diplomacy. He thinks if you
make money everything is all right."

Ultimately, the government determined that the Jedinaks had used
Guardian as a piggy bank, siphoning off money for themselves with
sweetheart loans and using S&L funds to pay for personal travel and
other non-business expenses. It also said the Jedinaks mishandled
major commercial investments and caused the S&L to misreport its
financial condition.

Even without the Jedinaks' involvement in the day-to-day management of the thrift, the government concluded that Guardian was a lost

cause. Regulators seized the S&L in June 1991, making it the twenty-third thrift it had taken over in Orange County since the crisis began. The final straw had been the decision to write down the value of Guardian Center, the company's gleaming headquarters on Beach Boulevard in Huntington Beach. The Jedinaks had paid $55 million for it in 1988; now it was worth less than half that. The write-down left Guardian's financial condition so precarious that the OTS believed it had no choice but to put the S&L into government receivership.

✳ ✳ ✳

Over at Long Beach Savings, things were going better, so well in fact that Arnall closed the main office in the company's namesake city and moved the headquarters to Orange County, into the high-rise on Town and Country Road that had long been home to the S&L's sub-prime lending operations. It made sense, now that subprime was Long Beach's main line of business. Arnall relocated there, too, knocking down walls and turning three offices into an expansive executive suite, complete with a private kitchen, for himself. He also adopted a new name for the company: Long Beach Savings morphed into Long Beach Bank, FSB, as in "federal savings bank." Many thrifts were renaming themselves in just this way, in an effort to distance themselves from the taint of the S&L scandal.

Arnall's greater physical presence signaled his determination to put his own imprint on the mortgage unit. He brought in a coterie of management consultants. Workers arrived one Monday to find that, over the weekend, the entire headquarters on Town and Country Road had been taken apart and put back together. Cubicles had been rearranged and employees were informed that they were being shifted into different jobs. The idea behind the reorganization was to make the loan operation run with the speed of an assembly line. If Long Beach could already move a loan from application to approval in forty-eight or seventy-two hours, the thinking went, couldn't a more streamlined process produce a same-day "turn time"—taking a submission from a mortgage broker in the morning and coming back with a yes or no by the end of the day?

The reorganization was a disaster. Turn times got worse, not better, with it sometimes taking four days to convey the decision back to the broker. "They took something that really wasn't broken and broke it," one longtime employee said. The problem was that many Long Beach employees had been shuffled into jobs they weren't familiar with, and, the truth was, examining loan applications required that real people exercise real judgment. It wasn't a process that could be modeled on an assembly line. In the subprime world, each borrower's story was different. People had credit problems, interruptions in their job histories, or other complicating issues. Borrowers needed hand-holding, and their applications needed scrutiny to ensure their loans made sense. After Arnall scrapped the existing systems in favor of the consultants' new efficiency theories, Long Beach's loan volume plummeted from $90 million to $30 million a month.

When some managers objected to the changes, the consultants made it clear they were in charge: The train had left the station, and either you were on it or you were off. The arrival of a gang of consultants often doesn't bode well for managers who represent a company's past, even if that past has been successful. It eventually dawned on Schuerman that Arnall was using the consultants to engineer a "nonviolent coup" in the mortgage division. Now that Arnall was settled into the Orange County offices and focusing on subprime, he was determined to make some personnel changes. He wanted to get rid of the top aides who had built the business that had kept Long Beach afloat during the S&L crisis. "Once it was working well, Roland wanted it all for himself," one former Long Beach executive recalled. Arnall fired Rank, the S&L's quality-control guru, as well as Rank's top aide in operations, Dennis Rivelli. Schuerman lingered for a few more months. At staff meetings, Arnall brushed aside his input. Then Arnall started holding key meetings without him. Schuerman thought it came down to a "control thing. He had the illusion I was trying to be more important than the company." All classic entrepreneurs, in Schuerman's view, were driven by a strain of paranoia; when you're trying to build an empire and taking on the world, you tend to eye people with suspicion, as impediments to your ambition to gain more power and more success.

Schuerman didn't like getting pushed out, but he wasn't the sort to hold grudges. He joked with Arnall about it: if Arnall really wanted to get rid of him, Schuerman said, Arnall could have saved the company money by forgoing the outside experts and simply giving Schuerman half of what he'd spent on consulting fees. Arnall put a good face on the split. He threw Schuerman a going-away party, inviting some of Long Beach's allies on Wall Street to come out to the West Coast to see Schuerman off.

Schuerman was set to receive a substantial sum on his exit since, under his original agreement with Arnall, he had been given a stake in the business. Schuerman recalled that Arnall paid him some money to go away. It wasn't as much as Schuerman, who had helped build the mortgage division from scratch, thought he was due. But knowing Arnall's reluctance to pay people what he owed them, Schuerman felt lucky to get anything out of him. "He fucked me," Schuerman said. "But within reason . . . within tolerance levels."

* * *

In the fall of 1992, Russ and Becky Jedinak made an appearance at the Mortgage Bankers Association's national convention in San Francisco. An old business associate, on his way to a cocktail party at the St. Francis Hotel, ran into the couple on an elevator. Becky, he recalled, was wearing a blue dress. Russ had on a $1,000 suit. On his breast pocket, Russ wore a name tag issued for conference attendees by the trade association. He'd crossed out "Guardian Savings" and written, by hand, "Quality Mortgage."

The Jedinaks were back in business, little more than a year after regulators had shut down their S&L. Their new venture, Quality Mortgage USA, was an independent mortgage lender rather than a bank or S&L. This absolved the Jedinaks from having to obtain a license from state or federal regulators. The couple controlled Quality through a holding company, and in some states conducted business through affiliates sporting other names, such as Express Funding. With federal authorities still investigating the Jedinaks' role in Guardian's collapse, it seemed best to build a bit of legal insulation into the corporate structure. Still, Quality Mortgage was essentially the same company as Guardian, with many of the same employees and many of the same independent brokers feeding loans into the Jedinaks' subprime fiefdom.

The Jedinaks' problems at Guardian didn't dissuade Wall Street from assisting the couple in their new start. They got help from Donaldson, Lufkin & Jenrette, an investment bank that was expanding its reach after hiring many of Michael Milken's former underlings from the wreckage of Drexel Burnham Lambert's Beverly Hills offices. DLJ took a 49 percent stake in Quality Mortgage and helped bankroll the company's loans and package them into mortgage-backed securities. Quality was, according to one top DLJ executive, "the first subprime/ Wall Street joint venture"—the first time a player on Wall Street had taken an ownership stake in a subprime lender.

Quality was aggressive about pushing loan products that made it easier for borrowers to qualify. These included "Quick Qualifier" loans and "stated income" loans that didn't require documentation of borrowers' wages—the sort of loans that someday would become ubiquitous but were not common during the 1990s.

DLJ's financial support allowed Quality to ramp up quickly and spread across California and then the rest of the nation. Russ Jedinak hired staff in bunches and pushed for leapfrog expansion into new markets, making do with whatever quarters he could find. James Gartland, a mortgage broker in Orange County in the early '90s, stopped by a Quality office one day to talk to the wholesale rep who was his contact at the lender. Fishnets and starfish hung on the walls. A fax machine sat on the bar. Gartland's wholesale rep was working at a table inside a red upholstered booth. The space had previously been occupied by a seafood restaurant, and there wasn't time to waste on redecorating.

Jedinak traveled far and wide, usually behind the controls of his jet, a four-seat Cessna Citation. He rented hotel ballrooms and invited brokers to attend his road shows—and to bring their latest loan files with them. He gave away Sony Walkmans and other prizes, offering the brokers an extra half-point commission if they would march to the back of the room and submit their customers' applications on the spot to Quality's loan underwriters. As Jedinak flew his jet across the country, he sometimes looked down and saw the lights of a city he'd never visited in his life . . . and decided that he *had* to open a branch there.

When he gathered his sales force together, he let them know the sky was the limit, for them and for Quality Mortgage. At company meetings, top-producing loan reps won time inside a money machine, a booth that blew a tornado of cash around. Whatever bills they could grab and stuff in their pockets, they got to keep. At one event, Jedinak illustrated the fierceness of Quality's salesmanship and competitive instincts by strutting into the room with a full-grown lion on a leash. At another he had armed security guards march in with bags of money and dump the cash into a big pile. Then he stood on the pile, announced he was standing on a million bucks, and gave a speech about how much money his sales reps could make if they worked hard and dreamed big.

* * *

Just as Long Beach Savings had competed with Guardian, now Long Beach Bank, FSB, found itself competing with Quality. They were bitter rivals. The Jedinaks' company was more willing to take on risky borrowers, and to offer creative loan products and cut prices to make a deal happen. "Anything aggressive, Quality was doing it first," recalled Adam Levine, an account manager at Long Beach in that era. "Quality pushed Long Beach pretty hard. We had to respond." If Quality came up with a loan product with a 3.99 percent initial "teaser rate," Long Beach had to at least come within shouting distance, rolling out a loan with a 4.99 percent teaser. Long Beachers thought of Quality Mortgage and Long Beach as "the evil twin and the good twin," Levine said. Long Beach's loan reps considered themselves to be more professional. They were required to wear ties. They were encouraged to think of themselves as bankers, and viewed Quality's reps in the field as equivalent to car salesmen. Folks at Quality dismissed Long Beachers as corporate types, with their button-down business attire and written policy manuals. "Long Beach was more particular than we were," said Jude Lopez, who joined the Jedinaks at their new venture. "They really couldn't compete with us."

With their company's more aggressive style, Quality's field reps often stole deals from Long Beach by undercutting Long Beach's prices. "They used to follow us around, sometimes figuratively, sometimes literally," Levine said. He realized his competition from Quality would ask brokers about loans that Long Beach had already approved—and offer a better price for the same loan on the spot, without underwriting it, because the Quality rep knew Long Beach had already checked the borrower's qualifications.

Some Quality employees were creative about handling the headaches that came from borrowers with less-than-impressive credentials. One manager told the *Orange County Register* that a top Quality executive disguised the company's loan delinquency rate with accounting legerdemain, shifting money from loan accounts that were current and applying the money to accounts that were delinquent, then later switching the money back to the right place. The Jedinaks saw those kinds of actions as "signs of initiative and loyalty," the manager said.

Quality's freewheeling ways also left it open to legal attacks from unhappy borrowers. The Jedinaks found themselves fighting off dozens of lawsuits, spending $2 million a year in lawyers' fees. The allegations were similar to complaints that had been aimed at their previous company, Guardian. The lawsuits claimed Quality socked customers with unfair fees and misled them about their loan terms. A class-action suit in Alabama charged that Quality "corrupted hundreds of small mortgage brokers by offering them—and paying them—illicit commercial bribes" to betray borrowers who thought the brokers would get them the best rates they qualified for. Quality's hidden commissions compromised the brokers, encouraging them to steer these customers into loans with "artificially inflated" interest rates, the suit claimed. In a case in Hawaii, a borrower accused two Quality affiliates of "manipulation and deception" as part of a "continuous cycle of unlawful predatory practices." Her first loan through a Quality affiliate had a starting rate of 8.9 percent. But the adjustable rate soon climbed past 11 percent. Her payment rose from $1,674 to $2,016 a month. Mortgage rates in the marketplace were beginning to come down, so she called and asked if she could refinance into a lower, fixed rate. According to her court claims, Quality's affiliate promised she could get a lower rate, and get some extra money for Christmas and to renovate her home. Instead, she said, the interest rate on the new loan turned out to be higher, she didn't get any extra cash, and the lender charged her nearly $20,000 in up-front fees to put her into a loan that didn't help her at all.

Lopez thought the accusations against Quality were unfair. Quality did what it could to police the independent brokers who were feeding it business, he said, but it could only do so much to protect consumers from themselves. "People will sign anything, sad to say," he said. Quality, Lopez believed, was simply operating under the rules of the game at the time, which, more and more, were being set by Wall Street and the investors who bought mortgage-backed investments. "It wasn't a conspiracy to cheat people," he said. "Wall Street tells you: 'You make this loan, I'll pay you a bunch of money,' so what do you do? If you don't make the loan, you're out of business."

* * *

Quality wasn't the only mortgage lender that was running into legal problems. Lawsuits were bubbling up around the country, attacking what consumer lawyers and neighborhood activists were beginning to call "predatory lending." The targets of these actions were the consumer-finance companies that had shifted their focus from small personal loans to home-equity loans. The biggest target was Fleet Finance, the Atlanta-based subsidiary of Fleet Financial Group, New England's largest bank. Fleet Finance, the *Boston Globe* said, was the "jewel in the crown of its parent company." While Fleet Financial Group's traditional banking operations were bleeding red ink, its consumer-finance unit was pulling in profits of $60 million a year. Wall Street helped Fleet put together home-equity securitizations worth hundreds of millions of dollars each. Fleet Finance took a different tack from Long Beach and Quality, both of which did larger-sized mortgages, focused on cash-out refinancings, and generally charged lower rates than consumer-finance lenders. Fleet Finance, in contrast, made its money by teaming up with mortgage brokers and home-improvement contractors who were talking minority and low-income home owners into taking out smaller mortgages with interest rates of 15, 20, even 25 percent.

In Atlanta, Fleet worked mainly with a group of seven mortgage brokers that consumer lawyers referred to as "The Seven Dwarfs." The brokers had written agreements to feed business to Fleet; many sold nearly all of their loans to the lender. By operating in this way, consumer attorneys said, Fleet was insulating itself from legal claims over the slippery methods used to sell the loans to unsophisticated borrowers. Fleet said the brokers were completely distinct companies and that all business dealings were done at arm's length. Ultimately, the lender argued, it was up to the home owners to make sure they got a fair deal. "These people may be poor and illiterate, but no one puts a gun to their head and tells them to sign," a top Fleet official said. "This idea that Fleet should regulate the world is preposterous."

The charge against Fleet in Georgia was led by William Brennan. Brennan had studied to be a priest but had decided, amid the turmoil of the 1960s, that he could do more good as a lawyer. "It seemed the whole world was going by and I was missing it, especially the civil rights movement," he once recalled. In 1968 he joined Atlanta Legal Aid, a government-funded program that represented low-income people. In 1988 he started Atlanta Legal Aid's Home Defense Program. He became a one-man clearinghouse on the dark side of home loans, plying visiting reporters with photocopied stacks of lawsuits documenting the growth of abusive lending. Brennan worked late into the night and on weekends, and had trouble turning down a client in trouble; he couldn't say no, no matter how big his caseload was. Legal Aid lawyers see a steady stream of people who are abused by powerful institutions. It's hard for lawyers not to shield themselves from their pain by sorting the victims into various patterns and categories. But for Brennan, one colleague wrote, "[I]njustice was not a pattern or a category. Even if he had seen a particular case a thousands times before, he always gave the client the impression that he had never seen anything like it. The impression was more than a good acting job. I am convinced that in some profound way, Bill was always surprised at injustice."

Many of Brennan's clients were older black women. They were often cash-poor but house-rich. They had chunks of equity in their homes, which over the decades had built up as real-estate values rose and they had dutifully paid down their house notes. That equity, Brennan saw, made them a target for loan brokers, tin men, and home-equity lenders such as Fleet. "It's like finding a ten-dollar bill in the street and say-ing: This is mine, I'm gonna take it. Their attitude is: It's there for the taking."

Other attorneys were starting to pick up on the questions swirling around Fleet's Georgia-based mortgage unit. Howard Rothbloom was a young bankruptcy lawyer in Marietta, Georgia. In those days, bankruptcy law generally involved helping folks in financial trouble go to court and work out payment plans that would allow them to pay off their accumulated debts. As a judge told Rothbloom, the purpose of "Chapter 13"—a standard bankruptcy reorganization plan for individuals—was for the consumer to catch up on his or her past-due debts, not to challenge them. That changed for Rothbloom one night when he got a call from Lillie Mae Starr.

Starr, a sixty-two-year-old grandmother, had a story to tell. She had tried to borrow $5,000 so she could replace her home's aging, drafty windows. After fees were added in, she ended up with a loan of $9,200 against her home, and was paying an interest rate of 23 per-cent. The loan landed in the hands of Fleet. When she fell behind, the company threatened to foreclose. She refinanced her mortgage once, and then a second time, trying to get away from the mortgage com-pany. Fleet bought her loan again. Her house debt had ballooned to $63,000, and Fleet was once again threatening her home. "If you have a little place that's all your own, how can you lose it just like that?" she wondered. "That can't happen, can it?"

She already had a lawyer. He told her that her best option was to allow Fleet to take her house. She wanted Rothbloom to represent her instead, and fight to save her home. He agreed. Not long after, Roth-bloom's dad sent him a newspaper clipping. It was an article about Bill Brennan's fight against Fleet. Rothbloom picked up the phone and called Brennan.

Brennan persuaded Rothbloom that Starr's experiences weren't iso-lated. She was representative of a multitude of borrowers who'd been taken in by Fleet. With Brennan's support and advice, Rothbloom decided to expand the case into a bigger attack on Fleet's practices. It wouldn't be easy. Class actions are expensive and hard for lawyers who, like Rothbloom, don't have a big war chest or significant institutional backing. He did have a powerful ally, though, in his law partner, Roy Barnes, a longtime state legislator who'd run, unsuccessfully, for the Democratic nomination for governor in 1990.

At first blush, Barnes might not have seemed a likely candidate to join a crusade against a big national bank. Besides being a lawyer, he was also a banker. He and his brother had started a bank in Mableton, the small town where he had grown up in Cobb County, on the other side of the Chattahoochee River from Atlanta. The bank had helped make Barnes a millionaire. In the '70s and '80s, as a legislator from a rural district, he had cast more than a few conservative votes, including a vote against instituting a state holiday in honor of the Reverend Martin Luther King Jr. He had also voted to wipe out Georgia's limits on mortgage rates. But by the early '90s he'd come to regret his vote against a King holiday, and he had decided that his vote to take the lid off mortgage rates had been a mistake. The legislation, he said, had allowed mortgage sharks to prey on poor Georgians. "I am a capitalist through and through. I believe in charging interest," he said. "But you can't justify charging anyone 27 points up front and 24.9 percent interest, as we've seen. Those types of things should not be allowed by governments."

As Rothbloom filled him in on Starr's case, Barnes grew angrier and angrier. He had grown up in his family's hardware store and learned about fair dealing from his father, who always told him: "We trade with folks for a lifetime, not just for today." As a small-town banker, Barnes loaned money to people who had known him and his family all their lives. Some, he recalled, would tell him: "Roy, I've been down on my luck. You know my daddy and you know me. You know I'll pay it back." He couldn't imagine sticking borrowers with shoddy loans and then having to look them in the eye on the street in Mableton. And as a bank executive, he had a responsibility to the bank to make sure he didn't approve loans that wouldn't be repaid. "We knew that if we made that loan, we were going to have to collect it," Barnes said. "We weren't going to sell it to somebody in Europe."

Along with fighting in the courts, Brennan, Rothbloom, and Barnes used the power of the media to help balance the scales in their fight against Fleet. The bank's practices gained nationwide notoriety when Morley Safer and a film crew from CBS's *60 Minutes* came to Georgia. The story that aired in November 1992 was a portrait of what one borrower called "the vulture of the mortgage market." Safer gave Barnes the last word on Fleet's modus operandi: "Well, I don't know what you all call it up North, but down here in the South we call it cheating and swindling. . . . It's a type of bondage that is taking advantage of the most helpless, the least . . . the ones that have the least ability to fight back."

That exposure on television's most-watched news program brought more aggrieved Fleet customers to the lawyers. Rothbloom noted a large number of the borrowers had "Mae" in their names—Lillie Mae, Julia Mae, Hattie Mae, Essie Mae, and so on. To him, that disclosed Fleet's favorite demographic: older, black, southern women with modest homes and modest incomes. At first, many of Fleet's borrowers were embarrassed by their mortgage problems. They hesitated to come forward. But as they learned that they weren't alone, and that others were standing up to fight, the case took on the air of a social movement. Borrowers formed themselves into the Fleet Finance Victims Group, embarking on a series of protest actions they termed "Operation Fed Up." They packed legislative hearings in Georgia and in Washington, D.C., asking for new laws to protect them from abusive lenders. Congress began to consider federal legislation. As the decade progressed, the issue of predatory lending would keep growing.

*   *   *

Roland Arnall's S&L avoided lawsuits and negative publicity because, in the early years of its mortgage-lending program, Mark Schuerman, Pat Rank, and other executives had run a tight ship. With Schuerman and Rank out of the way, Long Beach's quality control began to deteriorate. As the company became more decentralized and a tier of less experienced managers were promoted, some employees succumbed to the pressure to do whatever it took to produce loan volume, one former Long Beach executive, Frank Curry, recalled. Curry had to fire two regional managers who had approved bad loans based on fabrications, such as inflating property appraisals and borrower incomes. The clash between sales and operations became more intense, and sales began to gain supremacy. Competition with Quality Mortgage also encouraged Long Beach to lower the safeguards that protected borrowers from overly enthusiastic sales practices. The consumer-finance types who had migrated to Long Beach now had more freedom to follow their gung ho instincts.

One of the consumer-finance transplants was Terry Rouch. He had gotten into the loan business a couple of years earlier, straight out of the U.S. Navy. He thought it was a great gig, sitting at a desk and talking on the phone, making a lot more money than he'd made in the service. He worked his way up to branch manager at Transamerica, then took a job as a loan officer at Long Beach in 1992. With commissions, he could make more than $70,000 a year as a salesman at Long Beach, almost twice what he'd been making as a manager at Transamerica. Good money for a guy still in his twenties.

Loan officers at Long Beach worked from prepared lists of likely customers, making call after call, trying to find people willing to refinance their homes to pay off credit cards or other bills. The key was to stay glued to your seat and book as many loan applications—"apps"— as possible. Slackers weren't welcome. Want to knock off at 5:00 or 5:30 P.M. and go to your kid's Little League game? Forget it. A manager would be all over Rouch or anyone else who dared to leave early: "Where are you going? How many apps have you done today? We need three more before you go home." Argue the point, and the response might be along the lines of: "What's more important? Putting food on your table for your kid, or going to the game poor?" Salespeople who didn't have the stuff to close deals didn't last long. Good closers, on the other hand, were rewarded with big money and trips that Arnall bankrolled: all-expenses-paid cruises or days and nights at luxury resorts.

Arnall made surprise inspections from time to time at Long Beach's loan-sales offices, usually with a district manager in tow. "He absolutely knew the day-to-day branch operations," Rouch said. "You can't say that Roland didn't know what was going on or how we were doing business." When Arnall showed up, managers sent out for beer and pizza, and the salespeople knew they were in for a late night. The boss and his aides would listen in to make sure the salesmen were working their call lists and making effective pitches to home owners.

Managers gave frequent critiques, pushing loan officers to be more forceful on the phone and not allow good leads to get away. "If you weren't hungry and weren't passionate," Rouch recalled, "the company didn't want you."

Loan officers focused on selling refinancings to people who were already Long Beach customers or, especially, folks who had mortgages with consumer-finance companies. Geographically, Rouch and his fellow loan officers at the Long Beach Boulevard branch in downtown Long Beach targeted South Central Los Angeles—Compton, Bell Gardens, Lawndale, Inglewood, and other communities where home owners tended to be elderly, African American, and Hispanic. In those days, telemarketing wasn't limited by many rules, or by heavy call screening. It was easy for Rouch to catch borrowers on the phone and, by demonstrating he knew the details of their current loans, get them talking until they were willing to provide their Social Security numbers and the other information necessary to start a new mortgage application. Rates on finance-company loans were still high, around 9 or 10 percent on a first mortgage and 12 to 15 percent on a second mortgage. Long Beach could beat those rates by rolling all of the borrower's home debt into a new adjustable-rate mortgage that started at 7.99 percent. Not only that, it could lower borrowers' overall monthly debt payments by paying off all their credit-card balances and adding that debt onto their mortgages. That was the key to the pitch. It was a sales technique many Long Beach salespeople had learned working for finance companies: *Forget the rates and fees. Sell the payment.* That meant focusing on the monthly payment at the initial interest rate and glossing over other terms, including the setup costs of the loan, the adjustable-rate features, and prepayment penalties that would cost borrowers thousands of dollars if they tried to get out of the loan by refinancing their mortgage once their interest rates and monthly payments increased. Borrowers in the prime market rarely had to worry about prepayment penalties, but they were commonplace on subprime loans. Subprime customers often had no idea these surprises were tucked away in their contracts.

Taking $2,000 in monthly mortgage payments and credit-card bills and rolling them into a single monthly payment of, say, $1,200 sounded good to most consumers. For some, it might even be a smart financial move. But what most borrowers didn't dwell on was the fact that the monthly payments were being reduced in part because short-term, unsecured credit-card debt was now being attached to their homes and stretched over a thirty-year period. If their financial situations took a turn, the extra mortgage debt could put their homes at risk. What's more, many didn't understand that the low monthly payments wouldn't last. For some Long Beach customers, even the temporarily lower rates weren't as low as they could have found if they had gone elsewhere. They may not have known it, but many weren't subprime borrowers at all; their credit histories were strong enough to qualify them for a lower-priced fixed-rate loan. The problem was that loan officers got bigger commissions when they stuck people with good credit into higher-rate loans, and investors were willing to pay Long Beach more for loans with higher rates but less risky borrowers.

Why would borrowers with good credit sign up for a subprime loan? Salesmanship. Credit scores weren't available to consumers in those days, so credit histories were more in the eye of the beholder. Borrowers generally believed it when loan officers told them their credit histories had some serious dings. They were the mortgage professionals, after all. Loan officers simply had to point out an old late payment or two—items often so minor that they wouldn't have disqualified borrowers from getting a prime mortgage—and exaggerate the blemishes into major issues. From there sales reps would suggest that the borrowers might not have what it took to qualify for a loan from Long Beach, and if the loan did get approved, it might cost them a bit more. But they were vague about exactly how much more. Thinking they were lucky to get the loan, borrowers would jump at the chance.

Wendell Raphael, a supervisor in the mortgage unit, became concerned about some of his employees' sales tactics after he took over as an area manager for Long Beach in late 1993. After the promotion, he visited the loan branches he oversaw in and around L.A.'s San Fernando Valley. He considered himself a "by-the-book-type guy," and what he found bothered him: "People taking shortcuts. People who would do anything to get a loan through: lie, cheat, or steal."

New federal rules had recently kicked in, requiring that mortgage

lenders provide an early, detailed estimate of loan fees and other closing costs to customers who were applying to refinance their mortgages. Lenders had to put the "Good Faith Estimate" in the mail
within three days after taking an application. It was the first chance
borrowers would have to see, in writing, what their loan terms were
likely to be. It was also the last chance, until just before the closing or,
in many instances, the day of the closing. Given the prices that Long
Beach charged, some loan officers thought it was better if borrowers
didn't peek at the Good Faith Estimate. As Raphael sat among his
employees and listened to them pitch loans over the phone, he heard
them encourage borrowers to ignore these disclosure documents.

When it came time to complete the deal, some Long Beach employees had still more tricks for keeping borrowers in the dark about the
terms of their loans. Long Beach representatives liked to close loans at
customers' homes late at night, between 8 P.M. and midnight, knowing
borrowers were less likely to ask questions if they were bleary-eyed
after a long day at work. An alternative to the late-night closing was
the midday rush, which involved having home owners sign their loan
papers during their thirty-minute lunch break. Either way, borrowers
were eager to get it over with, whether it was to get to bed or get back to
work, and less likely to catch details about the costs and hidden terms.

Customers were also at a disadvantage because some Long Beach
employees weren't above forging borrowers' signatures on the loan disclosures so that everything in the file looked aboveboard. "That was
pretty much standard procedure," Rouch said. Some workers saw the
disclosure paperwork as red tape, "junk paperwork." Even back in the
mid-'90s, Rouch recalled, sales managers sometimes taped documents
up on office windows, using the light streaming in to help them trace
borrowers' signatures onto documents they hadn't signed. The laser
printer paper in use in those days was thin, making it that much easier
to fake a signature.

Naturally, more than a few of Long Beach's borrowers fell behind,
because of fragile finances or because they hadn't understood the terms
of their loans. This wasn't necessarily a bad thing for Long Beach. It
created more business. Once customers got into a hole, they were vulnerable to whatever new sales pitch the company might toss at them.

When borrowers are struggling to catch up on their payments and worried about losing their homes, they'll take almost any deal that allows them to start over, no matter how costly. Long Beach refinanced borrowers again and again, giving them a bit more money but mostly piling up new closing fees and collecting more prepayment penalties.

Many loan officers, enticed by the financial rewards and feeling pressure from management to produce, couldn't help themselves. They did what everyone else was doing—and tried not to think about the consequences for borrowers. "You started to become like a robot," Rouch said years later. He tried to buck the system as best he could. Management wanted loan officers to charge at least 5 points in up-front fees and finance charges. Rouch charged existing Long Beach customers just 3 or 4 points when he refinanced their old loans, figuring they'd already paid Long Beach points on the previous loan and were going to have to pay a hefty prepayment penalty to rewrite their loan. He also secretly farmed out customers with good credit to banker friends who could get them better deals. He did that even though he knew that if he was caught sending business out the door, he'd be fired on the spot.

After three years, he was ready to move on. The pressure, the long hours, the take-no-prisoners lending style—all of it had worn him down. In 1995, he quit and took a job as a branch manager at a bank. He told himself: "I'm done with all of this."

∗ ∗ ∗

S&L regulators weren't oblivious to the kinds of loans Long Beach was making. There wasn't much they could say, though. Long Beach was profitable. The prices it charged borrowers were high enough to make up for the loans' sizable default rate, and it kept its default rate within reason by refinancing many borrowers when they started to get into trouble.

Financial regulators tend to focus on the "safety and soundness" of the institutions they oversee. As long as financial institutions are making money and seem to have an adequate capital cushion, regulators usually don't worry much about how they treat their customers. Federal examiners who looked at Long Beach in the early '90s focused less on subprime lending and more on other concerns. They worried that Long Beach, like Guardian Savings before it, had too many dicey commercial loans on its books, and that Roland Arnall was running the company too much as a personal fiefdom. They demanded that Long Beach improve its accounting practices and add members to its board who didn't have family ties to Arnall or others connected to the thrift.

Bob Labrador, Long Beach's treasurer, thought regulators' complaints amounted mostly to nitpicking, the equivalent of a neighbor who, seeing you're changing a tire, walks over and informs you that you have a flat. Long Beach was already working to reduce its exposure to commercial real estate, and Arnall was none too happy about questions and concerns voiced by the bureaucrats.

Still, Arnall knew he couldn't afford to get into a fight with the feds. He agreed to their restrictions. Long Beach and the Office of Thrift Supervision reached a "supervisory agreement," with Long Beach promising to make changes and write a series of detailed corrective plans. For Arnall, it was a delaying tactic. He had his own secret plan. He was going to remove himself and his company from the jurisdiction of the OTS forever.

In the fall of 1994, Arnall sold more than $500 million of his customers' savings deposits to one of his thrift's competitors, Home Savings of America. Then he and Labrador climbed into Arnall's car. Arnall's chauffeur drove them up the Santa Ana Freeway to La Palma, where the OTS's regional offices were located. Once inside, Arnall slapped down the paperwork that surrendered Long Beach's license to operate as an S&L. "Here you go," Arnall said. "I'm done." Long Beach Bank, FSB, which had begun its life as Long Beach Savings and Loan, no longer existed. Now his company would be an independent mortgage lender, Long Beach Mortgage Company, licensed by the California Department of Corporations. Arnall would no longer have to worry about thrift examiners peering over his shoulder.

As part of the transformation, Arnall laid off hundreds of employees. The company would be leaner and more sales oriented than ever. Many of the clerks and bean counters necessary for the operation of a savings and loan were no longer needed. Among those Arnall let go was Labrador, who had been working for the company since the early '80s. Another executive who parted ways with Arnall was Al Leupp, the company's chief financial officer. Leupp had worked for Arnall for more than twenty years, first as his accountant and then as an officer of the S&L. Leupp was the sergeant at arms of the place, former colleagues recalled, a voice of reason who tried to restrain Arnall's freewheeling ways and make sure he stayed within the letter of the rules. "If anybody was responsible for keeping Long Beach relatively clean and keeping the regulators out of our hair when they were closing other S&Ls, it was Al," Labrador said. Arnall wanted more and more loan volume, and Leupp tried to slow him down, cautioning that the company should seek a steadier growth curve. Arnall accused Leupp of disloyalty and obstructionism. Long Beach employees sometimes heard them yelling at each other behind the closed doors of Arnall's office. Nobody else in the organization ever yelled back at Arnall.

Finally, they'd had enough of each other. They worked out a severance that reflected the stake in the company that Arnall had pledged to Leupp. Arnall agreed to make regular payments on what he owed, but after a few months he quit mailing the checks. Leupp hired a lawyer to prod Arnall into paying what was due to him.

✳   ✳   ✳

Now that he was fully in control of his subprime operations, Arnall pushed his sales staff to drive loan volume even higher. Competition was getting tougher. Long Beach and Quality Mortgage were no longer the only game in town. By the mid-1990s, at least two dozen lenders had entered the subprime business in a big way.

The changes in the market were driven in part by changes in the law. In 1994, around the time Arnall was getting out of the S&L business, Congress passed the Home Ownership and Equity Protection Act, known to industry and consumer wonks as HOEPA. The law had come to fruition as a result of the efforts of Roy Barnes, Bill Brennan, and others who had battled Fleet Finance and other home-equity sharks in the courts and in the media. The *60 Minutes* exposé and subsequent congressional hearings had created the momentum needed to get HOEPA passed and signed into law by the president, Bill Clinton. Unfortunately, the law was an example of what consumer protection expert Kathleen Keest has called "fighting the last war." It wasn't aimed at subprime lenders like Long Beach. Instead it targeted hard-money and second-mortgage lenders that charged sky-high interest rates and double-digit up-front points. It didn't outlaw these high prices. But if a lender made a loan that met the law's definition of a "high-cost" loan, it had to follow more stringent rules; a mortgage would be considered to be a high-cost, or HOEPA, loan if the up-front points totaled 8 percent or more of the loan. The special class of loans that met these high-cost triggers couldn't, for example, include prepayment penalties.

Yet HOEPA's triggers were set so high that few loans were covered under the law. In the greater scheme of the marketplace, hard-money and consumer-finance lenders were already being pushed aside by Long Beach and other subprime specialists. The subprimers could charge fewer up-front points because they were making first mortgages of a much larger size. A lender that charged 12 up-front points on a $50,000 second mortgage netted $6,000 up front. But a subprime lender charging 5 points on a $200,000 loan could net $10,000. Many of the new wave of subprime lenders structured their loans so they would stay below HOEPA's triggers. After the law took effect in 1995, more than a few subprime mortgages carried up-front points totaling 7.99 percent, allowing lenders to continue including prepayment penalties and other features that strip-mined home owners' equity.

In the end, the new law's main effect was to rein in some of the most outrageous abuses, while hastening the rise of the Orange County–bred subprime-lending model. There were plenty of burgeoning subprime lenders ready to seize the opportunity. That's because Long Beach and Quality had hired and trained a small army of subprime mortgage professionals who were now striking out on their own. After getting pushed out by Arnall, Mark Schuerman had gone over to Royal Thrift, to open a subprime unit there, in offices just across the street from Long Beach Mortgage's headquarters in the city of Orange. Three other former Long Beachers—Pat Rank, Bob Dubrish, and Dennis Rivelli—launched another subprime lender, Option One

Mortgage, as a subsidiary of an Orange County S&L, Plaza Savings. Another new rival staffed by ex–Long Beachers was New Century Financial, a start-up that began life in Newport Beach. Steve Holder, an executive vice president under Arnall, was one of New Century's founders. He oversaw New Century's loan production and brought over a slew of former Long Beach employees to help get the enterprise going.

As he began to see more talent drain away, Arnall fought back with a combination of charm and litigation. When he learned that one longtime aide wanted to leave and go to work at Option One, Arnall flew to Northern California and slept on the underling's couch for two days until he agreed to stick with Long Beach. When another aide left to join yet another subprime start-up, Arnall sued, charging that the former executive had stolen Long Beach's trade secrets and had used improper means to try to lure key employees to follow him.

Over at Quality Mortgage, Russ and Becky Jedinak also found themselves fighting a wave of defections. The Jedinaks weren't always easy to work for. "They weren't too employee-friendly," said Jude Lopez, who generally admired the couple in the years he worked for them. "They liked paying their managers a lot of money and letting them deal with their people." Russ's business philosophy, it was said, boiled down to "bring in the business and we'll figure out what to do with it later."

The Jedinaks were driven, too, by a distrust of other people. "They thought everybody was out to screw them," one former executive said. "They spent days poring over contracts looking for that one word that would give them an advantage." In the world of subprime, though, maintaining a healthy suspicion was an occupational necessity. Boardroom intrigues were common. Competitors frequently raided one another's employees. By the mid-'90s, the Jedinaks found them-selves in a battle to keep their company together. Two waves of Qual-ity Mortgage employees—high-level executives, branch managers, and salespeople among them—left to form two new lenders, One Stop Mortgage and BNC Mortgage. In all, more than a dozen branches and more than one hundred employees walked out, Lopez said. The Jedinaks sued the splitters, accusing them of sabotaging Quality's business. They also dispatched teams of lawyers and managers to visit the branches that remained under Quality's control. The circuit riders checked copier usage and sifted through mortgage files to determine whether loans begun under Quality's auspices had been smuggled out to the unauthorized offshoots.

As they were siccing their lawyers on their former employees, the Jedinaks also were negotiating an end to the federal government's investigation of their conduct as owners of Guardian Savings. In December 1995, they signed a settlement with regulators, shelling out an $8.5 million penalty to the government. The feds concluded that the Jedinaks had operated Guardian in an "unsafe and unsound" manner and showed a "reckless disregard" for the law. Russ and Becky admitted no wrongdoing but agreed that they would never again be involved with an S&L or other deposit-taking entity.

The deal didn't affect Quality Mortgage, since it operated as a non-bank institution. With their problems with the feds behind them, the Jedinaks focused on keeping their new company afloat. They hired more people to replace the staffers they'd lost. Quality continued churning out $1 billion a year in subprime loans, with more than fifty branches and some six hundred employees in thirty-four states. But the combination of employee defections and rising borrower defaults had weakened the company. The Jedinaks' relationship with DLJ began to fray. They suspected DLJ had had a hand in the walkouts; DLJ, after all, had ended up with a 44 percent ownership stake in BNC, the company started by Evan Buckley, a former executive at Quality.

As tension mounted, DLJ came up with a solution. It decided to sell Quality. Russ and Becky didn't want to give up the company, Lopez recalled, but the deal was too good, worth tens of millions of dollars if they were willing to cash out their holdings. In 1996, DLJ and the Jedinaks sold the company for $65 million to a Dallas-based financial services company, Amresco, Inc. Amresco's president noted that Quality had been one of the top five subprime lenders in the country before its problems began. "We believe the infrastructure is there to get them back quickly," he said. "The machine is there. It simply needs some tender loving care."

4. Kill the Enemy

By the mid-1990s, securitization had come of age. Financial engineers were showing they could securitize any manner of asset—pools of delinquent child-support payments, security alarm contracts, electric bill payments, even the royalties from David Bowie's outer space-themed glam rock. All they needed was a stream of income that could be quantified and predicted. "You can securitize virtually everything," one Wall Street structured-finance virtuoso told *BusinessWeek*. "The imagination is our only constraint—and time, because you can't chase every deal." Asset-backed securities offerings were growing at twice the rate of run-of-the-mill corporate bonds, driven, as one Wall Street insider put it, by "an insatiable demand from investors." Big pension funds and insurance companies loved securities backed by subprime loans and other assets because they offered high returns yet still boasted high marks for safety from bond-rating agencies. The steep fees and interest rates paid by subprime borrowers helped make the securities an alluring alternative to U.S. Treasuries.

A few observers questioned whether asset-backed securities might be too good to be true. "When everybody wants to securitize, and everyone is willing to buy, and everyone thinks nothing will go wrong, there gets to be a feeding frenzy atmosphere, and you have to remain cautious," one securitization expert said. Such cautions, however, were brushed aside by the exuberance of the marketplace. Investors kept plowing cash into subprime. The investment banks, collecting large fees for putting the deals together, embraced the sector with increasing fervor. Just as Long Beach Mortgage and Quality Mortgage no longer had the field to themselves, Donaldson, Lufkin & Jenrette and Greenwich Capital found themselves challenged by a wave of Wall Street rivals who had begun to catch on to subprime's potential. Among these new competitors was an investment bank determined to make itself Wall Street's most important patron of subprime mortgages: Lehman Brothers Holdings.

* * *

Lehman Brothers traced its roots back a century and a half to when brothers Henry, Emanuel, and Mayer Lehman left Bavaria and their family's cattle business for new prospects in a new world. In 1850, they started a trading and dry-goods business in Montgomery, Alabama. Lehman Brothers became a slaveholder and champion of the Confederacy. Mayer, the youngest, was hailed as "one of the best Southern patriots."

After the war, the brothers relocated to New York City, helping to found the New York Cotton Exchange and trading in grain, sugar, coffee, and petrol. Soon the firm branched into investment banking, raising capital for the war-ravaged state of Alabama and, over the next century, helping to bankroll Sears, Roebuck and Co., TWA, Pan Am, Campbell's Soup, and Hollywood's biggest studios. Herbert Lehman, Mayer's son, won election as New York's governor and as a U.S. senator.

Bobbie Lehman was the last of the family dynasty to oversee the business. An art collector, owner of thoroughbred racehorses, and polo teammate of old-money icons Jock Whitney and Averell Harriman, Bobbie ran the company from 1925 until his death in 1969. Without his patrician hand to pacify various factions, Lehman Brothers lost its equilibrium. Coups toppled the firm's chairman in 1973 and again in 1983. The last palace intrigue left Lehman Brothers vulnerable, within months, to a takeover by American Express.

The two companies were a bad fit. Cultures clashed. American Express had to ante up billions to keep Lehman afloat. AmEx finally gave up, spinning off Lehman Brothers as an independent company in the spring of 1994. Lehman was free to stand on its own, but it was a shell of what it had been, a "narrowly focused pipsqueak of a bond house." The future didn't look good. "Can Lehman survive?" a headline writer at *Fortune* asked. The firm's costs were bloated, and it was entrenched in low-earning bond markets while rivals were making killings in stocks, foreign exchange, and complex financial "derivatives," which allowed investors to make bets on all manner of markets and companies.

The architect of Lehman's comeback was its new chairman, Richard S. Fuld, who had spent his whole career at Lehman, starting at the firm in the year Bobbie Lehman died. Fuld had grown up in upper-middle-class Westchester, New York, but his most important mentor in his early days at Lehman was Lew Glucksman, a foulmouthed bond trader who was driven, it was said, by "bristling class resentment." Glucksman hated the Ivy League–trained bankers who ran the place and took most of the profits for themselves. Fuld claimed his mentor's attitudes as his own. "Fucking bankers," he'd complain. He was pugnacious and driven, given to monosyllabic grunts that earned him the nickname "The Gorilla." In his book, *Greed and Glory on Wall Street*, Ken Auletta called Fuld a "'digital mind trader,' someone who spent so much time in front of his green screen or making rat-tat-tat decisions that he was no longer human."

As he rose in the company, Fuld gained a reputation for being a demanding boss. "He thought he could intimidate you out of losing money," one former colleague told *New York Magazine*. When he was asked to take over Lehman, Fuld said he'd had an anxiety attack and stopped breathing for almost a minute. He didn't want the job, and he didn't ask for it. The pressure was too much. But he decided it was up to him to guide Lehman in its time of need. He gathered around him executives who were hungry to get ahead and hadn't had the advantaged backgrounds of the Ivy League bankers who had run the firm in the past. "We'd all been poor and we didn't want to be poor again," an early member of Fuld's inner circle said.

The new CEO instilled a "pugilistic, almost paranoid view of the world" in his troops. "Every day is a battle," he told his leadership team. "You've got to kill the enemy." Lehman needed to make tough choices if it was going to regain past glory. Dick Fuld was the man to make those choices. He trimmed fat, laying off thousands of workers, and pushed Lehman to seek out newer, higher-earning businesses. One place where Lehman made its move was in the market for subprime mortgages.

To make this push, Lehman put together a team of PhDs and other experts, hiring people away from competitors such as Prudential Securities, which was already packaging a heavy volume of subprime loans into securities deals. Lehman ramped up its operation in the last half of 1994 and first half of 1995, arranging mortgage-backed deals for some of the nation's leading subprime lenders. These included Household Finance, Beneficial Finance, and The Money Store, a late-night and daytime TV fixture that used baseball stars Phil Rizzuto and Jim Palmer as its celebrity salesmen.

Along with the brand names, Lehman also put together deals with lesser-known lenders. In an earlier era, companies of all stripes came to Lehman and other Wall Street powers, hat in hand, asking for help putting together financing to expand their businesses. In the last decades of the twentieth century, things changed. Investment bankers' social status and long-standing relationships with clients no longer carried much weight. Companies that wanted to raise capital on Wall Street were savvy about playing one investment bank against the other as a way of snagging the lowest borrowing costs possible. As far back as the 1970s, an internal company report had warned: "The major corporate names which Lehman Brothers desires as clients are now solicited, not soliciting, parties." By the '90s, competition among Wall Street firms was intense even for the business of smaller fish that investment banks had once disdained.

Among the smaller lenders that Lehman hooked up with in the mid-'90s was First National Bank of Keystone, a local bank serving a small town (pop. 600) in the coalfields of West Virginia. Keystone Bank was hardly the kind of institution you'd expect to be doing business with Wall Street's elite. It had survived, fitfully, over a century of coal booms and busts, taking in modest deposits and making small loans to folks in and around McDowell County, one of the poorest counties in one of the poorest regions in the United States. A large

motto emblazoned on the side of its building proclaimed, "Time Tried—
Panic Tested," but by the late '70s the bank boasted just $17 million in
assets. Things changed with the arrival of J. Knox McConnell, a financier from Pittsburgh. As a boy growing up in western Pennsylvania,
McConnell had been befriended by light heavyweight boxer Billy
Conn. After McConnell came home from a stint in the army in the
years after World War II, Conn gave him some advice. "If I were you,
kid, I would be a banker," the boxer said. "They go to work at 9 A.M.
and leave at 2 P.M. and all day long they sit and look at the most wonderful stuff in the world: money."

McConnell worked at banks in Pennsylvania and Micronesia
before taking over First National Bank of Keystone in 1977. He was the
oddest of characters. He was said to be worth $23 million but drove an
aging Buick and wore the same $10 thrift-store sports coat every day.
A bachelor, he hired an all-female staff, explaining that such a setup
prevented interoffice romances. Locals called his workforce "Knox's
Foxes."

By the early '90s, the bank was still a small-time affair, doing well
simply by staying afloat amid hard times for the coal business. But
McConnell dreamed of being "the No. 1 banker in the country." He
was a first-rate schmoozer, jetting around the country to banking
conferences and seminars, trying to bag new contacts and ideas. "He
was extremely outgoing. He was very animated, a lot of hand gestures," a former business associate said. "If Knox was drinking a cup
of coffee and telling a story, you'd have to be at least five or six feet
away, because he would always spill coffee on himself and half the
people he was talking to."

In 1992, McConnell flew to California for a seminar that would
change the course of Keystone's history. One of the speakers was Daniel Melgar, a San Franciscan who billed himself as an expert on how to
make money by pooling loans together through the process of securitization. Melgar and an associate, Harald Bakkebo, a Norwegian businessman who made Orange County his U.S. home base, recognized
McConnell as an easy mark, federal regulators would later conclude.
On the five-hour flight back home, McConnell excitedly drew up plans
for making Keystone a competitor in the securitization business, by

buying up subprime home-improvement loans from around the country. He needed Melgar, Bakkebo, and others, though, to make the plan a reality. "Keystone knew nothing," one bank employee later said. "Keystone didn't even know what the word *securitization* was." Melgar and his cohorts arranged for Wall Street backing and provided a pipeline of loans, mainly from California, that fed the deals.

From the start, McConnell's securitization program was a flop. The four deals Keystone put together in 1993 and 1994 didn't perform the way the bank's advisers had promised. As 1994 came to a close, representatives of Keystone's Wall Street connection, ContiTrade, an investment banking subsidiary of Continental Grain Company, met with the bank's advisers and delivered harsh news. The quality of loans Keystone was buying was so weak, the program was sure to be a money loser going forward. Conti would have nothing more to do with the bank.

That didn't stop Keystone and its allies. After the unpleasant meeting with Conti, Melgar huddled with bankers from Lehman Brothers. The investment bank was glad to help. For Lehman, building a relationship with Keystone was another step in its drive to become Wall Street's top subprime player. Lehman touted its budding partnership with Keystone in the marketing materials it used to sell itself to other subprime lenders. For Keystone, Lehman's help meant the bank could buy more loans and do larger securitizations. "The sky is the limit," Melgar crowed.

∗ ∗ ∗

It wasn't long before Lehman's pursuit of smaller lenders brought it to the proving ground for the new breed of enterprising home lenders: Orange County. One target was First Alliance Mortgage Company, known as FAMCO. The company had been one of the first subprime lenders, along with Long Beach and Guardian Savings, to tap into Wall Street's bankroll. Its go-to financier was Prudential, which at the time was the Street's No. 1 packager of subprime investments. Lehman wanted to steal First Alliance away from Prudential, and it wanted to grab Prudential's top spot in the rankings.

In the summer of 1995, Lehman sent a vice president, Errington

"Eric" Hibbert, to Southern California to check out FAMCO. To be able to sell bonds backed by FAMCO's loans, Lehman needed to be able to assure investors it had done "due diligence" on the lender. It also needed to assure itself that the lender was financially healthy, so it wouldn't have to worry about FAMCO stiffing Lehman by failing to repay a "warehouse" line of credit, money that investment banks advanced to mortgage lenders so they could make loans.

Hibbert was an engineer by training. He had immigrated to the United States from Jamaica when he was ten, growing up mostly in Brooklyn, the son of a security guard and a department store clerk. After graduating from UCLA, he joined GTE Sprint as a junior engineer, but mostly found himself fetching coffee instead of doing real engineering. He returned to New York and took a job at a company that helped scrutinize securities deals backed by loans to home owners with good credit. After he snagged a job at Lehman in the late '80s, the firm sent him into the field to vet conventional mortgages it was buying from lenders that had yet to expand into subprime. By the mid-'90s, though, Hibbert was beginning to take a look at an array of less conventional mortgage lenders.

Hibbert visited FAMCO's headquarters in Orange County in July 1995. He talked with department heads. He inspected loan files. He met FAMCO's founder, CEO, and owner, Brian Chisick. Chisick, fifty-six, seemed "slick" to Hibbert. In fact, the whole place unsettled him—the way it sold its loans, the borrowers it targeted, the prices it charged.

"I thought the place sucked," Hibbert recalled later. "By the end of the day, I mean, I thought I needed a shower."

* * *

Like Eric Hibbert, Brian Chisick was an immigrant with working-class roots. He was born in London in 1939. His father was a cabinetmaker and his mother a homemaker. The family moved to Vancouver, British Columbia, when he was fourteen.

He learned about the sales business in his early twenties, selling *Encyclopaedia Britannica* door-to-door in Trail, British Columbia, a company town dominated by Consolidated Mining and Smelting Company of Canada. He was young, and it was one of those jobs, he joked, where he "walked in the snow uphill both ways." He got dropped off in the snow early in the morning, banged on doors until lunchtime, and then went at it again all afternoon. He recalled that the full sets of the encyclopedia could be bought in installments for around $350, with payments of "twenty-six dollars and change" a month. Those early experiences helped Chisick begin to form his views on the life of a salesman and the social benefits of salesmanship. In the years to come, one of his heroes would be Brian Tracy, the author and achievement guru who held that a salesperson is a "professional problem solver" and that "the ability to persuade and influence others is central to a happy life."

In 1963, Chisick and his wife, Sarah, moved to the United States, first trying New York but then, after a few months, resettling in Southern California. He shifted from job to job, working six months here, a year or so there. He sold photocopy machines. He sold greeting cards. He went into business for himself buying and selling distressed real estate. He handled foreclosures for a local mortgage company and did a couple of stints at a national lender, Aames Home Loans, in Los Angeles and Orange County, working as a loan officer, appraiser, and branch manager.

As Chisick entered his thirties, he grew tired of working for other people. He wanted to be his own boss, and Orange County, a landscape teeming with entrepreneurs, was the perfect place to make that happen. Around 1970, he opened First National Mortgage Company of Anaheim. At first, he couldn't afford any employees. So he took on every job necessary to launch his company, writing ads for direct mail and local shopper newspapers, doing appraisals, closing loans, recruiting investors. "I did the whole thing. A one-man game," he said. "On Saturday I'd come in and wash the floors and clean the toilet."

Soon he expanded, hiring loan officers away from his old employer, Aames. He set his sights wider, dropping "Anaheim" and renaming his company First Alliance Mortgage Co. He opened branches throughout California. He wasn't a one-man show anymore.

By the late 1980s, FAMCO had 180 employees and was putting out as much as $65 million in loans a year. As FAMCO grew, so did complaints about the way it made those loans. In October 1987, Myrtle and Elmer Rogers took the company to court in Long Beach. She was seventy-four. He was sixty-two and had suffered a stroke years before. He'd dropped out of school after sixth grade and worked as a laborer. She'd dropped out after ninth grade and worked as a nurse's aide. They lived in a small olive-green home in Long Beach and got by on $500 a month between them.

The trouble started when they helped a granddaughter buy a Toyota. The dealership referred the elderly couple to FAMCO for a loan. The car loan was secured as a mortgage against their house. They paid $206 a month for a year until they learned a "balloon payment" was due—meaning they owed the lender a lump sum of $16,500. They paid it off by taking out another loan from FAMCO, this one carrying an interest rate of 42 percent. Later they took out a third loan from the company to repay the second. By then their payments had risen to $400 a month, 80 percent of their income. There was no way they could keep up.

Myrtle Rogers thought Chisick's company would repossess her grandchild's Toyota. Instead, she said, the lender tried "to take my house away from me." Chisick said his loan officers explained the loans thoroughly and the couple was approved for the initial loan only because the granddaughter told FAMCO she was expecting a $20,000 insurance settlement from the death of her husband. Actually, the granddaughter received just $8,000, and put none of it toward repaying her grandparents' loans.

A jury deliberated four days. It returned with a $1 million verdict against FAMCO. "We're shocked, we're outraged and we're very disappointed, and we will appeal it to the California Supreme Court if necessary," Chisick said. "And above all, we are guilty of no wrongdoing."

After a series of appeals, Chisick recalled, the verdict was vacated. By then, Myrtle and Elmer Rogers had died, and their lawyers threatened to sue on behalf of their granddaughter. Chisick said he agreed to pay a modest settlement to make the case go away. "We did nothing wrong," he said. "It was a minority lady who didn't like the loan she got and they sued us."

* * *

Bigger problems were coming for FAMCO. In the summer of 1988, California's Department of Corporations launched an attack that threatened the company's very life. The agency charged FAMCO with discriminating against black borrowers and generally misleading customers about what they were paying on their loans. If the majority of residents in a zip code was black, the state's lawsuit claimed, that area was designated "Never Never Land," and all applicants from that zone were charged higher rates and fees by FAMCO. "In many cases, the victims do not even know they are victims," an agency official said. "They don't know that in a neighborhood a mile away, a white borrower got a better rate."

The case had gotten its start when half a dozen former employees came forward and provided statements accusing the company of misconduct. FAMCO's management said the company was the victim of lies told by disgruntled former employees. It denounced the state's action in the strongest terms. "What the department is trying to do is stage a Pearl Harbor attack against First Alliance Mortgage Co., crucify First Alliance in the press, and have them tried and convicted and sent to the Gulag Archipelago before there's any administrative or judicial process," a lawyer for the company said, equating the company with the U.S. Pacific fleet, Jesus on the cross, and Russian political prisoners in the same sentence.

Among the lawyers on FAMCO's defense team was Willie Barnes, who had been the state's commissioner of corporations before going into private practice. Leading the charge for the state was Robert N. Kwong, a young staff attorney three years out of law school. It was Kwong's first major case. The big firms on the other side buried him in paperwork. He began to worry FAMCO was using extra-legal tactics. The whistle-blowers claimed they were being followed. Department employees spotted photographers snapping pictures from behind pillars and bushes as the company's former employees shuffled in and out of the agency's headquarters. Kwong himself was working after hours one night in the department's deserted offices when the phone rang. When he answered, the voice on the other end told him he'd better lay off FAMCO. "If you know what's good for you, you better stop what you're doing." He got another threatening call at home.

He reported the calls to the state police, but there was no way to trace them or prove anyone connected to FAMCO was involved.

The Department of Corporations wanted to put the company under state receivership, essentially a government takeover of a private company. A judge said that was too drastic, but he allowed the case to proceed. More legal scuffling followed. Finally, Chisick settled. He agreed to pay $436,000. In addition, new hires as well as Chisick and his top executives were required to take sensitivity training conducted by the National Conference of Christians and Jews. "It was really insulting to even go to those classes," Chisick recalled. "It was complete crap. There was nothing meaningful there other than expounding the Golden Rule. And, my God, we lived by that already." The investigation, Chisick said, was simply a way for the state to squeeze money out of his company.

* * *

Putting the lawsuit behind him, Chisick made changes that would help turn First Alliance into a nationwide force. It started with a phone call from an Orange County financial consultant named John Dewey. In the first half of the '80s, right out of college, Dewey had worked for Lehman Brothers' real-estate finance group, helping put together bond deals that bankrolled big apartment buildings. Dewey eventually went out on his own, buying real estate and cultivating an interest in the new developments in the world of mortgage-backed securities. He knew some of the gang at ContiTrade, which was putting together deals for The Money Store and other lenders that showed that subprime loans—which were generally known as home-equity or B/C loans in those days—could be used as the ingredients for mortgage-backed securities deals, just like plain-vanilla residential and commercial mortgages.

Dewey figured he could do the same in California. He did his homework and found that FAMCO was the biggest second-mortgage lender in the state. For years, he learned, FAMCO had depended on a pool of a few thousand individual investors: doctors, lawyers, retired schoolteachers. As a loan was being put together for a borrower, FAMCO would match the loan with one or two investors who were willing to purchase the mortgage from the lender. In essence, the investors provided the money for the loan in return for the right to get repaid the principal along with a healthy chunk of the interest. On a typical $40,000 loan with an interest rate of 14 percent, FAMCO might pass on, say, 12 percent to the investors, keeping 2 percentage points for itself, along with the hefty up-front points it charged as an origination fee.

Dewey knew there was an easier—and more profitable—way to do things. He cold-called Chisick one day in 1990. "Brian," he said, "how would you like to lower your cost of funds by 300 basis points?" In industry jargon, 300 basis points meant 3 percentage points. In other words, Dewey's idea would allow Chisick to pass on to investors just 9 percent of the interest on a 14 percent loan, keeping 5 percentage points for himself.

How could FAMCO do that? Through the magic of securitization. By funneling a large number of loans into a mortgage-backed securities pool, Dewey explained, FAMCO could alter the risk-reward relationship in its favor. Instead of buying an individual loan, investors would buy bonds backed by the payment stream for all the loans in the pool. If a few loans went bad, it didn't matter as long as the overall pool of loans performed well. And if investors had less risk to wring their hands over, they'd be willing to take lower returns—9 percent instead of 12 percent—in exchange. On a $40,000 loan, that would add an extra $1,200 onto FAMCO's balance sheet.

It sounded good in theory, but Chisick wasn't initially sold on the idea. FAMCO had been doing well without Dewey and securitization. "I wouldn't give him the time of day," Chisick recalled. "I threw him out a couple of times. He kept coming back." Finally, "just to humor him, we said: 'We'll take every sixth loan and throw it in this silly thing called a securitization.'" As the profits poured in from the early mortgage-backed bond deals, Chisick warmed to the idea. When FAMCO was matching individual loans to individual investors, he said, state rules required the lender to deal only with investors based in California. Securitization, by contrast, gave FAMCO access to investors around the world.

Along with securitization, Dewey said, he turned Chisick on to another innovation: adjustable-rate mortgages. FAMCO had specialized in doing smaller, fixed-rate second mortgages. Dewey persuaded Chisick to do first mortgages with adjustable rates. As Roland Arnall had discovered, by doing a refinancing that paid off the existing first mortgage and threw in some extra cash, Chisick's outfit could make bigger loans. His customers were open to the adjustable-rate products. Subprime borrowers, Chisick said, "are very sensitive to price," and if they have a choice between a fixed-rate loan that has a $700-a-month payment and an adjustable-rate one that has an initial payment of $475 a month, they'll take the lower payments to start. In less than a year, FAMCO went from doing $100 million a year in fixed-rate second mortgages to doing $400 million in adjustable-rate first mortgages. It opened branches in Denver, Seattle, Chicago, and Miami.

In August 1993, as head of FAMCO's capital markets program, Dewey helped the company put together its first public mortgage-backed securities deal. Prudential Securities, Wall Street's biggest packager of subprime mortgage securities, sponsored the deal, selling more than $55 million in bonds to investors. Dewey was happy with the way things were going, and he went away that fall for his honeymoon, a two-week cruise across the Mediterranean. He returned to find himself out of a job. Chisick told Dewey he was being replaced by the assistant Dewey had trained. Chisick was loyal to his mortgage salesmen; he had no problem paying his top producers $100,000, $150,000, or more. But with the company growing rapidly, Dewey's pay package, based on a percentage of the securitization deals he put together, was poised to exceed $500,000 or more a year. To pay that much to a non-salesman who wasn't bringing in customers, Dewey suspected, may have been too hard for Chisick to stomach.

For Chisick, it was a matter of dollars and cents. No hard feelings. "I wasn't against him making money. I just didn't want him to make two hundred thousand dollars every time we did a securitization," Chisick said. "John didn't want to back down on his percentage. I told him, 'You've got to come down to reality.' And he didn't, so I fired him."

Chisick no longer needed Dewey. The connection to Prudential was solid. In early 1994, Prudential put together an even larger deal with FAMCO, selling more than $100 million in mortgage-backed securities.

∗ ∗ ∗

As FAMCO reshaped its business model, a fresh legal threat emerged. Robert A. Goldstein, an Oakland consumer attorney with more than two decades' experience suing banks and other lenders, was pushing a class-action suit, *Dunning v. First Alliance*, accusing the company of misleading borrowers about its finance charges. FAMCO denied the allegations and, according to a second lawsuit filed by Goldstein, began a campaign to intimidate him and destroy his case. First, Goldstein claimed, Chisick and others associated with the lender made under-the-table cash payments to some of Goldstein's clients to persuade them to drop their suit against the lender and instead file ethics complaints against Goldstein with the California bar. After that, Goldstein claimed, FAMCO contacted borrowers who might qualify for relief in the *Dunning* case and told them Goldstein was involved in fraud and was being investigated by the state. FAMCO also filed more than a hundred lawsuits across California accusing Goldstein of illegally soliciting clients. Then, Goldstein charged, things got *very* personal: FAMCO hired goons to beat him up. According to his lawsuit, the thugs attacked him twice, in June and July 1993, breaking his ribs and causing him "physical and mental pain and suffering." Soon after Goldstein filed his second lawsuit, FAMCO capitulated, agreeing to pay nearly $7 million to settle the *Dunning* class action. Goldstein's personal lawsuit was quietly dismissed. Chisick said he had had nothing to do with any assaults on Goldstein. He filed the multiple lawsuits against Goldstein in an effort to stop a "class action attorney holdup," he said. "We were new at the game, and we tried to protect ourselves."

Eric Hibbert, the Lehman vice president, visited FAMCO's headquarters in Orange County in July 1995, a few months after the *Dunning* settlement was inked. Hibbert knew little about the lender's colorful history in the courts. It took him just two days, though, to eyeball the company and come away with the sense that it was "a weird place." "It is a sweat shop. High pressure sales for people who are in a weak state," he wrote in a four-page memo he typed for his colleagues back in New York. He didn't like the fact that the company charged an average of 14 points as an origination fee on loans. He was especially disturbed by the large number of elderly home owners with FAMCO loans. More than a few were in their seventies.

On the one hand, Hibbert wrote, "you cannot help but be impressed by FAMCO's efficient use of their tools to create their own niche. On the other hand there is something really unethical about the type of business in which FAMCO is engaged." He called the company "the used-car salesperson of B/C lending. In a sense and more so than any other lender I have seen, it is a requirement to leave your ethics at the door. . . . So far there has been little official intervention into this market sector, but if one firm was to be singled out for government action, this may be it."

Hibbert's indictment of the company didn't faze Lehman executives. Business was business. In a follow-up report, they noted that FAMCO had been in business for twenty-three years and its management was "very capable and well informed about the goals of the company." Lehman was "impressed" by the company's operations. In late November 1995, a top Lehman banker wrote to FAMCO that "Lehman Brothers would enthusiastically welcome the opportunity to become a partner in your future growth." Lehman set up a line of credit for FAMCO and helped the company raise hundreds of millions in the mortgage-backed securities market over the next couple of years.

Still, Lehman was forced to play second fiddle to Prudential, which held on to its role as FAMCO's primary financier. Chisick's company was in the catbird position of picking and choosing the big-name investment banks with which it would do business. Lehman "chased us for years," he recalled. In 1996, when Chisick decided to sell stock in his company to the public, Lehman was among the Wall Street firms that lined up for a chance to manage the initial public offering. "Yeah, we had a beauty show of just about all of the major investment bankers out there, and they came in and told us their story," Chisick recalled. Lehman didn't get the job—it went to Friedman Billings and

Ramsey, which helped Chisick and FAMCO reap tens of millions of dollars by auctioning away a portion of his stake in the company.

Losing business to lesser lights didn't sit well with Lehman Brothers. The company hated to lose. Dick Fuld saw business as a form of war, and loyalty at Lehman was defined as adherence to his code; the CEO's combativeness was imprinted upon the organization from top to bottom. Though it would be years before Lehman had FAMCO where it wanted, the investment bank would keep up the chase.

In the meantime, Lehman's win-at-all-costs ethos translated into a series of victories in the subprime sector. Between 1995 and 1996, Lehman tripled the volume of subprime loans it folded into mortgage-backed securities deals, reaching almost $7 billion, a record that placed it second on the list of Wall Street's top subprime packagers. Only Prudential did better. All together, Prudential, Lehman, and other Wall Street firms more than doubled their volume of subprime mortgage-backed securities from one year to the next, topping $38 billion in 1996. Subprime was now big business.

5. The Big Spin

As 1996 began, Roland Arnall had freed himself from many of the obstacles that had stood in his way. He no longer had S&L regulators on his back, and many of the underlings who had impeded his drive for headlong growth were gone. But he had something else to worry about: the U.S. Justice Department had turned its attention to Long Beach, opening an investigation into the company.

The investigation was a lingering by-product of Long Beach's dance with the federal Office of Thrift Supervision in the early '90s. Along with concerns about the way Long Beach handled big commercial loans, OTS examiners had identified another issue: it appeared that Arnall's company charged higher prices to borrowers who were minorities, women, or elderly. The OTS had passed its findings on to the Justice Department's Civil Rights Division.

Giving up his S&L license had not gotten Arnall off the hook. The Justice Department had latitude to investigate discriminatory practices throughout American business. Bill Clinton's attorney general, Janet Reno, urged lawyers in the Civil Rights Division to aggressively probe examples of unfair lending practices. For Arnall, an entrepreneur who thought government bureaucrats had little clue about the real world, having Justice Department gumshoes snooping through his company's loan files was the stuff of nightmares. He was indignant. Alexander "Sandy" Ross, a lawyer in the Civil Rights Division who worked on the case, recalled that Arnall protested that the idea that he or his company could be guilty of discrimination was ludi-crous. What, Arnall asked, would his mother, who'd survived the Holocaust, think of such slanders?

Ross didn't buy Arnall's wounded denials. The Justice Depart-ment's statistical analysis exposed a pattern: minorities, women, and older borrowers were indeed more likely to pay higher prices, even when compared to whites, men, and younger borrowers with similar credit histories. African-American women over the age of fifty-five who borrowed directly from Long Beach were 2.6 times more likely than younger white men to receive loans with up-front fees and points totaling 6 percent or more of their loan amount. Older black women who got a Long Beach loan through an outside mortgage broker were nearly four times more likely than younger white men to pay high points and fees. "Long Beach has used a number of devices to obtain higher prices from African Americans, Latinos, women and persons over the age of 55," the Justice Department concluded. "Long Beach has directed its marketing efforts toward persons and neighbor-hoods, particularly minority neighborhoods, that Long Beach offi-cials believed might be susceptible to higher prices that would be demanded by the lender without stating the costs of its loans or that the costs of its loans was substantially higher" than prices charged by more conventional mortgage lenders. Long Beach's salesmen led bor-rowers to believe they were getting a good deal, the department said, in part by focusing on the monthly payment and avoiding questions about points, fees, and the annual percentage rate. The interviews that Justice Department lawyers conducted with Long Beach's loan officers were revealing. Some of the salesmen, Ross recalled, were frank about which borrowers they saw as easier targets than others, telling investi-gators: "When you've got an elderly black woman, you can pretty much sell them anything you want."

The loan salesmen's comments reflected, however crudely, the sociological facts of life in the home-loan marketplace. Borrowers who traditionally have been discriminated against tend to be less wealthy and have less access to low-priced credit or information about finan-cial matters. Blue-collar women and members of minority groups may also be less likely to have the sense of entitlement that prompts, for example, younger, more prosperous white men to expect the best deals possible. In the 1990s, many older African Americans were first-generation home owners who had bought their houses through the help of government loan programs. Because of the finance industry's history of "redlining" minority neighborhoods—steering clear of black and Latino quarters and leaving the field to more costly outlets, such as pawnshops or "hard money" and consumer-finance lenders—many also came from families that had less experience with mainstream banks and lenders.

There were—and are—many exceptions to these socioeconomic dynamics, and there are people of all races, ages, and genders who are savvy consumers, hard bargainers wise to the wiles of salesmanship. But successful salespeople know to play the odds, to focus on the groups and neighborhoods where the chances of closing a deal are higher. True or not, such biases often create their own reality. Just as teachers' expectations for their students tend to influence students' performance, salespeople's expectations about their customers shape what prices and products they sell the hardest to whom. Salespeople assume certain types of consumers—the "weak, meek and ignorant," as the executives running Charles Keating's S&L holding company put it—are more likely to be malleable. They're more likely to try to pull one over on these customers, attaching extra costs and upping the price. Over the long haul, this makes it more likely that women, the elderly, and minorities will end up on the receiving end of higher prices and dirtier deals.

In the spring of 1996, as lawyers on both sides were wrangling over the Justice Department's allegations, sixty-five-year-old Betty Lacey got a call "out of the blue" from one of Arnall's mortgage salesmen. The young man initiated a transaction that seemed to be a perfect example of how lenders like Long Beach targeted vulnerable consumers. Lacey owned a two-story house on the north side of Columbus, Ohio. Around her neighborhood, Lacey, a widow, was known simply as "Mom." For months, she'd been hiding a secret. Collection agencies were pressing her to pay thousands of dollars she owed to a home-improvement con-tractor. She couldn't keep up with the payments for the home repairs on the $623 a month she got from Social Security. The Long Beach mortgage salesman promised to solve her problem. He told her he'd pay off her creditors and put another $1,300 in cash in her pocket.

Lacey signed the paperwork for a $19,800 mortgage against her home. She didn't understand that almost $1,400 of the loan amount went to processing fees and other up-front costs, and that her interest rate would be 13.4 percent. Her house payments jumped from $158 a month under her old mortgage to $303 a month, close to half her income. Instead of paying off her old mortgage in two years, at age sixty-seven, she was now obligated to make payments to Long Beach into her nineties.

To make the deal go through, someone at Long Beach had included $1,000 a month in babysitting income on her application. Lacey said she never told anyone at Long Beach that she had a source of income other than Social Security.

Within three months, she fell behind on her payments. Long Beach filed for foreclosure. The only thing that saved her home was the intervention of Pamela Simmons, a lawyer with the Legal Aid Society of Columbus. Simmons saw immediately that Lacey had been stuck with an unfair loan. "She really didn't need to get another mortgage," Simmons said. "She's a very trusting person, and because she would never do anything like that to someone else, she doesn't anticipate that anyone would ever do anything like this to her."

* * *

Arnall hired a top legal figure, Richard Thornburgh, to defend Long Beach Mortgage against the Justice Department that Thornburgh had once run. As attorney general under Ronald Reagan and George H. W. Bush, Thornburgh had overseen the prosecutions of junk-bond salesman Michael Milken and many of the nation's worst S&L crooks. Now his law firm, Kirkpatrick & Lockhart, was one of America's most powerful corporate practices, a beneficiary of Thornburgh's reputation for integrity and reform-mindedness. Retaining Thornburgh and his partners sent the message that Long Beach had the resolve and the resources to stand up to the federal government.

Long Beach had other allies, too. The American Bankers Association, the Mortgage Bankers Association, and massive mortgage institutions such as Freddie Mac, Countrywide, and Citibank jumped in, pressuring the government to back off. Industry leaders were most worried that the Justice Department was looking at not only the mortgages Long Beach had made directly through its own loan officers but also the loans made through independent mortgage brokers, an arrangement known as "wholesale lending." Lenders shouldn't be put in the position of policing loan brokers, Long Beach's lawyers and industry officials argued. The Justice Department, they said, was trying to enforce price controls, in the process creating a "compliance nightmare" and sowing fear and confusion in the mortgage market. "Your action will potentially undermine the entire wholesale mortgage lending structure of financing housing in our country," the Mortgage Bankers Association wrote. Long Beach and its supporters suggested the lender had little control over its far-flung brokers; many of them sold the company only one or two loans a year and could take their business elsewhere if Long Beach rejected their loan packages. Long Beach's lawyers argued, as well, that if the company rejected a loan to a minority borrower because the broker had set the price too high, it could end up on the receiving end of a discrimination suit alleging that it had rejected the loan on the basis of race. It was a catch-22. "If you listened to Bill Clinton in the campaign, he was saying that the affirmative action laws don't guarantee equality of opportunity," an attorney from Thornburgh's firm told *Forbes*. "What's frustrating here is that the Justice Department is insisting on equality of result." Echoing the "Quota Queen" rap that had sunk Lani Guinier, Bill Clinton's original nominee for assistant attorney general for civil rights, *Forbes* slammed the administration's fair-lending enforcers as "Quota Cops" who were "constantly on the prowl for statistical disparities that suggest bias." In fact, *Forbes* offered, these statistical disparities "may be evidence of nothing more than sensible lending practices."

At the Justice Department, the investigation was led by Deval Patrick, the lawyer Clinton had tapped to head the Civil Rights Division after Guinier's nomination foundered. Patrick, still in his thirties, had a rich education in the politics of race in America. He had grown up in a tough neighborhood on Chicago's South Side. After earning a law degree from Harvard, he went to work for the NAACP Legal Defense

Fund, litigating racially charged death-penalty and voting-rights cases. At the Justice Department he was known as a steady hand who was reviving a Civil Rights Division that had languished during the Reagan-Bush years. Patrick made it clear that the Long Beach Mortgage case wasn't about social engineering, it was about following the law: the price of loans should be based on legitimate factors, including the borrowers' qualifications and the real risk the lender is taking on. Borrowers shouldn't be gouged because of their race, gender, or age. When it came to wholesale lending, the department asserted, it was misleading for Long Beach and its supporters to suggest that the lender passively gathered in loans arranged through outside brokers; in addition to approving pricing, the company had in-house underwriters review the loans to make sure the borrowers' qualifications and loan terms fit its guidelines. And the guidelines themselves gave brokers plenty of room to fleece vulnerable populations. Long Beach's standard practice was to set a base price that took into account each customer's risk profile, then to allow the broker to add as many as 12 additional up-front points that had *nothing* to do with the customer's creditworthiness. Even if outside brokers were sniffing out the borrowers and doing most of their paperwork, Long Beach was still making loans to these customers. A Justice Department lawyer explained that there was nothing radical about the feds' case. "You are responsible for the loans you make," he said.

For the mortgage industry, that rationale was as frightening as it was plain. The idea that lenders should be accountable for loans arranged through brokers was at odds with the industry's emerging doctrine of "plausible deniability"—the notion that lenders were just a cog in a giant mortgage-production machine, and that the folks making and bankrolling home loans should be protected from legal and regulatory exposure by as many layers of insulation as possible. By 1996, nearly one out of two mortgages was made through brokers, up from about one in five a decade earlier. The proliferation of wholesale lending and the rise of Wall Street securitization were creating a complex web of actors, from the brokers and the lenders to the investment bankers and the investors, as well as loan servicers and the myriad of shell corporations set up to stockpile the securitized loans. It was, in other words, an extensive lineup of buck passers who could argue that someone else—or no one at all—was responsible for predatory tactics used to arrange mortgages.

The mortgage industry's complaints about the case had some effect. In July 1996, Patrick declared a ten-day "cooling-off period," putting the department's threats to sue Long Beach on hold. Negotiations continued and, two months later, the two sides had a deal. Long Beach agreed to pay $4 million to settle the case. Some industry insiders grumbled that the deal was vague as to how, going forward, Long Beach should monitor the brokers with which it did business. Others expressed relief. The settlement was "not what we were fearing," one industry executive said. It didn't require that Long Beach limit broker commissions, and most of the refunds extracted under the settlement would go to customers who had received their loans directly through Long Beach's own loan officers, not through outside brokers. Even Patrick, the lead government attorney on the case, sounded a conciliatory note. "We recognize that lenders understand the industry in ways we don't," he said. "That is why there is so much flexibility in the decree."

One example of the flexibility built into the deal was the government's agreement that Long Beach could direct $1 million of the settlement toward consumer education—and that Roland Arnall could pick the nonprofit groups that would get the money. Arnall identified three respected organizations with track records for defending minority communities: the National Association of Neighborhoods, the National Fair Housing Alliance, and the Leadership Conference on Civil Rights. The leaders of these groups said Arnall impressed them with his candor and his commitment to raising standards in the home-loan industry. After the organizations spent the first million in seed money, Arnall renewed his support, providing regular contributions of as much as $450,000 a year to the organizations.

It was a testament to Arnall's networking skills that he parlayed an embarrassment for his company into an association that helped promote his image as a straight-shooting reformer. He was always looking to make friends in important places. Along with the activist groups, Arnall had made another convert as a result of the Justice Department case: Deval Patrick. Sandy Ross, the Justice Department staff attorney who had been involved in the nitty-gritty of the investigation, poring through loan files and interviewing loan officers, came away with a bad impression of Arnall. He thought Arnall was shifty; summoning up his mother to defend himself, Ross thought, seemed crass. Patrick, who negotiated the final deal, reached a different impression. "We sat around my conference table. We talked it through," Patrick recalled later. "And I'll never forget Roland saying to me: 'How am I supposed to explain this to my mother . . . that I'm being sued by the Justice Department for violations of human rights?'" Arnall was, Patrick believed, a man who "wants to do the right thing."

As time went by, Arnall would suggest that Long Beach had won, that he had beaten back the government's assault. In a sense, he had. From his misadventures with the Justice Department Arnall emerged better positioned than ever to establish himself as a recognized player in the world of business and in the halls of politics.

∗   ∗   ∗

In early 1997, with the Justice Department investigation behind him, Roland Arnall revealed new plans for his financial empire. He was splitting Long Beach in two. The company's wholesale operation would become a public company that would offer shares to all comers. It would keep the Long Beach Mortgage name. The company's retail lending unit would remain private—in other words, stay in Arnall's hands—and operate under a new brand. Long Beach had positioned itself for Arnall's latest tack by nearly doubling its loan volume, increasing production from $592 million in 1995 to more than $1 billion in 1996.

Arnall stood to make a nice chunk of money by selling stock in the wholesale spin-off. His timing was a bit off, however. It wasn't a good time for a subprime lender to come to market with an initial public offering. Other subprime mortgage companies had already rolled out IPOs, flooding investors with choices, and their share prices had dropped an average of 40 percent as early enthusiasm gave way to apprehension. Worse, the market had been shaken by news of a meltdown among the big subprime auto lenders. One of them, Mercury Finance, had announced that its balance sheet had been inflated by imaginary profits and its controller had vanished. FBI agents swooped in, raiding

Mercury's headquarters in Illinois. Accounting discrepancies soon began to show up among other subprime auto lenders that, like Mercury, had relied on aggressive cash-flow projections. Subprime auto lenders, the trade press intoned, had become "the walking dead," lurching into bankruptcy court or simply shutting down altogether. An executive with one Orange County–based subprime auto lender blamed "greedy investment bankers" for funneling millions to lenders that couldn't handle the cash: "It's like putting an Indy 500 engine in your Volkswagen. After the first curve, you go off the road." Investors who had been bullish on all kinds of subprime lending were suddenly skittish. "It's like when they told you Santa Claus wasn't real," one analyst told *American Banker*. A Lehman Brothers analyst said it was probably the worst time ever to go public with a subprime mortgage lender.

Arnall didn't have a choice. He was getting a divorce, and he needed money. He had left Sally, his wife of thirty-seven years, and wanted to cash out a slice of his holdings to settle their property distribution. He made it clear, she later claimed in court papers, that there was no hope of reconciliation, telling her: "Even if you get sick, I'm still going to leave you." In the summer of 1996, as he was reaching the end of the negotiations with the Justice Department, he pushed Sally to sign a quickie divorce. "I'm your best friend," he told her. "You don't need a lawyer."

Arnall handled his wife in much the same way as he managed hirelings and business associates: he blustered and bluffed. He was cagey, searching for every advantage and keeping information about his finances to himself. He hid the existence of some assets, she later claimed, and lied about the value of others. During their marriage, she said, he considered Long Beach "his as opposed to ours." Now that they were divorcing, he wanted her to give up any claims to the company, no matter what California's marital property laws said. He offered her $1 million to walk away.

Sally was at his aged mother's bedside when she died. Minutes later, Sally recalled, he walked in and resumed his demands that she accept his terms for the divorce: "You better take care of this now." Things weren't going well with his company, he said. If she hesitated, she might have to settle for almost nothing down the road, and have to pay half of Long Beach's settlement with the feds. Later, when she read in the newspaper about the IPO for the separate wholesale business, he told her, "It has nothing to do with you."

He wore her down. She agreed to settle for $11 million and two homes. She believed she was getting half of everything.

What she didn't know was that, even in a time of market turmoil, Long Beach Mortgage's IPO had created vast wealth for her soon-to-be-former husband. The maneuver had garnered $162 million from investors, much of which went to Roland Arnall. And on top of that windfall, Arnall maintained control of a property with significant value: his company's retail lending operations.

He named his new retail-only lender Ameriquest Mortgage. "Long Beach" had a sunbaked California cachet. But it was, in the end, parochial. "Ameriquest" spoke of something bigger, grander, patriotic, heroic. It reflected Arnall's ambitions for the future.

He'd seen what Angelo Mozilo was doing at Countrywide Financial, which was based just up the highway in Los Angeles County. Mozilo, like Arnall, was a self-made man. He had been born in the Bronx, the son of a butcher, and started in the mortgage business as a fourteen-year-old messenger boy. He founded Countrywide with a partner in 1969 and built it, by the mid-'90s, into the nation's largest mortgage lender, carrying a portfolio of more than $100 billion in loans. He dressed flashily, sported a deep orange tan, and drove Rolls-Royces, "often," the *New York Times* noted, "in a shade of gold." Following Mozilo's example, Arnall didn't want to be just the biggest subprime lender in America. He wanted to be the biggest mortgage lender of any stripe. If he had his way, Ameriquest would be his platform for overtaking Mozilo as America's home-loan king.

* * *

Carolyn Warren went to work for Roland Arnall not long before the separation of Long Beach's wholesale and retail sides. She didn't know much about the mortgage business. Her experience included stints selling enrollments for a computer training school and weight-loss plans for NutriSystem. That was enough to qualify her for a job as a retail loan officer. In her interview, a manager explained that the lender helped people caught in a bind. Bill collectors were breathing down their necks. The company refinanced their mortgages and gave them cash to pay their debts. It seemed like a fun way to make a living and do some good, Warren thought.

She was assigned to a post in a high-rise in Bellevue, Washington, across the lake from Seattle. Training was brief and mostly on the job. She learned early on that after she finished walking a customer through a loan application over the phone, computers at the company's headquarters in Orange County spit out paperwork that was sealed in envelopes and quickly sent to the would-be borrowers. The printouts included the Good Faith Estimate, the disclosure required by the federal government. A coworker told her she should give borrowers a heads-up that they'd be getting something in the mail from the home office. Then, he said, Warren should explain the papers were meaningless, computer-generated flotsam, stuff that had nothing to do with their actual loans: "Don't even open them. Just throw them away. That's just an automatic disclosure." Warren was as fooled by her colleague's patter as the borrowers were. She didn't understand how crucial the Good Faith Estimate was in making sure that people fully understood the loan they were getting and that lenders like Long Beach weren't taking advantage.

Changing names hadn't changed the way things worked inside Arnall's network of retail loan branches any more than the Justice Department settlement had. The pressure to increase mortgage volume still ruled as Warren and other retail salespeople began working under the Ameriquest banner in 1997. At weekly meetings in Warren's branch, a manager would go around the table and make clear, employee by employee, how well or how badly each loan rep had done. Sales numbers were marked across a white dry-erase board. Those who fell short of their quotas were expected to come into the office on Saturday to make up the difference.

The people in the branch responded by racking up production records. But management was never satisfied. A single record-breaking month wasn't enough. On the first day of the new month, the previous month's record was announced as the branch's floor for production.

For those who did well, there were rewards. When salespeople got their first fat commission check, managers encouraged them to go out and buy an SUV or a Mercedes, which would lock them into a car payment and a lifestyle that could be supported only by selling more loans. Top performers jetted down to Orange County, where they were feted and given chances at the Big Spin, a roulette game that offered a shot at winning cars and other prizes. The bigger their sales numbers, the more spins they got. Warren returned home with fourteen-carat-gold earrings and a mountain bike.

Another perk Warren won was an all-expenses-paid trip for two to the Grand Wailea Resort in Maui, a prize granted to a few dozen top performers across the country. She and her new husband made it their honeymoon, enjoying massages, snorkeling, and a jaunt over the islands in a helicopter. Ameriquest gave her so much spending money for the trip that she couldn't use it all; she came home with $500 in her pocket. Later, when she got her W-2 form laying out all the compensation she'd received for the tax year, she noted that Ameriquest had blown $7,000 hosting her and her husband in Hawaii.

As the money and swag flowed, Warren began to have qualms about the way she was earning her perquisites and paychecks. She realized the prices Ameriquest was charging its customers were steep, in many cases much too steep considering the borrowers' creditworthiness. Just before the Hawaii junket, a coworker came to her, flushed with guilt about a deal she'd just done. "I feel kind of embarrassed by that loan," the woman said. She had put a borrower in a mortgage that cost him thousands in up-front fees but barely lowered his monthly payments. The monthly savings wouldn't catch up with the fees for decades, undoubtedly long after he'd refinanced out of the loan.

Warren asked her friend: How did she pull it off?

She'd flirted with him, the friend conceded, and the guy hadn't noticed the fees. She felt bad, she said, but she couldn't help herself. "I wanted to go to Maui *so bad*."

As Warren realized how Ameriquest was treating its borrowers, it became harder for her to go to work every day and sell its products. Her production flagged. After two years, she left Ameriquest. "I couldn't do it anymore," she said.

6. The Track

Ca-chunk. Ca-chunk. Ca-chunk. *Ca-chunk.* The big front bumper of the Ford Bronco mowed down the row of evergreens, shearing off one after another at its base. Greg Walling was behind the wheel, buzzed out of his mind on booze and pot. He and two buddies had thought it'd be hilarious to take the four-wheel drive he'd borrowed from the dealership where he was sales manager, South Bell Ford, and put it to its intended use, four wheeling through a snow-blanketed city park in Bloomington, Minnesota. They cut doughnuts in the grass and slammed through the pines before bouncing down an embankment and miring the Bronco nose-first in mud.

The cops took Walling into custody, sticking him in the backseat of a squad car while they inspected the devastation. Inside the car, Walling recalled that his driver's license listed an old address. What if he just ran off? The cops wouldn't be able to find him, he thought. He kicked out the back window of the cruiser and crawled out. He hid underneath one of the trees that he had felled. From his hideaway, he could see cops on foot and police cars moving about, searching for him.

After a while, he figured the coast was clear. He crawled out and began the walk home.

Two policemen approached him as he strolled down the street.

"What are you doing?" they asked.

"Just out for a walk," he said.

One of the officers reached out and brushed some pine needles off Walling's coat. They slapped cuffs on him and led him away.

* * *

People back home in Baudette, Minnesota, wouldn't have expected this kind of behavior from Walling. He was a nerdy Boy Scout who wore thick black glasses and was senior class president and captain of his school's football and curling teams. He never drank in high school, because he knew that if he got caught, he'd be barred from getting his varsity letters at the school's big end-of-the-year sports banquet.

Baudette (pop. 1,500) lies hard against the Canadian border. When Walling was growing up in the 1960s, it was even more out of the way than it is today. His family could only pull in one TV station on its antenna, and that was a government station broadcasting from Winnipeg. He grew up on a television diet of hockey and the Canadian Football League. Baudette was known to the outside world only because of its self-designation as the Walleye Capital of the World. Fishermen came from all over to try their luck in the Lake of the Woods.

Walling's father owned a boat repair shop in town. When Greg was twelve, his dad gave him an old boat engine to mess with. Greg took it apart and left it in pieces in a box. Months later, he reassembled and repaired the engine. It turned out he was as good at fixing engines as his dad and, when he put his mind to it, faster, too. Within a couple of years, his dad began leaving him in charge of the shop. Fishermen would come in, frustrated because their vacations had been spoiled by a sputtering motor. Would they really leave their engines in the hands of a fourteen-year-old kid? It was in those moments Walling learned his first lessons in salesmanship. He sold himself to dubious customers, asking smart nuts-and-bolts questions and projecting a sense of competence and conscientiousness.

Later, when he attended college in Duluth, he sold Weatherbeater and Easy Living paint at Sears. He liked it that the department store never failed to make good on its money-back guarantee that the paints would cover any surface in one coat. If you don't believe in the product you're selling, he thought, you're just a con artist. He dropped out of school and went through a series of jobs: salesman at a used-car lot near the North Dakota border, bartender at a skid-row watering hole in Grand Forks, hired hand at a plastic-bag factory in Bloomington. It was during those years that he developed a taste for alcohol and marijuana.

In the mid-'80s, he landed a job at South Bell Ford in the Twin Cities suburbs. He turned out to be a good salesman. He was a big teddy bear of a man, a guy who seemed so friendly and genuine that people naturally trusted him. Soon the dealership promoted him to sales manager. He lost that job after mucking up the Bronco and doing $17,000 in damage to the city park. He avoided jail by paying restitution and graduating from an alcohol treatment program. He went back to work in the car business. He vowed never to drink again.

He'd been sober for ten years when he got a call in the summer of 1997 from a headhunter working on behalf of a mortgage company he'd never heard of. He almost hung up the phone. But the headhunter told him that he could make at least $120,000 a year selling loans for First Alliance Mortgage Company. That caught Walling's interest. He was making good money at his new dealership, $75,000 a year, but he was working long hours, late into the night on weekdays, and on Saturdays, too. His wife, Julie, joked that she was a single mom. FAMCO, in contrast, promised that he'd only have to work a standard nine-to-six, Monday through Friday shift.

A series of intensive telephone and face-to-face interviews followed. The mortgage company explained that it wanted great salesmen, the best of the best. It was looking to grow by hiring high-earning car salesmen who were pulling in a minimum of $100,000 a year. It was making an exception for Walling because Minnesota was a lower-wage state.

Patty Sullivan, FAMCO's training director, flew out to the Twin Cities to do a series of interviews with Walling and other candidates, in anticipation of FAMCO's expansion into Minnesota. Sullivan had worked for several years in auto sales, including a period when she co-owned a car dealership, before coming to FAMCO, first as a loan officer and then as the chief of training.

During their interview, Walling recalled, Sullivan asked: Had he ever told a white lie to make a sale?

Long pause. A dead giveaway. Of course he had.

"You mean like the one I'm getting ready to tell you?" Walling joked. She scribbled some notes and moved on.

The company convinced Walling that he'd be able to make unfathomable amounts of money, and yet do it without working the kinds of hours he was working at the dealership. It would be a new life for him. He'd be able to bond with his wife. He'd be able to get to know his children again. And he'd be part of an elite corps, the best sales force in the mortgage business. He'd do whatever it took to get the job and keep it. Only later did he realize what a great sales job FAMCO had done on him, the guy who fancied himself as a salesman no one could put anything past. "Those fuckers," he'd grumble. "They sold me completely."

* * *

In September 1997, Walling boarded a plane in Minneapolis headed for California. When he landed at John Wayne Airport in Orange County, he knew he was far from his Minnesota homeland. He and eleven other trainees had been shuttled to FAMCO's new headquarters in Irvine for an intensive one-month immersion in the FAMCO way. All but one of them had been recruited from the auto sales business. He shared a rental car with two other trainees. Riding around Orange County in their rent-a-car during downtime, gaping at the palm trees and gleaming office towers, they were an odd trio: Greg, the Minnesotan from a town so small it made Lake Wobegon seem like a metropolis; Steve, a rotund, fast-talking, gold-chain-clad New Jerseyite; and Brent, a tall, quiet, fifty-ish Mormon from Utah. Whenever Walling started dropping profanities, Steve tried to cut him off. "The Mormon, Greg. The *Mormon*," he'd say. Still, as different as they were, they recognized each other as part of an exclusive brotherhood. They were salesmen, individuals who shared potent talents that few possess. The ability to size up people and quickly figure out what makes them tick. The power of suasion. The killer instinct to close deals.

They spent days and nights memorizing FAMCO's massive sales presentation, the "Track," short for "A Loan Officer's Track to Run On." The presentation had thirteen basic steps. They sounded innocent enough: *1. Smile and Break the Ice; 2. Complete the Worksheet; 3. Complete the Statement of Obligations; 4. Tell the FAMCO story;* and so on. But as Walling and the other salesmen learned the steps, one by one, they could see where it was going, how it built, how it played on people's hopes and worries, and how it inexorably guided the borrowers into a certain view about the way credit works.

Even for a successful salesman such as Walling, the attention to detail in the Track was remarkable. Every interaction and every word passed between the borrowers and the salesman was an opportunity to cultivate the impression the company wanted to create—to build trust, a special understanding that reached across the two sides of the table. Under the Track, Walling and other loan officers were taught to "meet" borrowers three times. First, the sales rep walked into the waiting area and introduced himself, asking if the borrowers wanted coffee or a soda pop. Then he returned with the customers' beverages and "reintroduced" himself. Once he had led them into his office, he excused himself, explaining he had to retrieve their paperwork. Upon his return, he introduced himself for a third time, shaking hands, and offering a wide, friendly smile. Using this approach, Walling saw, customers would begin to think of their loan officer not as a company functionary but as a friend. After all, they had met the loan officer not once but three times. The relationship had evolved.

The Track positioned loan officers not just as friends but also as problem solvers. Customers came in with a solution in mind. The loan was a solution, and it was up to the loan officers to find out what the problem was. Find out the problem, and you had a window into the borrowers' psyches. "Finding the pain," the sales reps at FAMCO called it. That required asking question after question. Most people like to talk about themselves. Even people who are initially hesitant to open up will wear down under skillful, empathetic questioning. The loan officers were taught to ask open-ended questions rather than ones that required yes-or-no answers: How hard has it been for you since the divorce? How does it feel to wake up every day worrying about your credit-card bill? Fixing up your house for your daughter's wedding reception is a wonderful idea—how does it feel to be able to show her how proud you are of her?

A good salesman is always ready with credible responses to customers' concerns and doubts. Salesmen call this "overcoming objections." In the argot of sales, any question was considered an "objection" if it sought to elicit specific information that the salesmen didn't want customers to know. If borrowers asked a direct question, Walling would answer, "No problem, no problem." Then he'd talk fast, changing the subject, using the "rebuttals" he had learned from the Track, which made an art form of avoiding answering a question without appearing to avoid answering. If customers pressed him for an answer on exactly what their rates and fees were going to be, Walling learned, the proper response was, "May I ignore your concern about the rate and the costs if I can show you that these are minor issues in a loan?"

The genius of the Track, though, was that it played offense rather than defense. Instead of waiting for borrowers to bring up objections, the sales presentation sought to defuse those objections before the customer could even bring them up. It did this by undermining the borrowers' trust in the annual percentage rate, or APR—the government-crafted measure of the cost of credit, which combines not only the annual interest rate on the loan but also the prepaid finance charge, the origination points that the lender takes up front.

During their training, Walling and the others were expected to take copious notes and encouraged to tape-record their classes. But not on the day the class covered APR. FAMCO flew in a top-selling talent from its Chicago branch to teach that session. Sullivan, the training manager who had recruited Walling, left the room. The sales maestro told the students: Put down your pens and pencils. Cut off your tape recorders. *This is just between you and me.*

This was Step 8, the Mortgage Savings Presentation. FAMCO called this step the "Monster," a reflection of its importance and its power. The Monster's attack on APR, Walling learned, involved a bit of mathematical razzle-dazzle. A loan officer was to begin by correctly pointing out that over the life of a thirty-year loan, borrowers pay back considerably more than what they originally borrowed. Fair enough. Next came a series of leading questions, all designed to prompt borrowers to "realize" for themselves that *time* was their enemy, not the interest or fees. The loan officer would direct them to a hand-drawn chart comparing two hypothetical loans, one labeled "Smith," the other "Jones." Smith and Jones had borrowed the same amount and had the same rate and fees. But Smith paid off his loan in fifteen years while Jones paid hers over thirty. Smith, of course, ends up shelling out fewer total dollars on the loan than Jones because the lender collects interest for a shorter span. But strangely, the loan officer gently pointed out, Smith's annual percentage rate was *higher*.

What the loan officer wouldn't say was that this was because the cost of the up-front points was spread out over a shorter term, driving the average annual cost of credit higher. Instead, the loan officer would prod borrowers into saying that the interest rate and fees really didn't matter, that what mattered was for the borrower to make extra payments and pay the loan off earlier.

Persuading reasonably educated people that by paying higher fees and interest they would actually save money was quite a coup. It was logically persuasive—and entirely misleading. The truth was borrowers could always save money by paying their loans over a shorter period. In fact, they could save the most money by taking a lower-cost loan and then doubling up on their payments to settle that loan in a shorter time.

In the years to come, as FAMCO's sales techniques became an issue in court, Brian Chisick and his top aides denied there was anything underhanded about the Track or the Monster. "There was absolutely nothing misleading or deceptive about it," Chisick said. "You don't have to gild the lily to sell people money. You can be straightforward." Patty Sullivan said she trained salespeople to be honest with borrowers about their loans. "It was very important to not run away from the fees," she said. "My instructions were to the loan officers: 'Don't be afraid of the fees. It's what we charge. Be direct, don't run away from them, don't hide the ball.'" One purpose of the company's sales pitch, she said, was "to talk a little bit about how loans work, to begin to bring to reality people's expectations about interest rates. In other words, to begin for them to understand that even if they don't get the rate that they really want, they can still save a tremendous amount of money on their mortgage by paying it off ahead of time."

* * *

After FAMCO's trainees memorized the Track, they worked on their delivery. It was important to put a personal stamp on the presentation, to make it sound so natural that customers would have no idea they were being walked through a rehearsed script. The salesmen practiced on one another and on videotape. Watching themselves on tape was eye-opening. All their tics were evident. Walling learned to slow down, to not be afraid of silence, to not use filler words like "you know." One trainee had an especially tough problem. He had a scruffy black mustache and a receding hairline. Whenever he asked a question, he leaned forward and put a big grin on his face. His brow would come down and it made him look, well, evil. It took a lot of practice to get rid of that deal breaker.

Walling could see that by perfecting the Monster, he'd be able to bend customers to his will. He told himself he could live with a little deception if it meant making a sale. Besides, FAMCO managers assured Walling and the other trainees that the lender would also give borrowers some benefit, by paying down credit-card debts or providing a chunk of cash out of their equity. The company's executives were quick to note that their customers had weak credit records; that made them bigger risks and, Walling thought, that meant there was nothing wrong in charging them more. If they'd been more financially responsible, they wouldn't need a subprime loan.

During the interview process, Walling recalled, company representatives had told him that FAMCO usually charged 10 or 12 upfront points for originating a loan. Near the end of their month in Orange County, Sullivan gave the trainees their passwords and had them log on to the company's computer system. She instructed them to pull up a program that would display a sample loan. Walling and the others in the room noticed something immediately: the loan terms included more than 20 points. A murmur rose around the room. Ten or 12 points was a lot. Twenty points seemed a bit beyond the pale. But

Walling pushed the thought aside. It was too late to quit now. He'd already given notice at his old job. He was committed.

As the class was getting ready to leave, Brian Chisick made an appearance. Chisick was now fifty-eight, a broad-shouldered, handsome man with the tanned look of a California surfer. Until just a few years earlier, Chisick had personally taught the loan officer classes. Now he was too busy. His company had gone public and had expanded to sixteen states and into his native United Kingdom. Chisick, Walling recalled, told his newest set of disciples that the only thing keeping the company from expanding was the need for more bodies. If he could put more salesmen out in the field, FAMCO was going to be an unstoppable force. His confidence seemed to fill the room. He gazed at the eleven trainees who had made it through the loan officer boot camp and told them: We are the best in the business. FAMCO is going to change your life. Is there anybody here who thinks you can make too much profit? Is there a law against making a profit?

No one in his audience could disagree.

* * *

Financial regulators cultivate an aura of colorlessness. They work in a profession shadowed by the specter of bank runs. State and national regulation of financial firms, after all, grew out of the panic-fueled bank failures that were common during the Depression. Regulators live by a code that emphasizes "safety and soundness" above all. They dress conservatively. They say little to the media. When consumer complaints come in, regulators generally err on the side of shielding the institution unless the evidence is overwhelming.

Chuck Cross was a different animal. He didn't have much patience for bureaucratic niceties. In the early 1990s, after working as a bank examiner for the federal government and Washington State, he left to take a private-sector job, managing the headquarters of a mortgage brokerage based in Bellingham, Washington, near the Canadian border.

It was an education. He discovered that some loan officers simply wouldn't give customers the federal truth-in-lending disclosure, which outlined the APR and other key details about their loan's costs.

Once one of his managers walked into a branch and found one of his employees sitting at a typewriter at 1 A.M., using a blank W-2 tax form to create a fake financial profile for a borrower who needed a boost in his income to qualify for a loan. Cross fired the ones he could catch and, when he returned to the Washington State Department of Financial Institutions, he brought an understanding of how things worked in the real world. He wanted to do something to clean up the bad practices in the mortgage industry. He was frustrated, though, because the nature of government regulation meant he was constantly running about two years behind the bad guys. A new company would open shop or an old one would invent a new scam. Borrowers were so taken in by the lenders' wiles that they had no idea they'd been fleeced until six months or a year later. Usually they didn't realize something was amiss until their interest rate zoomed upward, or they got a bill for unpaid property taxes and realized that the reason their monthly payments had been so low was because the lender hadn't included local taxes and property insurance in the deal. The borrowers would spend another six months trying to work the issues out with their lenders. After they filed a complaint with the state, they would take a place in line behind the other complaints that had streamed into the understaffed agency. By the time a complaint got investigated and the state took action, two years had typically passed. The borrowers' memories had faded. The loan officers who'd done the dirt had moved on to another lender in another state. Lawyers for the lender, mean-while, were skilled at using the law to gunk up the process. If the complaint ever got to court, the borrowers usually had already lost their homes, and the whole thing could seem like ancient history to the judge assigned to the case.

Cross decided there was only one way to break through the inertia. Get pissed. Make it a personal mission to get the bad guys, to "pop them between the eyes" and let them know you meant business. Bank examiners were used to politely requesting documents and working out quiet solutions. That didn't work with the aggressive band of lenders that were flooding the market. They were cocky. They didn't think bureaucrats had any right to tell them how to run their operations. Cross broke through the intransigence by using lines like this: "Today my settlement offer is twenty-five thousand dollars. Pay up or tomorrow it's thirty thousand."

First Alliance Mortgage represented a bigger challenge than the local lenders he had been bird-dogging. Cross's office had been fielding complaints about FAMCO since 1995. It also was getting complaints about a smaller lender that was owned by one of Brian Chisick's sons. The complaints lodged against Jamie Chisick's operation, NationsCapital Mortgage, mirrored the concerns that had been raised about his dad's company: sky-high fees and bait-and-switch salesmanship.

Cross had no investigative help. He took FBI courses to teach himself how to conduct law-enforcement interviews. As much as he wanted to take on the big cases, he took stock of his agency's limited resources and decided to start small. Instead of going after FAMCO first, he figured, he'd go after Jamie Chisick and NationsCapital and work his way up the food chain.

In September 1997—just as Greg Walling was starting his training at FAMCO's headquarters in Southern California—Cross and his agency ordered that NationsCapital stop making loans in Washington State. That was just a first step. Cross pushed on, continuing to look for evidence, with the hope of forcing the company to cough up millions in refunds to customers.

NationsCapital refused to turn over its records. Cross caught some luck, however. NationsCapital's branch manager and loan officer in Washington State were nervous types. The state's aggressive action had freaked them out, and they couldn't stop themselves from talking to Cross. Even luckier, the branch manager had previously worked at FAMCO. Sitting in the branch talking with the pair, Cross spied a binder on a shelf and walked over and grabbed it. It was a training manual that outlined a sales presentation, one that was identical to FAMCO's Track.

The branch manager, trying to be helpful, also admitted something startling. For a month, he said, while Cross was battling to get a look at NationsCapital's loan paperwork, a NationsCapital employee had been holed up in a storage shed sanitizing the company's files, stripping out documents that didn't look proper. The files were held in two-hole-punch folders. Later, when Cross got his hands on the folders, he found hundreds of tiny scraps of paper, the tops of the documents that had been ripped out. In an administrative hearing, he presented the presiding officer with a plastic baggie full of the slivers of paper he'd recovered.

* * *

In 1997, Tom James was running a satellite office on the South Side of Chicago for the Illinois attorney general. He knew the neighborhood well. It was one of the biggest African-American enclaves in America. He'd grown up there before moving to the suburbs with his parents when he was a teenager. Now he was back, as an assistant attorney general. In the 1960s and '70s, strides in civil rights and new fair-lending rules had helped a wave of middle-class black families to buy homes, often with government-backed loans, and by the '90s, their paid-off mortgages made them a target for mortgage brokers, tin men, and other sharpers. At first, James found himself grappling with small-timers. He had gone after a preacher, the Reverend Anthony T. Coleman. James filed a lawsuit charging that Coleman had used a Christian radio show and his ATC ("Always Through Christ") Ministries to enlist credulous schoolmarms to invest in what turned out to be a real-estate scam. The attorney general's office eventually won a default judgment against Coleman, obtaining a judge's order banning him from working in the mortgage business in Illinois. Because Coleman left the state and didn't return, James said, the agency wasn't able to extract monetary compensation out of him. Still, James figured it was a victory to have, in essence, run the mortgage-peddling preacher out of town.

James soon learned, though, that mortgage sleaze was more than just a local issue; states lines couldn't contain or keep out bad lenders. This became clear one day when John and Gloria Celeketic walked through his door. The Celeketics were immigrants from Serbia. They'd moved into a basement apartment in Chicago, worked hard, saved their money, and eventually bought the building where they lived, along with several other "two-flat" apartment buildings.

They'd gotten a loan from First Alliance Mortgage Company to pay off some credit-card debts. Something, they had decided, was wrong with the loan. But they weren't sure what. They brought their paperwork to James's office. He read through the stack and saw that FAMCO had rolled a $19,500 origination fee into the $141,000 mortgage.

There must be a mistake, Gloria Celeketic said. They hadn't borrowed $141,000. They'd borrowed just $118,000. James pointed to the figures on the documents. It was true that they'd only gotten about $118,000 on the loan, enough money to pay off their old mortgage as well as their credit-card debts. But adding in the $19,500 origination fee and other closing costs had pushed the amount they owed much higher.

Gloria looked at her husband. Then she burst into tears.

The Celeketics were smart business people. They were not unsophisticated borrowers. James thought: they've been tricked by a pro. Nobody could do that kind of damage by accident.

He picked up the phone and called the state's division of financial institutions. He asked if the agency had gotten any other complaints about FAMCO.

There was a long silence on the line.

It turned out that dozens of consumers had filed complaints against the company. But the colleague on the other end of the line reported that the agency had decided not to move on FAMCO; its paperwork was pristine. It made sure the *i*'s were dotted and the *t*'s were crossed. People knew what they were getting. At least that's what the documents said.

James decided to do some digging. He looked at the paperwork himself. He talked to borrowers. He started to appreciate, he said, that FAMCO had perfected a system for using the official mortgage paperwork to confuse borrowers and obfuscate the facts. He had to give FAMCO credit: it was a brilliantly executed fraud, a work of art.

Proving that wouldn't be easy. Just as FAMCO anticipated borrowers' objections, it anticipated potential legal attacks from regulators such as Chuck Cross and consumer-friendly lawyers such as Tom James. Its history of regulatory dustups back in California had taught it the art of legal self-defense. The Track didn't really rely on outright lies; it took small truths and fudged language and then arranged everything in such a clever way that the larger truth of what borrowers were paying was clouded over. The company had indeed made sure borrowers had signed and initialed in all the right places, officially acknowledging they knew exactly how much they were paying.

But many didn't know what they were signing. Again and again, investigators in Washington, Illinois, and other states encountered borrowers who appeared genuinely shocked when they were told exactly how much FAMCO had charged them. James, Cross, and the other law enforcers stalking FAMCO across the country began sharing information. They realized the case was too big and too complicated for one jurisdiction to handle. By comparing notes and reverse-engineering what they could glean about FAMCO's sales presentation, they began to develop a working model of how the Track worked. But to prove their case, they needed more. They needed an insider.

* * *

Greg Walling was uncomfortable. This was a loan he didn't want to make. A home owner had heard that interest rates were falling, and he'd come into FAMCO's new branch in Bloomington looking to refinance his mortgage. He didn't need cash out or bills paid. He just wanted to lower his rate. That was a problem for Walling. There was no way FAMCO was going to lower the man's rate. FAMCO usually *raised* its customers' mortgage costs. And without credit cards to pay off or some cash out, there was no way Walling could tell himself that the borrower was getting some benefit in exchange for paying 15 or 20 origination points to FAMCO.

He excused himself. He went to a manager and told him his concerns. The manager reacted, Walling later recalled, with a blast of invective, screaming: "You stupid motherfucker! Do you want to keep this job? Go back and find some goddamn benefit."

Walling wanted to keep the job. He was making lots of money. Soon he could be making $150,000, $200,000, even $250,000 a year. The only means he could think of for providing the borrower some "benefit" was to shorten the length of his loan, playing off the Monster's time-is-the-enemy riff. He wrote the man a ten-year loan, and charged him $10,000 as an origination fee, less than what FAMCO usually assessed. Paying his mortgage over ten years instead of twenty or thirty would save the man money over the long haul. What Walling didn't tell him, though, was that if he just doubled up his payments on his current mortgage he'd save money, too, and he wouldn't have to pay $10,000 in points plus miscellaneous closing costs.

As they were nearing the end of Walling's spiel, the borrower, an Asian immigrant, asked in a broken accent, "So Greg. Is this a good deal I'm doing?"

Walling looked down at his telephone. He could see the red light was on. That meant his manager was listening over the intercom.

Walling's impulse was to say, No, it's not a good deal. This is the stupidest thing ever. Get the hell out of here and run as far away from this place as you can.

Walling looked down at the phone again. The light was still red. He wasn't going to wave the customer off the loan.

But he didn't want to just say Yes, it was a good deal.

That would be an outright lie.

So he said: "I don't want to answer that question. I want *you* to come up with the answer."

What, Walling asked, had he said he wanted to accomplish with the loan?

"To save money," the borrower said.

Wasn't he saving thousands of dollars by paying off his mortgage in a shorter time?

The borrower couldn't argue with that.

"Thank you Greg," he said. "I save lots of money."

∗ ∗ ∗

Greg Walling had become a con artist. "I became a thief," he would say later. "And unfortunately, I found I was a very good thief." He told himself that he wasn't as bad as others at FAMCO. It was a bit like his weight. He was a big guy, big framed. But if he hung around people who were truly fat, he didn't feel so bad.

In his more lucid moments, though, it was hard to explain away what he was doing. This was especially true after he learned that most of his customers weren't really subprime borrowers. Their average credit score was around 700, good enough, generally, to get the best prices available on mortgages.

He began having trouble sleeping. His buddies in AA could see the change in him. They'd all been coming to the same meeting for years. Now, in meetings, he was quiet, withholding. He couldn't be honest about what he was doing at work. The others knew how dangerous it was when a reformed addict started lying to himself, explaining away his behavior. They told him he was prostituting himself. He needed to get out.

But the money he was making was just too good. Walling had been sold on a new life. He couldn't give that up.

He tried arguing with his manager about the ethics of what they were doing. The manager, Walling recalled, said he didn't care; his goal was to retire by the time he was forty-five. He told Walling he had put everything he had in a trust so that, even if he got sued, no one could get at his money.

With his manager eavesdropping on his presentations through the office intercom, Walling had no choice but to do exactly what FAMCO expected of him. If he deviated from the Track, his manager would announce over the intercom that Walling had a phone call. Walling would pick up the phone and pretend he was talking to another customer. On the other end, the manager would be yelling at him for not sticking to the script. In one instance, Walling said, a top exec visiting the Twin Cities branch from headquarters in Orange County listened in on one of his sales pitches. When Walling excused himself to go to his manager's office, Walling said, he and his manager and the executive eavesdropped as the borrowers discussed the maximum amount they would be willing to pay on their loan. It was as if borrowers were playing poker and had shown their "hole card." FAMCO had them exactly where it wanted them.

Walling's qualms about what he was doing began to dampen his killer instinct. He was having trouble closing deals. FAMCO required loan officers to close 60 percent of the deals that came through their doors. He fell short. When the company brought a second loan officer into the branch, Walling knew his time was running out. The branch wasn't doing enough business to justify two salesmen. After hours, he began copying every document he could get his hands on, and smuggling out training videos and recordings of his boss doing sales pitches. He wanted any ammunition that might help him save his job.

In February 1998, FAMCO fired him. He was angry. The company had promised him a new life, then snatched it away. He went to a lawyer, who told him there was little chance he could win a wrongful dismissal case. Walling took a job at another lender, Hometown Mortgage. Hometown charged borrowers 1 or 2 origination points. When Walling told his coworkers how much he'd charged people at FAMCO, he got one of two looks: disbelief or disgust. He quit the mortgage business and went back to his old car dealership. One day, he was parked in his office at Freeway Dodge, stewing about FAMCO. He wondered if anyone had ever filed a complaint against the company. He dialed the number for the Minnesota attorney general's office. He had no intention of being a whistle-blower. He was just curious.

An agency phone operator answered, and Walling explained he was calling to check on a business.

"Are you trying to file a complaint?" the operator asked.

"No," Walling said. "Just looking for information."

"What is the name of the company?"

"First Alliance Mortgage," Walling said.

The worker said there was someone in the office looking into FAMCO. She'd put Walling through.

Before Walling could say no, the phone was ringing in Prentiss Cox's office.

*   *   *

Other states, including Illinois and Washington, had already been investigating FAMCO by the time Minnesota got involved. The state was late to the party not because its consumer cops weren't aggressive, but because FAMCO hadn't started doing business there until late 1997, when Walling had helped open the Bloomington branch. The first complaint came into the attorney general's office a few months later. Prentiss Cox, an assistant attorney general, didn't believe it at first. A lender charging 20 origination points? It must be a typo, he thought. It must be 2 points.

But it was true. And when Cox sent an investigator to pull mortgage documents at the local courthouse in St. Paul, she found FAMCO had charged borrowers an average of just under 22 points. When the investigator knocked on doors, she met borrowers who, as in other states, were stunned to learn how much they'd actually paid.

Like Tom James, his counterpart in Illinois, Cox had been chasing mostly run-of-the-mill consumer cases. He didn't know anything about subprime lending. But as with Chuck Cross in Washington State, Cox had private-sector experience that helped inform his work as a consumer defender. Before going to law school, he had worked in the food industry. He had developed a knack for numbers and an understanding for how markets and businesses work. Cox could see FAMCO was making lots of money by charging prices that had nothing to do with borrowers' credit records or the riskiness of their loans.

Cox was well into his investigation of FAMCO when the call from Walling came through.

Walling was nervous. Cox asked what his interest in FAMCO was.

Walling hesitated, then said: "I used to work for them."

Long pause.

"What did you do for the company?"

"I was a loan officer."

A longer pause.

Cox asked what his name was. Walling wasn't sure he wanted to say. Cox pressed.

Walling told Cox his name.

Yes, Cox said, he'd heard of him.

Now there was an even longer pause on Walling's end.

Finally, Walling said, "I don't know why I called. I guess I don't feel right about some of the things I did there."

Cox persuaded Walling to come in for a meeting. Walling brought his wife, Julie, with him for support. He carried a small briefcase with a couple of hundred pages of documents, about a tenth of the stash he'd collected before leaving FAMCO. He wasn't ready to commit. What if FAMCO came after him? What if a customer sued him? Would the state try to prosecute him? Cox said the state was interested in the company, not individual employees. But he made no promises. It was unlikely borrowers would sue Walling, but there was nothing to stop them from doing so.

Walling walked Cox through the Monster, letting Cox play the role of a customer. Every time Cox "objected"—asking about the loan's price tag or other details—Walling had a ready answer. As he finished, he told Cox: "There's nothing in the world more dangerous than a sales presentation in the hands of a salesman."

Afterward, he thought about his customers. Cox had mentioned several of them by name. Some, Cox said, were on the verge of losing their homes. If Walling had any shred of denial left in him, that burned it away. He thought about the lessons of brutal honesty he had learned in AA. Alcoholism is a disease built on lies and self-delusion. AA's twelve-step creed urges alcoholics to make a "searching and fearless inventory" of themselves, and to be willing to make amends to the people they've hurt.

Walling decided he would do whatever he could to help Cox. He had copied his cache of documents as an act of self-preservation, to hang on to a job that, he believed, required him to lie and cheat. Now he would use them to help expose FAMCO. He couldn't give people back the money he had stolen, but he could do something to make sure it didn't happen to anyone else.

7. Buried

By the spring of 1998, Gary Ozenne had been living in his house on Crestview Street in Corona, California, for twenty-two years. Corona was a bedroom suburb in Riverside County, just east of the Orange County line. Ozenne and his wife had picked out the lot in a subdivision called Summerfield and watched as Standard Pacific, an Orange County–based homebuilder that was now expanding into California's Inland Empire, had put up their home. They'd picked the middle-priced model of the three ranch homes available. It cost them $41,000. The four-bedroom stucco house had a fireplace and a big backyard. The couple and their seven-year-old son, Scott, moved into the house in 1976, the bicentennial year. This, Ozenne decided, "was our piece of America," the place where they would live for the rest of their lives.

In 1991, though, he had taken a risk that put his dream in jeopardy. After twenty years in the computer business, he quit his job as a sales rep at Microsoft. He started his own company, Residential Fire Sprinklers, which installed and serviced fire-suppression systems for homes and businesses. The company had done well for a while, but eventually it faltered. Ozenne fell behind on his mortgage, and his lender began threatening to foreclose. He cashed in his Microsoft 401(k) and filed for personal bankruptcy, hoping for a second chance.

Things started to look up when he learned that the government had ordered the recall of eight million defective sprinkler heads. He would be okay, he thought, if he could refinance his adjustable-rate mortgage into a fixed-rate loan, and get a little cash out of his home equity to get his business moving again so he could take advantage of the recall. The hitch was that, with his late payments and his bankruptcy filing, his credit record was terrible. Bank after bank turned him down. Then he remembered a postcard he had received in the mail from Ameriquest Mortgage. The card told him he was "more than a credit score." Ozenne called Ameriquest and talked on the phone with a salesman who told Ozenne that if he would withdraw his bankruptcy petition, the lender could give him a good deal on a loan. Ameriquest sent him a Good Faith Estimate that described his loan as a thirty-year mortgage with no prepayment penalty and a fixed interest rate of 10.5 percent. The rate was more than 3 percentage points higher than the going rate for fixed-rate mortgages at the time—but not bad considering his credit history. The deal seemed to be the solution to Ozenne's problems.

Nothing about the new mortgage, though, turned out the way he expected, Ozenne later claimed. The loan closing took place in April 1998, at a coffee shop on Main Street in Corona. Ameriquest sent a representative bearing Ozenne's loan documents. As he read through the paperwork, Ozenne saw that what the lender was offering was nothing like what he had been promised. The loan carried an adjustable rate that started at 14.5 percent. It could never go down, but it could climb to as high as 20.5 percent. The thousands he had been told he'd receive as cash out had disappeared, and the contract included a prepayment clause that would force him to pay a big penalty if he tried to refinance.

Ozenne tried to object to the bait and switch, but the Ameriquest functionary said he couldn't answer any questions. He was just a courier. If Ozenne signed the papers, the courier suggested, he'd have time to fix any discrepancies before the loan became official. Under federal law, he had a three-day "right of rescission." He could change his mind about the loan within three business days.

Ozenne had been backed into a corner. The lender's assurances had persuaded him to abandon other strategies for saving his house, prompting him to quit looking for other loans and to withdraw his bankruptcy petition. So he signed.

Then he began calling the Ameriquest manager who had negotiated the deal with him over the phone. For nearly three days, he said, the manager didn't call back. Ozenne finally left a message saying if he didn't hear back from the manager, he was going to cancel the deal. A couple of hours before the three-day period was up, the manager faxed him a letter urging him to stick with the deal. If he made his payments on time, the manager said, he could refinance into a better loan in twelve months. Ozenne decided he had no choice. He let the deal go through. Soon after Ozenne tied his fortunes to Ameriquest, the lender handed off his mortgage to one of its allies. A document was filed in the county courthouse verifying that the mortgage on the house at 861 West Crestview Street in Corona, California, had been assigned, "for value received," to "Lehman Capital, a division of Lehman Brothers Holdings Inc., 3 World Financial Center, New York, New York 10285." Gary Ozenne's loan had become part of the global mortgage machine.

* * *

As Gary Ozenne and other borrowers signed loans and more dollars flowed in from Wall Street, Ameriquest began hiring new salespeople and opening new branches around the nation. Travis Paules was one of the company's hires in 1998, recruited away from a consumer finance company to open an Ameriquest outpost in Camp Hill, Pennsylvania, a suburb of Harrisburg, the state capital.

Paules was twenty-eight. He had been working for three years in nearby Lancaster for American General Finance. He wasn't, he later recalled, an upstanding guy. He smoked pot every day, boozed, gambled, frequented strip clubs when he had a little extra cash. One thing he did have going for him was a work ethic. His mother had been a disciplinarian. She'd hated laziness. When he was thirteen, his father had given him a copy of Napoleon Hill's *Think and Grow Rich*, the bestselling guide to striving and success. At American General, he was a "company man," a by-the-book branch manager, always on time and diligent with his paperwork. He cut no corners because American General made it clear that it didn't want him to cut corners, and that he should balance the need for loan production with the need for sound loan underwriting. "I played within the sandbox they allotted me," he said. "I always liked to say: My personal morals aren't good, but I have good business morals."

He was earning just under $50,000 a year. An acquaintance who worked at Ameriquest suggested he could make a lot more at the up-and-coming mortgage lender. As much as $150,000 a year, running a branch. She was just a loan officer, she said, and she was making a hundred grand. Soon after, Paules's supervisor at American General told him that he'd have to wait on the promotion he had been expecting, and that he shouldn't expect more than a 3 percent raise for the year. Paules picked up the phone and dialed Ameriquest.

About the only guidance he received before he opened the branch came from his new supervisor. She suggested he bring a list of American General employees and borrowers with him. He could draw from the employee list as he recruited for the new branch and hit up American General's customers with offers to refinance their debts. Paules thought that sounded strange. It wasn't the way he'd been taught to operate at American General. He quickly learned, though, that Ameriquest was a different company from the one he had worked at before.

Soon after he started, he traveled to Las Vegas for an Ameriquest managers' conference. The lender had booked rooms at the MGM Grand, the world's largest hotel-casino complex, replete with nightclubs, waterfalls, and theme-park rides. Here was a company, he mused, that knew how to reward and motivate its employees. There was free liquor and a "money machine" booth that, like the one Russ Jedinak had set up at his sales seminars, offered exuberant branch managers the chance to grab as many wind-churned bills as they could stuff in their pockets. The training sessions seemed to be an afterthought.

Before he left Vegas, a senior executive suggested they make a "side bet." It was a ritual at Ameriquest; bosses spurred underlings to greater production by betting on what their numbers would be over a specific time period. If Paules could get his branch to hit at least $1.5 million in its first full month of operation, the company would multiply the standard commissions for Paules and his employees by a factor of 1.5.

Back home in Pennsylvania, he leaned heavily on his list of American General customers. The branch recruited more than a dozen customers away from his previous employer and by the end of the month it had booked twenty-one loans in all, a company record for a new branch. Those twenty-one mortgage contracts translated into $1.6 million in loan volume.

Paules had won his bet and made a lot of money for himself and his staff. He swaggered a bit as the new month began. But he quickly learned that last month was old history. At Ameriquest, you were only as good as your current month. The branch had exhausted the leads from his pool of American General customers. As the new month came to an end, the office's numbers had dropped dramatically. While fellow branch managers listened in on a conference call, a supervisor chewed him out, counting off a roll call of epithets that described his performance: "one-month wonder," "king for a day," "shitting the bed."

Paules regrouped, aiming to prove he was a top producer. If he'd done everything by the book at American General, it was because that's what had been required of him. At Ameriquest, he followed cues that let him know that he needed to be creative about booking loans and making money. It wasn't a case of an innocent being corrupted. It was a case, he said, of an unprincipled personality finding a place that encouraged his self-serving instincts. "It's hard to have a guilty conscience if you don't have a conscience," he said. "Anything that benefited production—that benefited me and benefited my wallet—I'd do it."

About the only check on his behavior was the risk of getting caught. At Ameriquest, the risk was low, if you covered your tracks and didn't get too out of control. He let his workers fiddle with about 10 percent of the loan files, only the deals where changing a number or creating a fake document would provide a significant boost to the branch's commissions. He didn't allow his employees to alter pay stubs or tax documents, though he did allow them to use Wite-Out to alter the monthly benefit amounts listed on a couple of elderly borrowers' Social Security award letters.

He learned from his colleagues that one of the best ways to game the system without endangering yourself too much was to employ what they termed the "Whoops Technique." If a borrower had an annual income of $56,000, for example, he might instead report it as

$66,000. If somebody in underwriting caught the discrepancy, he could explain that it was a typo—a single mistaken keystroke.

If a borrower really couldn't afford the deal Ameriquest was writing for them, Paules learned, there were ways around that, too. As long as borrowers made their first payment, the loan officers and managers who'd put together the deal could collect their commissions. If you gave a borrower enough cash out of the deal, they could afford to make their monthly payments for a little while, at least. Another way to ensure the borrower could make the first payment was to work out a deal with the title company that helped collate the final loan documents. The title company could slip an extra charge onto a customer's loan balance, and then book a credit for that amount to serve as the customer's first payment. The best part was that this sly arrangement also allowed loan officers to promise mortgage applicants that Ameriquest would make their first payment for "free."

Once Paules started taking shortcuts and playing around in what Ameriquest workers called the "gray area," it was hard not to go further. "An inch becomes a yard," he recalled. "And a yard becomes ten thousand yards real quick." Many of the tactics that Ameriquest employees used spread informally, through back channels and over break room bull sessions. Simply by hinting that top-performing Ameriquest branches were cutting corners to post big production numbers, Paules could nudge his underlings into employing a bit of their own derring-do to bring in loans. If somebody wasn't figuring it out for themselves, he paired them with an experienced coworker who could demonstrate the tricks of the trade.

For those who'd already become proficient at these sleights of hand, he used various incentives to encourage them to push their production ever higher, including one that he'd learned at his first management seminar with the company: the side wager. Paules approached two of his salesmen with a proposition. Like Paules, they were young and wild. They liked to party. He promised the pair that if they could top their previous monthly bests, he'd stay after hours with them on the last business day of the month and host a private party for them—complete with a stripper. The pair won the bet, and their party. The next month, Paules increased the stakes. If the two sales-men could once again set personal records, he'd hire *two* strippers. Again, the salesmen beat their goal and Paules rewarded them—and himself—with an alcohol-fueled celebration in the office that didn't let up until early the next morning.

The branch was performing so well, many months it outdid all of Ameriquest's other Pennsylvania locations combined. Paules earned $170,000 in his first eight months at Ameriquest, more than he'd earned in all four years he'd spent at American General. After fourteen months as a branch manager, Paules was promoted to area manager. He was now overseeing his old branch and five others in the state. He hadn't made it to his thirtieth birthday yet, and he had six branch managers, forty loan officers, and various support staff reporting to him.

Higher up the line, Ameriquest's senior management put policies in place that encouraged managers to prod their employees to squeeze as much profit out of borrowers as possible, even those who had solid credit histories. The company awarded bonuses to area managers, Paules said, if more than 80 percent of the loans produced under their supervision included prepayment penalties. Hitting that target, he said, could put another $5,000 a month in his pocket.

Management also controlled employees by keeping count of just about everything they did. It counted the number of loans made each month by every branch and every loan officer, tracked how much rev-enue the sales reps had built into the deals, even noted how many phone calls reps were making in any given time span. The company's computer system allowed senior executives to monitor loan officers' telephone usage. It wasn't unusual for Paules to pick up the phone and find his regional manager on the other end of the line, demanding to know why a particular loan officer had only made, say, eight sales calls in the past hour. Paules's job was to go out and let the salesman know he better get himself into gear.

Paules generally didn't find too much cause to yell at the people who worked under him—they were fun to party with and they were making him lots of money. But the pressure got to him a few months into his tenure as area manager. He was demanding more and more volume from his sales corps. Near the end of one month, his branch managers assured him that he could expect big numbers for the month. Paules reported the projections up the chain of command. When things shook out, though, production for the six branches was far below what he'd predicted. His regional manager berated him. In turn, Paules summoned all of his branch managers to a conference call and screamed at them like he never had before. His face grew a deeper shade of purple with each expletive he spat out. "Get out of your fucking glass offices and get out on the fucking floor with your fucking people!" If their salespeople didn't start producing, he told the managers, the solution was simple: get rid of them and hire someone else. If the loan officers couldn't close loans, the branch managers needed to step in and do it for them. Paules later calculated that he'd set a personal record: he'd used various forms of "the f-word" perhaps five hundred times in the fifteen to twenty minutes he was on the phone. Only later did one of his managers confess: Paules had been pushing them so hard that they'd been afraid to tell him the truth, and instead had given him rosy projections for how loan volume was shaping up for the month. They thought they could always find some trick to catch up.

* * *

Between 1995 and 1998, subprime mortgage lending more than doubled, topping $150 billion a year. The growth had less to do with consumer demand than with the availability of capital. Wall Street's securitization machine created a seemingly bottomless pool of money that subprime lenders could use to make loans. Just as real-estate developers found a way to hatch new projects so long as financing was available, subprime lenders were bound to increase their efforts to sniff out borrowers in every corner of the land.

Securitization drove growth partly by lowering barriers to entry. Subprime shops with no track record and little capital opened for business, bringing in big bucks by selling stock through an initial public offering. "You get a company, do an IPO, securitize some assets, and you're off to the races," the CEO of one subprime mortgage start-up said. Securitization also fueled growth by changing the profit dynamics, allowing lenders to book instant "gain-on-sale" profits by estimating how much money would be paid on their loans over the long haul. "Securitizations are all about guesswork," *BusinessWeek* explained. "First, companies guess how much revenue they can expect at a particular time. Then they guess how much of that money they will need to back their bonds safely. Finally they guess how much cash will be left over—and book that as profit." It was a bit of bookkeeping sleight of hand that dressed up a company's balance sheets nicely—so long as loan volume grew at a robust pace and senior managers didn't give in to the temptation to inflate their profits with wildly optimistic projections of their cash flows.

When that had happened in the subprime auto sector, subprime mortgage professionals argued that they were different from the car-loan guys; they were more scrupulous with their bookkeeping and, besides, their business was underpinned by the bedrock of the nation, the home owner, rather than deadbeats driving secondhand Camaros and Toyotas off car lots. By the fall of 1998, however, news reports indicated that the subprime mortgage business had accounting problems of its own. Green Tree Financial, the nation's leading mobile-home lender, acknowledged it had inflated its earnings by $200 million. The confession was especially embarrassing because Lawrence Coss, Green Tree's CEO, had become America's highest-paid chief executive, nailing down more than $100 million in 1996. Other home lenders ran into trouble as well. Borrower defaults were rising. Even worse, lenders reaching for more volume were poaching one another's customers, driving up refinancing rates, and interrupting the stream of payments that were supposed to buoy the loan pools assembled by Lehman Brothers and the other Wall Street investment banks. This undercut the aggressive balance-sheet assumptions that had allowed them, à la subprime auto lenders, to record quick, fat profits.

With their accounting tricks under examination and their stock prices falling, subprime mortgage lenders were in a vulnerable spot when, in the summer and fall of 1998, world financial markets plunged. Investors around the globe had been spooked by the cascading effects of debt crunches in Asia and Russia and by the near collapse of Long-Term Capital Management, a multibillion-dollar hedge fund that was intimately involved with some of Wall Street's biggest players. The financial industry was battered by falling stock prices and fears of disaster. Lehman Brothers' stock price fell from a high of $85 in mid-July to less than $25 in early October. Rumors flew that Lehman was on the verge of going under. One top Lehman executive got a panicked call from his mother; she'd heard from her hairdresser that Lehman was about to file bankruptcy. Lehman's CEO, Dick Fuld, swore that his company was in good shape and asked the government to investigate whether speculators were spreading fictions in the hope of profiting from Lehman's fall.

Financial shocks usually produce a pullback from lenders of all stripes, as easy money gives way to caution. Amid the debt crises of 1998, investment bankers reduced their risk profiles by shutting down the lines of credit that subprime lenders had used to bankroll their loans. Hedge funds and other big investors, meanwhile, abruptly quit buying slices of the subprimers' securities deals. By the fall, the market for subprime mortgage-backed securities had essentially shut down. Without the flow of cash that allowed them to make loans and securitize them on Wall Street, many subprime lenders were dead in the water. Companies whose stock prices had approached $20 or $30 a year before saw their shares fall to $1 and, in some cases, zero. Dozens of subprime operations filed for bankruptcy or begged for deep-pocketed buyers to come in and save them.

* * *

Among the lenders hurt by the chaos was Brian Chisick's First Alliance Mortgage. A deep freeze in the capital markets was the last thing FAMCO needed. It had enough to handle as it tried to fight attacks from government agencies. The U.S. Justice Department and authorities in Illinois, Minnesota, Washington, and four other states were investigating the company.

The combination of the market troubles and FAMCO's growing record of litigation prompted Prudential, the lender's main financier on Wall Street, to reevaluate their relationship. Two days before Christmas 1998, Prudential informed Chisick it was cutting off FAMCO's warehouse line of credit. When Chisick heard the news, he knew it was a terrible blow. "I cried," he later recalled. He understood that losing the credit line would make it impossible for FAMCO to keep making loans. FAMCO executives scrambled to find someone else, anyone else, on Wall Street to be its banker. Most investment banks didn't want anything to do with FAMCO. Only one was willing to help: Lehman Brothers. After years of Lehman pursuing FAMCO, now FAMCO was pursuing Lehman.

Lehman said it would consider approving a temporary line of credit, then perform a "due diligence" review early in 1999 to decide whether to move forward with FAMCO. Executives from the two companies scrambled between Christmas and New Year's to get the temporary line in place. It was down to the wire. If FAMCO didn't have a credit line before the end of the year, its accountants wouldn't be able to verify that the lender was a "going concern." Lack of a "going concern" designation would make it clear FAMCO was out of business.

They got the line in place on December 30.

∗ ∗ ∗

Eric Hibbert returned to work at Lehman a few days later, after a long Christmas vacation. The phone rang. It was a call from a fellow Lehman executive. Knowing that Hibbert had written the scathing report about FAMCO back in 1995, the colleague was calling to tell him Lehman was getting involved with the company again. Hibbert's first reaction, he said later, was something along the lines of "Arrrgggghhh." Or, translated: "They suck."

The colleague assured Hibbert that FAMCO was an improved company. He noted that Francisco Nebot, who had been an executive at Shearson Lehman Mortgage in the late '80s and early '90s, had taken over as FAMCO's chief financial officer. Hibbert thought Nebot was a "pretty good guy." He agreed to go out to California and take a second look at FAMCO.

With the temporary line of credit in place, the question was whether the short-term relationship should become a long-term one. After his visit, Hibbert weighed in with a memo. It was more optimistic than the one he had written back in 1995. He said Nebot and Jeff Smith, the company's marketing director, were strong managers. He said FAMCO was "absolutely amazing at ferreting through large databases to find its target customer." But Hibbert added that Chisick, the

CEO, was "undistinguished" and that the company's leaders seemed almost blasé about the fact that the company was "the subject of more litigation than any non-bankrupt firm in this sector." FAMCO officials' explanation for the flood of litigation, Hibbert said, "revolves around conspiracy theory. The firm believes that a variety of people are out to get them," ranging from a private consumer lawyer in Northern California to Chuck Cross, the Washington State banking regulator who was compiling a thick dossier on FAMCO. Hibbert thought some of the company's practices violated the spirit of truth-in-lending laws and allowed for the possibility of a "wide range of abuses." If the lender didn't change its practices, Hibbert predicted, it wouldn't survive the forces lined up against it.

The consensus among Lehman executives who were vetting the lender's record, however, was that FAMCO was a better place now and that, with Nebot helping run the show, things would continue to improve. According to the report of a Lehman review team, "negative considerations" included FAMCO's litigation problems and the "headline risk" that Lehman could garner bad publicity for being involved with the lender. But the team believed the positives outweighed the negatives. These included the expectation that aggregate fees for the initial securitization deal would total as much as $4.5 million. Going forward with FAMCO, the team said, would signal Lehman's continued commitment to the subprime market and allow it to maintain its position as a dominant player in mortgage securitization. As far as Lehman was concerned, it didn't make sense not to do business with FAMCO. As one Lehman executive later testified: "We are in the business of doing transactions, providing financing. That's what we do. So we approach opportunities in a way to say: 'All right. Let's see how we can do this, if we can do it. . . .' That's how we make money."

* * *

That philosophy of doing business meant that by the beginning of 1999, Lehman was no longer second best in subprime. The investment bank had finally vaulted past Prudential to become Wall Street's top underwriter of subprime mortgage–backed securities, packaging $17.6 billion in subprime mortgage securities in 1998. It held more than 21 percent of the subprime market, almost twice the share held by Prudential, which fell to No. 2. The subprime lenders that Lehman partnered with included BNC Mortgage, one of the spin-offs from Russ Jedinak's subprime operations, as well as companies that in one way or another had grown out of Roland Arnall's S&L: Option One, Long Beach Mortgage, and Arnall's latest venture, Ameriquest. In one transaction later in 1999, for example, Lehman packaged nearly $800 million of Ameriquest mortgages into a securitization deal, supporting Arnall's company as it tried to establish itself after the split that had sent Long Beach Mortgage on its separate way.

Another company Lehman worked closely with was Delta Financial, a subprime lender headquartered on Long Island. Lehman and other investment banks helped Delta raise more than $5 billion through securitization deals, allowing Delta to increase its loan volume from $100 million a year in the mid-'90s to nearly $1.5 billion a year by the late '90s—and to stay in business even as state and federal authorities began investigating the company.

Delta operated in more than twenty states. It gained a reputation in working-class Queens and Brooklyn as New York City's most predatory lender. Government authorities and customers' lawsuits accused the company of targeting vulnerable home owners, particularly older black women, and working with brokers who pressured and intimidated borrowers into taking out loans they had little hope of repaying. Home owners who fell behind on their mortgages suddenly found that their interest rates jumped from the low teens to 24 percent, as the result of a "default" clause written into Delta's contracts. Some had to cut back on food and medicine to keep up with their payments, state officials said. One lawsuit charged that Delta and a mortgage broker took advantage of a developmentally disabled brother and sister who owned a house together. The pair's physical and mental disabilities were "open and obvious." And because they were in a "precarious financial condition," they were doubly susceptible to "coercion and undue influence." When the brother refused to sign the papers at the broker's office, the suit said, the loan salespeople told him that, if he didn't sign, "he would be left at said location and would not be driven back to his home, and that other severe consequences would follow."

* * *

As many investors ran for cover during the late '90s crisis in sub-prime, Lehman used the turmoil to sift through the wreckage and pick up bargains. The investment bank was interested in two descendants of Russ and Becky Jedinak's Quality Mortgage USA: BNC Mortgage and Amresco. Lehman took an ownership interest in BNC, the start-up that emerged during the mid-'90s employee defections at Quality. It also struck a deal for a lending partnership with Amresco, a Texas-based lender that had snapped up the remnants of Quality after the rebellion had weakened the Jedinaks' subprime empire. Like many other subprime lenders, Amresco was struggling to stay alive. It was more than willing to throw in with Lehman. Amresco and Lehman named their joint venture Finance America.

Lehman also wanted something more out of its relationship with FAMCO than the fees and interest it collected on warehouse lending and securities underwriting. Lehman demanded that Brian Chisick grant the investment bank stock warrants in FAMCO. These would afford Lehman an option to buy a portion of the common stock in Chisick's company. Chisick wasn't happy about the idea, but he didn't have much choice. Lehman, he knew, was "the only game in town." He had to bend to its will if he wanted to stay in business.

Thanks to Lehman, FAMCO survived its near-death experience. By March 1999, Lehman was able to roll out a $115 million securitization of FAMCO loans. With a new year well under way, things were looking up across the financial markets. Lehman and other Wall Street houses had supplied cash to support the Federal Reserve's efforts to diminish the effects of Long-Term Capital's implosion. Global markets were calming down. With 1998 behind them, FAMCO and other subprime lenders hoped 1999 would be a better year for their corner of the markets, too.

* * *

The tandem-axle dump truck groaned as it climbed the twisting lane out of the valley and snaked its way through miles of strip-mined landscape. It was heading for Burke Mountain. Big trucks were a common sight in McDowell County, in the heart of West Virginia's southern coalfields. What was unusual about this truck was its cargo. It wasn't hauling coal or dirt. It was filled with bank records.

On this day in August 1999, the truck made two trips back and forth between the town of Keystone and the C&H Ranch, a mountaintop compound dominated by a manor house that locals called "The Ponderosa." In town, the truck backed up against the side of an old schoolhouse that was being used to warehouse records for First National Bank of Keystone. Workmen threw boxes of documents out a third-floor window to the truck bed below. Up on the mountain, the truck dumped the boxes into a trench, ten feet deep and one hundred feet long. Then the workers filled in the hole with dirt and seeded the soft soil with grass.

Top bank executives had good reason to bury the records. They knew the feds were closing in. They didn't want investigators to see what was contained in the papers and microfilm. With the help of the international cast of financial consultants who had connected the bank with Lehman and other Wall Street firms, little Keystone Bank had for years pulled off an elaborate fraud. It was a scheme marked by kickbacks, money laundering, extortion, bribery, hush money, front companies, fake bank accounts, doctored ledgers, falsified board minutes, even a fugitive on the run. There were two distinct groups of white-collar bank robbers, according to the feds. There were the insiders, key bank officers who embezzled tens of millions of dollars. And there were the outsiders, those who scammed the scammers, manipulating the insiders and fleecing the bank out of tens of millions more.

The insiders were led by J. Knox McConnell, the man who had engineered Keystone's rise from a struggling small-town bank to a national force. When he had taken over the bank in 1977, he had brought with him two top assistants: his longtime lover, Billie Jean Cherry, and her friend and protégée, Terry Lee Church. He installed them as the managers of "Knox's Foxes," his all-female staff.

The trio became the town's leading citizens. Glad-handing his way around Keystone's Main Street in his thrift-store suit, McConnell greeted younger men as "Cousin" and older ones as "Uncle." He talked about running for governor. He was a big supporter of Republican candidates on the state and national levels. He cultivated a friendship with George H. W. Bush and earned the nickname "Knoxie" from Barbara Bush. Cherry and Church, meanwhile, bought up property around McDowell County, including most of Main Street. Church built a ranch, the C&H, and started a Harley-Davidson dealership with her husband. Cherry got herself elected mayor and opened a bakery and a bed-and-breakfast. Next door to the B&B, she had an exact replica of Shakespeare's Globe Theatre built as a treat for a playwright friend. In one way or another, Cherry and Church signed almost every paycheck in town. Cherry also gave $5 to local schoolchildren for each A they earned in school. "These people," one ninety-three-year-old retired schoolteacher recalled, "you had all the confidence in the world in them."

The outsiders were part of a global network that included individuals, corporations, and trusts located in Georgia, Pennsylvania, Nevada, Norway, Luxembourg, New Zealand, islands in the South Pacific and the Caribbean, and, naturally, addresses in America's haven for corporate crime, Orange County, California: Costa Mesa, Newport Beach, Huntington Beach, and the city of Orange. The far-flung financiers and their companies provided Keystone expertise and connections, along with a steady source of the product that was crucial to Keystone's scheme: subprime mortgages.

*   *   *

Complexity and shadows are corporate looters' best friends. The more complicated assets are, the harder it is to put a value on them. That makes it easier for slick operators to inflate the assets' prices and entice investors to risk their money—and keep regulators and journalists from stirring up too much trouble. In the '90s, the melding of subprime loans and "asset-backed" securitization made it easy for fraudsters to cook their books and dupe borrowers and investors alike.

To pull off its scam, McConnell's bank needed a continuous upsurge in the volume of subprime loans it packaged into securities. Without it, Keystone's losses on earlier securitizations would catch up with the bank and sink it. The only way to hide the red ink was to do progressively bigger and bigger deals. The larger the deal, the more Keystone's asset base grew, giving the bank accounting wiggle room to conceal losses and allowing it to lure more deposits, which in turn provided it with the cash to close still bigger deals. In this manner, Keystone had embraced the same Ponzi-like stratagem that subprime auto lenders had used to inflate their balance sheets.

McConnell and the two California-based financiers who had introduced him to the subprime securitization business, Daniel Melgar and Harald Bakkebo, had not achieved much success with their initial securitizations through ContiTrade, the investment bank that served as underwriter on the deals. The quality of the loans had been lousy, and Keystone had trouble hiding this fact because the securitization deals had been so small. Keystone's biggest deal with Conti pooled $33 million in loans.

Under Lehman's guidance, Keystone's securitizations zoomed from $66 million to $279 million. In all, Lehman put together seven securitizations for Keystone from 1994 and 1996, totaling nearly $1 billion. The investment bank sponsored Keystone's Wall Street forays even though, as the Federal Deposit Insurance Corporation later said, the deals "had little, if any, chance of success." They were losers because, like the deals put together by Conti, they were stuffed with shoddy loans that defaulted at a brisk rate. The bank lost perhaps $75 million over the life of the Lehman securitizations, regulators later calculated. Lehman Brothers, Melgar, Bakkebo, and others involved in the deals did better, snagging millions in fees. "Keystone," the FDIC said, "was the only loser."

That, of course, wasn't what Keystone's financial reports showed at the time. Keystone simply made up profits out of thin air. It reported a "return on average assets" of nearly 9 percent in 1996, dwarfing the performance of banks in its peer group, which averaged a return of less than 1.5 percent. The bank's surging financial numbers won it acclaim as *American Banker*'s top-performing community bank for three years running.

As he was granting interviews to banking publications about his enterprise's extraordinary success, McConnell was fighting inquiries from bank examiners who suspected he was playing fast and loose. McConnell was known to cough up various curses when the subject of regulators came up. "I don't care for examiners at all," he said. "I think they ought to do away with them." The bank's federal overseer, the Office of the Comptroller of the Currency, wrote reports cataloging "unsafe and unsound" banking practices. It issued warnings. It fined the bank's board of directors.

The problem was that, for all of the OCC's efforts, the agency's scrutiny came mostly around the edges, addressing rule violations but not systematic fraud. Even Harald Bakkebo's indictment in a $200 million insurance fraud case in Louisiana didn't give regulators enough ammunition to shut down Keystone's pyramid scheme.

McConnell's personal fight against meddling regulators ended when he died of a heart attack in October 1997 at the age of seventy. He remained peculiar and full of contradictions to the end; on one occasion, Terry Lee Church claimed, he pulled a gun on her, and, at other times, he promised her and a string of other women that he'd named them as big beneficiaries in his will. Church and Billie Jean Cherry seized on McConnell's death to falsify documents and steal millions out of his estate and to further delay regulators' probes into the bank's activities.

The OCC didn't begin to close in on the criminal conspiracy until the summer of 1999, five years into the swindle. In response, Church and Cherry redoubled their efforts to cover up their crimes, burying thousands of documents on Church's mountain ranch and subjecting examiners to what one top federal executive described as a campaign of vilification and intimidation. The walls finally came tumbling down when examiners discovered the most audacious of Keystone's lies: nearly half of the $1.1 billion that the bank claimed as assets didn't exist. The First National Bank of Keystone, the investigators discovered, was carrying $515 million in loans on its books that it had already sold.

On September 1, the OCC declared the bank insolvent and the FDIC moved to take control. Many locals were stunned. They rose in anger against the blue-suited government bureaucrats and their "Gestapo-like tactics." Someone spray-painted "Auditors Go Home" in huge letters on a building within sight of the bank. Most townspeople couldn't believe that their hometown bankers had done anything wrong.

"These are good people, the kind that will do anything for you," said a former teller at the bank. "I just don't believe there is fraud here."

By October, investigators had unearthed the documents on Church's farm and issued an arrest warrant for her, commencing a series of criminal prosecutions and civil lawsuits that parceled out blame for the bank's failure. Seven Keystone employees were convicted of crimes, including obstruction, embezzlement, and fraud. Outsiders linked to the case were not charged with crimes, but were instead targeted by civil suits filed by the FDIC. Daniel Melgar denied wrongdoing but agreed to pay $1.1 million to settle the government's claims. A jury awarded the FDIC a $161 million verdict against Bakkebo, a judgment the government had little hope of collecting. Bakkebo had fled the United States after Melgar posted bail for him on the Louisiana insurance fraud charges. He died in Norway in 2006, shot in the head by an unhappy business associate.

The FDIC's insurance fund took a $664 million hit, money paid out to cover account holders' losses up to the statutory maximum of $100,000 per customer. Many locals, though, had deposited amounts well above that limit. Joe Constantino, a seventy-one-year-old retired furniture-store manager, lost $123,000 in uninsured savings. Beginning in the 1970s, he'd saved 10 percent from each paycheck for retirement. "That money was for me and for my wife," he said. "She's seven years younger than I am, and I wanted to make sure there was something there for her." He never imagined their life savings weren't safe.

✳ ✳ ✳

In the spring of 2000, executives at Lehman Brothers heard some disquieting news. The *New York Times* was working on a story about Wall Street's funding of predatory lending. Bill Ahearn, a PR executive for the investment bank, had pieced together information about the article from contacts in the mortgage industry, as well as what he described as "sources at the *Times*." The *Times* hadn't contacted Lehman Brothers yet, but Ahearn said it was likely that the story would focus on Lehman's relationship with FAMCO and would be paired with a similar story on ABC News' *20/20*, which had started collaborating with the newspaper on enterprise projects.

The lead reporter on the investigation was Diana Henriques, one of the country's most enterprising reporters. She had written for the *Philadelphia Inquirer* and *Barron's* before joining the *Times*. Her work had sparked reforms and criminal prosecutions. Ahearn dismissed her as "essentially anti–big business and a zealot. The stories she writes tend to focus on what she views as average people being disadvantaged by big corporations, usually for profit. We or any sub-prime lenders simply won't be able to talk her out of her impressions of the industry."

Lehman later learned Henriques had a reporting partner: Lowell Bergman. He, too, was a dogged investigator. Before coming to the *Times*, Bergman had been a producer for CBS's *60 Minutes*. His breakup with CBS had been dramatized in a big-budget movie, *The Insider*, that recounted Bergman's fight to broadcast a tobacco industry whistle-blower's story. Al Pacino had been tapped for the Bergman role.

Henriques and Bergman's story marked the first in depth look by a mainstream media outlet at Wall Street's links to subprime. The article opened with Bernae Gunderson, a softball umpire and paralegal in St. Paul, Minnesota. She and her husband had been socked with $13,000 in up-front fees because, the story said, a FAMCO branch manager told her "mostly lies" when she tried to clarify how much she was paying. The *Times* felt comfortable saying so without any hedging because Bernae's husband, Scott, had hit the record button on their answering machine during her phone conversation with the branch manager.

When Bernae saw the $13,000 figure on the loan documents, she had called FAMCO to figure out what it meant. She asked the manager to confirm that they'd borrowed just under $47,000.

"Right, your amount financed is $46,172," the manager assured her. "That doesn't change."

"Right, right," she continued. "And then the thirteen thousand goes on top of that? And then interest is charged?"

"No, no, no," he said.

His answer, according to the *Times*, should have been "yes, yes, yes." The $13,000 was paid on top of the $46,172, bringing the Gundersons' mortgage debt to around $60,000 and requiring them to pay interest on the fees each year for the life of the loan. The fees accounted for roughly 22 percent of the couple's house note.

The branch manager told the *Times* that he had just been following the script that FAMCO had trained him to use. Greg Walling, the former loan officer who had worked in the branch that had made the Gundersons' loan, also appeared in the *Times* story, observing that FAMCO charged customers with good credit the same amount in fees that it charged customers with terrible credit. He noted, too, that FAMCO's office outside Minneapolis happened to be just down the hall from a conventional bank branch: "I wanted to tell some of my better customers that every step they took from my door to that bank would save them one thousand dollars."

Chisick replied that his loan officers were "specifically trained to insure borrower understanding of all aspects of their loan." Lehman decided against granting what Ahearn predicted could have been an "awkward and embarrassing interview" with the reporters. The investment bank hoped it would be a "one-day issue" without any "legs." In a written statement, Ahearn told the reporters that Lehman believed FAMCO had stepped up its efforts to prevent abuses. And when Lehman sold bonds backed by FAMCO's loans, it conducted careful reviews to ascertain that investors knew what they were getting, Ahearn said. But the investment bank's responsibility only went so far. Lehman was an "underwriter, not a regulator," he asserted.

The one-two punch of a front-page story in the nation's most prestigious newspaper and a network news magazine feature increased the pressure on FAMCO. The bad dose of publicity was sure to draw even more lawsuits and more attention from government law enforcers. Lehman continued funding the company's loans, but it demanded that Brian Chisick come to New York to discuss the latest problems. Chisick refused. He took the position that there was nothing new in the reports—the allegations against his company had been out there for a long time, and Lehman was fully aware of the details.

What FAMCO needed was a new strategy, a better way of defending itself against the legal attacks. Eight days after taking the media hit, Chisick made a move. He put his company into bankruptcy. It didn't seem to make sense. FAMCO was a profitable company. But the bankruptcy filing accomplished something Chisick couldn't accomplish otherwise: it put a temporary freeze on aggrieved borrowers' claims for restitution from the company. If they were going to get any money out of FAMCO, they were going to have to get in line with other, better-positioned creditors, including Lehman Brothers. Under bankruptcy law, creditors that have outstanding loans to a bankrupt corporation generally get first dibs on whatever money's left in the company. Consumers with as-yet-unproven claims often end up fighting for scraps.

Indeed, in the context of the subprime industry, Chisick's decision wasn't unusual; it was predictable. Bankruptcy was a tool regularly used by subprime lenders to avoid financial responsibility for questionable or reckless lending policies. Mortgage lenders lived by booms and busts. Hundreds of small to midsize home lenders went bankrupt every year. From 1998 to 2000, during the subprime mortgage shakeout, most of the largest subprime lenders went bankrupt. Between them, these failed lenders had issued more than $125 billion in mortgage-backed securities. There was little money left over, however, to compensate borrowers. As Christopher L. Peterson, a law professor who investigated subprime, wrote: "If an individual or class of victims obtains a large judgment, the lender's management can simply declare bankruptcy, liquidate whatever limited assets are left, and possibly reform a new company a short time later." Managers of abusive lenders "are indifferent because they are typically paid in full, or even give themselves raises, as their companies plow into bankruptcy."

For its part, FAMCO blamed its bankruptcy mainly on "unwarranted negative publicity." "These unfair and inaccurate stories have devastated the company's thirty-year reputation and acutely hindered the company's relationships with businesses, consumers and regulators," Chisick said in a statement. Still, Francisco Nebot, FAMCO's president and CFO, acknowledged that, along with the bad publicity, the bankruptcy had been prompted by the fear of additional lawsuits and proposed state and federal laws that would limit the up-front fees lenders like FAMCO could charge. Nebot said the company was spending $7 million a year in legal bills to defend itself. He added that Chisick was suffering because of the recent events. "He's known some of the employees for twenty-five years. He's taking this very hard. There were a lot of tears."

After the news broke, spokesmen for the mortgage industry distanced themselves from FAMCO. They made noises about "bad apples" and "rogue lenders." An executive vice president for Ameriquest told the *Los Angeles Times*: "If you're running a clean company, there is nothing to worry about."

* * *

On the street, protesters chanted, "Black or poor, we pay more." High above the street, inside lower Manhattan's World Financial Center, a gaggle of government officials and fair-lending experts convened a public hearing about the pain that American home owners were suffering at the hands of unscrupulous lenders—and about the banking heavyweights that served as the predators' financial patrons. In May 2000, in and around the cluster of office towers that served as headquarters for Lehman Brothers and Merrill Lynch, Wall Street was being put on trial in absentia. Organizers had asked the top financial firms to send envoys to speak at the hearing. But none of the corporate invitees showed up. "We're in one of Wall Street's houses, but Wall Street's not here," the head of a lending watchdog group announced. The Street's role in predatory lending was under intense scrutiny. Community activists and politicians around the country were connecting the dots and pointing fingers. "The bottom-feeders in society are reaching up to the titans of society. We need to break that link," Senator Charles Schumer, a New York Democrat, said at the hearing. U.S. housing secretary Andrew Cuomo spoke of "con men who are being financed by some of the biggest players in the market." Cuomo gave the high-level money men a bit of an out, saying, "I don't think that Wall Street investors are aware of the problem." But he added that he was certain they would quickly distance themselves from the bad actors once they learned the truth. "It's not going to be enough to say, 'We didn't know.'"

The speakers at the hearing articulated a straightforward solution: hold banks, Wall Street houses, and big investors accountable for the loans they were funding. If the evidence showed little guys down the food chain were peddling predatory loans, the money men should cut off the flow of cash. From the point of view of investment bankers and mortgage lenders, it was a scary argument. It represented a mortal danger to the mortgage machine that Wall Street had built, flying in the face of the home-loan complex's doctrine of deniability, which put distance between the financiers of loans and the dirty tricks on the ground level that were used to draw in borrowers.

As the 2000 race for the White House heated up, the subprime industry's leaders felt as if they were under siege. States and cities were trying to pass laws and ordinances that clamped down on subprimers' grubbiest practices. The Clinton administration was pushing to tighten federal lending rules. Robert Pitofsky, chairman of the Federal Trade Commission, declared that the subprime market demonstrated "some of the most abusive, anti-consumer overreaching I have ever seen." Even Alan Greenspan, a true believer in the let-the-market-sort-things-out strain of capitalism, fretted publicly about "abusive lending practices" that targeted impoverished neighborhoods and vulnerable populations.

Federal banking regulators questioned Lehman's relationship with Delta, the Long Island–based lender that had recently reached a multimillion-dollar predatory-lending settlement with New York State authorities. When Lehman asked the Office of Thrift Supervision to approve its purchase of a small S&L, the agency brought up Lehman's financing of Delta's loans. "We had concerns about Lehman's involvement with Delta Funding and we had to get behind it," the OTS's deputy director said. Lehman promised the agency it wouldn't finance lenders that engaged in predatory lending or underwrite securities backed by their loans. It was a paper commitment without teeth, but it did show that federal regulators were starting to worry about what was going on in the subprime market.

No federal official was more concerned than Donna Tanoue, Clinton's chief at the FDIC. She and her aides found themselves trying to untangle a puzzle: Why were they seeing a surge of bank failures during a booming economy? Eleven banks had gone under in eighteen months, producing a $1 billion hit to the deposit insurance fund that Tanoue oversaw. As she and her staff sifted through the wreckage,

they noted that six of the eleven had been heavily involved in subprime lending and that the losses from those institutions were out-
sized compared to the losses at the others. The failure of Keystone
alone was expected to account for two-thirds of the FDIC's payouts.
Further analysis revealed other subprime-related risks lurking among
the nation's banks. Institutions with significant involvement in subprime lending made up little more than 1 percent of federally insured
banks, but they accounted for 20 percent of the banks on federal regulators' list of troubled institutions.

Tanoue wanted to require banks with high concentrations of subprime assets to keep more cash on hand to cover their higher risks.
She also argued that banks that bought subprime mortgages from
other lenders should do a better job of inspecting the loans. "To effectively combat predatory lending, we must sever the money chain that
replenishes the capital of predatory lenders and allows them to remain
in business," she said.

The FTC and the Justice Department continued to pursue squirrely
mortgage shops, most notably Associates First Capital Corporation,
then the nation's largest subprime lender. For a time, Associates had
been a subsidiary of Ford Motor Company, and, after a stretch operating as an independent company, it had been acquired by Citigroup in
a $27 billion deal. The FTC hadn't flinched, launching a lawsuit against
Associates and Citi, charging that the subprime unit had abused its
"relationship of trust" with borrowers by inducing them to take out
high-priced loans that were inflated by overpriced insurance premi-
ums. If the FTC could prove its allegations, Citi could be on the hook
for as much as $1 billion.

* * *

Another lender that was starting to draw tougher scrutiny was Ameriquest. ACORN, the national advocacy group for low-income folks,
staged protests around the country against Arnall's company and
conducted a demonstration at the Washington, D.C., offices of Salomon Smith Barney, a Citigroup subsidiary that had bought some $3
billion in loans from the lender. At Salomon's office building on K
Street, the capital's lobbyist lane, an ACORN activist wore a shark

costume. He toted a sign that said: "No more loan sharks. Stop predatory lending." ACORN also funneled complaints to the FTC from thirty Ameriquest borrowers. Among them were Manuel and Guadalupe Alvarado, Mexican immigrants who had bought their first home in Orange County, California. They said an Ameriquest salesman hounded them for months to refinance, promising to lower their monthly payments. Instead, the loan raised their monthly house note from $1,125 to $1,342 and sucked away $11,000 in fees. "This loan doesn't make any sense," the couple's real-estate agent said.

The FTC opened an investigation. Just four years after his old company, Long Beach Mortgage, had settled with the Justice Department, Roland Arnall was battling another incursion from the feds. He took comfort, however, in the friendships he'd formed with civil rights and consumer activists in the aftermath of the Justice Department deal. The leader of the consumer-education consortium that Arnall had helped start defended Ameriquest in a variety of media outlets. Ricardo Byrd told the *New York Times* that he considered Ameriquest "one of the enlightened lenders." He told the *American Banker* that Ameriquest was "one of the few companies in this industry that is being aggressive about making sure that consumers aren't being abused. They're spending money to do that. I wish I could get more companies to put up money and not give lip service that they simply want the industry cleaned up." Byrd said Ameriquest had spent hundreds of thousands of dollars to support the consortium and hold conferences. ACORN wasn't impressed. "It's not about whether or not you can sponsor another conference," a spokeswoman said. "It's about whether you're having an impact in these neighborhoods. Ameriquest loans are having a negative impact." The scuffling continued for months, with ACORN calling Ameriquest and its ilk "slimy mortgage predators" and a top Ameriquest official responding: "How do you defend yourself against something you didn't do? This is very hard for us. It's like being asked, 'When did you stop beating your wife?'"

ACORN's demonstrations got the attention of one important person at Ameriquest: Adam Bass. Bass was a lawyer. He was the company's general counsel and senior executive vice president. He was also Roland Arnall's nephew. His aunt Sally had been Roland's first wife.

After the divorce, Bass had taken on an increasingly public role at the company, serving as Arnall's right-hand man. He was Ameriquest's point person on legal and legislative matters. He was known among activists and policy makers as a passionate advocate for his uncle's empire.

Bass agreed to conduct direct negotiations with ACORN. "Bass was smart and shrewd," Wade Rathke, ACORN's founder and president, said. "He got the big picture, so he moved quickly to resolve the headache." Bass recalled that when ACORN first targeted Ameriquest, "we felt unfairly harassed. But ultimately we decided to hear what they had to say. We found out we could learn a lot from them, and things have improved substantially."

In July 2000, the two sides announced they had reached a deal. Ameriquest agreed to launch a $360 million program that would channel as many as ten thousand home loans through ACORN chapters in ten cities around the country. The loans would carry no prepayment penalties and no more than 3 points in up-front fees. Ameriquest also unveiled a succession of "best practices." These included a promise of "full and timely disclosure of loan terms and conditions in plain English" and a commitment to determining whether borrowers could really afford their loans.

Ameriquest's promises were vague, without many specifics on how the company would carry them out. But ACORN and other watchdog groups that had financial ties to Ameriquest were elated. They portrayed the proclamation as an unprecedented victory for consumers, a model that the rest of the subprime lending industry should follow. "Working families deserve a fair deal in our society, and these new standards will help make sure they get a fighting chance for success in our economy," Wade Henderson, the chief executive of the Leadership Conference on Civil Rights, said. "Ameriquest has long been recognized for its strong ethical standards, and these 'Best Practices' will show every lender that good corporate citizenship is also a good way to do business."

The FTC found itself in a quandary. In the mortgage world, community activists often provide the impetus for government inspections. They help investigators locate aggrieved borrowers and provide the outside pressure that's often needed to counterbalance industry lobbying. With ACORN backing off and other watchdogs declaring it unthinkable that Arnall's company could act unscrupulously, the FTC was swimming against the tide. Why fight on alone? The agency closed its inquiry into Ameriquest. It said its decision shouldn't be construed as determination that the company had been blameless. But the move might as well have been a declaration of innocence.

Arnall had once again beaten back a threat from the government. And he had again turned a minus—allegations of sleazy practices— into a plus. Ameriquest would continue to roll out new "best practices" and continue gathering accolades from watchdog groups. One of the nation's most unprincipled lenders had succeeded in branding itself as a pacesetter that was "raising the bar" for ethical standards.

Ameriquest's victory was a sign that the subprime industry had the savvy and the clout to overcome efforts by bureaucrats and activists to force it to change its ways. For all the talk about reining in the unsavory habits of lenders, consumer defenders made only modest gains in the last years of the Clinton administration. Even as its appointees launched investigations and asked questions about the changing nature of American finance, the White House became a cheerleader for deregulation. It worked with Republicans in Congress to tear down the walls between commercial banks and investment houses such as Lehman, and to keep complex financial "derivatives"—the insurance-like bets on the price movements of investments and goods—outside the purview of government inspectors.

In flush economic times, the powers that be in government and finance don't spend much time worrying about worst-case scenarios or consumer protection. The FDIC, with its focus on banking fundamentals, wields little influence during booms. The immense power of the Federal Reserve, on the other hand, grows even stronger. In the '90s, pundits and policy makers hailed Alan Greenspan as the "Maestro" and treated the Federal Reserve with awe. "Whatever the Fed said was just God's words," the FDIC's Donna Tanoue recalled. While Greenspan was willing to offer strong words about shady lending, he had no enthusiasm for sweeping regulatory solutions that, as he saw it, interfered with the free market. It was better, Federal Reserve officials argued, to handle the problem on a case-by-case basis.

Some members of Congress, meanwhile, worried that a "rigid approach" to policing subprime could squeeze the flow of credit to underserved communities. "I know there are 'bad actors' out there, but I am also concerned that you could be cutting off some very worthy borrowers," Representative Carolyn Maloney, a New York Democrat, said. As she tried to get modest reforms in place, Tanoue felt as if she were getting hammered from all directions—from the Federal Reserve, from Congress, from industry insiders. "What the FDIC is proposing is ludicrous and makes no sense," said William Dallas, CEO of San Jose–based First Franklin, one of the country's largest subprime lenders. "I would think that lenders are smart enough to cover their risks on these loans and I don't think the government should stick its nose in this."

Tanoue kept fighting, but her time in Washington was short. George W. Bush's disputed victory over Al Gore brought changes to the nation's capital. By the summer of 2001, Tanoue was out at the FDIC. Bush came to Washington as a crusader against big government and regulatory intrusions. His administration had no interest in keeping on a Clinton Democrat who was making speeches about getting tough on the financial industry's excesses. Over at the Justice Department, Sandy Ross, too, could feel the chill as the new administration took over. Ross, who had worked on a string of fair-lending investigations, including the Long Beach Mortgage case, realized that the department's new management didn't have much interest in chasing lending discrimination. After higher-ranking officials refused to allow frontline staffers to file the lawsuit they had prepared against Associates and Citi, Ross decided it was time to go. He took early retirement.

8. Boil

Things were going well for Eleanor Kas in the summer of 2000. She had two decades of experience in the advertising business, and she'd landed a new job as a vice president and creative director at DDB Worldwide. DDB was one of the planet's biggest ad firms, riding a wave of success from its unforgettable "WHASSSUUP!" spots for Budweiser beer. Kas had an important assignment. She was preparing to introduce Ameriquest Mortgage to a nation of television viewers. Ameriquest executives had approved the storyboarded concept, "Affirmations," which showed home owners using their Ameriquest loans to respond to emergencies and care for their children. Everything seemed to be a go.

Then Ameriquest's owner got involved. According to Kas, the trouble began during a casting session for the commercial. Roland Arnall didn't like that the cast of characters included an African-American couple, empty nesters who were marrying off their daughter. "Why are there blacks in this commercial?" he wanted to know. Arnall's underlings explained that the on-camera demographics had been already hashed out. He let the issue drop for the moment. But he had more questions. He wanted to know about the woman playing the single mom who needed money to buy a computer for her children. What was her background? A producer indicated that the actor was Greek-American. "No. No Greeks," Arnall said. "They're too obscure."

After the meeting, Kas, who is Greek-American, was shaken. She

thought Arnall was racist, and his objections to including black customers in the ad didn't make any sense. Many of Ameriquest's borrowers were black. In fact, she noted, every piece of direct mail that
DDB had prepared for Ameriquest had showcased African Americans. And her agency's most successful campaign of all time—the
"WHASSSUUP!" spots—had used African Americans to sell Budweiser to a target audience of mostly white, mostly blue-collar, males.

Kas tried to put the unsettling encounter behind her. By the time
she showed Arnall what she hoped was the final cut, the Greek actor
was gone and the black family was limited to twenty seconds of the
sixty-second commercial. That still wasn't acceptable to Arnall. What
ensued, Kas claimed, was an increasingly unpleasant dialogue.

"You made the wrong commercial," he said. "You can't use blacks
to sell to my target audience. My target audience is a white, blue-collar
construction worker who drinks beer."

"Excuse me," she said. "Can you repeat that please?"

"I said, my target audience is a white, blue-collar construction
worker who drinks beer!"

"Interesting," she said.

"Yes, interesting, Miss Creative Director," he said. "Interesting that
you don't know a thing about marketing!" By now, Kas claimed,
Arnall was pounding the table with his fist, spittle flying from his lips
as he scolded her. "You don't understand my target audience. You
made the wrong commercial! Are there any questions?"

✳ ✳ ✳

Soon after, according to Kas, Ameriquest put DDB "in review," threatening to pull its business unless she was taken off the account. DDB
fired her. She sued, claiming DDB, Arnall, and Ameriquest had conspired to make her a scapegoat for the squabbles over the commercial.
Arnall and Ameriquest—along with DDB—denied that Arnall had
engineered her firing. They said there was nothing untoward about
her dismissal.

Whether Arnall was behind Kas's firing or not, it was evident that
Ameriquest's owner was still intensely involved in the workings of his

company. He had lofty goals, and specific ideas about how to achieve them. Ameriquest and other subprime lenders had expanded in large measure by promoting themselves to African-American consumers in inner-city neighborhoods. This had brought Arnall a history of problems with government authorities and community activists who had accused him of ripping off black borrowers. In the future, Ameriquest would continue to make a large share of its loans to minority borrowers, but the company and its founder would work hard to obscure that fact and strive to tap into a larger pool of borrowers, reaching out to white suburban home owners by using the products and sales techniques it had perfected in minority neighborhoods. Many Americans of all races and classes were having a hard time balancing their household budgets as medical bills and credit-card balances piled up. "Eighty percent of Americans are two paychecks away from subprime," one industry maxim went. People living a step or two from the financial edge were often susceptible to pitches from Ameriquest and other lenders that specialized in refinancings that rolled their consumer debts into mortgages against their homes. It was a perfect time for Ameriquest to make a push to become a national brand. Arnall's vision for the DDB television spots was a reflection of his desire to position Ameriquest as a mainstream company serving Middle America; in time, the lender would declare itself "Proud Sponsor of the American Dream."

The first year of the new decade would also prove to be a watershed for Arnall on a personal level. He got married for the second time. Unlike his first wife, Sally, who had stayed at home and raised their children, his new bride was a businesswoman. Dawn Mansfield had earned her M.B.A. from Virginia's College of William and Mary in the early '80s. She spent a season as a ski instructor in Mammoth, California, and then lived for a while on her family's farm, taking care of her one-hundred-year-old great-grandmother. Later she got her real-estate license and started a one-woman firm, marketing land for development and even selling the family farm. Then she moved into commercial real estate, working in the business for two decades, including a few years as a vice president at Sam Zell's Equity Office

Properties, the nation's leading owner of office buildings. She met Roland Arnall in 1995 and, in 1998, started work at his holding company, overseeing its real-estate division.

When she and Roland were married two years later, the ceremony was performed by California's governor, Gray Davis. Davis and Arnall had known each other since Davis's days as chief of staff to Jerry Brown. Davis owed considerable gratitude to Arnall. When Davis had run for governor in 1998, Arnall promised to find at least twenty supporters who would be good for a quarter of a million dollars each. His efforts spurred Davis's fund-raising to stratospheric levels. "Roland was responsible for Gray becoming governor," one top Davis strategist said.

Not long after the wedding, Davis appointed Dawn Arnall to a state post that allowed her to put her love of animals to use, as a member of California's Veterinary Medical Board. Roland, meanwhile, made her cochair of his lending enterprises. The couple would be partners in marriage, in business, in politics, and in philanthropy. Together they would give away millions to politicians and charitable cases. Dawn described herself as the more detail-oriented half of the pair. Roland, she said, was a force of nature, driven by big plans and big dreams. "I called him a typhoon," she said. "He was very visceral."

By the early months of the new Bush administration, the economy was slowing. Unemployment grew. Hard-hit home owners began defaulting on their mortgages in growing numbers. Eleven percent of subprime mortgages were at least sixty days in arrears by the summer of 2001, the highest figure since Moody's Investors Service had started tracking subprime mortgage delinquencies a decade earlier.

This news caused little concern on Wall Street. On the contrary, the volume of subprime home loans packaged into securities deals, which had fallen in 1999 and 2000 in the aftermath of the Russian debt crisis, shot to record levels in 2001. Investment banks securitized nearly $95 billion in subprime mortgages for the year, an increase of more than two-thirds over the year before. Pension funds, insurance companies, and other large investors were hungrier than ever for securities backed by subprime home loans. The steep climb in sub-prime delinquencies, Dow Jones Newswires reported, simply was "not enough to keep investors from snapping up the high-yielding securities." With the economy worsening, the values of stocks and corporate bonds were falling, and investors were moving their money elsewhere. "People are getting away from some of the more risky stuff that's been affected by the stock market," a Moody's analyst noted. "They need to put cash somewhere."

The emerging players in the market for subprime securities included managers of investment vehicles called collateralized debt obligations. CDOs were a form of securitization. They pooled together income from various investments, often junk bonds and other corporate bonds, and sold securities backed by the income streams from the underlying assets. Starting in 2000, Wall Street CDO managers had begun buying mortgage-backed securities as the raw material for their deals. In the years to come, CDOs would become an integral part of Wall Street's mortgage juggernaut, driving growth by soaking up subprime mortgage bonds, plowing them into their CDOs, and then selling slices of the CDOs to investors around the world. In this way, the profits from American subprime mortgages were parceled out far and wide. So were the risks.

It was the emergence of what Mark Adelson came to call "dumb money." Adelson had worked in the mortgage business for years, first as a junior associate for a law firm that represented Long Beach Savings and Guardian Savings in the early days of subprime securitization, then as a structured-finance expert for Moody's Investors Service. As CDOs began to enter the mortgage sector, Adelson worried. Most of the CDO managers he met were kids with math degrees. They hadn't been around long enough to experience the ups and downs in the mortgage market. They plugged data into statistical models and predicted cash flows and yields. Things went well as long as the mortgage market grew and housing prices continued to rise. The numbers geeks thought their success was a function of the brilliance of their math skills and their risk models. They believed they had created a moneymaking machine that could transform dicey assets into safe, high-yielding investments. They didn't understand,

Adelson thought, that solid knowledge of lenders' fundamentals was crucial to predicting how the loans and the bonds they backed would perform over the long haul. They had no concept of "putting their boots on the ground" and sifting through loan files and asking tough questions to people who worked on the front lines of the business. "It's not a math problem," Adelson said. "It's a phone call about what somebody's business practices are. It's real business."

In the near term, though, CDOs and mortgage-backed deals worked out well for the financial engineers, the bankers, and the investors. Subprime could flourish even in hard economic times as long as three things happened. First, home values needed to keep rising and lending standards in the subprime market needed to keep loosening, so that borrowers had the ability to refinance out of loans they couldn't afford and temporarily stave off default. Second, Wall Street investors needed to keep pouring money into the market, so that lenders could increase their loan volumes. This allowed lenders to obscure their true borrower default rates. (It usually took borrowers a year or two to collapse under the weight of an unaffordable loan. By then, if the lenders and securitizers had dramatically increased their volume, the defaults would be a percentage of a much enlarged base, and the default rates would still appear, on paper, to be relatively low.) Third, lenders needed to "price their risk" correctly, meaning they charged enough in fees and interest to all borrowers that they could cover the losses caused by a sizeable percentage of loans that did go into default. As one market analyst put it as the market heated up in 2001: "The issue isn't whether subprime loans produce higher losses, or substantially higher losses. They do. Everybody knows that, or the loans wouldn't be subprime. The question is whether you've priced adequately."

* * *

Ameriquest was one of the subprime lenders that were happy to charge their borrowers stiff prices for the privilege of becoming part of the growing boom in higher-risk mortgages. To match the consumer interest generated by its advertising campaign, as well as its owner's obsessive desire for growth, the company was bringing in hundreds of new workers to fill out its growing sales force.

One of them was Stephen Kuhn. Kuhn fit the profile Ameriquest was looking for. He was in his twenties, enthusiastic, a good communicator, and had some sales experience—but no experience in the mortgage business. Ameriquest didn't want its new hires to know much about mortgages; it wanted blank slates who could be taught to sell home loans according to Ameriquest's instructions. "We didn't want anybody with experience," recalled Travis Paules, the Pennsylvania area manager. "You wanted people who were hungry. Motivated. You wanted to brainwash them your own way."

Kuhn was certainly motivated. And he was a natural salesman. He made his first sale when he was ten years old. His father had bought a new car and put up a "For Sale" sign in the window of the family's old Chrysler. The car was hard to start on cold days, so Stephen's dad was willing to let it go cheap. Stephen had other ideas. He loved riding in the Cordoba with his dad. He didn't think it should go for nothing. Stephen was playing down the street when he overhead that somebody's older brother was looking to buy a used car. Stephen went into salesman's mode: his dad had a great car for sale—a 1978 Cordoba, maroon with a 318 V-8 engine under the hood. His pitch worked, his dad collected the money for the Cordoba, and Stephen had, for the first time, experienced the high of making a sale. It wouldn't be the last time. He was a good talker, an extrovert who liked to be in the middle of things. He had a bit of a stammer on words that began with *st*—not a great thing for someone named Stephen—but he thought that just made his sales pitches seem more authentic and trustworthy. By the time he was twenty, he was going to college and holding down a part-time job at a shoe store in Kansas City, Missouri, peddling Doc Martens and other high-end footwear. Then he and his girlfriend had a baby. They set up house in his parents' basement. He quit college and started selling shoes full-time. He got promoted to assistant manager. He thought he was doing great.

One day near the end of 2000, Kuhn got a call from a manager at Ameriquest. He'd seen Kuhn's résumé on Monster.com. He wanted

Kuhn to come out to a suburban Kansas City branch, in Gladstone, Missouri, to talk about a job opportunity. Like Greg Walling's audition for FAMCO, Kuhn's interview was odd. Nobody asked about his qualifications or experience. Instead, he got a sales pitch: the branch manager was selling Ameriquest to him—or, rather, selling Kuhn on how much money he could make at Ameriquest. How much, the manager asked, did Kuhn earn selling shoes? Around $23,000 a year, Kuhn replied. The manager scoffed: "I make that much in a *month*." How would Kuhn like to make $100,000 a year? How about half a million dollars a year? The possibilities were unlimited, if he could hustle and sell. There were perks, too. The manager pulled out his car keys and tossed them on the table. He'd won his BMW in a sales contest.

Kuhn began his new job in early 2001. He was twenty-one years old, and he was a loan officer, or in the company's idiom an "account executive." In branch offices all around the country, young salesmen such as Kuhn were spending most of their workdays on telephones, calling home owners who were struggling with heavy credit-card debts. The idea was to catch them on the phone and explain how they could improve their financial destinies by tapping the "equity" tucked away in their homes. Say they had bought a house a few years earlier for $100,000. Now, the value had grown to $150,000. And the balance on the mortgage used to buy the house now stood at $80,000. That meant the home owners had $70,000 in equity stored up.

As he was making his pitch over the phone, Kuhn cross-referenced real-estate databases to see how much the home owners had originally paid for their houses. Then he multiplied the number of years they'd owned the place by 5 to 7 percent a year, to come up with a ballpark estimate of how much the house was worth and how much equity they had in the place. He built anticipation, asking the person on the other end of the phone to hold on a few moments while he came up with a figure. When he finally told them he figured they had $50,000 or $100,000 to play with, *that* got their juices flowing. The sensation of found money can be one of the greatest joys in life. If someone is struggling to get by, it can also provide a sense of salvation. That, as much as anything, was what Kuhn and other Ameriquest loan officers were selling.

They prepped borrowers for what they were going to have to pay for this rescue by using their lack of knowledge about their own credit histories against them. The motto among Ameriquest's account executives was, "Beat them down and then build them back up." In the early 2000s, most consumers didn't have access to their credit scores. Just as Terry Rouch's coworkers at Long Beach Bank had discovered in the 1990s, Kuhn and other Ameriquest sales reps learned it was easy to pick out the record of a late payment here or there and convince borrowers that their credit records were worse than they really were. After successfully beating them down, Kuhn could build them back up by promising to come up with a loan that would help them improve their credit records. This also helped nudge borrowers toward accepting that they might have to pay a bit more than the going rate.

Just how much more? Following the industry standard, Ameriquest trained its loan officers to be vague. Many people didn't ask for quotes on fees or interest rates, and if they did, loan officers were taught to answer the question without providing specifics. Armon Williams, who worked as a loan officer in Grand Rapids, Michigan, had been grabbing a paycheck day by day as a substitute teacher before he landed a position at Ameriquest. He was desperate to keep his job. When he talked to home owners on the phone, "I was afraid if I told them the truth about the loan—about how much the fees were—that they wouldn't sign that loan. If they didn't sign that loan, I wasn't going to have a job." When someone asked what Ameriquest's prices where, he responded: "That's a great question. I'm glad you asked that question. Since we are a national mortgage lender we have access to some of the most competitive rates in the industry." He promised he'd find the customer the "best rate for your individual situation."

Kuhn guessed that half of Ameriquest's customers didn't know what their interest rates were until they sat down to sign the loan papers, and nine out of ten didn't know what the up-front fees and closing costs were. The training at Ameriquest was so bad, Kuhn recalled, that many of his coworkers "would quote the rate and they wouldn't know what the hell they were talking about. They would just pull a rate out of the air."

The Good Faith Estimate required by the government usually

wasn't any help. Ameriquest often mailed out disclosures that were inaccurate, lowballing the interest rates and fees or failing to reveal that the loan carried an adjustable rate. But those distortions weren't enough for the company; to prevent even a little truth from slipping through, Ameriquest continued the tradition, dating back to the days of Long Beach Bank, of suggesting to customers that the disclosures were generic computer printouts, pro forma sample loans provided by the company's main office in Orange County as a point of comparison. They had nothing to do with the actual loan being offered and should be thrown in the trash, customers were told. One former employee recalled that managers conned inexperienced loan officers into misleading customers about the Good Faith Estimate. "We'd have conference calls with our area manager," he said. "They just basically told us: 'Oh, that's the worst case scenario. It doesn't have anything to do with the loan.' We all just kinda ran with that."

* * *

As they were misleading customers about the details of their loans, Kuhn and other salespeople were also finessing the official mortgage paperwork with a variety of misrepresentations, exaggerating borrowers' incomes and their home values. One former loan officer and branch manager testified that inflating property appraisals served the "dual purpose of both making sure the loan was approved by the home office as well as making the loan more attractive to sell to investors." Loan officers pressured appraisers to inflate valuations by $10,000 or $20,000, and sometimes by $100,000 or $200,000, and to lie on their reports about the properties' defects. In one instance, a loan officer demanded a $500,000 valuation in a town where the most expensive house was worth no more than $425,000, recalled Michael Filip, an appraiser in New Jersey. Other lenders asked for higher values, too, Filip said, but they'd simply take you off their appraiser list if you didn't cooperate. Ameriquest salespeople, on the other hand, "got mean and angry. It was almost like a different breed of people. They were just nasty, aggressive, yelling loan officers." If one appraiser didn't hit the number needed, branch workers commissioned another, and, if need be, another, and another, until somebody came in with a high-enough value. Appraisers who didn't cooperate saw their business with Ameriquest evaporate; those who did got all the business they could handle. Appraisers even used inventive camera angles to make homes appear more valuable. "You can make the biggest piece of shit look like a mansion," Kuhn recalled.

Kuhn and his coworkers were adept, too, at making loan applicants' financial profiles look better. Fraud was so ingrained in the culture that employees developed specialties in document alteration and fabrication. One coworker was better at forging a mortgage history, to remove loan applicants' late payments on previous loans. Another was better at doctoring a W-2 tax form and making borrowers' incomes look bigger.

When it came time to finalize the paperwork, it was unlikely borrowers would catch any irregularities. Some borrowers couldn't read, or didn't have the savvy to understand the complex stack of documents that was set before them. Those who did try to wade through the paperwork were often surprised to find out that the rates and fees were much higher than they had expected, or that they were getting an adjustable-rate loan instead of a fixed-rate one. Loan officers were "intimidating, mean, whatever it took" to get customers to sign, Kuhn said. And if you couldn't get it sold, he said, you took it to a manager and the manager "would start beating up on them. Fifty percent of my customers were bullied into doing their loans." At least once a month, Kuhn camped out in a customer's driveway, waiting for the person to come home so he could try to "corner them and force them into signing the documents." Some loan officers played off the bait and switch by telling borrowers that a mistake had been made, or a new problem with their credit history had come up during the underwriting of the loan. If the borrowers signed the documents, they assured them, Ameriquest would "fix" their loan with a refinancing in six months or a year.

Kuhn's salesmanship helped him produce impressive numbers. In his first month at Ameriquest, he booked eight loans, earning more than $10,000 in salary and commissions, about half of a whole year's salary selling shoes. In his first year at Ameriquest, he made nearly $100,000. He was earning so much that he didn't give much thought to the kinds of things he was doing to make that money. All that cash in his pocket made it easier for him to justify Ameriquest's prices and tactics. He told himself—as he'd heard often enough from the senior management—that the company was doing a favor to borrowers who had nowhere else to turn for credit.

Kuhn won a promotion to branch manager before the end of 2001, not long after his twenty-second birthday. In his new position, he began to get an insider's view of how management drove the day-to-day routines at the branch level. He was on the phone constantly with higher-level managers, going through his branch's production pipeline loan by loan. Every loan counted; the prospect that a deal was slipping away would bring an explosion of anger and threats from his bosses. If a salesman was having trouble bringing a deal home, the higher-ups told Kuhn: "Tell him to do whatever it takes to close that loan or it's his ass."

* * *

Rarely does corporate misconduct flow from an explicit blueprint. A culture that encourages fraud communicates through informal channels: break room discussions, information swapped over drinks at corporate gatherings, unwritten systems of rewards and punishments. In the workplace, people tend to do what everyone else around them does. In an unhealthy workplace, they worry less about whether something is right or wrong than whether it's the day-to-day norm. "You're a creature of your environment," Travis Paules recalled. "You don't have to be. But most people fall into that trap."

The culture of cheating and exploitation flourished at Ameriquest because it was synonymous with success. Christopher J. Warren was just nineteen years old, he said, when he was hired in 2001 as a loan officer at an Ameriquest branch in Northern California. His "managers and handlers," he wrote in a long essay about his years in the mortgage business, "taught me the ins and outs of mortgage fraud, drugs, sex, and money, money, and more money." One manager, Warren claimed, handed out crystal meth to salespeople to keep them alert and working long hours. Most of the staff in his branch, Warren said, manipulated documents or made false statements on borrowers' loan applications. He said an Ameriquest vice president explained to him that investors audited just 10 percent of the mortgages in the company's loan pools; if investors found a loan with misrepresentations, the company simply replaced it with another and then moved the bad loan to another pool and hoped it wouldn't get audited the next time.

Warren figured that $75 million out of the $90 million in mortgages he sold in his two and a half years contained some sort of "material fraud" that slipped through Ameriquest's loan-approval system undetected. Eventually he learned how to hack into the company's computer system and approve his own loans, waiving requirements for documentation and other conditions. His performance, he claimed, earned him $700,000 during his tenure at Ameriquest, as well as free trips to the Super Bowl, Hawaii, and Las Vegas. The company also tapped Warren and other sales champions for management training at its Orange County headquarters.

Big earners with flexible ethics quickly moved up from frontline sales positions to management slots, running branches and clusters of branches and whole regions and hiring, training, and supervising others who wanted to rise in the organization. When Travis Paules hired or promoted employees at the branches he oversaw in Pennsylvania, he looked for people just like himself. If they worked hard and prospered under him, he protected them. "If somebody was producing," he said, "you didn't want them to go." When one of his salesmen got caught altering a borrower's insurance documents with Wite-Out, Paules took the blame with Ameriquest's human resources department. Paules received a written reprimand. He knew he wouldn't be fired because his production record was too good. He covered for the salesman, he said, even though he knew the guy was thoroughly unscrupulous, someone who loved committing fraud for the kicks of it. "He would just do it to see if he could get away with it. He was good at what he did." The salesman lasted another five years at the company before he was finally fired.

At the same time, Paules came down hard on anyone who didn't meet the company's expectations for production. In 2001, Ameriquest transferred him from Pennsylvania to Maryland, making him area manager of the group of branches that had the weakest sales record in the nation. He knew exactly what to do. He stalked into the branch in Catonsville, in suburban Baltimore, and fired ten of the twelve employees on the spot. He hated laziness, and he'd decided they were lazy, losers who didn't have what it took to make it at Ameriquest. He always liked to say, "If you don't have Ameriquest tattooed on your ass, you shouldn't be here." Laziness was contagious, and Paules wasn't going to let the slackers infect his new hires.

"You're not going to give me a month?" one of the fired workers pleaded. "You're not going to give me *any* reprieve?"

There was no reprieve. Over the next year, Paules recalled, he ended up firing nearly every single salesperson in his area.

Paules, though, was far from the most tyrannical boss inside the company's sprawling hierarchy. Racism, sexism, and callousness festered in many Ameriquest offices. The company hired many African Americans, Hispanics, and women, but in most branches and regions, the workplace culture and management ranks were dominated by young white men who flaunted their wealth and their power within the company. Some of the ugliest allegations of workplace discrimination involved a toxic mix of sexism, ageism, and racism. According to former employees, an area manager in the Midwest stood up at sales conferences and bragged that his territory had a dazzling production record because he'd created an "Aryan Nation" of tall, young, blond-haired, blue-eyed white men, a cadre he was grooming to run the company someday. One former employee testified that the executive explained that women with children couldn't maintain the commitment to be successful; blacks were too hard to fire; and workers over forty couldn't cut it in a high-energy young man's game. Instead of being punished for his remarks, the man was put in a position of more power, winning a promotion to regional manager. Ameriquest denied any illegal or unethical conduct by the company or its employees. "We have over three thousand employees, and we base all employment decisions on merit," a spokesman said. "Factors such as race, religion, marital status, gender or age play no part whatsoever in our decisions."

* * *

As Travis Paules moved up in the company, going from branch manager to area manager, he didn't have to give up the party-'til-you-drop philosophy that had served him well as he hired strippers and boozed with his top salesmen. Now he just partied in nicer locations. At one company gathering at a resort in Utah, some of his peers rented a ski-slope condo for several nights so they could party after hours, beyond the reach of prying eyes. When Paules strode into the party pad, he said, he caught his favorite aroma: marijuana. Two "eight balls" of cocaine were laid out on a glass table in the middle of the celebration. Cocaine, he'd soon learn, was the drug of choice at Ameriquest. He and several of his fellow area managers snorted lines until the sun came up.

The events that Ameriquest hosted for its most successful employees made Paules feel as though he was living the life of a "mini rock star." He rocked out to bands like Smash Mouth and Third Eye Blind, which put on private performances for Ameriquest employees. He took a ride in a hot-air balloon. He played paintball in the California desert.

Increasingly, in 2001 and 2002, the company's multimillionaire owner made his presence felt among Ameriquest's managers. To Paules, it seemed clear that Roland Arnall knew what was going on in the company's far-flung branch offices, and that he had a big hand in how it operated on the ground. One day, when Paules was visiting the home office on Town and Country Road, he ended up on the same elevator as Arnall, and the boss invited him into his office for a chat. Arnall peppered him with question after question about how things were going in the field. "He was definitely sharp," Paules said. "Of all the people I ever worked with, he's the only person that ever intimidated me. He was just so focused, and so goal-oriented."

One of Arnall's rules, Paules recalled, was that no one in the company was allowed to say "if." They had to say "when." If an area manager was caught saying "if" during a meeting, Arnall would "fine" the guy $20 on the spot, the cash going into a kitty that was donated to charity. If a regional manager said "if," the fine increased to $100. Arnall had had no hesitation about stopping one of his executives in the middle of a presentation and invoking his "no-if" policy.

Arnall had other ways of spreading his gospel of positive thinking. At one meeting, Paules said, Arnall waded into a circle of area managers. He looked each one in the eye. His gaze was intense, glaring, Paules remembered. As usual, the boss wanted to know how quickly the company could increase its loan volume numbers. At the time, the best branches were producing no more than $5 million a month each; Arnall wanted to know if these managers thought they could get their branches to post $15 million. This was crazy, Paules thought. He knew how hard it was to get a branch to $2 million or $3 million, much less $5 million or $15 million. One by one, Arnall asked each man in the group if his branches could get to $15 million. Each one said yes. When Arnall pointed to Paules, he looked the CEO in the eye and said, "Yes, sir!" with a whatever-it-takes fervor.

At Ameriquest, that's the way things worked. The boss set impossible goals, and then the sales corps went out and made his ambitions a reality. Within a year or so, many branches in Arnall's empire would be hitting the number he'd demanded. In August 2003, Ameriquest's Annapolis, Maryland, branch—one of the offices under Paules's supervision—became the first in the company to hit $20 million in a month. Soon top branches would be reaching the $25 million or $30 million mark.

As Roland Arnall was firing up his troops, Wendell Raphael was struggling to rein in the zeal and audacity of employees like Travis Paules. Raphael had worked inside Arnall's lending operations for nearly two decades, from the late 1980s into the new century, as Long Beach Savings became Long Beach Mortgage and then a portion of the company split off into Ameriquest. As an area manager for Long Beach Savings in Los Angeles, he'd seen the decline of standards in the early to mid-'90s, as the sales ethos gained the upper hand within the organization. He was there as the Justice Department and FTC investigated the company. Through it all, he managed to hang on to his by-the-book approach. In January 2000, soon after he took over as vice president of operations, he fired more than twenty salesmen and managers for fraud. Raphael discovered that a branch in Florida was using the same appraiser for all of its loans, a fact that had been hidden because the appraiser was doing business under multiple company names. A close examination of the branch's loan files made it obvious that this man was a "rubber-stamp" appraiser who would deliver whatever value the loan officers and branch manager asked him to provide.

Raphael tried to tweak Ameriquest's systems in an effort to squelch the dirty employees who were willing to do anything to book loans. It didn't do much good. He'd close one loophole and they would quickly find a way around it. "The more that we changed the system, the better they got at beating it," Raphael said. "The better we got, the better they got." The other problem, he said, was management. Senior executives weren't willing to make system-wide changes that would end fraud. It was one thing to fire one or two or even twenty employees who got caught, red-handed, engaging in fraudulent practices. It was quite another, he found, to admit that fraud was endemic—and that the very practices that were fueling the company's phenomenal growth had to be stopped. During a telephone conference to determine what to do about a gaggle of employees who had been caught falsifying paperwork, Raphael recalled, one top executive suggested sorting out the offenders this way: employees who were involved with fraud on five or more loans would be fired; employees involved in fraud on fewer than five loans would get a warning and keep their jobs. "I was dumbfounded," Raphael said.

Raphael tried to use Ameriquest's loan approval software as a weapon in his battle. For example, he asked Ameriquest's computer geeks to install a fix that would discourage employees from gaming the appraisal process. On some loans, branch staffers went through as many as seven or eight appraisals on a single house. They were ordering appraisal after appraisal until they hit the value needed to get the loan approved. "You dial until you find a guy," Raphael said. "There's always a guy." He asked the techies to reprogram the system so it would accept entry of no more than five appraisals.

Usually, the computer fixes he requested would upload on a Sunday. On Monday, by 9 A.M. Pacific time, Raphael would begin hearing from sales staffers in the Midwest and East, whose workweeks had started. They had quickly caught on to the change, and they were upset about it. "You're killing our business," one regional manager told him. "This is going to slow down production." Later, he would get a summons from upper management. Invariably, he said, he would be told to remove the fix. "I'd be told to undo whatever I'd put in." That was the case with the block on excessive submissions of appraisals. He was ordered to delete the change in the system's code.

By 2002, Raphael decided to move on, to get out of operations and find something else to do. The moment he realized it was time to leave, he said, came during a meeting of senior managers. Someone jokingly asked a company attorney if he was worried, given all the fraud that was turning up, what might happen to him if the FBI raided the place. Without missing a beat, the lawyer nodded in the direction of Raphael and replied, "No. I'm counsel. If the FBI comes in here, they want *Wendell*."

9. The Battle for Georgia

The photo was taken in the early years of the Bush administration, as a deregulatory fever swept the nation's capital. Five white men in dark suits and power ties face the camera. They're posed around a four-foot-tall stack of documents held together by red tape. Four of them hold gardening shears. The fifth grips a chain saw. Leaving nothing to the imagination, the backdrop reads "Cutting Red Tape." Among the five are representatives of the American Bankers Association and two other financial trade groups, as well as John Reich, the vice chairman of the FDIC. The man wielding the saw is James Gilleran, the head of the Office of Thrift Supervision. The regulators and lobbyists were making an announcement: the financial industry was finally going to be freed from excessive regulation.

In the early 2000s, the federal agencies that kept an eye on the practices of the nation's banks and mortgage lenders went to great lengths to be hospitable to them. Financial institutions could choose which agency they wanted to regulate them. The Office of Thrift Supervision and the Office of the Comptroller of the Currency, which policed nationally chartered banks, depended on fees paid by their licensees to determine their budgets and their clout within Washington's bureaucracy. So they competed to show financial institutions which one of them could offer the softest hand in overseeing their lending practices. "Our goal is to allow thrifts to operate with a wide breadth of freedom from regulatory intrusion," Gilleran declared in one speech.

During the years of the home-loan boom, as abusive lending tactics thrived, the OCC took exactly two public enforcement actions against banks for unfair and deceptive practices in mortgage lending, both involving small Texas banks. Individual consumers with complaints had little hope of getting help from the agency. Dorothy Smith, a sixty-seven-year-old retiree from East St. Louis, Illinois, learned this after she ended up in a loan from First Union Bank that she couldn't afford. She was living on $540 a month in government benefits. A home-repair contractor offered to do work on her house and promised to help her get a loan to cover the work. The contractor hooked her up with a mortgage broker. The broker, according to a complaint later filed with banking authorities by Smith's attorney, submitted a loan application claiming Smith had a job at a senior citizens center that paid her $1,499 a month. Fees and closing costs on the $36,000 mortgage from First Union totaled $3,431. She would be required to pay $360.33 a month and then, at age eighty-three, come up with a balloon payment of more than $30,000. When her attorney filed a complaint on her behalf with Illinois banking officials about the loan, they forwarded it to the OCC, which had sole jurisdiction over First Union. In 2002, the OCC responded: "We cannot intercede in a private party situation regarding the interpretation or enforcement of her contract. . . . The OCC can provide no further assistance."

The lending industry had succeeded in pulling off what students of bureaucracies call "regulatory capture." The OCC and OTS considered their role to be not watchdogs but partners and defenders of the institutions they were supposed to police. Along with turning a blind eye to banks' and S&Ls' bad practices, the agencies protected their turf, closing the paths available to other agencies that tried to stop institutions from misbehaving. In particular, the OCC and OTS labored to ensure that state consumer-protection officials kept their hands off national banks and S&Ls. They invoked the power of federal "preemption" to quash lawsuits and state investigations, and to exclude these institutions from state consumer-protection laws. It was unfair, the agencies said, to require that national banks and S&Ls follow a patchwork of state laws. Better, they said, to have uniform standards that were national in scope. Besides, the OCC explained, there was "no evidence of predatory lending by national banks or their operating subsidiaries." The agency said it knew this because it used "sophisticated surveillance tools" to home in on "the highest risks" in the lending marketplace.

It was true that many of the diciest subprime lenders, including Ameriquest, weren't regulated by federal banking authorities. But many subsidiaries of national banks and S&Ls were players in the subprime market and they were, increasingly, employing questionable lending tactics. In 2002, bank examiners in the state of Washington concluded that National City Mortgage was violating state lending laws by packing illegal fees into mortgages. The state's Department of Financial Institutions asked the lender to justify its overpriced array of charges. The mortgage company contacted the OCC, which oversaw the lender's parent, National City Bank. The OCC informed bank officials that the state had no jurisdiction over National City Mortgage. National City attached the OCC's letter to its reply to the state department. The state's regulators, the company said, should back off. They dropped their investigation.

∗ ∗ ∗

The Clinton administration's efforts to regulate subprime had been makeshift and inadequate. Clinton appointees had tried to do *something*, though—they had filed lawsuits against big lenders and talked about the need for Wall Street to use its power of the purse to clean up dirty lending. After George W. Bush moved into the White House, his administration did even less to fight predatory lenders, rewriting the rules of the marketplace in a way that made it even easier for lenders and their financiers to take advantage of consumers. To the new officials in Washington, the free market was a self-correcting machine, one that required not even a modest level of Clintonesque tinkering.

The only federal agency that continued to show much concern for mortgage lending abuses was the Federal Trade Commission. Although it had dropped its Ameriquest investigation in early 2001, the FTC decided to move forward on two big cases it had started under President Clinton. The first involved First Alliance Mortgage Company. The FTC, private attorneys, and officials in several states had all taken their claims on behalf of FAMCO borrowers into the company's bankruptcy proceedings in federal court in Orange County. The government officials and private attorneys reached a settlement with the lender in March 2002, announcing an agreement that earmarked more than $60 million to help relieve the financial straits of as many as eighteen thousand borrowers. As part of the deal, Brian and Sarah Chisick agreed to release $20 million of the fortune they had personally made from their lending ventures. They also agreed to a ten-year ban on engaging in home mortgage lending in Arizona, Massachusetts, and New York, and a lifetime ban in California, Florida, and Illinois.

A few months later, in September 2002, the FTC concluded its biggest predatory-lending investigation. Citigroup agreed to pay two class-action settlements totaling $240 million, to be paid out to as many as two million people who had taken out mortgages or smaller personal loans from Associates, the consumer-finance unit that Citi had purchased in late 2000. The FTC trumpeted the deal as the largest consumer-protection settlement in the agency's history. But the amount was considerably lower than the potential exposure Citi had in the case—analysts initially estimated its exposure at $1 billion. And simple math showed the settlement allowed for an average payout of perhaps $120 per victim, even though borrowers had lost hundreds and often thousands of dollars each through what the FTC described as "systematic and widespread deceptive and abusive lending practices." Some fair-lending advocates thought the settlement constituted a cost of doing business for Citi rather than a real penalty. "They let Citigroup off absurdly cheap," one consumer watchdog complained.

* * *

To consumer-protection officials in Minnesota, Iowa, and other states, the FAMCO and Citigroup cases seemed to be last gasps in the federal government's efforts to fight subprimers' abuses. Both investigations had been launched in the '90s, and state officials, hearing the free-market rhetoric from the Bush administration and Congress, didn't have much hope that Washington, D.C., would get behind new initiatives to combat predatory lending.

Financial regulators and attorneys general in several states vowed to attack the problem on their own. In Washington State, Chuck Cross and the Department of Financial Institutions unleashed a bare-knuckle assault on Household International. Like many consumer finance companies, Household had moved away from its old model—making small personal loans and second mortgages—and followed Long Beach Mortgage and Quality Mortgage into offering high-priced first-mortgage loans that were folded into mortgage-backed investments by Lehman Brothers and other Wall Street banks.

Cross's agency had been getting an increasing number of complaints about Household. When he sent staffers from the agency on routine examinations, they found no serious violations. The paperwork in Household's loan files seemed to be in order. Cross decided there had to be more. He notified the company he was conducting an "expanded examination"—a euphemism for an investigation—and began interviewing aggrieved borrowers. He wrote a thick report detailing exactly how Household was screwing its customers. Household, the report said, used a variety of tricks to "mislead and confuse" borrowers. For example, it charged borrowers up-front "discount" points that were supposed to allow them to "buy down" their interest rates but in fact did nothing to reduce their rates. One couple received a Good Faith Estimate from Household that disclosed the discount points in an absurdly ambiguous range of $0 to $9,425. On the actual loan, the borrowers ended up paying $10,486 in discount points, and their interest rate remained sky-high—13.5 percent.

Household said the state's report was inaccurate and inflammatory. It went to court and won a restraining order to block its public release. But Household couldn't bury Cross's findings, because law enforcers in other states were also investigating. Household blamed its problems on a "rogue office" in Bellingham, Washington. Cross and regulators in other states knew this was a facade, because they had compared notes. If investigators were finding the same grubby practices in upstate New York that others were finding in Washington State, it probably wasn't a coincidence. "We realized how national this stuff was," Cross recalled. "It wasn't a few loan officers and a few rogue branches. This was a pattern and practice of deceiving customers."

With Washington State, Iowa, and Minnesota leading the way, the front against Household grew to include dozens of states. The coalition's leaders demanded that Household change its lending practices and pay reparations to its borrowers.

As negotiations between the lender and the investigators proceeded, the states appeared ready to cut a deal that would require Household to pay a settlement in the neighborhood of $100 million to $200 million.

Cross didn't think it was enough. Household had been the nation's largest subprime mortgage lender in 2001. It had made more than $18 billion in subprime home loans, roughly 10 percent of the subprime market. The company had earned $3.6 billion across 2000 and 2001. In the fall of 2002, when the states' coalition gathered at a hotel in downtown Chicago to hash out their strategy, Cross told the other members of the states' negotiating team that they were about to make a huge mistake. "We can't do this," he said. "We cannot settle with these guys for what we're talking about. It's just wrong. We will not be doing our jobs if we let this thing go through. These guys are criminals."

The debate over how much money to demand from Household ping-ponged among the regulators, with the room divided between "hawks" like Cross, who wanted to extract a whopping sum from the company, and "doves," who thought a lesser sum was appropriate. The difference of opinion wasn't so much a disagreement over how harshly Household deserved to be punished. It was more a difference over how far the states could push Household. If the states locked in on too large a figure and refused to budge, some worried, Household might refuse to settle. "There were a number of people who were kind of afraid: 'They're going to walk away and then what are we going to do?'" recalled Dave Huey, an assistant attorney general in Washington State. The only alternative then would be years of litigation that would delay getting relief for victimized borrowers. Better to cut a deal for a lesser sum, the doves thought, and get money into consumers' pockets as soon as possible.

Prentiss Cox, the assistant attorney general from Minnesota, initially sided with the doves. He felt there was only so much the states could get out of Household, given the agencies' limited resources and their need to hold together a diverse coalition. But as the case progressed, he realized the states were in a better bargaining position than he'd thought. Household, he saw, needed a settlement to put the matter behind it. A nationwide legal assault could spook the company's funders, driving up Household's borrowing costs and cutting into its profits. Wall Street prefers bad news that's over and done with; it doesn't like uncertainty. It could deal with a multimillion-dollar settlement, because that would demarcate the costs of the company's legal problems. Cox began to move over to the hawks and argue in favor of a larger settlement. In contrast to Cross, who had a reputation as a firebrand, Cox was known for having a more measured demeanor. His support for the higher dollar figure—and his analysis of the leverage that the states had over Household—helped shift the expectations held by the group.

On October 2, 2002—Cross's birthday—Household capitulated. It agreed to a $484 million settlement, to be paid out to as many as three hundred thousand borrowers. The company also agreed to change its practices; it committed, for example, to reduce its up-front fees to no more than 5 percent of a loan's value. State law enforcers hoped the agreement would serve as a template for the standards that should be expected of the nation's subprime mortgage lenders. In the end, all fifty states and the District of Columbia signed on to claim a share of the settlement for their citizens.

It was a victory for consumers, but the deal also had benefits for Household. By settling on a nationwide basis, Household had been able to diminish its legal problems for a fraction of what it was likely to cost the company to fight thousands of individual borrower claims. Washington State officials estimated that borrowers would get back about 25 percent of what the lender had squeezed out of them through its "deceptive misconduct." They said it was the best the states could do under the circumstances. "We were ready to force the company into bankruptcy if we had to, but we knew that if we did, consumers would never see a penny," Cross told reporters.

Wall Street liked the deal. Word apparently leaked before the public announcement; Household's stock price rose 25 percent on

October 10, then another 7 percent after the official word came on October 11. "Investors appear to be betting Household International Inc.'s regulatory problems will abate in the wake of its huge settlement with dozens of state regulators and attorneys general," the *Wall Street Journal* noted. "Analysts say the Prospect Heights, Ill., lender can easily afford the payment, even though it is the largest consumer-lending settlement ever." Mortgage-backed securities packagers also remained bullish on Household. Soon after the big legal settlement was announced, Lehman Brothers issued $574 million in bonds backed by mortgages originated by the lender.

HSBC, the world's second-largest bank, liked the settlement as well. Soon after the agreement was finalized, HSBC revealed it was angling to spend $14 billion or more to purchase Household. Sir John Bond, HSBC's chairman, said the proposed deal would help his company gain ground on the globe's No. 1 bank, Citigroup. "We see this as a fantastic opportunity to buy a national franchise in America," Bond said. "The U.S. consumer is the engine room of world growth."

✳   ✳   ✳

Chuck Cross, Prentiss Cox, and other state consumer watchdogs were beginning to see that the subprime lending industry was out of control. The problems were systemic, not a matter of a rogue lender or two. During the meeting in Chicago that cinched the Household deal, Cox and a few others were waiting in a room as Household officials, huddled elsewhere, discussed whether to accept the proposal that had been put on the table. The state negotiators felt confident they had a settlement. They were both exhausted and elated. All that was left now was to wait. Prentiss Cox took this moment to scribble a note. He walked over to Tom Miller, Iowa's attorney general and the man who had headed the Household investigation. He handed Miller the piece of paper, in a wry imitation of schoolchildren passing notes in class. Cox had a succinct question for Miller, one that was starting to germinate in the minds of many of the state law enforcers. "Who's next?" the note asked.

Miller was known as an advocate for consumer protection. But as an elected official and someone who had worked to bring factions together to create multistate settlements, he had cultivated a reputation for having an easygoing, evenhanded manner. He was not one to venture opinions or make pronouncements lightly. So it meant something when he added his scribble to the paper and handed it back to Cox. His one-word answer to Cox's question: "Ameriquest."

* * *

As state law enforcers were thinking about their next investigative campaign, the issue of predatory lending was heating up in state legislatures and city councils. Local governments in Los Angeles, Chicago, and other cities responded to the growing numbers of foreclosures within their borders by passing municipal ordinances that restricted lenders' practices. Philadelphia passed a tough ordinance in April 2001. It forbade lenders from doing business in the city if they charged exorbitant fees or interest rates, or made loans with no regard for a borrower's ability to pay. Some subprimers declared they would no longer make loans in the city. Within weeks, however, the crisis was over; industry leaders had persuaded the Pennsylvania legislature to pass a state law that prohibited Philadelphia and other localities from limiting mortgage lending. After Los Angeles, Oakland, and Atlanta approved ordinances, an industry group, the American Financial Services Association, filed lawsuits that delayed implementation of the local rules. Subprime mortgage leaders prepared for a full-pitched battle. The president of another trade group, the National Home Equity Mortgage Association, asked members to give cash to its political action committee to help "keep our legislators focused on what their job is—and that's promoting free enterprise."

With their efforts thwarted on the local level, and with little hope of getting help from Congress, home owners' advocates focused their efforts on the nation's statehouses. When the Georgia general assembly met in 2002, consumer defenders pressed for a law that would hold financiers and investors accountable for the proliferation of bad lending. They argued that securitization and the demand from Wall Street for more mortgage-backed assets were driving predatory-lending practices on the ground. Victims of abusive loans were often powerless to defend themselves. Their loans passed through many hands in the mortgage food chain, and it was hard for them to find someone to sue. They were generally prevented from raising legal claims to save their homes from foreclosure because the entities that now owned their loans and collected their payments were far removed from the company that had signed them to the mortgage. Going after loan brokers or small-fish lenders who had put together the mortgage deals often was pointless. The flow of money from Wall Street allowed lenders and brokers to open up shop, make thousands of loans, and then shut down if lawsuits or regulatory investigations became a problem. Then they could move to another state or reopen under another name. As law professor Chris Peterson observed, "In the new marketplace, mortgage loan originators serve not only an intake function—using marketing strategies to line up borrowers—but also a filtering function. As thinly capitalized originators make more and more loans, *claims against the lender accumulate, while the lender's assets do not.* The lending entities are used like a disposable filter: absorbing and deflecting origination claims and defenses until those claims and defenses render the business structure unusable." At that point, the "filter" is used up and discarded, with the lender declaring bankruptcy or settling with borrowers for a fraction of the money it charged them. Either way, the lender had already served its purpose in the mortgage-backed securities machine.

The only way to ensure accountability was to follow the money—to move up the chain and hold securitizers and investors responsible for the loans they were buying and selling. Without this sort of accountability, any effort to stop lenders from making reckless or predatory loans would fall short. Georgia state senator Vincent Fort, a Democrat from Atlanta, called the existing system "the legal laundering of bad loans. Neither the originators nor the holder of the loan is willing to take responsibility." He believed that mortgage contracts should carry "assignee liability," attaching legal responsibility for fraud to investors and others who purchased a stake in the loan.

The industry's leaders were horror-struck. Assignee liability, they said, would dry up the lifeblood of the home-loan industry, the flow of money provided by securitization. Financial types had a name for this flow of capital: "liquidity." "Consumers and advocacy groups need to understand that capital flows and securitizations offer lower costs to consumers," explained Adam Bass, Roland Arnall's nephew and a top executive at Ameriquest. If the flow of Wall Street capital was cut off, Bass said, lenders would become like physicians who couldn't afford malpractice insurance. "Like doctors who can't give care without insurance, we can't lend without the liquidity provided by the securitization markets."

In 2001, with help from Bill Brennan, the Atlanta Legal Aid attorney who had worked on the Fleet Finance case, Senator Fort had tried to get the legislature to pass a tough predatory-lending bill. Fort built momentum by convening town hall meetings around the state. "It's about as hot an issue as I've ever dealt with," he told reporters. A lobbyist for the Georgia Association of Mortgage Brokers said Fort's public forums were nothing more than "fear-mongering." "I think it's unfortunate that the senator chooses to have such lopsided hearings in that format, by making it a parade of victims," the lobbyist said. "I could put together the statistics through the lenders in Georgia that he is way off base that this thing is an epidemic." The bankers and lenders won the day. Fort's bill died.

Fort and Brennan returned to the issue, determined to try again, when the legislature reconvened in 2002. They made a good team. Brennan was a white attorney and consumer advocate who had come of age politically during the civil rights movement. He carried himself with the air of an absentminded professor, which belied his encyclopedic knowledge of lending laws and his passion for helping the needy and neglected. Fort was an African American who had grown up in a factory town in Connecticut and had come to Atlanta as a graduate student in the late '70s. He became a history professor and a community organizer who fought against bank branch closings in southside Atlanta's black neighborhoods. One thing Fort and Brennan had in common was a willingness to speak their minds. When bankers and mortgage brokers argued that Fort's bill would cut off access to credit and drive subprime lenders out of the state, Brennan replied that that would be a good thing. "People don't need access to predatory lenders," he said. "That's like saying people need access to poison, or children need access to mumps."

Fort knew predatory-lending legislation had little chance a second time around unless he could find a new, high-profile ally. There was only one place to turn: Georgia's governor, Roy Barnes, the country lawyer who'd taken on Fleet in the '90s, going on *60 Minutes* and accusing the company of "cheating and swindling." After he and his law partner, Howard Rothbloom, had settled with Fleet, Barnes had turned his attention to another run for the state's highest office. He won the governor's office resoundingly in 1998, after campaigning across the state as a down-home politician, clad in scuffed shoes and rumpled suits. Fort knew that if Barnes decided to put his full weight behind the bill, it had a great chance of winning approval in the general assembly.

Barnes was a master of the legislative process. He'd been elected to the assembly at the age of twenty-six, the youngest Georgia legislator since Reconstruction. In his two decades in the state house, he'd made friends and learned how to work the levers of power. As governor, he'd pushed through a stunning array of legislation, including a bill that had reduced the size of the Confederate Stars and Bars on Georgia's flag. But whether he would now get involved in the predatory-lending issue was an open question. Despite his legal campaign against Fleet, Barnes was also a small-town banker with a history of pro-business politics. Some wondered whether the governor would wade into such a contentious debate.

In February 2002, Barnes removed any doubt about where he stood. He announced that he was introducing a tough, anti-predatory-lending bill that included strong assignee liability language. "We're going to get back to the basics of truth in lending," he said. Everyone who knew Barnes understood that once he'd declared himself in a fight, he wouldn't back down.

The banking industry wasn't going to roll over for Barnes. Lobbyists from inside and outside the state camped out at the capitol building. They poured money into the campaign accounts of key legislators. They bore down on Senator Fort and Chris Carpenter, the governor's legislative liaison. The message, both recalled, was that these were matters too big for small-time politicians in Georgia to concern themselves over. "They were so pejorative to us," Carpenter said. "It was like a schoolboy pat on the head: 'You just don't understand. This is so much bigger than you.'" Barnes was so incensed by the industry's opposition that he gathered the state's top bankers together for a breakfast meeting and chewed them out. If they didn't back off, he warned, he would do a nationwide search for a new banking commissioner and hire "the biggest long-haired, sandal-wearing, earring-wearing consumer radical I can find."

Ameriquest was a big player in the debate in Georgia, as it was in California, Minnesota, and other states that were considering new mortgage rules. In Roland Arnall's early days as a developer and S&L proprietor, he'd given money to politicians largely out of a desire to style himself as a power broker and to socialize with the influential. Now, though, with his business interests spread out across the country, much of his political largesse was targeted at influencing state and local officeholders as they considered anti-predatory-lending legislation. Wherever there was a fight over lending laws, Arnall and his associates sprinkled campaign contributions: they gave more than $10 million in California, $180,000 in New Jersey, and $160,000 in Georgia. In all, Arnall, his companies, and his executives contributed at least $20 million to state and federal politicians during the boom years of the mortgage business. That was ten times the amount that Countrywide Financial, the nation's largest home lender, shelled out to politicians.

Arnall's nephew, Adam Bass, maintained a high profile in Georgia. Barnes's aide Chris Carpenter arranged for Bass to meet with Vincent Fort to discuss the legislation. By this point, Fort was furious with Ameriquest. Bill Brennan had filled him in on the company; Brennan's Home Defense Program had seen several borrowers who had ended up with Ameriquest loans they couldn't afford. Many of them were widows on fixed incomes. Fort met with Bass anyway, as a courtesy to Carpenter and the governor. Bass told him that Ameriquest had an impressive set of "best practices." Ameriquest, he said, was an industry leader in doing things the right way. Bass added, both Carpenter and Fort recalled, that Senator Fort was doing his constituents a disservice by discouraging companies like Ameriquest from lending to them.

Fort blew up. His deep-throated voice rose in anger. Nobody, he said, better dare suggest he didn't know what was best for the people he served. He heard from them every day in the street and on the phone. They told him the stories of how they were on the verge of losing the homes they'd worked hard to own. Bass and his company were getting rich, Fort said, by taking advantage of poor minorities. Then he stalked out. Bass, Carpenter said, was so shaken by Fort's blast and quick exit that tears welled up in his eyes. Asked later about the confrontation, an Ameriquest spokesman told the *Wall Street Journal* that the meeting "was a very candid conversation about complex policy issues."

* * *

In April 2002, the general assembly sent a compromise version of the Georgia Fair Lending Act to the governor for his signature. Barnes signed it more than once, touring the state and holding ceremonies in Atlanta, Macon, Augusta, and Savannah, with Fort at his side. "I have met the victims, seen the faces, heard the stories, and helped pick up the pieces," Barnes said. Along with placing tough assignee liability on investors and others involved in the mortgage process, the law also protected borrowers from loan flipping, put limits on prepayment penalties, and created stringent requirements for "high-cost" loans that carried higher rates and fees. It wasn't against the law to make high-cost loans, but doing so triggered enhanced consumer protections and penalties that could be used against lenders, securitizers, and investors.

In response, dozens of lenders vowed to stop making loans or curtail their business in the state. Ameriquest was among those that promised to pull out completely. That didn't bother Barnes. If Ameriquest was leaving the state, he said, Georgians should dance in the streets.

Industry officials talked of revising the law. As the next legislative session approached, Barnes was prepared to fight to keep it intact. He didn't get the chance. In November 2002, Sonny Perdue blocked

Barnes's effort to win a second term in the governor's mansion. Perdue, a Republican, beat Barnes with 51 percent of the vote. Experts agreed that record turnout in rural precincts, which had been goaded by Barnes's efforts to redesign the state flag, had doomed the reelection hopes of a man who had been one of the Democratic Party's rising stars. One of Perdue's first orders of business on taking office was to rewrite the Georgia Fair Lending Act. He and like-minded members of the legislature were determined to craft a more industry-friendly law.

They had powerful allies. These included the federal Office of Thrift Supervision. In January 2003, as industry officials tried to build momentum for revising the Georgia Fair Lending Act, the OTS announced that it was using its authority to block most of the law as it pertained to federally chartered S&Ls. The agency said the state law would subject national S&Ls to "increased costs and an undue regulatory burden" and thwart Congress's mandate that the OTS have exclusive responsibility for policing them. The federal agency's move put more pressure on the assembly to revise the law. Adam Bass said that unless the law was changed, the resulting "unlevel playing field" would prompt a rush of lenders applying for OTS charters that would allow them to escape the law's requirements. The fair-lending act, he said, "needs to be fixed; it was a mistake."

Georgia's law also came under attack from even more commanding powers: the credit-rating agencies, the investment banks, and the federally sponsored home-loan investment giants, Fannie Mae and Freddie Mac. These were institutions that could make or break the mortgage market. Fannie and Freddie said they would avoid buying loans designed as "high-cost" mortgages under the Georgia Fair Lending Act. In early 2003, Standard and Poor's dropped the biggest bomb of all: it announced it would no longer rate securitizations that might contain high-cost mortgages affected by the act. S&P said it was doing so because it believed that even the most advanced securitization techniques could not insulate investors and securitizers from legal liability. If they bought loans that violated the law, an S&P executive said, investors could be hit with huge jury verdicts. "There's no way to quantify the punitive damages," the executive said. "We cannot issue a rating on the underlying collateral." S&P's competitors, Fitch and Moody's, followed suit, announcing that they, too, would look askance at pools of loans that included mortgages from Georgia. In the wake of S&P's decision, the trade press reported that Lehman Brothers, Credit Suisse, Greenwich Capital, and other investment banks had begun cutting off lines of credit to lenders that continued to originate loans that might fall under the law's guidelines.

Georgia's home-loan industry spun into chaos. "I can assure you we have a major crisis down here," a spokesman for the Georgia Association of Mortgage Brokers said. The joke was that, until Roy Barnes's lending law had passed, people in Georgia thought S&P was a chain of cafeterias. But now, almost everybody in the state knew what S&P was: a behemoth that was poised to shut down a large swath of Georgia's mortgage market. Lawmakers turned to S&P for help. S&P vetted proposed amendments and made recommendations for how the legislature could change the law to satisfy the rating agency's concerns.

As word of the deliberations got around, the atmosphere within Georgia's gold-domed capitol grew tense. Consumer advocates wearing bright "Stop the Loan Shark" T-shirts jostled a legislator who'd voted to weaken the law. Mortgage brokers in loafers and polo shirts packed the hallways and hearings, taunting Fort and others who were struggling to maintain strong consumer safeguards. To Fort, it seemed like "war without weapons." When Bill Brennan tried to testify, a throng of mortgage brokers blocked his way, preventing him from entering a committee room. Brennan asked for a police escort to lead him through the crowd. "He couldn't get a job in the real world," one mortgage broker sneered.

It came down to a vote in the Georgia senate, which Perdue and the Republicans controlled, but just barely. On the final day of the fight, the senate debated the bill for two and a half hours. The most electric moment came when one of Governor Perdue's floor leaders announced that a letter was in transit from Freddie Mac. The mortgage powerhouse, he said, was giving the legislature just forty-eight hours to change the mortgage law, or there would be "real bad consequences." That was enough to sway the chamber. Perdue's mortgage amendments slipped through the senate, 29 to 26.

It turned out, though, that the letter from Freddie Mac never came. Freddie Mac officials denied they had ever set a forty-eight-hour deadline for rewriting the law. The losers in the battle protested. "You have the governor's floor leader telling untruths about a phantom letter," Fort said. "When you can't trust the people who represent the highest elected official in the state to tell the truth, the people's interests aren't served." A spokesman for the governor claimed that Freddie Mac had intended to send the letter, but had backed off under pressure from consumer advocates.

The amendments gutted the original law's assignee liability provision, shielding investors from class-action lawsuits and putting tight caps on the damages that individual borrowers could collect from investors. Perdue signed the modifications into law on March 7, 2003. S&P, Fitch, and Moody's returned to business as usual in Georgia. Lehman and other investment banks resumed the steady flow of liquidity into the state's subprime mortgage business, and Ameriquest and other subprimers returned to making loans in the state. The industry's power play had worked. It had sent a message to other states about what would happen if they got out of line. Though other battles would follow in state legislatures and city councils, the damage was done. Consumer watchdogs who had hoped to use state and local laws to defeat predatory lending would, instead, find themselves crushed by the power of the mortgage industry.

10. The Trial

The Ronald Reagan Federal Building and Courthouse in Santa Ana, California, is a sleek, eleven-story high-rise draped in glass and Italian marble. It's set in the heart of Orange County, an expanse of planned suburbs and shopping malls that Reagan once described as the place "where good Republicans go to die."

In early 2003, in a courtroom inside the Reagan Courthouse, a group of plaintiffs' attorneys tried to lay the sins of subprime into the lap of Wall Street. They aimed to show definitively that Lehman Brothers had helped sustain First Alliance Mortgage Company's fraud-driven business practices. Given the industry's success in thwarting state and local consumer protections, the case represented what many considered to be one of the last best hopes for stopping the subprime mortgage machine. Beating Lehman in federal court, consumer defenders believed, would send a message to Wall Street that there was a price to pay for gleaning profits from abusive lenders. Maybe, they thought, a big jury verdict could put the fear of God into the Street and force investment banks to exercise some real control over the lenders they financed.

The case was a long shot. The borrowers and their attorneys were taking on a mighty investment bank in a courthouse named after one of America's staunchest advocates of free enterprise, and taking on subprime in the industry's birthplace and headquarters—a county where as many as fifty thousand locals drew their paychecks from the

mortgage business. As the housing and mortgage boom grew, Orange
County became the kind of place where many home owners could
step out of their front doors and rattle off a list of friends and neighbors who depended on the home-loan industry: a mortgage company
owner across the street, a loan officer two doors over, a mortgage
broker down the block. The plaintiffs and their lawyers also had to
contend with the county's political conservatism. As a land long pop-
ulated by John Birchers, Goldwaterites, and Reaganites, Orange
County tends to look down on anyone who might encroach on the
creative powers of the market, including government regulators and,
especially, trial lawyers who harry businesses with class-action suits.
Industry spokespeople had long dismissed the drumbeat of litigation
against Orange County's subprimers as the machinations of lawyers
sniffing around for deep pockets. During his testimony inside the
Reagan courthouse, FAMCO's owner, Brian Chisick, played up this
sentiment by quantifying his company's legal problems: "Lawsuits
brought by borrowers, very few. Lawsuits brought by attorneys after
fishing for clients, very many."

It's true that anyone can file a lawsuit over just about anything. But
for consumers, winning a lawsuit—or even getting a day in court—
isn't easy. Like most lenders, FAMCO required its borrowers to sign
an arbitration clause, which meant all disputes between consumers
and the company were decided not by a judge and jury but instead by
an arbitrator in a private proceeding. Because the for-profit firms that
offer arbitration services depend on the corporations that hire them
for their income, critics say they tend to favor companies over consumers. FAMCO's arbitration clause was the first hurdle that Steinbock and Hofmann, a three-lawyer firm based in San Jose, had faced
when it began suing the company in the mid-1990s. To get a day in
court, the firm had to prove FAMCO had bamboozled borrowers into
signing the arbitration agreement.

Sheila Canavan, an associate attorney with Steinbock and Hofmann, took on the FAMCO case as a crusade. The firm counted about
half a dozen FAMCO borrowers among its clients. The lender had been
fighting off attacks in the courts since the 1980s, and it employed
some of the nation's top corporate law firms to handle its lawsuits and

regulatory matters. Canavan, on the other hand, had just returned to the law after taking time off to raise her children. Friends warned her and the firm's partners, Phillip Steinbock and David Hofmann, that taking on FAMCO was going to bankrupt them, in much the same way the lawyers depicted in *A Civil Action* had lost everything pursuing the big chemical companies they claimed had poisoned drinking water in a small town in Massachusetts. Through the late '90s, the FAMCO case consumed Steinbock and Hofmann's staff, which racked up big bills for court reporters and document copying while no money came in the door to cover those costs or pay the lawyers' salaries. Steinbock and his wife sold their home and moved into a cramped town house. Hofmann burned through a modest inheritance he'd collected a few years before.

Among the firm's clients was Velda Durney, a widow in her seventies who got by on Social Security and a small pension. Durney had gotten in touch with FAMCO after getting a barrage of telephone and mail solicitations from the company. She needed $10,000 to paint her house and put in new carpeting. When she visited FAMCO's offices in San Jose, she later testified, her loan officer promised he would treat her like he would treat his own mother. He convinced her that as part of the deal she should also pay off her existing mortgage along with some credit-card debt. Later, as she signed a stack of loan papers, another FAMCO employee flipped through the pages so she could sign the bottom of each page without seeing what was written above. She would later say she knew nothing about the arbitration agreement, and hadn't realized until weeks later that she had agreed to pay more than $13,000 in points and other up-front costs on a loan of barely $51,000. Steinbock and Hofmann and FAMCO's lawyers fought for two years over whether Durney had known what she was doing when she'd signed the one-page arbitration contract. In 1999, a California appeals court gave her a big victory: it ruled FAMCO had fooled her and other borrowers into signing arbitration agreements. The court rejected the lender's demand that an arbitrator hear Durney's case.

The ruling was not an end but a beginning. State attorneys general, the Justice Department, and the FTC all joined Steinbock and Hofmann in the legal campaign against the lender. Things became even more complicated in the spring of 2000, when the weight of litigation—and fallout from the *New York Times–20/20* exposé—prompted Chisick to take his company into bankruptcy. Now, FAMCO customers who wanted financial recompense not only had to prove they'd been defrauded, they also had to fight for their place in line with the lender's other creditors, including Lehman Brothers.

After FAMCO settled with the FTC and others in early 2002, FAMCO's bankrupt shell had been drained of all of the money that had been left in the company. Borrowers would get payments of a few hundred or a few thousand dollars each, a fraction of what their advocates claimed the lender had stolen by slipping exorbitant fees into their loans. To make up the difference, Sheila Canavan and other consumer attorneys placed their sights on Lehman, the deepest pockets of all. They demanded that Lehman not only pay borrowers compensation for "aiding and abetting" FAMCO, but that the investment bank be forced to forsake some $80 million in debts that Lehman had recovered from the bankruptcy estate.

To give the plaintiffs a better shot at prevailing, Canavan invited Richard "Dickie" Scruggs, one of America's most successful litigators, to serve as lead attorney. Scruggs was a former navy fighter. In 1998, he had led the legal campaign that forced the big tobacco companies to agree to a $248 billion national settlement. If anybody had the cash and the courtroom flair to take on Lehman, Canavan figured, it was Scruggs. Except he wasn't sure he wanted the job. He had never handled a predatory-lending case before and besides, he told Canavan, he was thinking about retiring.

Scruggs agreed to fly out to California to hear Canavan out. She picked him up at his hotel in her Toyota Previa. Not wanting to launch into explaining the complicated case while she was behind the wheel, she popped in the recording of Bernae Gunderson's telephone conversation with the FAMCO branch manager in Minnesota. Scruggs listened for a few minutes, then turned to Canavan. "This is just a simple case of fraud," he said. He agreed to take the case.

He brought in a crew of lawyers and support staff from Mississippi, including Don Barrett, a litigator from Lexington, Mississippi, with a down-home courtroom style equal to Scruggs's own. Scruggs's team invested a huge amount, channeling, by its calculation, more than $9 million in time and costs into the litigation. Helen Duncan, one of Lehman's lawyers, said Scruggs wanted $1 billion from Lehman, but said he would be willing to settle for $500 million. Lehman countered with a much smaller offer. Scruggs replied, she said, that he had a war chest of cash that would allow him to fight the case to the end. "God didn't give me all this money to settle" for spare change, he said.

* * *

The trial began on February 13, 2003, presided over by U.S. district judge David O. Carter. The first witness to testify was Terry LaFrankie. He had worked as a loan officer for FAMCO for just six months in 1999, but he had learned many of the company's secrets. When he spotted an advertisement the lender had placed in the *Cincinnati Enquirer*, he could tell FAMCO was seeking the cream of the nation's salesmen. "They were looking—to lose my humility—they were looking for me." LaFrankie thought of himself as a "one-call closer," a salesman who could talk just about anyone into signing on the dotted line, "right then and there." Some people read the *Financial Times* for the news of the day, or Mark Twain for entertainment, he explained to the jury. One-call closers read books on psychology and salesmanship, with titles like *Creative Visualization* or *Persuasion* ("a very dangerous book as far as the information in it," LaFrankie noted). FAMCO's sales presentation, LaFrankie told jurors, was designed to "flow a little deception into the process." It was effective because it allowed loan officers to probe deeply into borrowers' psyches. "If you don't find the true pain," the saying at FAMCO went, "you won't write the loan." Matt Winston, who in 1999 worked for FAMCO in Illinois, testified that he and his fellow loan officers sometimes called around to other branches to compare weekly totals—not of loans booked but of how many customers had broken down and shed tears. On one occasion, Winston testified, a manager gave him a $50 bonus for making a borrower cry. The engineers of FAMCO's Track believed that the relief borrowers got from identifying a possible solution to their inner pain would prevent them from asking too many questions, Winston explained.

Along with the salesmen, the borrowers' lawyers also demanded testimony from Brian Chisick, the man who had built FAMCO from scratch and guided it over the better part of three decades. "If you want to stay in business for twenty-five years, you can't do it any way other than being completely straight and forthright with your borrowers," Chisick told the jury. The borrowers' attorneys hoped they could squeeze some admissions out of Chisick that would help their case or, at least, that he would undermine FAMCO's position with his demeanor. Chisick's spell on the witness stand was peppered with exchanges like this:

> Q. Did you ever instruct loan officers to charge elderly people who are not really with it only a maximum of 18 points, as opposed to 20.9 points?
> A. Yes.
> Q. All heart.
> A. Thanks.

Chisick was a hard witness to shake concessions out of. After the borrowers' attorneys complained that Chisick was being vague and unresponsive, Judge Carter ruled that the "consistent ambiguity" of his answers had reached a "threshold of evasiveness" that made it difficult for the plaintiffs' attorneys to conduct their examination. Scruggs and Barrett kept pushing, asking question after question in excruciating detail. Chisick responded to one line of questioning by saying: "You are beating this to death, but I agree, yeah." He maintained that his company's attackers were twisting facts and smearing his company.

When it came time to discuss FAMCO's practice of electronic eavesdropping, he testified that the company kept tabs on its sales force to make sure loan officers were doing their jobs properly. "I don't like the word eavesdrop," he said. "We would listen in, such as the telephone company and various other large organizations do, you know."

* * *

The jury also heard from FAMCO customers. They were mostly older folks who had none of the finesse and financial acumen of Chisick and his salesmen. Harriet Berringer was an eighty-six-year-old homemaker and the wife of a retired machinist from Fair Oaks, California. Borrowers' attorney Don Barrrett teased her about being a newlywed; she and her husband had been married for fifty-six years. Berringer said she and her husband had wanted $14,000 to pay off their credit-card debts. The loan officer persuaded them to roll over their existing mortgage, which brought the amount of the loan to around $66,000. But the loan ended up topping out at over $84,000, because FAMCO charged them roughly $18,000 in up-front points and closing costs. The couple couldn't afford their payments, and to save their house, they refinanced with another lender, taking out a special loan designed for elderly home owners known as a "reverse mortgage." The new loan allowed them to stay in their home but would mean that they would not be able to pass it on to their children and grandchildren when they died.

One of the younger borrowers who testified was Michael Austin. He was forty-eight, a machinist in Napa Valley. He explained what he did for a living: "You take a big piece of metal and you machine it down into a smaller piece that turns into something." He and his wife, Barbara, had three kids, ages five, sixteen, and seventeen. In December 1999, the Austins were behind on their mortgage. They were facing foreclosure. He called FAMCO. On December 13, he and Barbara went to FAMCO's branch in Pleasant Hill, bringing their youngest child with them. The office, Austin recalled, had "lots of glass, lots of brass. Lots of carpet. Real nice. . . . Very impressive." He explained his problems to the loan officer. Following the Track to the letter, the loan officer built a connection with Austin by explaining that he, too, had had some serious money problems. The salesman seemed like "Mr. Nice Guy," Austin said.

As they were going through the preliminary loan disclosures, Austin spotted a document that indicated that the loan's annual percentage rate would be 15 percent. Austin told the loan officer, "I'm not going to take out a loan for 15 percent." The loan officer, Austin testified, assured him: "Don't worry about it. It's not a binding document. . . . It's just an estimate. . . . Nothing we're doing here means anything." After they'd gone through the loan, Austin said, the loan officer took copies of the preliminary documents and put them in an envelope. He handed the Austins an envelope when they left. When they got home and opened it, Austin said, all that was inside was a handful of FAMCO advertising flyers. "I was bewildered. I really didn't know what to think." The couple called FAMCO, and the loan officer promised a courier would deliver the documents to them. When the courier didn't show, the salesman explained that the messenger had been in a car accident on the way to the Austins' home.

Mike Austin decided he didn't want to get the loan after all, and that he would instead try to save his home by filing for bankruptcy. The loan officer called him at work. "The guy sounded like he was going to break down and cry over the phone: 'You've got to do it. You're going to lose your house if you go through with bankruptcy. . . . You're going to ruin your credit forever. . . . C'mon Mike, this is a good deal. . . . This is what you want. This is what you need.'"

Austin relented. He and Barbara returned for a second visit to FAMCO's offices. When they arrived, Austin said: "Now, I'm going to leave with documents this time, right?" After they signed the final loan documents, the loan officer said he had to run; he had to go pick up his kids. "Don't worry about it," he told the couple. "You'll get all the documents you need in the mail."

It was two weeks before the paperwork arrived. When he read through it, Austin saw that he and his wife had borrowed around $86,000, not the "sixty-seven-odd thousand" that he had thought they borrowed. He read and reread the documents. "It never changed," he told the jury. "It still was '86' no matter how many times I read it."

* * *

Just after 8:40 A.M. on the sixth day of the trial, February 26, 2003, the plaintiffs called a new witness to the stand. The clerk asked for his name, and its spelling. "Gregory M. Walling," he said. "It's W-a-l-l-i-n-g."

It had been four years since Greg Walling had bumbled his way into becoming a whistle-blower, dialing the Minnesota attorney general's office on a stray impulse, hoping to satisfy his curiosity. Since then he had tried to do what he could to help those who were working to expose FAMCO's tactics. He had signed a sworn statement about his experiences at FAMCO for Prentiss Cox, the assistant state attorney general. He'd also given a deposition in one of the various threads of litigation tangling around FAMCO. This was different, though. He was testifying in front of a judge, a jury, and teams of lawyers in the middle of subprime country, the very place where he'd been tutored on the Monster and the other steps in FAMCO's sales script.

While the other two loan officers who had testified had seemed to enjoy their tenure as witnesses, bantering with the lawyers, Walling took little pleasure in the experience. On the witness stand, he wasn't the self-assured salesman who could talk to anybody about anything. He was a man racked with guilt about the things he'd done in his time at FAMCO. He talked so fast that the court reporter had trouble keeping up. The judge had to order breaks to allow the stenographer to rest her hands.

Walling told the jury about the power of the Track. "The Track was everything. I mean, it . . . it basically took you from a good salesman to a refined professional. It did everything—it covered every single step we ever did." It taught him how to get strangers "to disclose intimate personal details of their life, to give you the ability of—my analogy is reach inside of them and grab a hold of their heart. If I felt like reaching inside of them and doing whatever I wanted to their heart and soul, that Track gave me the ability to do that. I mean, people would break down in tears. There would be arguments between spouses in front of you, and you are leading it. It's a play. It's a play. You are up on stage, and you are acting out the part, and it's just like the audience is acting a part and—" He could have gone on, but a lawyer for Lehman cut him off with an objection.

Walling was nervous not only because of his audience of judge, jury, and lawyers, but because he had spotted someone he knew listening to his testimony from the courtroom's benches. Halfway through his questioning, Scruggs asked Walling whether he remembered most of his customers at FAMCO. Walling said he remembered many of them.

> Q. Do you see one of them sitting here in the courtroom today?
> A. Unfortunately, yes.
> Q. And would you point him out to the Court and the jury.
> A. The man in the front row with the blue coat.

Scruggs asked the man to stand up and then turned back to Walling.

Q. Do you recognize this gentleman?
A. Yes, I do.
Q. What is his name?
A. Clarence Winc—I know him as Wendy because his name is Clarence Wincentsen.

Wincentsen had been one of Walling's customers back in Minnesota. And Walling remembered him well. Wincentsen and his wife had been the rarest of consumers. They had a credit score that topped 800. Credit scores typically run between 300 and 850. Average scores run in the upper 600s. Anything in the 700s is excellent. And 800? "Eight hundred credit scores you don't see," Walling told the jury.

The other thing that had struck him about the Wincentsens was the fact that they had more than $300,000 in the bank. They were about as far from subprime customers as you could get. But Walling and FAMCO sold them a subprime loan anyway, charging them, Walling recalled, upward of $12,000 in points for a mortgage refinancing that netted them $15,000 in new money, which they used to pay off a car loan.

The other thing about the Wincentsens that Walling remembered was they had remarked that they hadn't brought their reading glasses with them the day they came into Walling's FAMCO branch. He had used all the tricks he'd been taught, running them step-by-step through the Track, tightening in with the Monster, and then eavesdropping on them when he left the room. It had been easy to sell them that loan. They'd been so happy with Walling that they'd signed a testimonial praising the fine service they'd received from FAMCO. Groping for the words to explain his guilt over what he'd done to Wendy Wincentsen, Walling said, "Kind of what made me remember him, is that even a thief has morals and ethics."

Q. I'm sorry?
A. I said even a thief has morals and ethics.

Lehman attorneys asked that Walling's answer be stricken as "non-responsive." The judge agreed. Walling tried to keep going. "Okay. He was one of those people—" The judge cut him off.

* * *

After presenting evidence of First Alliance's practices, the borrowers' attorneys then turned to the issue of what Lehman knew and when it knew it. Lehman had known as far back as 1995, the plaintiffs' attorneys said, that FAMCO took advantage of its customers. The memo from its own vice president, Eric Hibbert, had compared FAMCO to a seedy used-car lot, a place where you had to "leave your ethics at the door." An even bigger paper trail had piled up throughout 1999, when Lehman was serving as FAMCO's go-to financier on Wall Street. In February 1999, in a case involving Steinbock and Hofmann's clients, a California appeals court concluded: "FAMCO trained its employees to use various methods, including deception, to sell its services." In March, a state judge in Minnesota ordered that FAMCO halt its misleading sales tactics, calling them "smoke and mirrors." In September, the judge approved a settlement in which FAMCO agreed to pay $4,000 to $6,000 to more than one hundred customers the lender had signed up in Minnesota.

None of this, the borrowers' attorney said, gave Lehman pause. Throughout 1999 and into early 2000, Lehman funneled money to FAMCO to fund loans to home owners and securitized $425 million in FAMCO's loans into mortgage-backed securities deals. Even after the *New York Times–20/20* piece, Lehman kept funding FAMCO's loans, bankrolling nearly $12 million's worth in the eight days between the story's appearance and the lender's bankruptcy filing. What, the borrowers' attorneys asked bitingly, would it have taken to lead Lehman to conclude that there was something unethical about the way FAMCO did business? How many attorney general investigations would it take to scare Lehman away? Was seven not enough? Would eight have been enough?

* * *

Lehman's attorneys spent a good deal of time trying to blunt the impact of Hibbert's 1995 memo. They suggested that, at the time he wrote the report, Hibbert—and Lehman itself—had been neophytes in the subprime business. "It was a new industry, relatively," Hibbert testified. "It was unknown within Lehman. We had done no subprime deals. We had bought no subprime loans. It was a new business for us. . . . We really did not have a team of people who worked with sub-prime mortgage lenders or mortgage loans." Later, however, under cross-examination, Hibbert acknowledged that, before his review of FAMCO, Lehman had put together investment deals backed by mort-gages from a variety of subprime lenders, including names such as Household, Beneficial, the Money Store, and Aames. "Hibbert was not 'Alice in Wonderland' when he wrote his report," Scruggs told the jury. Hibbert had seen other subprime lenders, the litigator said, and he could draw on others at Lehman who had experience in subprime. A marketing memo that Lehman had submitted to FAMCO in mid-1995 had crowed about its work with subprime lenders as well as its team of Ph.D.s and other experts in securitizing subprime loans.

In making their defense, Lehman's lawyers argued that allegations against FAMCO and Lehman were part of a larger campaign that was unfairly assailing the subprime lending industry. Fourteen days into the trial, a week after Governor Perdue had signed the amendments that gutted his state's protections for mortgage borrowers, Lehman attorney Helen Duncan raised the specter of the Georgia Fair Lending Act as an example of misguided attempts to label legitimate business practices as predatory. Out of the jury's hearing, Duncan explained to the judge, "What I want to show is what happens when lenders leave the state, and when they leave the state, then those people who are subprime borrowers do not have the option of obtaining that type of financial borrowing. Because what's been painted in this courtroom is how terrible First Alliance is. How terrible subprime lending is. How it's gouging. How Lehman stands to profit from this. And what I'm trying to show here is that without subprime lending, you would have a lot of people who would not have access to the market."

* * *

For all the expertise and resources that Lehman put into defending its honor, the investment bank's top executives were nowhere to be found

in the courtroom. This was not a venue where Dick Fuld and his lieutenants wanted to be seen. Instead, the company sent a group of what
borrowers' attorneys mocked as "nice young men in middle management."

One of them was Frederick Madonna, a senior vice president who
earned roughly $400,000 a year. He went way back in subprime. In the
late '80s, while at Moody's, he'd help prepare ratings for Guardian
Savings, and then, after moving to Greenwich Capital, he'd worked on
deals involving Long Beach Bank. Madonna testified that Lehman
didn't believe it had ever been proven that FAMCO executives or
employees had committed fraud. "They, in our eyes, have not been convicted of anything," he testified. "We had had no reason to believe borrowers were being harmed." Besides, he said, FAMCO's practices were
no different from those of other subprime lenders. "This company was
very much like other companies in the business at the time," he said.

Another Lehman executive who testified for the defense was Steven
Berkenfeld, a managing director who had spent most of his career at
Lehman. He was in his forties, the eldest son of a structural engineer
and a homemaker. He had earned his law degree from Columbia
University. Berkenfeld said Lehman officials didn't object to going
forward with FAMCO in late 1998 and early 1999 because they had a
sense that the lender's problems were "old history"; it was a "new company" that had added new managers and strived to put its legal issues
behind it. If there were "violations of statutes" at FAMCO, Lehman
wanted to make sure those violations were corrected. "We take the
f-word very seriously," Berkenfeld said. "I don't understand why anyone would think that we would want to finance a company that was
engaged in fraud." All the scrutiny from state authorities actually had
a positive side, he suggested; FAMCO was less likely to break a law if
regulators were watching closely and attorney general offices were
pursuing actions against it. "Any rational person would say it's less
likely that someone will speed if there's a cop following 'em than if
there's no cop in sight."

One of the borrowers' attorneys, Phil Steinbock, pressed Berkenfeld on how he and his colleagues defined fraud. Steinbock read a line
from the 1999 California appeals court decision that said FAMCO

had trained its employees "to use various methods, including deception," to peddle its loans.

"That is not saying the conclusion that there is fraud," Berkenfeld said. "Fraud is a very serious term in our mind. To say that they trained their brokers to use deceptions, to me—and I'm not trying to mince words here—but it's not equivalent to saying that there was systematically a pattern of defrauding or committing fraud in the origination of loans."

It was on this point that the plaintiffs and the defendants parted ways starkly. Attorneys for the borrowers asserted that the deceptive salesmanship woven into the Track and the Monster was no small matter—deceiving your customers on a consistent basis constituted systematic fraud and tainted everything else the company did. What was more important to the integrity of the mortgage business than making certain that borrowers understood their loans?

For Lehman officials, though, what was said to borrowers wasn't as important as what was on the face of the documents. If the paperwork was in order, properly filled out and properly signed, there could be no fraud, Lehman maintained. Lead defense attorney Helen Duncan argued, "You can't not read the documents and then say, 'Well, I was justified in relying on what you told me.'" She added that Berringer and other borrowers had ample opportunity to review their documents or consult others for advice. "I don't think these borrowers were as dumb as plaintiffs' counsel want you to think they were," Duncan told the jury.

Lehman's lawyers took the position that First Alliance wasn't engaged in fraud during the span from December 1998 to March 2000 when Lehman served as the lender's sole lifeline to Wall Street. As good lawyers always do, however, they had a fallback position: if FAMCO had engaged in fraud, they said, Lehman didn't know and wasn't involved. "What's the fraud? The fraud is lying to people at the closing table," Duncan said. "Even under their theory, Lehman is not at the closing table." If FAMCO was lying to its borrowers, "it was lying to us, too."

In his closing arguments, borrowers' attorney Don Barrett mocked Lehman's multilayered defense. "First they tell you . . . 'No fraud was committed.' Then they tell you, 'Well . . . the plaintiffs can't prove fraud was committed.' And then—'Well, okay, but you can't prove we knew about it.' And then finally they tell you, 'Well, okay. So we knew it. We thought they were going to change. . . .' Lehman clearly ignored the basic rule of human relations—that you predict people's future behavior based on what they've done in the past."

The borrowers' attorneys asked the jury to award $85 million to the forty-seven hundred borrowers FAMCO signed up for loans in 1999 and early 2000. Barrett said he wasn't asking for "fluffy" damages for emotional suffering; he simply wanted the jury to award "the money that the class members were cheated out of," the difference between what they thought they were borrowing and what they actually borrowed. Barrett and the other plaintiffs' attorneys asked that Lehman be held responsible for 100 percent of the award. FAMCO, they said, would not have survived into 1999 or 2000, and could not have made any of the loans in question, without the financing provided by Lehman Brothers. "In Lehman's big scheme of things, First Alliance and the Chisicks were small fry," he said. "Dime a dozen. Easily replaceable." Lehman could easily have declined to work with FAMCO, and without Lehman's backing, "these loans would not have been made, not a one of them."

Barrett's request was necessary because of a seemingly insurmountable legal constraint on the plaintiffs. Under the 2002 settlement, FAMCO could not be held liable in this trial. The jurors were not allowed to know that, or to know how much FAMCO had agreed to settle for in 2002. How the jury sliced up the responsibility for the verdict was as important as how big the verdict would be. Any percentage that was attributed to FAMCO would be meaningless; it wouldn't increase the borrowers' recovery by a dime and it would decrease any liability owed by Lehman.

✳ ✳ ✳

The trial lasted fifty-six days, spread over five months, with the last nineteen days taken up by jury deliberations. The jury was charged with answering three questions: Did FAMCO defraud home owners? Did Lehman know about the fraud when it bankrolled FAMCO? And did Lehman assist FAMCO in perpetrating the fraud?

On June 16, 2003, the jury announced its decision. To all three questions, the answer was "yes." It awarded the plaintiffs $50.9 million in damages—more than $10,000 for each of the borrowers. As auspicious as that was for the plaintiffs, the next part of the verdict was bitterly disappointing. The jury attributed just 10 percent of the fault to Lehman. That translated into less than $5.1 million. Given the investment bank's profits and access to capital, the figure was the equivalent of spare change. A Lehman spokeswoman said the firm was "disappointed with the jury's finding on the question of liability. We continue to believe that no one at Lehman Brothers was aware of any wrongdoing that may have been committed by individual loan officers at First Alliance." Still, Lehman was "pleased that the jury understood how minimal Lehman Brothers' involvement was in any wrongdoing." The borrowers' attorneys were frustrated. Barrett wondered whether they'd done too good a job of nailing FAMCO, creating such disgust for the lender that the jury focused its anger too much on FAMCO and not enough on Lehman.

Lehman had one more hurdle to cross before it could be free of exposure from its FAMCO misadventure. During the jury trial, Judge Carter had also been conducting a shadow trial to determine whether Lehman Brothers should be required to pay back some $80 million it had diverted from FAMCO's bankruptcy estate as repayment for money FAMCO owed to the investment bank. The trustee appointed to oversee the bankruptcy proceedings had asked the judge to order Lehman to return the money to the estate. This would make more money available for borrowers involved in the 2002 settlement. With backing from the plaintiffs' attorneys, the trustee argued that Lehman should forfeit the rights to the money, because its support of FAMCO's frauds amounted to "inequitable conduct." Whatever the jury had decided, the judge's ruling on this issue could make or break the effort to punish Lehman.

Carter came back with his decision on July 30, six weeks after the jury had weighed in. His twenty-four-page ruling laid out in detail the relationship between FAMCO and Lehman. He concluded that "Lehman's financing constituted significant, active and knowing participation in the First Alliance fraud, thereby substantially assisting First

Alliance in its fraudulent lending practices." But was that enough to deprive Lehman of the rights to the $80 million? As bad as Lehman's conduct was, Carter said it didn't meet the heightened legal standard required, under bankruptcy law, to sustain the trustee's claim on behalf of the borrowers. Lehman's misconduct didn't bring about the lender's bankruptcy, the judge said, and so it was a separate issue from the distribution of FAMCO's assets after its failure. The claim against Lehman was denied, and with it the last opportunity to hold the investment bank accountable for funding FAMCO's wrongdoing.

In dollars and cents terms, Lehman had escaped almost unscathed. That made it easy for Lehman and other investment banks to dismiss the whole matter as an aberration. In the aftermath of the trial, there was little evidence that the verdict had discouraged Lehman and other Wall Street firms from continuing to work hand in hand with the subprime industry. "This case should have made a difference," Sheila Canavan, who had done as much as anyone to bring Lehman into the dock, said years later. "Instead, the slap on the hand which Lehman received emboldened Wall Street. And the rest is history."

A few days after Judge Carter's decision, industry sources told *National Mortgage News* that Lehman Brothers was planning to exercise options to buy a larger stake in BNC Mortgage, the Quality Mortgage offshoot in which Lehman had owned a minority interest since 2000. For all the legal problems and bad publicity that subprime had brought Lehman, subprime was still an essential part of the firm's future. Lehman wasn't turning back. The same was true for the rest of Wall Street. Over the next two years, the hunt for subprime customers would become a feeding frenzy.

11. Feeding the Monster

By the summer of 2003, Robert Braver had enough of spam e-mail. He decided to do something about it. He opened an e-mail with the subject line, *Lowest home rates won't last long*. The e-mail professed to be from Prince Darnell at oxq6ajdxmj@fabulousomars.us. Braver clicked on the link in the body of the e-mail, which promised him a great deal on a mortgage. That took him to a Web site called fastfree-quotes.com. He filled out the rate-quote form on the site. He didn't use his real name. After all, he knew Prince Darnell was a nom de plume. If the sender of the e-mail wasn't going to give him a bona fide name, Braver didn't feel obliged to reveal his personal information. He identified himself as Maren Eliason of Norman, Oklahoma. He clicked submit, and his trap was set.

Soon after, he got a call from a salesman from Ameriquest Mortgage, asking if he was interested in a loan. Braver repeated his test more than twenty times over a span of more than a year, producing a series of ghostly communications between fictional characters. Gregory Annapolis followed a link e-mailed by Colleen West. Clayton Fountain followed the link e-mailed by Glenna Manley. And so on. Almost every time, the result was the same: a call from a fast-talking sales rep from Ameriquest promising to tailor a loan to his needs or help him become "debt free."

Braver had uncovered a subterranean marketing machine that was flooding the nation's in-boxes with come-ons for home loans—and helping to plant the notion in Americans' minds that *everyone* was getting a new mortgage and, if they hesitated, they'd miss out on the chance of a lifetime. Mortgages and the real-estate boom became a hot topic of discussion at backyard cookouts, the subject of TV shows such as *Flip This House,* and a ubiquitous presence on the Internet. The influx of unsolicited mortgage e-mails burgeoned, soon to account for as much as 44 percent of all spam, surpassing pharmaceuticals and porn as the No. 1 subject of spam. The mortgage boom was partly fueled by a relentless stream of e-mail pitches like these: *Guaranteed lowest rates on the planet . . . You could get $300,000 for as little as $700 a month! . . . Approval regardless of credit history!*

Many people couldn't resist. They clicked the links and typed in their personal details. Lead-generating vendors collected prospects' information and sold it to Ameriquest and other lenders. The lenders then contacted the would-be borrowers by phone or regular mail. Braver thought the e-mails were tools in a bait-and-switch campaign that lured borrowers by telling them they had already been approved for what were, in fact, impossibly low rates. Braver challenged one of his callers from Ameriquest about how the e-mail that had connected him to the lender could promise he had been preapproved for a $400,000 mortgage at a 3.25 percent fixed rate. That was more than his house was worth, Braver said. "Aren't y'all obligated to honor that?" Braver said. "Let's do it. Sign me up." One of the salesmen explained that such an offer was simply a "best case scenario." "Every single borrower is an individual situation," the sales rep said. "We're not like a cookie-cutter lender."

Braver had other reasons to be concerned about the influx of spam touting home-loan deals. He ran an e-mail and Internet hosting company in Oklahoma. He saw mortgage spam as a costly threat to the health of his business. Braver's investigation convinced him Ameriquest was a major enabler of the surge in mortgage spam. He sued Ameriquest and a gaggle of its lead vendors, many of them based in Southern California. He charged that the lender and its vendors had conspired to send out billions of e-mails that used fake sender names, fake return addresses, misspelled words, and other tricks in an effort to evade spam filters and mislead consumers.

Ameriquest said it wasn't responsible for the actions of third parties that provided it with leads. It eventually settled the case on undisclosed terms.

Ameriquest's spam-aided hunt for customers was part of a larger marketing blitz, one that was bigger and more aggressive than any ever seen in the history of the mortgage industry. Not so long before, Ameriquest had been an obscure company in an obscure corner of the mortgage market, relying on old-fashioned direct mail and telemarketing to reach customers. In this earlier time, loan officers' telephone lists were "green sheets," computer printouts with a list of prospects that, one manager recalled, "wasn't much better than just what you'd find in the phone book." Things had changed. Ameriquest seemed to be everywhere. It was hard to log on to your computer, turn on a television, or go to a ball game without seeing Ameriquest's Liberty Bell logo, designed, the company said, to "symbolize America and the quest for a mortgage." Flip on PBS, and there was Ameriquest, a sponsor of the wildly popular *Antiques Roadshow*. Surf the Internet, and you were likely to encounter a pop-up or banner ad extolling Ameriquest's service. By late 2003, the company was the fifth biggest U.S. advertiser on the Web, with 1.9 billion ad "impressions" a month. Click over to a random cable channel late at night and you might come across a game show legend hosting a slickly produced infomercial that explained how Ameriquest could help home owners change their lives and their lifestyles: "Hi. I'm Chuck Woolery. You know, owning your own home, well, it's always been the biggest part of the American dream. It's the cornerstone for a lifetime of memories. A place of comfort. A source of pride." Woolery strolled along the sidewalk of a sun-dappled, tree-lined street. "Your house is also a financial investment, and buying or refinancing one can be complicated, even intimidating," he continued. "Now wouldn't it be fantastic to have a friend, a neighbor who would help you through this process? Well, that's exactly what an Ameriquest mortgage specialist does." As Woolery kept talking, the screen faded to images of smiling Ameriquest loan officers from hometowns around the nation: Schaumberg, Illinois. Sugar Land, Texas. Egg Harbor, New Jersey. Miramar, Florida. Friendswood, Texas.

* * *

On Tyson Russum's first day on the job at an Ameriquest branch in Tampa, Florida, he was herded into the conference room with a couple of other new hires. The three of them watched a training video. It wasn't the typical in-house video with a modest budget and modest production values. Instead, branch officials popped in a copy of *Boiler Room,* the Hollywood movie starring Ben Affleck, Giovanni Ribisi, and Vin Diesel. The fast-paced film, released in 2000, followed a stock-broker wannabe at a securities brokerage that sold worthless shares in nonexistent companies. The veterans showed the neophyte how to close sales over the phone by manipulating unsuspecting customers. "The impression I got was that they were trying to get across to us that it's basically make the sale at any cost," Russum recalled. "And that kind of set . . . the mood for the next eleven to twelve months that I was with the organization."

Boiler Room was a reference point many Ameriquest employees used to explain how things worked at the company. Brien Hanley worked for Ameriquest in the Kansas City suburbs. He described the environment inside the branch this way: "Lot of gung ho, lot of macho, lot of sexual harassment for the women. Kind of like the movie *Boiler Room.* Our office's claim to fame. The perfect movie for working for Ameriquest. That was the favorite movie. My boss always talked about it." Sales reps and managers recommended the movie to one another and passed DVD copies around. "That was your homework—to watch *Boiler Room,*" Lisa Taylor, who worked as a loan officer in Sacramento, recalled. Managers, she said, hoped new workers would pick up on the movie's feverish, anything-goes ethos: "the energy, the impact, the driving, the hustling." For the gang at Ameriquest, Affleck had the movie's best lines. Affleck played a savvy operator already wealthy beyond most people's dreams. "Anybody who tells you that money is the root of all evil," he told the hungry-eyed trainees, "*doesn't fucking have any.*"

Ameriquest loan officers focused less on the object lesson of the movie, which came when the FBI swooped in and arrested the con artists. Sometimes, though, they'd make dark jokes about their employer's over-the-line tactics, alluding to the movie's closing moments: "I wonder when the feds are coming?"

* * *

For those who gave themselves over to the breakneck pace of life inside Ameriquest, the rewards were dazzling. Twenty-three-year-old salesmen made $100,000 a year. Twenty-six-year-old branch managers grossed $200,000, $300,000, even half a million dollars a year, and boosted their takes higher as they climbed within the company's ranks. Many would become millionaires as they made Roland Arnall a billionaire. One longtime Arnall aide, Wayne Lee, pulled down more than $5 million in salary and bonuses in his year as CEO of Arnall's holding company, ACC Capital. After he left the company, Lee garnered a consulting contract from Arnall that put almost $35 million in his pocket.

For the big earners and top executives, working at Ameriquest and other subprime lenders often seemed like a nonstop party. In 2003, Ameriquest flew Stephen Kuhn and a horde of other salesmen and managers to Southern California, rewarding them for having a great year with a trip to the Super Bowl. The company put them up in a luxury hotel in Huntington Beach. Then it chartered a bus to carry them down to San Diego for the game. The booze was free and the atmosphere was raucous. One regional manager, bantering back and forth with a colleague over who was a bigger fish within the company, shot back with a killer line: "Let's compare W-2s. I made over two million dollars. What did you do?"

At sales conferences and managers' meetings, employees were treated to a steady stream of celebrity athletes and musicians. At one meeting, the surprise guest speaker was baseball legend Cal Ripken Jr. He shared with them what baseball had taught him about customer service. "Fans are essentially customers: You've got to win each of them one at a time, or you will lose them. You can't let one fan—or one customer—go away unhappy."

Back home in Texas and Florida and Maine, managers spent larger and larger wads of the company's money, taking their staffs out on the town, treating them to $80 steaks, shrimp cocktails, $15 cigars. During Dave Johnson's first week as a branch manager in Michigan, his area manager picked up Johnson and other branch leaders in an Escalade limo and took them out for a seven-course meal. Then they headed to one of the hottest nightclubs in Detroit, where Johnson's supervisor sprang for half a dozen bottles of Dom Pérignon. The fun had a purpose: managers used their expense accounts to reward salespeople and to motivate them to work crazy hours and take the bosses' production numbers to new heights. "It's amazing what alcohol can do," Mark Glover, the loan officer who worked in Ameriquest branches around Los Angeles, said. "A guy takes ten of us out, spends five thousand dollars on dinner and drinks, we like that guy. We were like: 'This guy's cool. We're going to do all we can to help him out.'"

* * *

In the overheated world of subprime, where money, liquor, and cocaine flowed easily, down-and-dirty sexuality often came with the territory. According to dozens of industry insiders, the trading of sexual favors became commonplace in the mortgage business. Some wholesale reps offered sex to brokers who were willing to send loans their way. One mortgage broker recalled that his office often got visits from "minimally trained and minimally dressed" wholesale reps in short skirts. They asked him and his colleagues to come party with them at Ruth's Chris Steak House. "There were some indecent proposals made," he said. "That was part of building the relationship." Among the testosterone-fueled fraternity of mortgage brokers, this sort of behavior came to be expected. "Women who had sex for loans were known very quickly," Sharmen Lane, a former New Century wholesale rep, recalled. After she turned down one mortgage broker who propositioned her in his office, he refused to send loans her way. "I didn't want to be a mortgage slut," she said. *BusinessWeek* titled its story on the phenomenon "Sex, Lies, and Subprime Mortgages."

The flip side of subprime's sexual politics was the Neanderthal tendencies of many of the men who dominated the industry. Lisa Taylor encountered a wide array of "disgusting, demeaning, and demoralizing conduct" while she worked as a loan officer at one of Ameriquest's Sacramento branches. Men in the office discussed what color panties or thongs the women were or should be wearing, and which women they were "doing" and which ones they'd like to "do." Men frequently made explicit references to women's bodies, referring to Taylor's breasts as "twin towers" and "midgets in there." One supervisor, she claimed, began to "constantly touch, fondle, and adjust his genitalia" in front of her and other women. Taylor complained to human resources about the sexual harassment as well as what she termed management's policy of condoning and participating in altering and forging loan documents. Ameriquest fired her in 2003. The reason company officials gave? They said *she* had sexually harassed a customer. Taylor sued, charging that the reason given for her firing was a pretext and the real reason was her complaints about fraud and sexual misconduct.

Humiliation and intimidation became a way of life for some Ameriquest employees. Keeping people in their place—making it plain they were expendable or held a less than equal status—encouraged them to conform. Nazik Santora, a credit analyst in the company's Orange County operations, learned this one day when she made a mistake handling a customer's loan application. She filed the application on a Saturday, instead of, as was required, on a weekday. She fixed the problem on Monday. She thought that was the end of it. But then, Santora claimed, two supervisors ordered her and two other workers who had made the same error into a car belonging to one of the managers. The group drove to a self-service car wash, where the managers ordered the three minions to wash the vehicle. The managers, Santora said, stood by, laughing and joking and taking photos; they required her to stand in front of the shiny-clean car so they could take her picture with her head bowed in shame. Soon after, she said, they hung blown-up versions of the photos in a prominent corridor in the office, over a huge, all-caps caption, "Don't let this happen to you."

A manager at one of the lender's Northern California outposts was a military vet who, according to a lawsuit filed by some of his former employees, bragged he had permission from human resources to impose any kind of physical exertion he wanted on his sales corps.

He demanded that loan officers stand at their desks until they booked their first loan application of the day, a process that might take hours. He made sales contest losers do push-ups, wear wigs, and wash the winners' cars. When anyone complained, he said they were weak and weren't manly enough to do the job. When a woman in the branch had a miscarriage, former employees claimed, he didn't ask how she was doing. He yelled at her for missing work.

* * *

Ameriquest's onetime rival in Orange County, FAMCO, built a brilliant sales force by recruiting the best of the best. Then it drilled them exhaustively until they learned, by heart, the meticulously crafted sales presentation, the Track, and its key component, the Monster. Ameriquest built its sales juggernaut in a different way. It hired people in droves, trained them little, pushed them to meet huge expectations, and hoped that a small percentage would turn out to be superstars. The rest were expendable. Either they left because they couldn't take the pressure or they were fired because they didn't produce. The process was simple. Hire a dozen new salespeople, and one or two would be successes. Hire a dozen more, and repeat the process until you had a branch full of sales dynamos. Then ratchet the sales quotas higher and higher. "I don't think there's a day that went by that I wasn't told I was going to be fired," recalled Omar Ross, who worked as a loan officer for Ameriquest in Michigan. "I was told I was going to be fired at least two hundred times." Supervisors stayed on him even as he rose to become one of the top-producing salesmen in the company, beating his monthly quota for producing loans and making lots of money for the lender. "They would tell everybody: 'Omar did ten. How come everybody else can't do ten?' Then in private they would turn around and say: 'Why can't you do more? You're slacking. You're capable of doing more.'"

In many branches, turnover reached 100 percent, even 200 percent a year. It wasn't unusual for a salesman to begin a job at Ameriquest and, six months later, find he was the longest-tenured loan officer in his branch. One of Stephen Kuhn's coworkers who had made the Super Bowl trip with him in January 2003 came home and had a lousy February. He'd put up big numbers in prior months—big enough to win the trip—but a single bad month was enough to get him fired. "He was shit-canned," Kuhn said.

The pressure to produce began to get to Kuhn. After he became a branch manager, he saw a bigger picture of how Ameriquest was treating its customers. Many nights, he had to drink a twelve-pack of beer to get to sleep. He asked for a demotion. He wanted to go back to being a salesman.

Even that didn't work for him. He felt trapped. To hang on to his job, he had to put borrowers in deals that sank them deeper into ruin. One of his customers was a veterinarian who was having tax problems. The IRS was threatening to close down his business. Kuhn arranged a loan for the veterinarian that "had no benefit whatsoever. It was a terrible loan." Another customer was a small businessman, the owner of a Chinese restaurant. Kuhn put the man into a stated-income loan that raised his payments by $200 a month, even though he was struggling to keep up on his existing mortgage. "He was desperate," Kuhn said. "So I was told to take advantage of him." Kuhn said a supervisor ordered him to cut and paste documents to make the loan go through, telling him, "It's a three-hundred-thousand-dollar loan. Get it done." The borrower was facing foreclosure on his existing mortgage, so Kuhn forged his mortgage history so it looked like he'd never been late on his mortgage.

By the summer of 2003 Kuhn couldn't take it anymore. He told his manager he was having trouble dealing with things, because he thought Ameriquest's rates, fees, and business ethics were terrible. Soon after, on a day when Kuhn was out sick, his manager left him a cell phone message telling him it would be in everyone's best interest if Kuhn and Ameriquest parted ways. Kuhn called back and asked why he was being fired. The only answer the manager would give him, Kuhn said, was, "I think you know."

* * *

Mark Glover was another of the young workers who walked through Ameriquest's revolving door. He hadn't held a steady job for years. A friend who worked in the mortgage business suggested he try Ameriquest. "They hire everyone," she said. Glover started as a loan officer at

Ameriquest's downtown Los Angeles branch the day after Christmas 2002. He should have fit right in. He was a fast talker, and he had a loose definition of right and wrong. For years, he said, he'd been a regular in L.A.'s club scene, a heavy cocaine user who acted as a drug courier and engaged in check and credit-card fraud to bankroll his lifestyle. He'd learned how to fabricate fake IDs and other documents he needed for pulling off financial scams. The kinds of things that his coworkers at Ameriquest were doing, he said, had long ago become almost second nature to him.

He was tempted to put his skills in fabrication and forgery to use at Ameriquest. He knew that, at Ameriquest, "anyone who wasn't doing bad things was getting replaced. The people who were doing the illegal things were the ones making the money and getting the promotions." But he hesitated. He was going back and forth to the county court-house a few blocks away, dealing with the check-fraud charge that had been hanging over his head for months. His lawyer was trying to work out a deal that would let him off with probation. He and his fiancée had a son who was almost a year old. He was afraid if he got caught fabricating mortgage documents, he'd end up in jail for sure. He was haunted by the thought of his son having to visit him behind bars. He decided to draw a line. He'd work hard and talk fast to sell loans, but he wouldn't do any cut-and-paste or Photoshop jobs. He wouldn't falsify documents. Strange as it seemed, the experienced fraudster decided he was going to be the cleanest loan officer in his branch. Or as clean as anyone could be working at Ameriquest.

He maintained that policy after he transferred across town to Ameriquest's Santa Monica office. That didn't make him popular with his coworkers, Glover said. In a place where employees were expected to do whatever it took to get the job done, Glover's attitude made him an outsider. His discomfort grew as he saw the ways in which many of his coworkers lied to their customers. When borrowers objected to rates or fees they hadn't expected, Glover said, loan officers worked to "massage them through it" and get them to sign. They told borrowers: "That will come off after the loan is funded." Or: "That's only for the first month." Salesmen at Ameriquest took pride in their ability to befuddle and bemuse. Once, Glover said, a loan officer who'd just cinched a high-profit deal bragged: "I just raped this customer for 5 points and 10 percent interest!"

Glover stayed because he needed the job and the money was good. His days at Ameriquest didn't end until after a coworker filed a sexual harassment claim against her manager and asked Glover to share what he'd seen. A supervisor warned Glover that if he supported the woman's story, he'd lose his job. He told what he knew, and things went downhill from there. People in the office called him a "snitch" and a "mole." A supervisor told him to go home, take a few days off, "think about things." When he returned, he saw that someone had defaced a photo on his desk, using black ink to blot out his son's face.

Just before he was fired, Glover collected documentation on $30 million's worth of loans that he knew to be fraudulent. The documents came in handy when he sued the company for wrongful termination. Glover, who was biracial, claimed that he'd been subjected to "racial slurs and epithets" and "constant verbal abuse." He also charged that he had witnessed "deceptive business practices such as lying to customers about cancellation rights, interest rates, points, and closing costs." Ameriquest eventually settled the case on undisclosed terms. Glover thought Ameriquest had settled because, otherwise, it might have been forced to own up to the falsifications in the loan documents he had spirited out of the office. "They weren't going to do that," he said. "They knew I could have gone to every single one of those home owners and said: 'Your loan was done fraudulently.' "

* * *

If Ameriquest set a standard for hard-boiled tactics in the subprime market, it wasn't alone. As the market grew, it became crowded with lenders that frequently placed growth and profits over the well-being of their customers. These included big companies. They also included smaller ones that opened for business with no track record and little capital but still managed to get funding from Wall Street. Christopher J. Warren, the mortgage fraudster who had started in the industry as a nineteen-year-old salesman at Ameriquest, decided to strike out on his own after just two and a half years. In 2004, at age twenty-two, he opened his own mortgage company, WTL Financial, headquartered in

Sacramento. He got licenses to operate in California, Florida, Connecticut, and other states and eventually had 120 people on staff. Warren had a valuable supply of sales leads, he said, because before he'd left Ameriquest he had hacked into the company's computer system and stolen private information on 680,000 Ameriquest customers. He boasted that he had fashioned WTL on *Boiler Room*, the movie that served as a training tape for many Ameriquesters. He took the fraudulent tactics that he'd learned at Ameriquest, he said, and then threw in wrinkles of his own. He discovered that the investors and bigger lenders who bought WTL's loans never bothered to recheck the credit reports of the borrower, so WTL began falsifying borrowers' credit records, wiping away late payments and raising credit scores of 500 up to 700. If a bigger lender managed to spot a fraudulent loan, Warren would "fire" the employee who was responsible. Then he'd rehire the employee under an alias. Before his company went under, Warren claimed, it had sold $800 million in loans that were packaged into mortgage-backed securities. For him, that translated into earnings, between the ages twenty-two and twenty-four, of more than $2.25 million. He blew it all, he said, on twenty-four cars, five houses, and drugs.

Most of the big lenders targeting home owners for subprime loans were based in Orange County, within a fifteen-minute drive from Ameriquest's headquarters. New Century, a company founded in 1996 with a large contingent of folks who had learned the trade under Roland Arnall during his Long Beach days, operated out of a black-glass tower in Irvine. New Century billed itself as "a new shade of blue chip." It rewarded top-selling employees with trips and perks, such as classes at a Porsche-driving school and a party at a train station in Barcelona, Spain. One of the company's top salespeople was Sharmen Lane. She was a high school dropout who worked as a manicurist before she took a job at the lender. In 2003, Lane said, she booked more than $200 million in loans, taking a half-percent commission that worked out to an income of more than $1 million for the year—a success story that eventually encouraged her to strike out on her own as a motivational speaker and life coach, selling her rise from "manicurist to millionaire."

Long Beach Mortgage had been subsumed into the nation's largest

S&L, Seattle-based Washington Mutual, but it kept its headquarters in Orange County, in Anaheim. The trail of lawsuits against Long Beach showed that the company had changed little from the days when it had been owned by Arnall. Diane Kosch, a senior loan coordinator in Long Beach, said company executives pushed mortgage deals through even when she found questionable appraisals or other signs of fraud. They treated her and other "quality assurance" workers as an annoyance rather than a vital part of the process. "We were basically the black sheep of the company, and we knew it," she said. Long Beach put home owners in harm's way, ex-employees said, by pushing them into complex mortgages they didn't understand and couldn't afford. "They were just nasty products — just awful for the consumers," WaMu's former chief legal officer said.

One of the products favored by Long Beach, Ameriquest, and other subprimers was the "hybrid" adjustable-rate mortgage. The loans started out with a fixed rate that lasted for two or three years. Then they flipped, with a huge payment shock, to adjustable rates for the final twenty-eight or twenty-seven years of the loan term. These "2/28s" and "3/27s" allowed salespeople to lure in borrowers by quoting relatively low starting interest rates and monthly payments. Even if borrowers caught on that there was going to be a payment shock down the road, loan officers said they shouldn't worry, because the lender would roll them over into a better loan before the original loan began adjusting upward.

The inventive mortgage products emerging in the home-loan market were watched closely by the heaviest of the industry's heavyweights: Countrywide Financial's Angelo R. Mozilo. Mozilo's company had established itself as the largest mortgage lender in America by providing loans to home owners with good credit. Mozilo called his company "my baby." For much of his career, he had been cautious about the kinds of loans his company made. Countrywide had mostly steered clear of subprime as other lenders dived into the market throughout the 1990s. Mozilo worried that subprime loans were too risky, in some cases even "toxic."

Yet as Ameriquest and subprime expanded, Mozilo became fixated on Roland Arnall's success, according to Paul Muolo, an editor at *National Mortgage News* who interviewed Mozilo many times over the years. The two moguls met in the early 2000s, each trying to size up the other. Arnall wanted to surpass Mozilo as the biggest mortgage lender of any type. Mozilo wanted to know the secret of Ameriquest's runaway growth. Mozilo could see that Arnall's company was a giant sales machine, driven by bonus-hungry loan officers who used stated-income loans and other risky products to aggressively increase the company's market share. "He plays by his own rules," Mozilo said. "He's the guy who started stated-income, the guy who started no-documentation loans. All of his people were on commission." Mozilo learned more details about Arnall's tactics after Countrywide hired a group of former Ameriquest employees in New York. He was so concerned by what he heard, he said, that he forwarded the information to the state's attorney general, Eliot Spitzer.

While Ameriquest's methods may have made Mozilo uneasy, he wasn't so troubled that he kept Countrywide from joining the subprime gold rush. His company had survived decades of real-estate booms and busts, and he thought it had the brains and brawn to handle the risks of subprime better than the upstarts. Mozilo's competitive instincts beat out his caution. He couldn't accept being second or third. "It's a question of dominance," he told investors. He didn't like that Countrywide trailed Ameriquest in the subprime lending rankings. By 2003 Arnall's companies had captured nearly 12 percent of the subprime market; Countrywide did barely half as much subprime volume, with a market share of just 6 percent.

Besides, the real money in the mortgage business was now in subprime, not in prime loans. When Countrywide sold prime loans to investors, its average profit margin was 0.93 percent; when it sold subprime loans to investors, the company's profit margin nearly quadrupled, to 3.64 percent. The fees, interest rates, and prepayment penalties embedded in subprime loans made them much more seductive to investors.

* * *

In the fall of 2003, Countrywide, Long Beach, and other lenders doing business in the subprime market found themselves being muscled by a new Orange County–based rival. Argent Mortgage Company, which had begun making loans barely a year before, was racking up huge volumes as a wholesale lender, making subprime loans to home owners through independent mortgage brokers. Argent, it seemed, had come out of nowhere, and now it seemed to be everywhere. It sponsored the Argent Mortgage Indy Grand Prix for open-wheel automobile racers, as well as the circuit's rising female star, Danica Patrick. It was leasing huge swaths of office space in Orange County, in Rolling Meadows, Illinois, and White Plains, New York, announcing plans to hire hundreds of additional workers.

Argent wasn't a rival to Ameriquest. It was a sister company, another one of the ventures that Roland Arnall had dreamed up in his quest to become the king of subprime and, someday, the king of all home lending. The wholesale-lending operation had begun quietly in 2000 as a division of Ameriquest. It broke out in 2003, adopting the Argent name and operating independently of Ameriquest, with its headquarters in nearby Irvine rather than in the city of Orange, where Ameriquest maintained its home office.

Terry Rouch, who had worked for Arnall at Long Beach in the '90s, signed on at Argent as a wholesale loan rep. Friends inside Arnall's holding company, ACC Capital, assured him that the boss was committed to putting copious resources into the new venture. "It was Roland's baby," Rouch said. "He wanted it to be a classy company. If Ameriquest fell apart, Argent would be the one that was still standing." Argent's Orange County offices rapidly expanded from one floor, to two floors, then to five floors and ten, then spilled over into a second building. Argent, Rouch recalled, spent millions on extravagant multiday sales meetings for employees and ingratiated itself to mortgage brokers by offering the biggest producers a chance to win an all-expenses-paid cruise from New York City to the 2004 Olympic Games in Athens. "Roland saw us as huge global players," Rouch said. "The money that we threw out was unbelievable."

Argent's rise was readily apparent in Middle America. Argent had made no loans in metropolitan Cleveland in 2002. The next year, it booked more than three thousand loans, totaling more than $300 million, in Greater Cleveland. It was on its way to becoming Cleveland's biggest mortgage lender, in large part because of its eagerness to lend in African-American neighborhoods. In a metro area that was less than 20 percent black, according to the 2000 census, Argent made roughly half its loans to black home owners.

One of them was Elizabeth Redrick. She was seventy-seven years old, a retired hospital housekeeper who had lived in her three-bedroom house on East 147th Street for thirty-seven years. A mortgage broker-age promised that it could get her a loan from Argent, Redrick said, that would pay off a $3,600 personal loan and lower her mortgage pay-ment from $700 a month to $500. The loan she ended up with didn't pay off the personal loan or lower her mortgage payment. She got just $651 in cash out of the deal. In order to get the $651, she paid $5,400 in up-front fees. "That wasn't helping me," Redrick said.

Ed Kramer, an attorney with a local law clinic, Housing Advocates, Inc., took her case. He discovered that the broker had submitted two applications to Argent. One said Redrick was black and had an income of $1,871 a month. The other said she was white and earned $2,630 a month. Two loan applications with such different information should have been a red flag for Argent. The lender either knew or should have known there was something fishy about the deal, according to a civil rights complaint that Kramer filed on behalf of Redrick and other black Clevelanders who had obtained loans from Argent.

Kramer charged that Argent had colluded with a mortgage broker-age, which brought in the loans, and with Wells Fargo Bank, which purchased the loans from Argent after the ink was dry on the contracts. Argent, Kramer alleged, did little to make sure the broker wasn't prey-ing on minority borrowers by sticking them with loans they couldn't afford. "They didn't do their due diligence," Kramer said. "If anything, they encouraged brokers to provide any kind of information, whether it was correct or not. That's the reason Argent grew so quickly."

* * *

In November 2003, key members of the House Financial Services Committee held a public hearing in Washington, D.C., titled "Pro-tecting Homeowners: Preventing Abusive Lending While Preserving Access to Credit." Representative Bob Ney, a Republican from Ohio, presided. Ney was one of the mortgage industry's men on Capitol Hill. He had received roughly $500,000 in campaign contributions from finance, insurance, and real-estate interests since the late '90s, including at least $24,000 from the National Association of Mortgage Brokers and more than $30,000 from Wall Street firms such as Morgan Stanley and Lehman Brothers.

Ney was sponsoring a bill he called the Responsible Lending Act. Consumer lobbyists had another name for it: the "Loan Shark Protection Act." The legislation Ney was pushing as the chairman of a House Financial Services subcommittee was industry-written and industry-backed. As state legislators and city councils began to badger subprime lenders about their practices, Wall Street bankers and mortgage executives had looked to Washington for a solution to their problems. Ney's bill sought to restrict the legal liability of Wall Street banks that bought fraud-tainted mortgages, and to override state and local anti-predatory-lending laws. It had been crafted as a counterweight to a proposal, offered by North Carolina Democrats Brad Miller and Melvin Watt. That bill was modeled on their home state's landmark law; it would toughen federal lending standards but still allow states to pass even more stringent rules.

As he kicked off the hearing, Ney acknowledged that there were bad actors in the mortgage market. "I think that everyone in this room agrees that we must find a way to stop the practice of predatory lending." Then he pivoted to his real purpose in convening the hearing: protecting investors from states' effort to hold them accountable for abusive lending. "A lot of people don't even want to discuss this subject, but we know what happened in some of our states, including Georgia—the legislature had to come back and had to go through a lot of things because, frankly, a lot of people were shut out of the housing market, which is very unfortunate," he said.

Micah Green, the president of the Bond Market Association, testified on behalf of Wall Street. He noted that a friend had suggested he might feel uncomfortable at a hearing about preventing abusive lending, given the association's opposition to various state-level initiatives. Green said he didn't feel awkward. His group, he said, was steadfastly against predatory lending; it simply wanted to make sure that any

legislation attacking the problem didn't have unintended consequences. "I dare say this would be a significantly more awkward hearing for me if the title of the hearing is, 'Why is the secondary market
cutting off supply of capital to your constituents who may simply not
have stellar credit?'" It would be misguided, Green said, to shift liability for abusive lending from "the predatory culprit" to the investors
who buy large pools of mortgages that happen to include questionable
loans. Holding the investors responsible for those bad loans, he said,
would be like "banning motor vehicles on roads to reduce speeding
and other motor vehicle violations."

A law professor at Chapman University Law School in Orange
County, Kurt Eggert, held a different view. Eggert had spent years
investigating the role of securitization in encouraging the growth of
predatory lending. He submitted written testimony to the committee,
but he could not be sure lawmakers would bother to read it. When he
was given a chance to speak, he quickly hit his crucial points. The
"huge spike" in predatory lending that began in the '90s, he said, had
been driven by the rapid rise of securitization of subprime loans. "If a
predatory lender does not have access to the secondary market and if
they're forced to hold their own loan, it dramatically limits their ability to lend and to grow, because, as they lend, they're going to have a
portfolio of borrowers who are angry at them, who are not going to
want to pay and are going to want to sue them," he testified. "If, on the
other hand, they have access to the secondary market, what the predatory lender can do is make loans, sell it on the secondary market, get
the money back, and make new loans. They can churn and grow."

And the investors and Wall Street professionals? They were not
innocents who happened to foul up and buy a few dicey loans, Eggert
said. They had plenty of tools at their disposal—including the home
owners' loan-to-value ratios and credit scores—to detect whether
lenders were gouging people. He was getting to the essence of his
argument: "How do we make the securitizers do this job? The solution
is assignee liability. If you say your investors are going to pay the price
if you deal in predatory loans, then the ratings agencies will make sure
that they track it. Now—"

Ney interrupted him, letting him know that his allotted time was over. Ney thanked Eggert for his testimony. "It was fascinating," the law-maker said. Then he moved on. Wall Street and the mortgage industry had no better friend on Capitol Hill than Bob Ney. He would continue to talk about clamping down on predatory lending, while working to ensure that the financial industry would be protected from any restrictions that might threaten the profits generated by high-priced loans.

*   *   *

By the end of 2003, Roland Arnall's mortgage empire had become the nation's largest subprime lending enterprise. In just two years, his companies had increased their loan volume by 600 percent, going from $6 billion in loans in 2001 to $42 billion in loans in 2003. Ameriquest and Argent had blown away the competition. New Century had finished a distant second among the ranks of the largest subprime lenders, posting just over $27 billion in mortgage originations in 2003.

Subprime had more than recovered from its turn-of-the-century swoon; it had zoomed to record levels. The industry's overall loan volume topped $330 billion in 2003, almost doubling production over two years before. Investors pushed up the stock values of New Century and many other publicly traded subprime lenders to more than twice their levels a year before. It was no wonder stock investors were bullish on subprime: New Century was now claiming profits of nearly a quarter of a billion dollars.

How much money Arnall's companies were making off its remarkable sales production was a secret. As private companies, Ameriquest, Argent, and their sister ventures weren't required to disclose their profit-and-loss statements. *National Mortgage News* took a stab at a dollar figure, interviewing industry insiders and speculating that Arnall's lenders may have earned a stunning figure: as much as $1 billion in profits in 2003. "They're on fire right now," one mortgage veteran told the trade publication.

12. Chimera

With so much money to be made, and so much competition on Wall Street to buy subprime loans to fold into securities deals, it made sense for Lehman Brothers and other investment banks to control the means of production and buy directly into the mortgage-origination business. Both of Lehman's subprime origination platforms, BNC Mortgage and Finance America, expanded rapidly. Their combined loan volume increased from $3 billion in 2001 to nearly $11 billion in 2003. By 2004, Lehman had bought out its partners and owned both companies outright. The investment bank was now a full-service, "vertically integrated" subprime provider. It could make loans to home owners, package those same loans into bond deals, and then sell those bonds to investors, reaping fees at every stage.

In early 2004, soon after Finance America promoted him to regional sales manager, Cedric Washington had a night on the town with fellow members of the lender's California-based management team. Liquor was flowing, and the executives were swapping stories. One executive began talking about doctoring paperwork in loan files, Washington later claimed in a lawsuit against the company. Another executive shushed her. Washington asked what she had been talking about, but another member of the dinner party sloughed him off, telling him to pay no attention, the executive was simply "drunk again." Later, Washington said, he discovered the comments weren't drunken blather; he witnessed the executive change a loan document by forging the borrower's initials. He soon learned, his lawsuit claimed, that many managers and workers at Finance America were falsifying loan documents on a regular basis, doctoring W-2 tax forms, forging borrowers' signatures on disclosure documents, and selling stated-income loans to investors as fully documented loans. This last trick, Washington said, helped fool the investors who bought the loans into thinking they were less risky than they really were. The stated-income loans were slipped into groups of fully documented loans, and investors missed them because they only conducted spot checks on the loan pools. When he raised concerns with other executives in the company, Washington said, they promised to look into the problem but did nothing.

In one instance, Washington claimed, he discovered that an employee had submitted a loan that was secured against what was supposed to be a duplex. The structure wasn't a duplex; it wasn't even a home. It was a greenhouse. Washington worried that, as the worker's supervisor, he could get in trouble if he approved the loan. He complained to upper management. He wanted the company to cancel the deal, he said, but the lender pushed it through anyway.

By this point, Washington had had enough of Finance America. He resigned in March 2004, a few months after he'd earned his big promotion. The company retaliated, he claimed, by spreading lies about him—telling people in the lending business that Washington himself had committed fraud when he was working at Finance America. It was payback, he claimed, for his refusal to go along with the sleazy conduct of his coworkers at Finance America, a reflection of the company's "desire to divert the blame from the actual perpetrators."

✳ ✳ ✳

Washington wasn't the only employee within Lehman's subprime mortgage arms who ran into problems. Workers in BNC and Finance America offices around the country complained about the questionable loans flowing into the system during the mortgage boom. Dena Ivezic worked as an underwriter at Finance America and BNC in Downers Grove, Illinois. Management turned a blind eye, she said, as home appraisals were inflated, and salespeople did cut-and-paste jobs to fabricate W-2s and other documents. "You were basically told not to question anything," Ivezic said. Workers who tried to take a stand got nowhere, she said. "They were reprimanded for not being cooperative—not wanting to be creative about making deals work." Lehman didn't put much stock in the complaints of low-level workers. Ivezic worked at BNC for less than five months, so her experiences were "hardly representative of BNC's employee base," Lehman said.

The firm's worst employee uprising took place in BNC's Sacramento branch. The complaints came from a group of women who said the company's sales culture had gotten out of hand. Most of the women were underwriters. Their job was to vet the loans to make sure borrowers could afford them and that the deals met the lender's guidelines. Or at least that's what they thought. The company's wholesale loan reps worked with independent brokers, bringing in the loan deals that brokers had sniffed out. The sales reps didn't like it when underwriters raised questions about loans, especially when the deals had been submitted by brokers who brought them a lot of business.

One of the underwriters, Coleen Colombo, claimed she had flatly rejected a bribe from a coworker, who offered her money if she would approve a fraud-tainted loan. She met with a vice president to complain about fraud in the branch, she said, but the executive swept aside her complaints and she left the meeting in tears. Soon after, she claimed, a coworker began sexually harassing her, "intentionally rubbing his body against hers" and leaving her "uncomfortable and fearful." Others claimed they got similar treatment. "You would have thought he was the pimp and we were his prostitutes," said one woman who worked in the branch. "It felt like a dirty, sleazy place to work." Six former employees—all women—filed a lawsuit, claiming that managers punished employees for reporting fraud and allowed sexual harassment to fester at the branch. The women's attorney charged that some managers used sexual harassment as a tool to humiliate and intimidate employees who wouldn't go along with questionable loan practices.

Lehman Brothers said it investigated the women's complaints, questioning employees and hiring an outside investigator to review hundreds of loan files from the branch. The review, the bank said, found problems with a small percentage of loan files, mostly conflicts-of-interest among mortgage brokerage employees who sent BNC loan applications in their own names or in the names of family members. But it said the review found no evidence that BNC employees were slipping falsified documents into loan files. The women who had complained said the investigation was flawed at best, a cover-up at worst. Some of them appeared on the local NBC television affiliate to protest the way company officials had treated them. "They continue to string us along, not come to our rescue," Colombo told KCRA-TV. "We have suffered so much stress, and we've just had it."

* * *

Between 2003 and 2004, subprime lending grew by 60 percent. Lenders made $529 billion in subprime home loans in 2004. Ameriquest, Argent, and their sister companies led the way, making $82.7 billion in subprime loans for the year. That represented a 15.6 percent share of the market, and was almost double the $42 billion in volume that New Century, the nation's second-largest subprime mortgage lender, had produced. The idea that subprime had made Roland Arnall a billionaire was given a stamp of authenticity in the spring of 2004, when *Los Angeles Business Journal* estimated his net worth at $1.2 billion. By September, *Forbes* ranked him No. 106 on its list of the four hundred richest people in America, upping his estimated fortune to $2 billion. "I knew him when he was just a millionaire," Bob Labrador, Arnall's aide from back in the Long Beach Savings days, mused.

Ameriquest crushed the competition because Arnall was willing to spend money to make money. His mortgage juggernaut's advertising and marketing budget rose from $65 million in 2002 to $365 million by 2004. Countrywide paled in comparison, spending half as much. Like its sibling, Argent, Ameriquest invested much of its marketing budget in efforts to associate itself with America's most popular sports and sports stars. It sponsored dozens of professional baseball and football teams. It founded its own NASCAR race, the Ameriquest 300. It launched two blimps, *Ameriquest Airship Freedom* and *Ameriquest Airship Liberty*, into the sky over sporting events.

In the spring of 2004, the company announced that it had

committed to pay $75 million to have its name affixed to the stadium in Arlington, Texas, where the Texas Rangers played baseball. A fifteen-foot-tall replica of the Liberty Bell was installed in Ameriquest Field's left-field grandstand. It rang anytime a Ranger scored a run. Robert Braver, the Oklahoma Internet provider who was investigating the company's links to spammers, got calls from a slew of Ameriquest salespeople who talked enthusiastically about their employer's marketing presence. "It's incredible," one of them said. "We're the largest privately held mortgage company in America. We're the ones that just bought the baseball field. We do a *lot* of business."

As it raised its profile, Ameriquest positioned itself as an advocate for the nation's home owners. As the "Proud Sponsor of the American Dream," it described its mission as "helping people achieve their home-ownership dreams and financial freedom." In announcing a multi-year partnership that would make Ameriquest the "official mortgage company" of Major League Baseball, Arnall's nephew, Adam Bass, noted there was a "natural synergy" between baseball and home ownership. "Ameriquest belongs in baseball," Bass said. "Like baseball fans from all walks of life, we treasure the game as America's national pastime. We also appreciate that homeownership is the stake in the American dream of baseball fans and families across the country." One top Ameriquest executive told the U.S. Senate banking committee that Ameriquest and other subprime lenders had "contributed to the highest homeownership in the nation's history."

From its marketing spiel, it was easy to get the impression that the company was in the business of making home-purchase loans, with an emphasis on lending to first-time home buyers. That wasn't the case. In 2004, just one-quarter of 1 percent of its mortgages went toward home purchases; the rest were refinancings or home-improvement loans. Rather than promoting home ownership, Ameriquest's loans increased the odds that borrowers would end up in foreclosure, by increasing their monthly house payments and increasing the amount of debt they owed on their homes. The story was the same throughout the subprime industry. Best estimates were that less than 10 percent of subprime mortgages went to first-time home buyers during the market's boom years. One study estimated that for every family that gained a home thanks to a subprime loan, as many as two other families would lose their homes to foreclosure due to unaffordable loan terms. The pro-home-ownership line, though, was a useful tool for Ameriquest and other subprime lenders when they met with politicians and consumer watchdogs. It allowed them to talk about expanding access to the American dream and reaching out to African Americans, Latinos, and others who'd faced lending discrimination over the years—and to paint criticism of their business practices as an assault on home ownership and equal opportunity.

* * *

By June 2004, Travis Paules had settled into a new job at Ameriquest, as well as a new office. A few months before, he'd been promoted from area manager to regional manager, overseeing Texas and the rest of the southwestern United States. He was now thirty-three, and he was on pace to earn $700,000 for the year supervising forty-five branches and around six hundred employees. He and his assistant shared a two-thousand-square-foot office situated in prime real estate for Arlington, Texas: a centerfield skybox at Ameriquest Field. The front of the office was a ceiling-high glass wall that allowed Paules to watch Rangers' home games as he worked. The balcony could host parties of up to forty-three people.

His dreams were coming true. Someday, he imagined, he'd be the president of Ameriquest. He was more vested in the company now, and so he took fraud more seriously. "I became a little more tight on what I allowed," he said. "My first sixty days, I eliminated a lot of crap." He quickly fired a clique of employees at a branch in Houston that had set up a fraud-enabling operation they nicknamed "The Lab." With the help of special computer software, they could produce fake W-2 forms on which the income figures matched up perfectly with the tax and Social Security deductions.

For Paules, the goal wasn't to make the system squeaky clean. It was to make sure that employees didn't go too far overboard. It was okay to be greedy, but not so greedy you got caught. He'd always preached to his people that it wasn't necessary to play games with the documentation on every deal, just on the key ones that would help them make the most money.

He laid down the law on certain practices that were so blatant their perpetrators seemed to be asking to get caught. For example, he forbade his people from inflating home values by switching electronic appraisal profiles from one borrower's property to another. He knew other regions did it, but he told his employees that it was forbidden in the Southwest. "I better not catch you doing that," he warned. Still, he didn't say much about the more traditional means for inflating property values: letting appraisers know that if they didn't rubber-stamp the values needed to make the deals go through, the flow of assignments from Ameriquest would be cut off.

He knew that fraud was so ingrained in the company there was no way to stamp it out. You could fire half of the people in the company, he thought, and their replacements would quickly learn all the tricks and dodges from the half who remained.

His employer had little interest in doing a top-to-bottom restructuring to clean up its practices. Instead, the company preferred public relations gestures that diverted attention from its on-the-ground tactics. In mid-July 2004, Ameriquest and the Rangers celebrated the "grand opening" of Ameriquest Field by dedicating two Habitat for Humanity homes built by employees of the two organizations. Adam Bass declared, "Homeownership is the foundation of healthy communities." *Airship Freedom*—the company's "airborne ambassador"—floated in the skies above the stadium during the ball game between the Rangers and the Toronto Blue Jays.

* * *

The phone rang at the farmhouse with the gable roof in Blue Earth County, Minnesota. Duane and Gertrude O'Connor's thirty-four-acre spread was set among fields of corn and soybeans just outside Mapleton, a town of 1,600 that bills itself as the Curling Capital of Southern Minnesota. The O'Connors were worried about keeping up with the mortgage. Bills were piling up. So when Gertrude O'Connor answered the phone and a loan officer from Ameriquest Mortgage introduced himself, she was willing to hear the salesman's pitch about refinancing and rolling their credit-card bills into a new mortgage.

It was August 2004, and Ameriquest's high-octane marketing campaign was leaving almost no corner of America untouched. The subprime industry, which had begun by lending mainly in inner-city neighborhoods, had now spread into the heartland, targeting rural homesteaders and small-town householders. The O'Connors' patch of Minnesota farmland was as good a place as any to make a loan, as far as Roland Arnall's company was concerned. Gertrude O'Connor explained to the salesman that she and her husband were retired. Duane was sixty-seven and collected a pension and a Social Security check. He couldn't work even if he wanted to, because he suffered from Parsonage-Turner syndrome, a rare disease that made it hard for him to breathe and left fingers on both of his hands partially paralyzed. Gertrude was sixty-six and received Social Security as well as a check from the county to cover her in-home care for their thirty-six-year-old son, Brad, who'd been disabled by a car accident. She told the Ameriquest salesman that they had high credit-card balances, because of medical bills from Brad's accident, and because she and her husband had been forced to take out cash advances to cover their house note and car payments. The salesman said Ameriquest could help. He took the O'Connors' information and filled out a loan application for them over the phone. He told them the closing costs for the loan would be less than $9,500.

Soon after, Gertrude O'Connor got another phone call from Ameriquest. The caller said they'd been approved for a thirty-year loan with an initial interest rate that would stay locked for the first three years. Their payments would be $3,440 a month. She told the caller that sounded fine, but that she and her husband wouldn't pay any more than 8.5 percent interest.

The loan application that Ameriquest put together was replete with misrepresentations designed to make the O'Connors appear to be better risks both to the company's loan underwriters and to the investors who would buy securities backed by their loan and others like it. Ameriquest claimed that Gertrude O'Connor had worked for two years for a home health-care company, even though the truth was that she had received a home-care grant for taking care of her son for less than nine months, and there was no guarantee the grant would keep coming in. Someone at Ameriquest also shaved twenty years off the O'Connors' ages, listing her birth date as "03/19/1958" and his as "08/04/1957." In addition, Ameriquest valued the O'Connors' property at $445,000, substantially higher than it was worth, the couple would later claim.

Ameriquest scheduled the loan closing for August 17, at the Perkins Restaurant in Mankato, the largest town in Blue Earth County. According to the O'Connors, they never received a Good Faith Estimate or any other preliminary documents from Ameriquest in the mail, as required by federal law. The closing agent had come down from the Twin Cities to take care of the O'Connors' loan. "Sitting in a booth, he rushed them through the process, quickly shuffling through documents, providing only cursory explanations of the documents and directing the O'Connors where to sign," according to a lawsuit later filed on the couple's behalf. Soon after the signing, the O'Connors learned that the loan was different from what they had been told to expect, they said. The settlement costs weren't $9,500; they totaled nearly $17,000 of the $400,500 loan. The annual percentage rate was also higher than they'd expected: 10.166 percent. And instead of being fixed for the first three years of the loan, the rate was fixed for just two years. After that it could climb as high as 15.75 percent.

* * *

As it was dawning on the O'Connors that they'd been put in worse shape by their new mortgage, their loan was transferred into a pool of loans with the moniker "Ameriquest Mortgage Securities Inc. Asset-Backed Pass-Through Certificates, Series 2004-R11." Deutsche Bank acted as the trustee, overseeing the transfer of loans into the pool and acting as the custodian of the documents. The Swiss banking giant UBS served as the "lead manager" and "book runner," meaning that its securitization whizzes structured the deal and its bond salesmen took the lead in peddling the mortgage-backed securities to investors. Two of Wall Street's most powerful investment banks, Goldman Sachs and Merrill Lynch, served as "co-managers," pitching in to help UBS sell the bonds. Ameriquest liked to spread its business around. Unlike some subprime lenders, it no longer had a go-to investment bank; it was so big and so important to the market that just about everyone wanted—and got—a piece of the action. ACC Capital, Arnall's holding company, enjoyed lines of credit totaling more than $20 billion, provided by almost every major player on Wall Street. In addition to Deutsche Bank, UBS, Goldman, and Merrill, it could call on JPMorgan Chase, Citigroup, Credit Suisse, Bank of America, and Long Beach Savings' early backer, Greenwich Capital.

The O'Connors' mortgage was one of more than eighty-five hundred Ameriquest loans that UBS packaged into the deal around the beginning of November 2004. The securities were cobbled from mortgages from across the United States, from big cities such as Pittsburgh, Orlando, and Detroit, and from small towns such as Berlin, New Hampshire; Farmersburg, Indiana; and Sand Springs, Oklahoma. Nearly two-thirds of the loans included prepayment penalties. Roughly 27 percent were stated-income or limited-documentation mortgages, an indication that Ameriquest had done little checking to see whether the borrowers could afford the loans. Many borrowers in the pool were loaded up on debt, with high "debt-to-income" ratios that signaled they were struggling to get by. Four out of five mortgages in the pool were 2/28 adjustable-rate loans, which meant they started with a two-year teaser rate and then began zooming upward for the remainder of their thirty-year term. Most of their rates could climb as high as 13.5 percent after their initial two-year fixed-rate period.

The loans' stiff terms and the borrowers' debt loads and modest credit scores suggested that many of them wouldn't be able to repay their mortgages. Getting around these risks required some financial magic. UBS's securitization experts protected investors through what Moody's described as "various forms of credit enhancement." These included designing "subordinate" slices of the deal that would absorb the first losses if a large number of borrowers couldn't pay their loans. That meant that holders of higher-level slices of the deal wouldn't have to worry about losing their money, unless the defaults reached a catastrophic level. In addition, UBS's financial engineers added extra collateral—that is, they'd put in a greater dollar volume of mortgages than the total dollar value of the securities to be sold. They also arranged to set aside part of the interest payments on the loans in a rainy-day account, to be used to help pay off investors if too many borrowers defaulted.

None of this alchemy would make any difference if Moody's and other credit rating agencies weren't willing to give their seal of approval to the deal. Moody's, S&P, and Fitch played a crucial role in putting together securitizations. The veneer of propriety they provided helped assure pension funds, insurers, and other major investors that the securitizers were indeed turning high-risk assets—subprime mortgages—into the safest investments money could buy. The fees that the rating agencies collected buoyed their profits; just as subprime mortgages were more profitable for lenders than A-credit mortgages, the agencies made three times as much money rating complex securitizations than they made rating traditional corporate bonds. The pressure to play ball and give good ratings to mortgage-backed securities was enormous. "Everybody was looking to pick up every deal that they could," a former S&P executive recalled.

In the case of the loan pool holding the O'Connors' loan, the process worked as it usually did. The three rating agencies liked what Ameriquest and UBS had done in putting together the securitization. They awarded Triple-A safety ratings to the vast majority of the securities in the deal—$1.3 billion's worth of the $1.5 billion in bonds to be sold to investors. Many of the nation's top financial firms also liked what they saw. JPMorgan, John Hancock Insurance, Fidelity Investments, and Citigroup were among those that bought pieces of the deal.

* * *

In October 2004, Roland Arnall's home-loan combine announced the latest and grandest of its sports marketing ventures: the Ameriquest Mortgage Super Bowl XXXIX Halftime Show. The Janet Jackson wardrobe malfunction at the previous championship game had stoked controversy, and Ameriquest executives bet that sponsoring a kinder, gentler event would pay off for the company. "Eager to scrape the X-rated mud off the cleats of last season's Super Bowl halftime show, the National Football League will announce today that it has signed a fast-growing mortgage company to sponsor this season's show," *USA Today* reported. "It's expected to be one of the most widely watched in Super Bowl history." Bass called it "a historic day for Ameriquest" and said the company was pleased the NFL was demonstrating a "renewed commitment to provide an entertainment product that appeals to the American values of home and family."

Roland Arnall and Ameriquest were also making themselves a big presence in politics. For decades, Arnall had supported Democrats more often than Republicans. But that changed in the early 2000s. After giving $100,000 to his old friend Gray Davis as the Democratic governor tried to stave off a recall ballot initiative in 2003, Arnall transferred his backing to the election's victor, Arnold Schwarzenegger, pouring cash into the California GOP and political committees that supported Schwarzenegger's agenda. He was also busy on the national level. In the aftermath of the 9/11 attacks, Arnall issued a statement describing George W. Bush as "a leader with great integrity and courage who will rid the world of the scourge of terrorism." Arnall used his checkbook to show his support for the president as well. In the weeks leading up the November 2004 election, the Progress for America Voter Fund, an independent political group, aired TV commercials attacking Democratic presidential nominee John Kerry with the help of $5 million donated in Dawn Arnall's name. One of the anti-Kerry spots made fun of the senator's windsurfing foray, painting him as a politician who went "whichever way the wind blows." Another flashed images of Osama bin Laden and terrorist bombings around the world as an announcer intoned: "These people want to kill us. . . . Would you trust Kerry against these fanatic killers? President Bush didn't start this war, but he will finish it." After Bush won reelection, Roland and Dawn served on the president's inauguration committee. Contributions to the inauguration from individuals or corporations were limited to $250,000 apiece. *USA Today* reported that the Arnalls "found a creative way to pump more than the $250,000 limit into the event"—four of their companies each gave the maximum, for a total of $1 million. Overall, Ameriquest, its sister companies, and its leaders donated and raised more than $12 million for the president's reelection and inaugural festivities, making Arnall's subprime empire the single biggest source of political cash for Bush from 2002 through the 2004 election cycle, according to the *Washington Post*.

* * *

As he was positioning himself among the nation's political power brokers, Roland Arnall was also trying to position his companies among the nation's corporate elite. As 2004 came to an end, there were hints that a huge deal was in the offing, one that could take Arnall's companies to a new level. A few days before Christmas, *National Mortgage News* floated a story that Arnall was considering taking Ameriquest public. By offering stock to the public, the company could raise between $6 billion and $8 billion, an "industry official who was briefed on the deal" told the newspaper. If the deal could raise that much cash, it would be the third-largest IPO in U.S. history, behind only the $10.62 billion AT&T Wireless offering in 2000 and the $8.68 billion Kraft Foods offering in 2001. "They're talking about doing it by late March," the source said. Another source said JPMorgan Chase was expected to play a major role in bringing the IPO to market, and that JPMorgan's president, Jamie Dimon, had been negotiating personally with Arnall.

Nothing, it seemed, could stop Roland Arnall.

13. The Investigators

Ed Parker grew up in southeastern Louisiana, in a town called Bogalusa. He was born in 1954, just as the struggle against Jim Crow was beginning to gain momentum. By the 1960s, he recalled, "I was a little guy in the civil rights marches. I've seen some things in my life." His barber, Royan Burris, was a leader in the local chapter of the Deacons for Defense and Justice, a Deep South organization that fought against racism and, unlike the Reverend Martin Luther King Jr.'s disciples of "creative nonviolence," believed in carrying guns as a self-defense measure. Parker wasn't an in-your-face personality, though. He thought of himself as "basically a good old Southern boy. Quiet. Humble. I'll give you one hundred percent. I'll try to do what's right." After college, he worked as a sales manager for Goodyear and took management training at McDonald's before going to work in the banking industry. He learned how to do quality-control auditing of home loans. He eventually landed a job as a fraud investigator at Aames Home Loans in Los Angeles.

One day near the end of 2002, he got a call from a headhunter, an employment consultant who was recruiting for one of Aames's competitors, Ameriquest. The company, the headhunter explained, was looking to hire someone to build a fraud investigation team at its headquarters in Orange County. The company had an internal controls department, but that unit was responsible for other tasks in addition to checking on fraud complaints.

The company offered him a good salary, nearly $55,000 a year, and Parker took the job. He started work in January 2003. Soon after he began, he was handed a backlog of investigations that internal controls hadn't been able to complete. The most serious one involved Ameriquest's branch in Grand Rapids, Michigan. Company officials suspected that appraisers were inflating home values at the urging of the salespeople in the branch.

Parker ordered up production reports and loan files from the Grand Rapids office. As he pored over the documents, a pattern emerged. An appraiser would turn in his report on a piece of property, and the mortgage application would be declined because the home value wasn't high enough to support the loan. Then, a day later, a week later, two weeks later, a second and sometimes third appraisal would be submitted. This time, it would hit the value needed to get the loan approved. Most of loans had been made based on "verbal appraisals," meaning the appraiser had simply telephoned in the value and promised to send a written report later; in some cases, however, the written report still hadn't appeared. Parker was astounded that Ameriquest was closing loans without a hard copy of the appraisal. He realized he was on to something big.

He wrote up his findings and submitted them to Ameriquest's legal department, which oversaw Parker's work. By the middle of February, Parker was on a plane heading for Michigan, along with Ameriquest's human resources director and an outside attorney. They landed at Gerald R. Ford Airport, checked into a hotel, and then huddled for dinner, plotting the next day's strategy. They showed up at the branch first thing the next morning, unannounced. They called everyone together and explained they were from "Corporate" and needed to talk to the branch's employees about "concerns about policies and procedures." They called the employees into an office, one by one. Based on Parker's preliminary sleuthing, they'd determined who appeared to be the most and least culpable. They choreographed the interviews so that the worst offenders came last, giving them time to sweat a bit while their coworkers were being questioned.

They talked to nine employees. Each session unfolded virtually the same way. They began with a series of question: Had anybody at this branch ever asked them to do anything they shouldn't do? Have they ever done anything here they shouldn't have done? If we looked at your loan transactions, would we find anything wrong? The workers answered no to each question.

In the face of these denials, Parker and the two other corporate representatives began cracking open loan files and flipping through document after document and asking more specific questions. Is this your handwriting? Look at this document: What's wrong with this? Look at these three files: What are the chances that on all three the appraisals came back with the exact value needed to get the loan approved?

Each time, Parker recalled, the employee finally relented, realizing that denials were fruitless. Each in turn admitted the entire scheme. They had been taught how to "back into" the property values and loan-to-value ratios needed to get the loan approved. The appraisers who were providing the inflated values were paid a $250 rush fee on top of their normal fee. Parker wanted to know why no one had spoken up and reported the fraud. The employees said they feared that if they weren't "team players," they'd be out of a job.

Ameriquest shut down its Grand Rapids operation for months, before starting anew with a fresh staff. The company also had to repurchase hundreds of Grand Rapids loans from the investors who had bought them. Then the loans were repackaged and resold as "scratch and dent" mortgages, problem loans that Ameriquest was forced to sell at discounts.

Parker was pleased with the results of his first big investigation. He believed he had helped set a precedent within the company: fraud would not be tolerated. Over the long haul, this would mean that fewer borrowers would end up in such predicaments. As for himself, he thought he was making a name within the company. "I'm thinking: I'm on the way up."

He soon discovered that the reputation he was making didn't necessarily endear him to his coworkers. One executive, he said, told him the sales force looked on him as "Darth Vader." A coworker asked: "Are you causing problems again?" Another time, during a meeting of executives, the discussion turned to a possibly fraudulent loan file, and a colleague said: "Don't give it to Ed. If you give it to him, that one file will multiply and become hundreds of files." He thought these were jokes, but later he began to believe the jokes had a message behind them.

For the time being, though, the company needed to have Parker in place. By the end of 2003, the California attorney general's office was fielding a large number of complaints about the company. It wanted Ameriquest to clean house, and in particular to look at stated-income loans made in four counties: Alameda, Santa Clara, Monterey, and Los Angeles. The fraud team pulled more than twenty-five hundred loan files going back two years. Its research indicated that many Ameriquest workers in these counties were falsifying borrowers' incomes on the application paperwork. They weren't subtle about it; they didn't seem to want to go to the trouble of making up a variety of fictitious jobs. Again and again, Parker said, the investigators found loans on which the husband was listed as a computer consultant and the wife was listed as the operator of a housekeeping service. On many mortgage applications, the loan officers didn't bother to list any kind of occupation at all. According to the team's tally, 48 percent of the loan applications they reviewed left the occupation line blank, described the borrower as a consultant, or listed him or her as an "owner" without specifying the name of the company or the type of business.

In March 2004, Parker turned the team's findings over to Ameriquest's lawyers, which forwarded the information to the attorney general's office, to demonstrate that the company was serious about dealing with fraud. It was the last full-scale investigation, Parker said, that he was allowed to do at Ameriquest. More and more, he said, his superiors wanted him to focus on "ones" and "twos," smaller cases that didn't have a big impact. The company had had to buy back lots of loans in the Grand Rapids case, and that had cost the company lots of money. "I was bad for business," Parker said.

Management instructed his unit to limit the scope of its inquiries, to only examine three months of loan files when it investigated a branch rather than six months or a year. "They thought we looked at too many loans," Parker said. Reducing the number of loans reviewed

ensured that, even if the team found fraud, the number of loan buy-
backs would be minimized. As the months went by, Parker said, he
found himself marginalized, removed from meetings and key decisions.

He began to wonder if the fraud team had been created mainly as
window dressing. As Wendell Raphael had learned before him, it was
one thing to respond to complaints and catch one or two or twenty
employees who were committing fraud. It was another thing to document that fraud was widespread throughout the company. Kelly J.
Dragna, who worked as an investigator under Parker, said senior
executives let the fraud team know they weren't interested in getting
to the root of the problem. "You're like a dog on a leash," Dragna
recalled. "You're allowed to go as far as a company allows you to go. At
Ameriquest, we were on a pretty short leash. We were there for show.
We were there to show people that they had a lot of investigators on
staff."

This was driven home to Parker and his investigators when they
were assigned to look into some loans made by a branch in Mission
Valley, California. Two loans raised red flags about whether branch
employees were falsifying not only borrowers' incomes but also their
ages, so that the inflated incomes would seem plausible. One borrower
was sixty-seven, but the loan application prepared in her name said
the borrower was forty-one and was making $4,000 a month as a con-
sultant. Another borrower was seventy-four, but the loan application
indicated the borrower was forty-four and was making $8,000 a
month as a consultant. The two borrowers' cases had drawn the attention of a television reporter in San Diego, Parker said, and the company wanted to be able to tell the TV station that it was taking care of
the problem.

The company boxed up all of the branch's loan files and transported them to Parker's team in Orange County. Management sent
word, however, that the investigators shouldn't open the boxes. Parker's
investigators looked anyway. As they pulled open more and more
files, they saw that falsified incomes and ages were problems that
went beyond the two borrowers' loans. When company executives
found out what the team was doing, Parker said, they weren't happy.

"They said: 'Don't look anymore,'" he recalled. "They didn't want to know."

* * *

In the aftermath of the Household case, government authorities from Iowa, Minnesota, Washington, and a few other states formed an interstate working group, to compare notes on bad mortgage lenders and coordinate actions against the worst offenders. Ameriquest had been one of the two names that had come up in their discussions to determine which lender should be the target of the next multistate investigation. The other was Wells Fargo Financial, a subprime-lending arm of Wells Fargo Bank. The members of the working group knew they could only take on one big case at a time. Even when they combined forces, their resources were limited. Washington State's Chuck Cross took charge of scoping out Wells Fargo. Minnesota's Prentiss Cox oversaw efforts to gauge Ameriquest as a candidate for state action. By the end of 2003, Ameriquest had emerged as the better candidate. The states were getting a higher volume of complaints against Ameriquest, and Ameriquest was now the No. 1 subprime mortgage lender in the nation.

Soon after the state coalition agreed to focus on Ameriquest, Cox got a call from a lobbyist for the company. The lender's general counsel was going to be in the Twin Cities and wanted to meet with Cox. Cox wondered whether this was a coincidence, or whether there had been a leak about the investigation. Had somebody tipped off Ameriquest that the states were scrutinizing the company? It was just as likely, though, that the company was being proactive, trying, as Roland Arnall's companies always did, to establish good relations with people in positions to help or hurt the company.

In his meeting with Cox, the Ameriquest lawyer talked up the company's "best practices," which it had recently updated. A long lineup of fair-lending advocates had praised Ameriquest's new and improved standards. On paper, Ameriquest's pledges did sound good, especially in an industry with a history of dirty tactics. But Cox was skeptical. "Whenever companies come in with their best practices, you can basically throw them in the trash can," he recalled. "It tells you nothing about what they're really doing."

Cox sent Ameriquest a request on behalf of several states for a "data dump" of paper and electronic documents, including selected loan files and e-mails. To sift through the enormous database of e-mails that Ameriquest provided, Cox tried several search strategies. One of the best was to do keyword searches for profanities. These called up some interesting exchanges. One was an e-mail from a manager to his sales staff: "We are all here to make as much fucking money as possible. Bottom line. Nothing else matters."

Interviews with former employees were also revealing. In Washington State, former Ameriquest employees told investigators that management had put them under constant pressure to sell loans and break the law. One manager's favorite motivational technique, they said, was to tell his salesmen, "I just hired your replacement," and then give them one more chance to hit the phones. The former employees also reported that supervisors trained them to hide the loan disclosures from borrowers. One manager told his workers: "You can either make the sale or you can make the disclosure. But you can't do both."

David Huey, an assistant attorney general in Washington State, came to believe that the misrepresentations in Ameriquest's sales program were "an effect, not a cause." In his view, the lender's 2/28 and 3/27 adjustable-rate mortgages were such terrible deals for consumers that the only way to sell them was to lie to borrowers and play hide-and-seek with the disclosures. Arnall and his senior executives claimed they had no idea that fraudulent practices were occurring at the branch level, Huey said, but their aggressive push to market 2/28s and 3/27s suggested Arnall and his people knew more than they let on. "I'd be real surprised if he didn't know exactly what he was doing," Huey said. "They put these products out there knowing full well that somebody who understood the market and was acting in their own best interests would not take these loans. The only way to sell them was to make misrepresentations and hide the negative features."

The documents and interviews with former employees painted a picture of a new kind of home-loan marketing. Ameriquest's model incorporated some of the practices that investigators had identified in the FAMCO and Household cases: bait-and-switch salesmanship and other tactics designed to mislead borrowers about the costs and terms of their loans. But Ameriquest sales reps' reliance on inflated borrower incomes and inflated home appraisals lifted predatory lending to new heights. These fabrications allowed the company to sell bigger loans that carried bigger fees. By leading borrowers to believe their homes were worth more than they really were, the company made them feel richer, emboldening them to load up on more debt. And by inflating both property values and incomes, the company was able to sell them in larger numbers to Wall Street investors. Cox and other investigators could see this was more than a classic fraud problem. It was, Cox thought, a problem of "wildly inappropriate lending. It was about the complete deterioration of prudency in lending. The whole thing had spun out of control."

By the fall of 2004, the state authorities were ready to make their move. They agreed to come to Orange County and meet at Ameriquest's headquarters on Town and Country Road. The company had gone all out to present a strong defense. It hired a contingent of former state attorneys general and former government regulators. The states' representatives were low-paid civil servants, up against a phalanx of high-priced legal talent. "There were maybe eight former AGs and a former chief justice of the Texas Supreme Court in the room," Huey said. "I remember sitting there thinking: 'What is it costing them for one day? These guys aren't cheap. They cost what? Five hundred, six hundred, seven hundred dollars an hour? And you've got their rooms and flights.' It was just astronomical what the company was spending to influence us."

At the initial meeting between the two sides, Cox laid out the framework of the states' case. Ameriquest's lawyers countered that the states had no viable legal theory. There was no harm to borrowers, the company's lawyers said. If borrowers were being hurt, they asserted, Ameriquest's default rates would be much higher. And where, they asked, was the harm in an inflated appraisal? Borrowers benefited from higher appraisals, they said, because they could borrow more money than they could otherwise. The discussions grew tense, with lawyers talking over one another. No one was giving much ground.

* * *

One figure conspicuously absent from the discussions was Roland Arnall. Chuck Cross sensed that Arnall was the ultimate decision maker. The executives and lawyers in the room from Ameriquest could argue the company's case, but if anything were to be settled between the states and the lender, Arnall would be calling the shots. It was his money at stake.

In the midst of the negotiations in Orange County, Ameriquest officials came to the states' representatives with an idea for easing the tension. Everyone needed a break, and Arnall wanted to invite the folks from the states to dinner. It would allow them, company officials explained, to get a feel for the people at the corporation and what it stood for. The state representatives were unsure about how to respond. Some, including Cross and Prentiss Cox, didn't think it was a good idea to be socializing with the people they were investigating. Others thought that it couldn't hurt to meet and talk with the Ameriquest contingent in a more informal setting. And even Cross was curious to at least meet Arnall. "We'd never even seen the guy," Cross recalled. "This was our opportunity to meet with the guy and hear him tell the story of Ameriquest."

That evening, a shuttle bus pulled up to the hotel where the state officials were staying. The driver transported them to an undisclosed location. "We didn't even know where the hell the bus was taking us," Cross recalled. The bus deposited them in front of a nice restaurant. The driver, promising to come back later, drove away.

The two sides mingled before dinner was served. Arnall worked the room, shaking hands and coming off, Huey said, like a regular guy rather than one of the world's richest men. Huey recalled that Arnall told a story about getting mugged in Washington, D.C. The billionaire and one of his lawyers had been robbed at gunpoint; they had turned over their billfolds and went on their way, unharmed if not unshaken.

Among the dignitaries representing Ameriquest was Deval Patrick, the former assistant U.S. attorney general for civil rights who had led the investigation of Arnall and Long Beach Mortgage in the mid-'90s. Now he was in private practice, a troubleshooter for companies that were under fire; he'd already served on the boards of Coca-Cola and Texaco as they faced allegations of racial discrimination and human rights violations. As the states' investigation against Ameriquest heated up, Arnall had asked Patrick to join the board of Ameriquest's holding company, ACC Capital. Arnall made a big show of introducing Patrick to everyone at the dinner, Huey said. "He was pushing Deval Patrick and wanting everybody to know that he had brought Deval on board. This was supposed to make us happy and satisfied that he was on the up-and-up, trying to do a good job. We were a pretty cynical lot. We were definitely not impressed."

When it came time to sit down and eat, the public employees saw that the seating chart had been as meticulously planned as it would be at any wedding banquet. Each table had assigned seating, and it appeared to the states' team that they had been strategically dispersed, so that the most vocal of their group were separated and so that they sat beside Ameriquest representatives who might be able to impress or influence them. Tom James, the assistant attorney general from Illinois, was placed beside Deval Patrick, the only other person of color in the dinner party.

The state officials noted, too, that, at each place setting, the restaurant had laid out a menu offering a limited selection of superb courses. There were no prices. Cross and others began asking questions. They were on limited budgets. Chuck Cross's per diem from the state of Washington's Department of Financial Institutions allocated him roughly $30 for dinner. Ameriquest officials told them: "Don't worry about it. Everything is taken care of." That was unacceptable to the public servants. Their states had ethics rules that forbade them from being wined and dined by the subjects of enforcement actions. There was no way they were going to allow Arnall to treat them to an evening on the town. Cross and several others talked about leaving, although they weren't sure how, because the bus was gone and they didn't really know where they were. "It was like the Hotel California," Cross said. "We couldn't leave." The matter finally seemed to be settled when Ameriquest executives promised they would get a bill at the end of the night.

Arnall and other Ameriquest leaders gave speeches. The company was sorry for any bad things that had happened in its lending operations, they said, and the states could be certain that, moving forward, the problems were being fixed. One of the Ameriquest lawyers whom Prentiss Cox knew and had come to like leaned over to him and whispered, "This was not my idea." Cox thought the speakers' apologies seemed strained and perfunctory. As Arnall spoke, Cox made a show of getting up and pouring wine for people at various tables around the room. He knew what Ameriquest had been doing to borrowers all over the country, and a few apologies weren't going to wipe that away.

As the dinner broke up, Cox and his colleagues asked for their tabs. Ameriquest officials put them off. They promised to produce the bills during the next day's negotiating session. The next day, though, company officials again equivocated. Soon, they promised, the company would send them the bills. After the public officials went back home, they debated the subject during phone conferences and in e-mails, trying to resolve the issue. Finally, bill or no, Cox decided he would send Ameriquest a personal check, for around $50, to cover his meal. Others followed suit. An Ameriquest lawyer called and informed them that, actually, the cost of the meal and wine was just under $100 a head. The state officials mailed a new round of checks. Ameriquest, Cross and Huey recalled, never cashed their checks.

Some felt they'd been tricked, made suckers in a parody of Ameriquest's bait-and-switch lending tactics. If Ameriquest thought the dinner was going to somehow sway its antagonists from the states, Cross said, the whole thing had backfired. To him, it seemed an object lesson in how Arnall believed he could get away with whatever he wanted by winning friends and buying influence. Cross subtracted the amount for the uncashed check from his family's joint bank account. From time to time, his wife suggested it might be time to reconcile their balance. The check was never going to be cashed. Cross, stubborn, refused. The symbolism of letting Ameriquest win didn't sit well with him. "We'll carry this difference to the end of time," he told her.

14. The Big Game

In the fall of 2004, I was traveling around the country, helping film-maker James Scurlock with *Maxed Out*, his documentary about debt, American style. I'd been writing about subprime lending since the early '90s, as a freelance magazine writer and as a staff reporter at the *Roanoke Times* in Virginia. Scurlock had asked to tag along with a camera as I met borrowers and discussed their run-ins with lenders. We traveled to Pittsburgh, Brooklyn, Queens, and rural Mississippi. In Pittsburgh, Rich Lord, a local reporter, set up some of the interviews. At the end of the day, Rich and I sat in the study of his home in the South Hills section of the city and brainstormed about where our investigations of predatory lending should go next. Rich had reported extensively on Household. I'd been investigating the rise of Citigroup's subprime dynasty for two years. Rich and I asked the same question of each other that state law enforcers had asked after the Household settlement in 2002: "Who's next?"

Rich suggested that Ameriquest deserved attention. He had touched on the company in his book on predatory lending, *American Nightmare*, but he knew there was more to tell. Ameriquest had become the nation's largest subprime lender and, knowing the tactics that often fueled the industry's leaders, it made sense to us to take a close look at the company. Soon after I returned to Virginia, I logged on to PACER, the federal court system's case database. I found citations for dozens of lawsuits filed across the country by borrowers and ex-employees of the lender. One case I pulled up was *Kuhn v. Ameriquest* in the U.S. District Court in Kansas City. Stephen Kuhn claimed in his lawsuit that Ameriquest had fired him for complaining about its unethical practices.

I telephoned Kuhn at his home, and we talked for an hour or more. "Have you ever seen the movie *Boiler Room*?" he asked. By the time we got off the phone, he had given me the names of several former coworkers who also had stories to tell about Ameriquest. I found other former employees through court records and other contacts. Many had been shaken by the pressures in Ameriquest's workplace. "I couldn't live with myself if every day I was screwing people out of their investment," a former loan officer in Michigan told me. Another said that he and four others in his branch in Michigan quit because of the drive to sell overpriced deals by "targeting the weak." "We just couldn't take it anymore," he said. "They just had you. Once they sign you on for that salary they pay, they own you."

I took what I'd found to the *Los Angeles Times*. Ameriquest was headquartered in the paper's backyard. The *Times*'s editors liked the story. They hired me on a freelance contract and paired me with a business staff writer, Scott Reckard. Scott was an experienced investigative reporter who'd written about FAMCO and helped expose a number of Ponzi schemes in Southern California.

One thing Scott and I discovered as we talked to former employees was that Ameriquest was ignoring its "best practices" pledge not to solicit its own customers for refinancings within twenty-four months after their initial loan with the company. Former employees told us that Ameriquest had a "portfolio retention" unit, based near Sacramento, employing hundreds of workers who did nothing but try to "flip" the company's own customers into new loans.

We could see that Ameriquest's system was devised to back borrowers into a corner. When customers complained about the costs of their loans, loan officers assured them not to worry, that if they made their payments on time for twelve months, the company would refinance them into a lower-cost loan. In addition, the payments on the company's 2/28 adjustable-rate mortgages always shot upward at the end of the two-year introductory period, almost ensuring that borrowers would be stuck in desperate straits that would require them to refinance with Ameriquest or another lender—and pay a hefty prepayment penalty.

Lawsuits in St. Louis and Alabama provided more evidence that the company had violated its anti-loan-flipping pledge. It refinanced one Missouri borrower within six weeks of selling him his initial loan. The company refinanced two other Missouri borrowers, Rodney and Karen Ellsworth, within eight months. When they were signing up for their first loan, their suit said, the company promised them it wouldn't charge them a prepayment penalty if they refinanced with Ameriquest rather than a competitor. In fact, the company hit them with a prepayment penalty of $7,490. In just eight months, the prepayment penalty and Ameriquest's fees and points had claimed more than $21,000 of the equity in the couple's home.

To test what we were hearing, Scott asked an industry analyst to crunch some numbers on Ameriquest's lending. The data showed that nearly one in nine mortgages made by Ameriquest in 2004 was a refinance of an existing loan with the company that was less than twenty-four months old. That was a higher rate than for any of the competitors included in the analysis. This was an important point—Ameriquest's anti-flipping pledge had been one of the things that had helped persuade the Federal Trade Commission to drop its investigation of the company in 2001.

When Scott talked to a source at the FTC, however, the official said it was hard to know what to make of the company's high rate of refinancings among its own customers. "I'm not aware of any change in their policies," he said. "There could be a concern if they are misleading consumers into a refinancing that doesn't benefit them. But I don't think we'd have a concern if they were saving people money by refinancing them because rates have dropped." This answer belied the fact that Ameriquest seldom lowered people's rates and that its refinancings almost always put people in worse positions, adding in more fees and ratcheting their debts higher.

The official acknowledged that the FTC hadn't kept close watch on Ameriquest since closing its investigation four years before. But if there were major concerns about the company, he told Scott, his agency would probably be aware of them. "We read the trade press pretty carefully, things like that. I haven't heard a lot of complaints raised."

Had he checked his own agency's records, he would have seen that the FTC had received 466 complaints about Ameriquest from 2000 to 2004, more than three times the number registered against Countrywide's subprime mortgage unit and New Century Financial combined.

* * *

Scott and I scrambled throughout January 2005 to nail down the story. We knew the Super Bowl halftime show—with ex-Beatle Paul McCartney tapped as the headliner—would bring a new level of public attention to Ameriquest. In the weeks leading up to the Super Bowl, Scott struggled to get Ameriquest officials to answer questions about the lender's policies and practices. The company's PR officers finally sent over a written statement that was short on specifics: Ameriquest held itself "to the highest standards" and didn't tolerate improper behavior by its employees. Our story ran on February 4, the Friday before the championship game. It cited thirty-two former employees in all who said they had witnessed or participated in unethical conduct at the lender.

Things went better for the company on Sunday. The ads it had picked to premiere during the broadcast were wicked and funny, and would be listed by critics as two of the best spots that aired. In one, a man talking on a cell phone in a convenience store is mistaken for a robber, then beaten and maced. In the other, a man preparing a surprise dinner for his wife has a cooking mishap that makes things look very bad when she walks in the door and finds him with a knife in one hand and her cat in the other. Both ads ended on Ameriquest's tagline: "Don't judge too quickly. We won't." It was a clever way of suggesting that the company was sympathetic to folks with bad credit or other problems, without coming out and saying it was a subprime lender that catered to the "Bad credit? No Credit? No Problem!" demographic.

The reaction to our reporting was initially muted. The story was picked up by the *Chicago Tribune* and the Associated Press, but it didn't get much national play. In mid-March, however, Ameriquest publicly acknowledged, in a securities filing, that it was in talks with authorities in twenty-five states over its practices. The lender said it had "valid responses" to the states' concerns. A company official told Dow Jones Newswires: "When you do hundreds of loans a day, a couple may come out bad."

Scott and I followed up with a story about three women in Tampa who didn't know each other but had some things in common. Each had gotten a mortgage from Ameriquest, and each of their loan applications had been supported by a 401(k) retirement statement that showed exactly the same balance: $25,456.53. The retirement nest egg belonged to only one of the women. A cache of Ameriquest documents smuggled out by a former employee showed that Wite-Out and tape had been used to create new versions of the statement that carried the other two borrowers' names. When Scott showed the mutual fund statement to the other two women, they were surprised. "Oh, my God," one said. "Are they saying I owned money? I wish I had money."

One of the roadblocks we faced in our reporting was the company's secrecy about its revenues and other financial numbers. Roland Arnall's holding company, ACC Capital, was organized as a private corporation that was under no obligation to reveal its financial data to the public. This suited Arnall's personality well. He liked to keep his financial matters private. The less his competitors knew about him, the better advantage he had over them. Rolling out an initial public offering might have brought more sunlight to the internal workings of his companies, but the bad publicity over Ameriquest had persuaded him to set aside plans to go public.

Scott and I got a break when a source told me how to get hold of the financial statements for ACC Capital. We knew Arnall had been making good money, but I was stunned when I squinted over the documents and saw exactly how much. Arnall's holding company had earned around $500 million in 2002, and had indeed come close to $1 billion in profits in 2003, raking in a hair under $900 million. In 2004, the company's profits had swelled to $1.34 billion. In three years, Roland Arnall's subprime empire had earned more than $2.7 billion.

* * *

In April 2005, in the wake of revelations about squirrely tactics at the nation's largest subprime lending operation, the nation's most important banker, Alan Greenspan, weighed in on subprime, securitization, and other innovations that had transformed the mortgage marketplace. The Federal Reserve chairman didn't mention inflated appraisals or bait-and-switch salesmanship. He could think of no negatives. Deregulation, technological advances, and product innovations, he said, had helped increase home ownership to record levels. "As we reflect on the evolution of consumer credit in the United States, we must conclude that innovation and structural change in the financial services industry have been critical in providing expanded access to credit for the vast majority of consumers, including those of limited means," he said. "Without these forces, it would have been impossible for lower-income consumers to have the degree of access to credit markets that they have now."

Robert Gnaizda had been hearing these sorts of statements from Greenspan for years. Gnaizda had been a lawyer for migrant farmworkers before he'd become one of the founders of the Greenlining Institute, a civil rights group based in Berkeley, California. He had a reputation for getting powerful people to do what he wanted. Gnaizda had met regularly with Greenspan since the late '90s. Greenspan talked about helping poor people and minorities. But when Gnaizda urged him to use the power of the Fed to make sure subprime lenders were adequately supervised, the chairman balked: his free-market creed made it difficult for him to consider any sort of regulation, even when fraud and sleaze were increasingly becoming features of the marketplace. Greenspan later said he had "the impression that there were a lot of very questionable practices going on. The problem has always been, what basically does the law mean when it says deceptive and unfair practices? Deceptive and unfair practices may seem straightforward, except when you try to determine by what standard." Such circumlocutory logic was a recipe for inaction. Even when Gnaizda urged him to push for voluntary standards in the subprime market, Greenspan wouldn't budge. "He never gave us a good reason, but he didn't want to do it," Gnaizda said. "He just wasn't interested."

If Greenspan didn't take note of the allegations against Ameriquest, Gnaizda and the Greenlining Institute did. Greenlining had given its seal of approval to Ameriquest's "best practices" pronouncements. It had accepted $350,000 in donations from Ameriquest in little more than two years. Arnall, Gnaizda believed, had been open to Greenlining's concerns about bad tactics in the subprime business. "I've met with him many, many times. I like the guy," Gnaizda said. "He's highly intelligent, very incisive—a nuanced thinker. He's as impressive as any CEO we've met with, and I've met with at least forty CEOs over the last few years." After our *Los Angeles Times* exposé broke, Gnaizda tried to get in touch with Arnall. Ameriquest's owner was uncharacteristically unavailable. Other executives at the company were of no help either. They gave him "more of a lawyer's response, which was unconvincing to me," Gnaizda said. "Platitudes are always unconvincing to me." Greenling took the dramatic step of rejecting $200,000 in donations that Ameriquest had pledged to the group for the year—returning half that was already in hand and telling the company not to bother sending the rest.

Other watchdog groups that had benefited from Arnall's largesse made no plans to return the company's donations. Ameriquest had given as much as $800,000 to seven advocacy organizations in 2004, a portion of the millions it had sent their way over the years. "I don't expect any company to be perfect," Shanna Smith, the chief executive of the National Fair Housing Alliance, said. "But I do expect that when the flaws are identified, they correct them. And Ameriquest has that attitude." Whenever she brought individual borrowers' complaints about inflated appraisals or other issues to the company's attention, Smith said, Ameriquest quickly addressed the problem—sometimes fixing the loan, investigating the sales branch in question, or, in cases when consumers were simply having trouble keeping up, forgiving late fees and halting foreclosures.

Ameriquest's donations weren't unusual. Citigroup, Household, and others had donated millions, and funneled billions in special loan programs, to groups that had once been critical of them. Some consumer advocates wondered whether such relationships benefited borrowers as much as they benefited the lenders. Matthew Lee, a community activist based in the Bronx, said it made sense for Ameriquest to respond promptly to watchdog groups that could stage demonstrations or draw attention to the company's flaws. Lenders realized, Lee said, that "they only look bad if certain prominent players criticize them. So the energy that could and should have gone into making sure you're not screwing your own customers goes into making friends with possible critics."

It wasn't surprising, then, that ACORN's relationship with Ameriquest took some strange turns. ACORN made only a few loans under the $360 million loan program promised by Ameriquest, because the group was able to secure better mortgage products for its constituents through Bank of America. Still, Ameriquest maintained the association, donating about $100,000 a year to ACORN. The activist group later admitted it didn't do enough to monitor whether Ameriquest was living up to its best practices pledges. In 2004, ACORN started fielding a steady stream of consumer complaints about Ameriquest, including claims that Ameriquest employees were falsifying borrowers' incomes to qualify them for loans they couldn't afford. ACORN raised these issues with the company. Mike Shea, the director of the group's housing programs, said ACORN became so fed up with Ameriquest's unresponsiveness that it came close to filing complaints with regulators. After Ameriquest promised to get on top of the problem, ACORN decided to give the company another chance. "Some say we might have waited too long," Shea said. "But you try to give people the benefit of the doubt once they pledge to work with you."

* * *

Ameriquest also had its friends on Wall Street. The bad publicity and the investigation didn't stop investment banks and investors from snapping up Ameriquest's mortgages and mortgage-backed securities. One of the deals that Ameriquest rolled out that spring did so well that a trade publication, *Asset Securitization Report*, published the headline: "Ameriquest Unscathed by Legal Woes." Investors were so eager to buy bonds issued in the $1.2 billion deal that some slices of the deal were "six to eight times oversubscribed." The trade paper said "the company made sure to cover its tracks and smooth the way" for the transaction. "They talked to investors and made the market comfortable," one source told the publication. "There was a significant amount of global investor demand for this deal," another source said. Along with the deals marketed under its own Ameriquest Mortgage Securities label, Ameriquest and its sister companies sold billions of dollars in mortgages over the next few months directly to Lehman Brothers, which pooled the loans into its own mortgage-backed securities deals.

Wall Street's securitization machine was crafted to absorb a large percentage of loans that were bad for borrowers and, in the long run, likely to end in default. As long as the deals were structured properly and real-estate prices continued to rise, investment banks and investors didn't have to worry much about the quality of loans in the pools. Securitization could insulate investors from the risks of predatory lending without discouraging predatory lending itself. As a result, legal researchers concluded, investors could safely invest in top-rated subprime mortgage bonds even when the underlying loan pools were "replete with questionable loans."

Prentiss Cox understood how important Wall Street and securitization were to keeping the subprime hustle going. He hadn't grasped the big picture when he worked on the FAMCO case for the Minnesota attorney general's office. He thought FAMCO was an anomaly, one of perhaps a handful of rogue companies that dotted subprime's landscape. By the time he was deep into the Household case, he understood how the flow of cash from Wall Street helped fuel unsavory tactics among lenders. As he led the investigation of Ameriquest, he grew more concerned about the size and destructiveness of the subprime business. Nobody seemed to care about what was happening to borrowers, and nobody at the top of investment banks and subprime lenders was willing to acknowledge the risks they were taking with their companies and the financial system. "It's hard to get a clear vision when your heads are buried in cash," Cox said. During one meeting with Ameriquest representatives, one of the company's lawyers quipped: "Prentiss, on a bad day, you would say every lender in this industry is fraudulent." Cox shot back: "I'd say that on a good day."

Ameriquest and other subprime lenders argued that the real culprits were rogue loan officers and mortgage brokers, unscrupulous property flippers and other real-estate scammers, and, finally, borrowers who lied about their incomes and assets in order to suck more cash out of their homes or buy bigger homes than they could afford. Lenders, they said, were victims, not perpetrators. "All lenders fight fraud because it costs them money," an Ameriquest spokesperson told the *Los Angeles Times*. "Ameriquest is no different." The Mortgage Bankers Association agreed, writing a letter to the newspaper: "It is a serious, and sometimes criminal, problem when lenders mislead consumers. It is arguably a more serious problem, however, when lenders are misled by criminals that seek profit or property."

Cox didn't think the argument rang true. There might be hundreds, perhaps even thousands, of cases in which lenders had been defrauded, but that was because they had made themselves vulnerable to low-level frauds by lowering their loan-approval standards and by hiring inexperienced workers and pressuring them to produce loan volume at all costs. Any fraud against lenders, Cox thought, paled in comparison to the millions of borrowers who had been victimized by lenders' abuses. And the argument that average borrowers had pulled off a far-ranging spree of fraud against big lenders? That made no sense to him. Many borrowers had no idea that their incomes had been inflated on their loan paperwork, and they had no power over the real-estate appraisers who worked in cahoots with lenders to inflate their property values. "Nobody walked in and said, 'Hey, why don't you give me one of those loans where the rate is going to explode in two years, and by the way, I can't afford it, so can I lie about my income?' That's not what happened," Cox said. For Cox, the equation between borrower and lender came down to this: "Do you put the blame on individuals who are struggling to get by? Or do you blame sophisticated people who consciously designed a scheme and aggressively sold it to borrowers?"

Ameriquest and other lenders also argued that market demand provided the best evidence that they were on the up-and-up. If they were preying on their customers and putting them in loans they couldn't repay, why were investors flocking to plow their money into the industry, and why were their mortgage securities performing so well? Cox's rejoinder was that the mortgage pools were riskier than the people investing in them thought them to be. The unprecedented rise in home values had helped to hide the abusive nature of the loans. "Imagine," he said, "what would happen if the housing bubble burst?" The results, he believed, would be catastrophic.

* * *

Cox had all of this in mind as the state law enforcers debated how much money they should demand from Ameriquest. It was a repeat of the intramural debate in the Household case, with hawks wanting the states to hold out for a big dollar figure, and doves arguing for a lower figure that would smooth the way for a settlement. Cox and a few other hawks believed the states should demand $1 billion and settle for no less than $900 million. If they settled for less than the $484 million that Household had paid out, he told his colleagues, it would establish that the penalties for predatory lending were indeed just a cost of doing business. The doves argued that the states were fighting a tough battle with few resources, against a company that had friends in high places and wasn't shy about hiring expensive legal talent. Besides, they pointed out, Ameriquest executives and their lawyers were crying poverty. Ameriquest didn't have enough money to pay a mega-settlement, they said. A billion dollars was out of the question.

Where were all the billions that ACC Capital had made in profits over the past three years? Long gone. The money had been transferred to the conglomerate's owner, Roland Arnall. He had good lawyers and good accountants. ACC Capital was a labyrinth of companies set up to enrich its owner and insulate his fortune from legal assaults. Arnall owned Ameriquest Capital Corporation, which owned ACC Capital, which in turn controlled Ameriquest, Argent, and other subsidiaries. As big as the organization's profits were, money seldom lingered inside the corporate shell. Once it flowed into Arnall's personal accounts, it was for the most part out of the reach of any lawyers or bureaucrats who might want to get their hands on it. "The money was there,"

Washington State's Chuck Cross said. "It just got moved from one pocket to another." Cross argued that the states should file civil claims personally against Ameriquest's owner. Arnall had created the culture and he was the one who profited from it, Cross believed.

Cross couldn't persuade the group that going after Arnall made sense. The law provides sturdy protections for corporate owners; only in the most extreme cases are litigants allowed to "pierce the corporate veil" and hold owners financially responsible for their companies' misbehavior. That left the states in a difficult position. If they demanded too much money, Ameriquest might refuse to settle or file bankruptcy. That would force the states to spend years tied up in court.

That would have been fine with Prentiss Cox. He thought the states should be prepared to fight the case as long as it took. They could create a legal and media maelstrom that would strike fear in Ameriquest, the mortgage industry, and Wall Street. It was time, Cox believed, to "step on the neck" of the subprime industry. Subprime's house of cards was going to fall, and the consequences would be painful. When that happened, Cox told his colleagues, "I want us to be able to hold our heads up and say we did everything we could to stop this."

By mid-summer 2005, it was clear there would be no billion-dollar payout by Ameriquest, or even a half-billion-dollar one. The company and the states had tentatively agreed on a settlement of around $300 million. It was far less than what Household had settled for two years earlier, in a case involving far fewer borrowers. It represented about 12 percent of the profits of Arnall's holding company, ACC Capital, from 2002 to 2004. All that remained was for the two sides to work out the portion of the settlement that would set out the reforms Ameriquest would be forced to make in its practices.

* * *

As investment bankers and their clients kept pouring money into the subprime market, a few Wall Street insiders were starting to question how much longer their employers could keep the game going. One morning in 2005, Lawrence G. McDonald, a vice president at Lehman Brothers, sat in on yet another presentation about the opportunities that Lehman was creating for itself in mortgages and real estate. Afterward, Alex Kirk, a top official in Lehman's bond business, took McDonald and another colleague, Larry McCarthy, aside. McDonald knew Kirk, his boss, as a man who chose his words carefully. That's why he was surprised by what Kirk told them.

"The housing market is all 'roided up," Kirk said. "The whole fucking thing is ridiculous. This market is on fucking steroids."

It was the first time, in hundreds of hours of discussions at Lehman, that McDonald had ever heard anyone utter a bad word about the company's mortgage business. In the year that he'd been at Lehman, McDonald had seen how the mortgage guys on the fourth floor of the firm's Midtown Manhattan headquarters dominated the investment bank's culture and politics. McDonald was one of Lehman's most successful traders, once making $5 million in a single day on a single trade. But he came to feel "slightly second class" in comparison to the mortgage guys, who were producing the profits that made Lehman go. The executives who ran the company's sprawling mortgage business, he said, had direct access to CEO Dick Fuld and his inner circle on the thirty-first floor. "Their words were not so much heard as acclaimed," McDonald recalled. "Whatever they needed—extra budget, permission for more risk, permission to invest colossal hunks of the firm's capital in their market—they got."

So it was a big deal when Alex Kirk voiced a dissenting opinion. McDonald recalled that McCarthy, Lehman's global head of distressed debt trading, was speechless for a few moments. Finally, McCarthy found his words. The real-estate market, McCarthy agreed, was "on borrowed time, and we have to get the hell out. Couldn't you just smell the hubris in there, that mindless fucking smugness?"

McCarthy believed Dick Fuld was the problem. When Lehman's risk managers said the company should "hit the brake pedal," McCarthy later said, the CEO was instead "hitting the accelerator." Fuld, he said, wouldn't listen to anyone outside his inner circle. "Other than six or seven people, no one really knew him. It was like he was in his own world on the thirty-first floor," McCarthy recalled. "He was never in touch with the troops. In my four years there, he never came down to the trading floor. Not once."

Another Lehman manager who was concerned about the risks in the real-estate market was Michael Gelband, the head of capital markets and a member of Lehman's executive committee. In the summer of 2005, Gelband gave a well-attended presentation that spelled out, in explicit detail, the dark side of the mortgage market. He described the proliferation of "no-doc" mortgages and other toxic loans, sold by commission-hungry salesmen and then off-loaded to Lehman and other Wall Street banks. Gelband, McDonald said, predicted that the house of cards could soon collapse, perhaps in 2007 or 2008, producing serious consequences for the U.S. economy.

Gelband's warnings didn't do much to slow down Lehman's mortgage operations. Its BNC and Finance America units posted their best years ever in 2005, originating $26 billion in subprime mortgages between them. Lehman's subprime securitization team continued cranking out product, packaging $54 billion in subprime mortgage–backed securities for the year—more than any investment bank had ever packaged. Lehman also placed high among the leaders in "Alt-A" mortgages, originating $40 billion in Alt-A loans in 2005, ranking behind only Countrywide and IndyMac in the category of loans that fit somewhere, on the risk and pricing scales, between A-credit loans and subprime. The money coming in from Lehman's high-risk bets on home mortgages and commercial real estate had helped produce a surge of profits never before seen in the company's history. The firm that had barely survived the '90s earned a record $3.2 billion in 2005.

With encouragement from Kirk and McCarthy, McDonald said, Gelband continued to use his position on Lehman's executive committee to try to persuade the firm to pull back from subprime and its increasingly large bets on commercial real estate. Fuld didn't want to hear it, according to McDonald. Instead, McDonald said, the CEO bullied and belittled Gelband, telling him during one meeting: "I don't want you to tell me why we can't. You're much too cautious. What are you afraid of?" Fuld's stance was that his company had been through downturns and crises before, and it had always emerged stronger and more profitable. Fuld's on-the-team-or-off-the-team mentality set the tone. Executives who were squeamish about risk taking weren't welcome. "It was quite hard to stand in the way," a former top Lehman official in London recalled. The company had good risk managers, "but the prevailing atmosphere was for fast growth and special fast-track treatment for what we now know were toxic deals."

* * *

As some Lehman executives began to worry about the exposure the firm was taking on in the mortgage market, Roland Arnall's flagship stepped up its advertising blitz. In the summer of 2005, Ameriquest unveiled a new TV commercial spot from the advertising aces at DDB Worldwide. As Mick Jagger and the Rolling Stones play to a packed arena, a woman dressed in a business suit squeezes through the crowd, jostled by fellow concertgoers. She is, viewers learned, an Ameriquest "mortgage specialist." Over the din, she manages to say: "Whether your dream is to buy a house or refinance, or see the Stones, Ameriquest can help." The ad closed with the Ameriquest Liberty Bell, the "Proud Sponsor of the American Dream" motto, and then the Rolling Stones' iconic giant tongue logo.

Ameriquest had put down a large sum—$4 million by one estimate—to sponsor the Stones' 2005–2006 U.S. tour. It leveraged its partnership with the band to generate leads for its salespeople through an online sweepstakes that allowed Stones fans to sign up for a chance to win free tickets. The commercials, the sweepstakes, and Stones-themed direct mail helped increase traffic on Ameriquest.com by one-third.

Ameriquest also leveraged the relationship to enhance its cultivation of politicians' good opinion, giving away Stones tickets to officials in several states. Among the recipients was California's governor. Schwarzenegger landed forty Stones tickets that he used as a come-on to raise money for his reelection. When the Stones opened their "A Bigger Bang" tour at Boston's Fenway Park in August 2005, political fat cats forked over $10,000 each to Schwarzenegger for a preconcert reception and front-and-center seats, or $100,000 each to watch the show in a luxury box with the governor. In Arizona, about thirty lawmakers attended a Stones concert through the patronage of Ameriquest. The lobbyist who arranged the outing said it was a "very cool opportunity" to boost the company's name; he said company officials wanted "to demonstrate . . . what their contribution is in our culture."

The company offered free tickets to nonpoliticians as well. Irv Ackelsberg, a lawyer with Community Legal Services of Philadelphia, had filed a petition with Pennsylvania's Department of Banking, charging that Ameriquest had a pattern of "unfair, deceptive and unethical conduct." Ameriquest had tried to smooth things over with Ackelsberg; company representatives had flown to Philadelphia and met with him over dinner to explain the company's side of things. Soon after, an Ameriquest official e-mailed Ackelsberg and offered him and a colleague tickets to one of the Stones concerts at Philadelphia's Wachovia Center. Ackelsberg was a huge Stones fan. "I think they were offering us four tickets, right up front," he recalled. "You know, sitting close enough so that I could catch Mick's sweat. I have to say this, the SOBs knew how to get to me; I never saw the Stones live, and the tickets were ridiculously expensive and they were going to give us VIP seats at that. There was a little voice inside me saying, Yo, Irv, are you f'in' nuts not taking the tickets?" But Ackelsberg couldn't, in good conscience, take payola from what he thought of as "subprime racketeers." He wrote Ameriquest back. Thanks but no thanks, he said. He said he would think about Ameriquest whenever he put the Stones on his stereo and cranked up "Sympathy for the Devil." He never heard from the company again.

* * *

Not long after the Stones played Philadelphia, Ameriquest's owner had some business to attend to down the road in the nation's capital. On October 20, 2005, the U.S. Senate Foreign Relations Committee took up the question of President Bush's nominee to be the new ambassador to the Netherlands: Roland Arnall.

The nomination was a testament to the melding of money and politics in America. By the fall of 2005, Arnall's net worth had grown to $3 billion, according to *Forbes*, which ranked him No. 73 on its list of richest Americans. Members of that list—and big campaign contributors—often are tapped by presidents to serve as ambassadors to second-rung allies. In the etiquette of the selection process, the fact that Arnall had been Bush's single-biggest pipeline of cash during the 2004 election cycle was deemed to have nothing, officially, to do with the nomination. Bush selected Arnall "after a careful and exhaustive search for a distinguished American" to fill the post, a State Department bureaucrat wrote in a letter to the Senate committee's chairman, Indiana Republican Richard Lugar.

By the time the committee held its first hearing on Arnall's nomination, it had received a stack of letters from supporters who described him as a man of principle. Among them were civil rights leaders whose groups had benefited from Arnall's contributions. Wade Henderson of the Leadership Conference on Civil Rights, Shanna Smith of the National Fair Housing Alliance, and Ricardo Byrd of the National Association of Neighborhoods called Arnall a "very good friend." Also included was a letter from Deval Patrick, who had led the Justice Department investigation of Arnall and Long Beach a decade before and then joined ACC Capital's board as state officials pursued a new investigation of Arnall's lending operations. Patrick was now a contestant for the Democratic nomination in Massachusetts' gubernatorial race. "This is a good man," Patrick wrote. "I always say the measure of a good company is not whether things always go well, but whether a company does the right thing when they don't. By that measure, ACC Capital and Ameriquest are good companies."

The hearing convened in Room 419 of the Dirksen Senate Office Building. Representative Tom Lantos formally introduced Arnall to the committee. Lantos, a Democrat from the San Francisco Bay Area, carried much respect on Capitol Hill. He was the only Holocaust survivor to have served in Congress and was the founder of the Congressional Human Rights Caucus. He referred to the nominee as "my dear friend Roland Arnall." He observed that both he and Arnall were "Americans by choice," immigrants who had come from humble beginnings. He noted that Roland and his wife, Dawn, were generous donors to many causes. Roland, Lantos said, was a man with a "half-a-century track record of cultivating a myriad of dynamic relationships in the business and cultural worlds, while at the same time effectively managing large corporate institutions."

When it came time for him to speak, Arnall began by introducing his family: "my lovely wife Dawn, my daughter Michelle, my brother Claude, and my nieces and nephews." He talked about his early life, and about his decades of experience in business and philanthropy. "I bring to this post an unwavering commitment to excellence," he said. "I have always been driven by a belief that excellence is achieved through strong and capable leadership. I have made 'Do the right thing' my motto."

Starting off the questioning, the committee chairman, Lugar, asked Arnall about the states' investigation of Ameriquest's practices.

"Mr. Chairman," Arnall replied, "even though I'm not involved in the day-to-day operations of my various holdings and various companies, which are quite substantial, I take full responsibility for anything that goes wrong anywhere. I also would like to tell you that I would consider our company the anti-predatory company. In the late eighties when we founded the company, we provided credit to folks who did not have the opportunity because of their credit history to borrow directly from the institutional banks. We analyzed that particular sector. We found that the risk could be quantified and that basically we could reduce the cost of borrowing to these people to an unbelievable degree compared to the finance companies and the inner-city companies who preyed on these people." Over the years, his companies had developed "an outstanding gold standard for non-prime lending. Non-prime lending at one time was not something that the major institutions were interested in. After having reviewed our history within the sector, major banks and major institutions have joined."

Lugar let the matter drop, but two Democrats—Paul Sarbanes of Maryland and Barack Obama of Illinois—burrowed in deeper. Sarbanes didn't buy Arnall's characterization of himself as an absentee owner. The senator quoted two high-level executives who'd told the *Los Angeles Times* that Arnall was a hands-on owner who knew much about the ins and outs of his companies. As for Ameriquest's proposed settlement with the states, Sarbanes said, $300 million seemed more like "a business expense. It doesn't really constitute a major deterrent."

During his turn to ask questions, Obama noted that he and Arnall had a friend in common: Deval Patrick. Still, Obama said, the allegations against Arnall's company were serious. They weren't technicalities.

Both Obama and Sarbanes suggested Arnall needed to see to it that the settlement was finalized and the investigation put behind him. "I'm wondering whether it is appropriate for us to send someone to represent our country with these issues still looming in the horizon," Obama said.

Arnall was conciliatory. "Thank you, Senator," he told Obama. "I've read up on your background, and I'm very impressed with your life history, and I can appreciate your concerns." He said, though, that he and his wife had recused themselves from the settlement talks. They were leaving negotiations up to the senior executives who would be running the company in his absence. He told Sarbanes: "These people know what the right thing is, Senator. Problems happened. They corrected it. Problems did happen. They corrected it. There are sixteen thousand employees. There are a lot of companies with sixteen thousand employees. From time to time, unfortunate stuff happens."

Sarbanes couldn't let that pass. Enough stuff had happened, Sarbanes replied, to provoke dozens of states to threaten to sue the company. "Innocent people were hurt—abused, really, in some instances—and it seems to me there ought to be an overwhelming desire here to set that situation straight and remedy it."

And that was it: the issue had been framed. Most Republicans thought Arnall should be approved on the spot and sent to the Senate floor for a vote. The Democrats wanted to wait, insisting that Arnall settle with the states before his nomination could be approved. Not everyone, though, believed it made sense to approve the nomination, even if Arnall coughed up money for the state regulators. Ira Rheingold, the head of the National Association of Consumer Advocates, thought it was strange that no one asked whether, settlement or not, a man who ran a company that preyed on vulnerable borrowers was the kind of person who should be representing America overseas. Paying cash to stave off further government action, Rheingold thought, shouldn't provide absolution.

With the GOP holding a Senate majority, Republicans held a 10-to-8 edge in the committee. One of the Republicans, however, was Chuck Hagel, an independent-minded Nebraskan. He didn't want to green-light a nominee while a "cloud of investigation" hung over his head. With Hagel siding with the Democrats, the vote was dead-locked.

The tie appeared to bottle up Arnall's nomination. Lugar, the chairman, had other plans. Most of the Democrats had voted by proxy, casting absentee votes on the question. It was standard practice in the Senate. Lugar ruled, though, that only the votes of the senators who were present should count. That changed the tally to 8 to 2 in Arnall's favor, sending his nomination to the full Senate. Democrats vowed to challenge the ruling by going to the chamber's chief parliamentarian. With the nomination still up in the air, Arnall arranged a private meeting to lobby Hagel to change his mind. He also hired Fred Field-ing, a former White House counsel to Nixon and Reagan, to lobby on his behalf.

* * *

Subprime mortgage lending rose to $665 billion during 2005, a 25 percent increase over the previous year. Ameriquest's legal and public relations headaches had hardly slowed its sales machine. Arnall's companies maintained their rank as the market leader, making just under $80 billion in home loans for the year, down barely $3 billion from the year before. It would be the last big year for Ameriquest and the rest of Arnall's subprime juggernaut. The state law enforcers tried to ensure that that would be the case.

In January 2006, the company and the states announced that they had put the final touches on their settlement. Many Ameriquest bor-rowers would be eligible to draw refunds of at least $600 from the $325 million settlement. In all, about seven hundred thousand Ameri-quest borrowers might be able to share in the money. The deal also imposed changes in the way Ameriquest did business. For example, it forbade the company from setting outlandish sales quotas for its loan officers or offering them a higher commission for sticking borrowers with higher prices and prepayment penalties.

Iowa attorney general Tom Miller said the Ameriquest settlement would help reform what "in some ways has been a very bad industry." He expected other subprime lenders to embrace similar reforms to avoid exposing themselves to investigations and lawsuits. Other observers were more skeptical that the settlement would force the industry to change. "I applaud the settlement that will come from Ameriquest," said former Georgia governor Roy Barnes, an advocate for tough rules against predatory lending. "But where Ameriquest will die down a little and maybe change their stripes, there'll be another company out there doing the same thing, and another, and another." Critics also pointed out that Ameriquest's sister company, Argent, hadn't been included in the settlement. Argent was free to keep growing without restrictions on the way it did business.

Consumer lawyers complained, too, that the payouts to Ameriquest's borrowers were small. In Jacksonville, Florida, Carolyn Pittman's attorney said the settlement wasn't going to make much of a difference for her client. "I don't think a few hundred dollars is going to help her." Pittman, sixty-nine, was still fighting to save her home after being flipped through a series of loans, the first one from Ameriquest, the second one from its former sister company, Long Beach Mortgage, and the third one again from Ameriquest. "I think they should go out of business because they're not treating us right," Pittman said. "I don't think they can change."

Ameriquest's $325 million payout was less than the company's annual advertising and marketing budget, and a fraction of the $1.34 billion that Arnall had earned from his mortgage operations in 2004 alone. As with the modest dollar judgment against Lehman Brothers in the FAMCO case, the Ameriquest settlement may have emboldened the subprime mortgage industry rather than making it pull back. It was, a Fitch Ratings executive told the trade press, "a manageable amount for the company." As Dave Huey, the assistant attorney general in Washington State, later said: "I think what happened is people read the settlement as, 'Whew, they're not going to put us out of business. It could have been worse. It could have been a whole lot worse. We're still making all this money. So let's go.'"

There was one other outcome of the deal. It cleared the way for Roland Arnall to go to Holland. Obama and Sarbanes, the two senators who had been toughest on him during his committee hearing, indicated that the bargain with the states had extinguished any concerns they had about Arnall's nomination. "Because a settlement was reached, Senator Obama will not seek to block Mr. Arnall's nomination," an Obama spokesman said.

On February 8, 2006, sixteen days after the settlement with the states had been announced, the U.S. Senate made its blessing official. The chamber confirmed Arnall as ambassador to the Netherlands, without discussion, on an uncontested voice vote. Adam Bass, Arnall's nephew, spoke for Ameriquest. "We take great pride in knowing that our company's founder will be representing our country abroad and know he will serve with honor and distinction," he said.

*   *   *

As Arnall put an ocean between himself and the controversies over America's subprime lending industry, his friends and allies back in the United States were still dealing with the fallout from the states' investigation into Ameriquest. In Massachusetts, Deval Patrick was fighting to become his adopted state's first African-American governor. His opponents made much of the $360,000 a year he had knocked down as a board member of ACC Capital. One of his rivals in the Democratic primary was Tom Reilly, the state's attorney general. "I've been on the side of the people," Reilly told Patrick during one of their debates. "You've been on the side of Ameriquest, the largest, most notorious, predatory lender in the history of this country."

Patrick dismissed the attacks on him, saying that Ameriquest was "using the situation as an opportunity to raise the bar for the entire industry," echoing the company's talking points. "I see my role in every company I have been associated with as trying to make it better," he said. "Sometimes problem solvers, if they're serious, get their hands dirty. That is exactly the kind of leadership we need in Massachusetts today."

Patrick's ties to Ameriquest didn't prevent him from capturing the Democratic nomination and then winning the gubernatorial election. He couldn't put Ameriquest entirely behind him, though. In time, his connection to Roland Arnall's company would come back to haunt him.

15. Collapse

George and Evelyn Lee had lived in their house on Irving Park Place in Saginaw, Michigan, for nearly three decades. He was eighty, a retired autoworker. She was seventy-three. In the spring of 2006, they decided their house needed some work. The roof leaked and the patio room was rotting away. A home-improvement contractor told them he could take care of everything; he would arrange for financing and they wouldn't have to pay anything out of pocket. It shouldn't have been a problem for the Lees to borrow money to make some repairs. They owed just $5,200 on their old mortgage, and the house was worth perhaps $35,000. Their credit rating was good, and George had a pension from the United Auto Workers.

The contractor showed up at their house with a salesman from a mortgage broker called Real Financial, LLC. Like the contractor, the man from Real Financial said he'd take care of everything. The Lees signed a "bewildering stack of paperwork, which was never explained to them," their lawyer later claimed. They were never given a chance to read the papers before the man "whisked all of the originals away with him."

What those papers said was that the Lees had signed for a loan from BNC Mortgage, the subsidiary of Lehman Brothers. The loan totaled $40,000, more than the house was worth. The interest rate on the loan started at 10.5 percent and could rise to 17.5 percent. If they wanted to pay the loan off early and get away from BNC, they would be charged a prepayment penalty. As compensation for arranging the deal, Real Financial took a $3,371 broker's fee. It also collected an $810 "yield spread premium" directly from BNC, as a reward for persuading the Lees to take out a mortgage that carried a higher interest rate than what they qualified for.

The contractor got just over $30,000 to cover the work, but, Evelyn Lee later alleged, the work the contractor performed was haphazard and inadequate; the contractor reused the old rusted flashing around the roof, cut their burglar alarm cable, and failed to do many of the renovations the Lees had been promised. George Lee didn't have the strength to complain. He was fighting cancer. He died in November 2006, soon after he and his wife had made their first payment on the loan.

By then, the Lees' mortgage had found a home in BNC Mortgage Loan Trust 2006-1. The shell corporation pooled together nearly four thousand other subprime home loans, and then spun off more than $800 million in mortgage-backed bonds. Evelyn Lee knew nothing of this. She just knew the work hadn't been done right and she was stuck with an overpriced loan. After her husband died, she decided she wasn't going to pay another dime to BNC. "Basically, we were cheated," she said. "That is what they did—and still expect to be paid every month."

Representatives of the loan trust filed for foreclosure against the house. Realizing she needed help, Lee went to the UAW-GM Legal Services Plan, which represents General Motors workers and retirees. An attorney with the law clinic, Sharon Withers, concluded that the mortgage professionals had inflated the appraisal on the Lees' home to get the deal done. She also discovered information that raised questions about the friends that BNC kept. The broker, Real Financial, had a history. It had been the subject of twenty-five complaints to Michigan financial regulators. BNC wasn't aware of the complaints because it hadn't checked with the state agency about complaints when it put Real Financial on its approved broker list. Instead, it simply checked to see whether the broker had a license in the state.

Withers filed a sharply worded lawsuit naming the contractor, the broker, and BNC as defendants. She said it was puzzling that BNC would allow the broker "to set up such a draconian, one-sided loan for the unsuspecting Plaintiff and her spouse, even rewarding the Broker with an additional yield spread premium on top of the unearned fees charged the Plaintiff at closing, while turning a blind eye to the results for their elderly and ailing victims. . . . It cannot be argued the Defendant BNC didn't understand the seamy details of what happened here, as the lender prepared the closing documents, reviewed the application and sent its agent Real Financial to the closing with a set of instructions for how to proceed." Lehman Brothers replied it wasn't to blame in the matter. "BNC was not aware of anything wrong with the Lees' loan because all it saw was the loan application, which was in good order," Lehman said. "Real Financial was not BNC's agent, and BNC gave it no 'instructions' whatsoever. We strongly believe BNC has been added to this case only as a 'deep pocket.'"

BNC wasn't the only Lehman Brothers unit where questionable loans were popping up. Another subsidiary, Aurora Loan Services, specialized in making Alt-A loans, the category that fit between subprime and A-credit loans. As Aurora became an important source of profits, Lehman installed its own managers inside the lender to keep watch over the operation. According to a securities fraud lawsuit later filed against CEO Dick Fuld and other Lehman executives, these managers were more concerned with keeping up the flow of mortgages into the securitization pipeline than with screening out dicey loans. One of the Lehman-installed managers, the suit said, "stormed out of a meeting and yelled at the vice president for special investigations, loud enough for everyone in the vicinity to hear: 'Your people find too much fraud!'"

By 2006, it was evident that many of the mortgages produced by Aurora were underpinned by inflated appraisals and other deceptions. An in-house special investigations team reviewed a sample of mortgages packaged into securitizations by Lehman's structured finance experts. It found that 40 to 50 percent of them had misrepresentations in the loan documents, according to a witness in the securities fraud case. One big problem was Aurora's "strategic partners"—lenders that funneled large numbers of loans to the company and received preferential treatment in the company's loan-approval process. Given the high volume of mortgages that Lehman's strategic partners provided during the boom times, Aurora's quality-control specialists could examine only a small sample of the loans as they came through the pipeline. When they found problem loans in a pool, the witness said, Aurora simply shipped those loans back. It didn't dig deeper into the pool to see if other loans were bad, too. A separate review looked at a sample made up mostly of loans that Aurora purchased from its strategic partners. More than 70 percent of those loan files showed signs of fraud, according to the witness.

One of Lehman's strategic partners was Arizona-based First Magnus Financial. A bankruptcy court trustee later charged that the father-son team that ran First Magnus had squandered a fortune through over-the-top spending that "would make even the most pampered and precocious movie star blush," installing themselves in a lavish headquarters adorned with a $170,000 waterfall. The U.S. Department of Housing and Urban Development concluded that First Magnus had paid illegal kickbacks to entice mortgage brokers to feed the company business. A class-action lawsuit charged that First Magnus promised low, fixed-interest rates that turned out to be a mirage; instead borrowers were trapped in overpriced, adjustable-rate mortgages with prepayment penalties.

First Magnus was a favorite of both Lehman Brothers and Countrywide. The two companies purchased nearly three-quarters of the loans that First Magnus originated between 2005 and 2007. Countrywide ended up saddled with more than $100 million in bad loans from First Magnus; Lehman got stuck with nearly $400 million in bad loans from the lender.

* * *

Questionable loans flooded mortgage pipelines throughout the industry. Steve Jernigan, a fraud investigator at Argent, Roland Arnall's wholesale unit, understood how bad things had gotten when he received a call one day in 2006 from a real-estate appraiser in Indiana. Jernigan was based at Argent's headquarters in Orange County. He'd dispatched the appraiser to check on a subdivision in which Argent had made loans. The appraiser wanted to make sure he had the right location. "I'm standing in the middle of a cornfield," he told Jernigan. The addresses on the loan applications, it turned out, were made up. The houses didn't exist. Jernigan pulled the files and found that all of the original appraisal reports had been accompanied by a photo of the same house. It sunk in that Argent had been swindled by fraudsters who'd taken advantage of the company's lack of concern for checking the documentation provided by loan applicants.

Lending standards and underwriting were so weak at Argent and many other lenders that it was easy for fraudsters to take out mortgages on houses that were overvalued or existed only on paper, then siphon off the proceeds of the loans for themselves. The fraudsters often used "straw buyers" who would take out the mortgages in their own names in order to hide the identity of the true borrowers. Some straw buyers were in on the scam; others were dupes who'd been fooled by con artists, who stole their Social Security numbers and credit histories by signing them up for fictitious "investment clubs." At Argent, Jernigan said, the drive to increase loan volume trumped concerns about fraud. Outside mortgage brokers and in-house sales people flooded the company's infrastructure with deals that should never have been made. Senior managers didn't care because questionable loans could be off-loaded and hidden in securitization deals, Jernigan said. The attitude, he said, was: "It's going to be sold about twenty minutes after it's funded, so there's no sense worrying about it."

A second Indiana case removed all doubts for Jernigan as to whether management was willing to take the problem seriously and clean house. Argent, along with Countrywide and other lenders, had been taken in by a con man named Robert Andrew Penn. Just a few years before, Penn had been a waiter in an Italian restaurant in Indianapolis. He had reinvented himself as a real-estate investor by enlisting the help of family and friends back home in Virginia. His mother was a lay minister and his sister was a beautician. They knew lots of folks in Martinsville, a struggling factory town along the North Carolina border where many of the mills had closed. Penn later admitted that he duped about a hundred people in Virginia, misappropriating their names and credit histories and using the information to take out loans to buy hundreds of overvalued properties around Indianapolis. The borrowers included truck drivers, factory workers, and a pastor. They thought they were joining a risk-free investment club. Federal authorities charged that Penn and his accomplices told the borrowers they wouldn't have to make any payments or take on any debts but would receive regular disbursements for letting the group use their credit records.

Argent made dozens of loans on the properties that Penn purchased. An Indianapolis real-estate agent warned Argent in 2004 that Penn may have been involved in mortgage fraud. The lender's Loan Resolution Department wrote the real-estate agent back, saying: "Argent would like to thank you for the information you provided and assure you that we will conduct all necessary investigations to secure our interests." But Argent didn't conduct a serious investigation of Penn's scheme, Jernigan said, until 2006, when it learned that Countrywide was preparing to file a lawsuit and make the scheme public. Then Argent scrambled to do damage control and get on top of the matter. By then, the loans had gone into default and Argent was out millions of dollars, stuck with properties that were worth considerably less than the loans that were attached to them. Argent, for example, had loaned nearly $500,000 for the purchase of a house on Easy Street in Indianapolis that turned out to have a market value of less than $300,000.

Jernigan spent weeks on the case, wallpapering a conference room with printouts of information on the Argent loans wrapped up in the scam. It was obvious to him that Argent's underwriters hadn't done the most rudimentary checking to make sure the loans were legitimate. One red flag that should have prompted a closer inspection was the fact that the loans were being made in Indiana to "purchasers" with home addresses in Virginia.

Eventually, Jernigan said, the investigation led him higher up Argent's food chain, to a senior executive who was "pretty much turning a blind eye" to the fraud. At that point, he said, a supervisor intervened. "I was pulled into an office," Jernigan said. The supervisor "looked me straight in the eye and said: 'You've got to stop.'" Upper-level management was off-limits.

* * *

In May 2006, Ameriquest Mortgage announced that it was shutting down all 229 of its branches and letting go thirty-eight hundred employees. It was an end of the boiler rooms that had dotted the nation, with their Power Hours and trash bins stuffed with empty Red Bull cans. The reforms required under the settlement with state authorities had made it impossible for Ameriquest to operate in its traditional freewheeling manner. Ameriquest said it would keep making loans through regional call centers in Arizona, California, Connecticut, and Illinois. Company officials talked about reengineering their business, but, in reality, the move was a prelude to closing shop. The company had served its purpose, producing billions for its owner, and now, holding fast to the boom-and-bust model of subprime, Ameriquest was preparing to fade into oblivion.

Its timing was perfect. By late summer, the boom times were over. The real-estate bubble had burst. Economists speak of soft landings and hard landings after an economic boom. The housing market's landing would be a hard one. After rising 58 percent from 2001 through 2005, home prices had stalled in many places, and they were falling in once-hot markets such as San Diego and Washington, D.C.'s Virginia suburbs. "It's just like somebody flipped a switch," one real-estate auctioneer said.

The real-estate market was so central to the economy that many financial leaders tried to put a hopeful spin on events. They suggested the worst would soon be over. Alan Greenspan, who had presided over the housing frenzy, had stepped down after eighteen years as chairman of the Federal Reserve. By autumn he'd settled into his role as elder statesman, declaring that he saw "early signs of stabilization" in the housing market. Countrywide chief Angelo Mozilo was even more optimistic. "We've already had the hard landing," he said. He expected the housing market to "tread water" in 2007. "In 2008, we'll have one hell of a year."

As the housing market stalled and plummeted, the first pain was felt in the subprime market. Subprime loans packaged into mortgage-backed securities in 2006 were falling into delinquency at the fastest rate in a decade. "We are a bit surprised by how fast this has unraveled," the head of asset-backed securities research at UBS said. Investors were demanding that Lehman Brothers and other Wall Street firms buy back loans that were rapidly going bad, and Lehman and other big players in turn were trying to get lenders down the line, such as First Magnus, to repurchase toxic mortgages. The chain reaction destroyed the mortgage machine that had served lenders, investment bankers, and investors for so long.

* * *

In early 2007, a month after being inaugurated as Massachusetts' chief executive, Deval Patrick got a phone call from Roland Arnall's nephew, Adam Bass. Bass, the vice chairman of Arnall's ACC Capital, had a favor to ask. Ameriquest was struggling to stay afloat. It was hoping to get an infusion of capital from Citigroup. Bass asked the new governor to make a call to the bank on behalf of Ameriquest.

Patrick called Robert Rubin, the chairman of Citigroup's executive committee and a former U.S. Treasury secretary. He vouched for the character of Ameriquest executives. Soon after the call, ACC Capital and Citigroup reached an agreement. The bank promised to pump $100 million in working capital into ACC, and ACC gave the bank an option to buy two of its holdings, Argent and AMC Mortgage Services, at a later date.

The sticky thing was that the state of Massachusetts exercised some oversight over both Ameriquest and Citigroup. Patrick defended himself by saying he had made the call not as governor, but as a private citizen. "As a former board member, I was asked by an officer of ACC Capital to serve as a reference for the company and agreed to do so," he said. "I called Robert Rubin, a former colleague from the Clinton administration and an executive at Citigroup, to offer any insight they might want on the character of the current management. The conversation with Mr. Rubin lasted at most a couple of minutes. Even though I made this call solely as a former board member, and I believe that was clear to Mr. Rubin, I appreciate that I should not have made the call. I regret the mistake." Massachusetts Republicans filed a complaint with the state ethics commission. One newspaper columnist, alluding to the fact that Patrick had become wealthy representing troubled corporations, described the incident as "a call by a rich man to a rich man on behalf of a rich man."

The ethics complaint was dismissed. But Patrick's relationship with Ameriquest continued to hang over him. The *Boston Herald* said Patrick's "radio silence on the subprime lending bust" was becoming "more awkward by the day." Between them, Ameriquest and Argent had had the second-highest number of foreclosure filings in Boston in 2006, the *Herald* noted. In the spring of 2007, the governor did begin to talk about the state's foreclosure crisis, asking the state's Division of Banking to help a terminally ill woman who was fighting Ameriquest's effort to take away her home. Massachusetts, Patrick noted, had set a record for foreclosure filings in 2006 and was on pace to break that record in 2007. "Behind those numbers are real families losing real homes," he said.

* * *

As Ameriquest and ACC Capital fought to stay alive, they were also facing an array of legal challenges. Ameriquest's settlement with the states had taken care of thousands of borrowers who were willing to accept the deal's modest financial payouts. In exchange, the borrowers had agreed not to press lawsuits against the company. But dozens of consumer attorneys continued to push private lawsuits against Ameriquest and Argent, and these lawsuits weren't covered by the states' settlement. For the borrowers hoping to win something out of these suits, it was a roll of the dice. Those who decided to "opt out" of the states' settlement were holding on for more financial relief. They were also taking a chance that they might get nothing.

To handle the flood of litigation, the courts consolidated all of the federal claims against the companies into a single multidistrict case to be overseen by a judge in the U.S. District Court in Chicago. A handful of attorneys were tapped to serve as lead counsels for the borrowers. These lawyers were confident they had the evidence to make a case for fraud and other misdeeds by Ameriquest and Argent. The big question was just how deep ACC Capital's pockets were.

If they were going to get real compensation for the borrowers, the attorneys would have to bring Roland Arnall into the case as a defendant and gain access to his billions. Doing so wouldn't be easy. The private attorneys were staring down the same hurdles that state officials had faced when it came to the issue of Arnall's accountability; it takes a heavy burden of proof to hold owners personally responsible for their companies' actions. In court papers, the borrowers' attorneys argued that Ameriquest and its sister companies were "the alter ego" of Arnall. It would be wrong, they said, to maintain "the fiction of the separate existence" between the man and the companies. Arnall "either established or ratified the policies and practices" that drove the fraud and exploitation that flourished under him. "Allowing Arnall to hide behind the corporate veil," the lawyers said, "would extend the principle of incorporation beyond its legitimate purposes and would promote injustice, unfairness and injury with respect to the thousands of borrowers who obtained loans from Ameriquest."

The borrowers' attorneys got a break in early 2007 when Wayne Lee added his name to the roll call of plaintiffs making claims against Arnall's companies. Lee had worked for Arnall in one job or another for fifteen years, starting at Long Beach Savings back in 1990. By 2001 he had risen to become president of Ameriquest's wholesale lending operation, the unit that would eventually operate under the Argent Mortgage flag. He built Argent into the giant that had helped make Arnall's companies the biggest source of subprime mortgages in America. In 2004, Arnall rewarded him by naming him CEO of his holding company, ACC Capital. That put Lee in charge of both Argent and Ameriquest. As Ameriquest was pressed by state authorities' burgeoning investigation, Lee said, he tried to reform the company's practices. He gave one example: Ameriquest allowed branch managers to supervise loan coordinators, the workers who determined whether a borrower qualified for a loan and on what terms. Under this structure, Lee said, branch managers had the authority and motive to exercise "undue influence" over the loan coordinators and force them to approve loans they shouldn't approve. Lee said he wanted to reorganize the company so that loan coordinators would no longer be under the thumb of branch managers or other sales personnel. Arnall, Lee said, rejected this idea. "Arnall blocked this and other reforms," according to a lawsuit Lee filed in Orange County Superior Court. Things came to a head, Lee said, in the summer of 2005, when Arnall told Lee that he should focus on Argent and let Arnall oversee Ameriquest. With Arnall usurping his authority, Lee resigned.

He didn't leave empty-handed. In exchange for Lee's agreement not to work for any competitors, Arnall promised him a $50 million consulting contract—$20 million up front, followed by $6 million a year for five years. After Arnall paid the signing money, Lee's story took a turn reminiscent of Arnall's parting with others who were close to him. In June 2006, two days before Lee was supposed to get his first $6 million installment, he was summoned to the office of one of Arnall's lawyers. The lawyer told him that Ameriquest wasn't going to pay him the rest due on the consulting contract, Lee said, and that if he tried to challenge this decision, ACC Capital would drag the case out for years in court.

Lee filed a breach of contract lawsuit that included his description of Arnall's efforts to block reforms at Ameriquest. It was not the kind of dirty laundry that Arnall or Ameriquest wanted aired in public. An attorney for the company called Lee's lawsuit "a ridiculous work of fiction."

For attorneys in the multidistrict litigation, Lee's allegations were tantalizing. Save for the one example, he hadn't been specific about the reforms Arnall had blocked. Still, it's rare that high-level executives are willing to turn on the bosses or companies for which they have worked. When they leave companies, even under unhappy circumstances, they can often count on "golden parachutes" or consulting contracts that help enforce their silence. "Non-disparagement" agreements or the threat that money will be cut off are usually enough to prevent executives from spilling embarrassing details about their ex-employers. Now, with his consulting contract voided and his claims about Arnall already on the public record, Lee seemed to be a great candidate for a witness in the case against Ameriquest and Arnall.

The borrowers' attorneys scheduled Lee for a quick deposition. He gave his testimony in Orange County little more than three months after he'd sued Arnall. The attorneys tried to verify and expand on the claims he had made in his suit. As they questioned Lee, they encountered a witness who preferred one- and two-word answers. *Yes. No. Uh-huh.* Lee didn't volunteer much new information. He also appeared to soften the claims he'd made in his lawsuit about the power that Ameriquest's branch managers held over loan coordinators.

> Q. And that's the structure that you attempted to change when you became CEO.
> A. Correct.
> Q. And it was blocked by Mr. Arnall?
> A. It was —I don't know if you'd describe it as a block as much as maybe, you know, he was concerned about the timing of it.

That answer was a change from what he'd said, unequivocally, in his lawsuit—that Arnall had blocked the reform. Asked whether he was worried about branch managers exercising "undue influence" over loan coordinators—the words he used in his suit—Lee replied, "The appearance of impropriety is more likely in that scenario."

> Q. What are some of the other reforms that Mr. Arnall opposed . . . you implementing in that time frame when you took over as CEO?
> A. That was the big one. You know, I mean as far as specific reforms, he didn't object to it. He actually agreed that we should do it. He didn't agree with my approach in how we were going to do it.

As the questions continued, the borrowers' attorneys did learn one thing of interest. In the three months or so that had passed from when Lee filed his lawsuit to when he sat down for his deposition, he and Roland Arnall had put their disagreements to rest. They had reached a settlement. Ameriquest Capital, the parent company of Arnall's holding company ACC Capital, had agreed to pay Lee $14.75 million. Of that, $200,000 went to his attorney. The rest was Lee's to keep. Ameriquest threw out the consulting contract's non-compete clause, allowing Lee to work for any other mortgage lender he wanted. All he had to do was drop his lawsuit and agree to a "mutual non-disparagement" clause.

As the deposition dragged on, the borrowers' attorneys continued to push Lee to talk about Ameriquest, Argent, and Arnall. It was of little use.

> Q. Do you in any way blame yourself for the ongoing litigation
>   against Ameriquest about its mortgage practices?
> A. No.
> Q. Do you think it's Roland Arnall's fault?
> A. No.

If they hoped to get the inside scoop on what was going on at the highest levels of Roland Arnall's corporate enterprises, they'd have to find it elsewhere.

* * *

Ameriquest Mortgage took its last loan application on August 1, 2007. A month later, ACC Capital announced Ameriquest was shutting down. Roland Arnall's subprime empire had reached its end. Citigroup took control of Argent. It also took over the servicing rights to $45 billion in loans made by Ameriquest, collecting monthly fees for its work to ensure that borrowers continued to send in their checks and investors got repaid.

The remnants of what had once been the nation's biggest subprime lending operation were now part of the nation's largest banking conglomerate. Like Ameriquest, Citigroup had had its own misadventures with subprime lending, including its $200 million-plus settlement with the FTC. Now, with subprime in disarray, Citi was betting that the market would come back in six months to a year, and it wanted to be positioned as subprime's next vertically integrated powerhouse. "In a deteriorating market, it was obvious that this was a good time to exercise this option," a Citigroup executive said. "Production can't be this bad forever."

In the last three months of 2007, Citigroup put Argent's lending on hold. It would bide its time until the market rebounded. The bank renamed the wholesale lender Citi Residential and kept Argent's wholesale mortgage reps, such as Arnall veteran Terry Rouch, on staff, with the hope that the recovery wouldn't take long. "They were feeding us propaganda about how good it was going to be once they got it going," Rouch said.

Rouch came to work every day at Citi Residential's offices in Orange County. His bosses told him that even though he couldn't book any loans, he should continue making contacts with the mortgage brokers out in the field. It was a strange time. He traveled around to various brokerage shops. It was like visiting a ghost town. The mortgage crash had devastated the region's home-loan businesses, especially the small guys that had fed loans to the big boys. He'd show up at a broker's office and find it empty. An eviction notice would be taped to the entrance. He'd push on the door at some offices and find them abandoned but unlocked. Borrowers' files—filled with enough personal information to make an identify thief rich—would be stacked on desks and spilled across the floor. Rouch went to an auction of the equipment from one defunct loan shop that had funneled loans to Argent. He bought two filing cabinets and discovered they were filled with confidential loan applications. He took them to a shredding service to dispose of them.

Citi Residential's own offices became emptier and emptier. At Argent's once-bustling headquarters, Rouch found an entire floor nearly unoccupied, with fewer than a dozen people working in cubicles that had been pushed together into one corner. "Where did everybody go?" he thought, shaking his head. Citi Residential started funding loans again in early 2008, but it had become apparent that a market rebound was still a long way off. Word came down that the group was going to be folded into CitiMortgage. Soon after, Citigroup laid off more than four hundred employees who worked in its mortgage business in Orange County. Rouch was out of a job.

* * *

By 2008, Orange County had lost thousands of jobs in the local mortgage industry. In a county where lavish living was the norm, the collapse of the mortgage market produced aftershocks. Auto dealers that had specialized in selling Porsches and other luxury cars to the county's high-flying mortgage professionals saw their sales fall to almost nothing. Mortgage workers were instead trying to unload their cars on consignment.

When laid-off home-loan workers tried to find new careers, many had little luck. A business writer for the *Orange County Register* wondered whether there was backlash against them. "We all saw the mortgage stars of the last several years clogging O.C.'s freeways in their tricked out Escalades and other fancy vehicles. I always viewed that sort of capitalistic hubris as just part of the Orange County scenery," he wrote. "But is it possible that some folks here secretly harbored resentment of those guys and gals during their heyday years, and now are indulging in a little schadenfreude?"

Other communities in California were suffering, too. In Pacoima, a blue-collar suburb in the San Fernando Valley with a population that is 90 percent Hispanic, one in nine home owners fell into default on their mortgages. A local Catholic priest, the Reverend John Lasseigne, first learned how bad the problem was when a family approached him after mass and asked him to pray for them because they were about to lose their home. After talking to more people, he realized there were thousands of families in his community with similar stories. He began devoting much of his time to negotiating with banks and politicians on behalf of local home owners, and organizing them to speak for themselves. The struggling borrowers were mostly Mexican and Central American immigrants who didn't speak English well. They were enticed to take out subprime loans to buy what turned out to be overpriced homes. "We have to take stands in aiding the needy and denouncing the injustices of society," Father Lasseigne said. "The financial entrapment that was part of this was unbelievable."

Four of the ten metropolitan areas with the worst foreclosure rates, one government study found, were in California: Stockton, Sacramento, Riverside–San Bernardino, and Bakersfield. Outside the state the hardest-hit cities were Detroit, Cleveland, Memphis, Miami–Fort Lauderdale, Denver, and Las Vegas. Roland Arnall's companies were the kings of foreclosure in these mortgage disaster zones. Ameriquest and Argent accounted for nearly fifteen thousand foreclosures over three years, more than any other subprime lender in the ten metropolitan areas. They had a foreclosure rate of nearly 40 percent in Detroit and 33 percent in Denver. Another Orange County lender, New Century, ranked No. 2 on the list. Arnall's old company, Long Beach Mortgage, came in at No. 3. It had a foreclosure rate of more than 50 percent in Detroit and more than 40 percent in Sacramento. In all, five of the six lenders with the highest number of foreclosures were based in Orange County.

* * *

So many banks and lenders went under that one enterprising Web entrepreneur started a site, called Mortgage Lender Implode-O-Meter, that kept a running tally of the industry's casualties. By January 2008, more than two hundred lenders had, according to the site, "imploded"—halting operations, filing bankruptcy, or getting gobbled up in a "fire sale" purchase. The biggest to go was Angelo Mozilo's Countrywide Financial. With his company drowning in losses, Mozilo was forced to ask Bank of America CEO Ken Lewis to rescue Countrywide from failure. Bank of America purchased the lender, once worth as much as $26 billion, for $4 billion.

Mozilo's home-loan giant had been done in by a program of reckless and unsustainable lending. He should have known better. He called one of his own company's subprime products—which combined an 80 percent LTV first mortgage with a 20 percent LTV "piggyback" second mortgage—"the most dangerous product in existence." He had also called out Ameriquest and New Century as "irresponsible players." Yet Countrywide followed Ameriquest and New Century into subprime and, making matters worse, began pushing other unconventional loan products, such as Alt-A mortgages. "We got caught up in it," Mozilo said.

Though Mozilo's company had come late to the party, once it was there its size and clout deepened the pain that subprime visited upon home owners and the financial system. Countrywide did little to pull back on its subprime push, even in 2006, when there were signs of an impending crash. "You have to make a choice—to get out or not. And they stayed," a longtime mortgage industry watcher told the *Los Angeles*

Times. "It's hard when you're following someone off a cliff to know when to stop." Paul Muolo, the *National Mortgage News* editor who knew Mozilo well, said Countrywide might have survived if its founder hadn't become fixated on competing with Ameriquest. "If he hadn't followed Roland Arnall down the subprime path this would never have happened," Muolo said. "It's ego and ambition that sunk him."

* * *

As Countrywide and other institutions struggled, senior officials at Lehman Brothers pronounced their company safe and healthy. They said Lehman hadn't made the kinds of bad choices that had sunk other financial firms. After posting another record year in 2006, pulling in $4 billion, it eclipsed its own record in 2007, reporting nearly $4.2 billion in profits. "We believe we have done a good job in managing our risks," a top Lehman executive said. One analyst noted that, "for many investors, it is not necessarily about beating expectations but the lack of skeletons in the closet. . . . Lehman seems to have fewer skeletons." When a Lehman competitor, Bear Stearns, imploded in March 2008, Bear was saved via a takeover by JPMorgan Chase. The Federal Reserve made the deal possible by providing a $29 billion loan. Again Lehman officials assured investors and shareholders that their firm was in good shape.

Soon, though, it became clear that Lehman wasn't as secure as it claimed. In June 2008, the company admitted it was facing a quarterly loss of nearly $3 billion. More concerns about Lehman arose in September, when the federal government was forced to take over Freddie Mac and Fannie Mae, the two federally chartered mortgage giants. On September 9, word leaked that Lehman's efforts to raise capital from a government-owned bank in South Korea had fallen apart. Lehman's stock plummeted 45 percent. The next day, September 10, Lehman acknowledged it would post another quarterly loss, this one totaling $3.9 billion. Lehman chief Dick Fuld described the crisis as "an extraordinary time for our industry and one of the toughest in the firm's history." He said the bank would survive. "We have been through adversity before and always come out a lot stronger." Behind the scenes, according to the *Wall Street Journal*, Lehman officials were scrambling to raise money, even as they were publicly assuring investors that all was well and that the firm needed no new capital. The *Journal* said the contrast between the firm's public statements and its closed-door maneuvers raised questions "about whether it crossed the line into misleading clients and investors."

Over the weekend of September 13 and 14, U.S. Treasury and Federal Reserve officials met with Wall Street's biggest players. They tried to figure out a way to save Lehman. The hope was that they would find another company willing to buy the firm, in much the way JPMorgan had snapped up Bear Stearns. The difference was that, with Lehman, federal officials were not going to risk government funds to orchestrate such a deal. With the feds unwilling to put up taxpayer money, both Barclays and Bank of America decided to pass on a Lehman takeover. As midnight neared on Sunday, Fuld was still on the phone, trying to find someone to save his company. No one would take on the risk. At 12:30 A.M. Monday, Lehman issued a news release. The firm, it said, would file for bankruptcy protection when courts in New York City opened that morning.

That Monday, September 15, was a blur of panic and desperate measures. To try to quell fears that Lehman's demise would spark a global financial disaster, government officials around the world injected more than $100 billion in short-term credit into banks. Investors asked the terrifying question: "Who's next?" One of the most likely to fall, it seemed, was American International Group, the nation's largest insurer. On Tuesday, Bush administration officials put together an $85 billion bailout for AIG. Federal Reserve chairman Ben Bernanke and Treasury Secretary Hank Paulson asked Congress to okay the most substantial government intervention in the financial markets since the Great Depression. In one private meeting, according to the *Wall Street Journal*, Paulson told lawmakers, "If it doesn't pass, then heaven help us all."

The pain filtered far beyond Wall Street. Iceland's three largest banks failed. Yu Lia Chun, a retired hospital orderly in Hong Kong with a sixth-grade education, lost $155,000, her life savings. Her bank had risked it on complex investments tied to Lehman Brothers' bonds.

"There is no way a person like me could understand any of this," she said. "Sometimes I feel like jumping off a building."

Ten days after Lehman's bankruptcy, federal authorities seized Washington Mutual, the nation's largest S&L. It was the biggest banking failure in U.S. history. WaMu had immersed itself in risky lending through Roland Arnall's old company, Long Beach Mortgage. Federal regulators had said little as the S&L embarked on a path of abusive lending that placed its borrowers in danger in the short term and the institution in danger in the long term. Former employees said WaMu's executives brushed aside risk managers who warned them about the S&L's practices. "Everything was refocused on loan volume, loan volume, loan volume," a former senior risk manager told ABC News.

* * *

Lehman's crash put the financial crisis at the forefront of the 2008 battle for the White House. The mortgage meltdown was a ticklish subject for both Barack Obama and John McCain. Obama's national finance chair, billionaire Penny Pritzker, had once been chair of Superior Bank, an Illinois-based bank that had failed in 2001 as a result, government investigators concluded, of questionable accounting and bad subprime loans. Two of McCain's top campaign aides had billed more than $700,000 as lobbyists for Ameriquest, an embarrassing fact given the lender's scandalous reputation and McCain's pose as an enemy of the lobbying industry.

As the crisis grew, Obama and the Democrats pointed fingers at the mortgage industry, Wall Street, and the Bush administration's passion for deregulation. McCain and the Republicans blamed the Community Reinvestment Act, a three-decades-old law that requires banks and S&Ls to make efforts to serve all parts of their communities, including low- and middle-income neighborhoods. They also turned on Fannie Mae and Freddie Mac, which had bought mortgages and bundled them into securities as a way of encouraging home ownership. "One of the real catalysts, really the match that lit this fire, was Fannie Mae and Freddie Mac," McCain said during a debate in October 2008. "They're the ones that . . . went out and made all these risky loans, gave them to people that could never afford to pay back."

But the CRA hadn't forced lenders to make subprime mortgages, or to push stated-income loans or other risky products. A study by the *Orange County Register*, the daily newspaper most familiar with subprime lenders, found that nearly three of every four dollars in subprime loans made from 2004 to 2007 came from companies that weren't covered by the law. Even the American Bankers Association, no fan of the CRA, said it "just isn't credible" to blame the law for the mortgage meltdown.

And though Fannie and Freddie did buy risky mortgages and lobby against better regulation of the home-loan market, they were minor players compared to the investment banks on Wall Street. In fact, Fannie and Freddie had entered the subprime sector after the boom in risky mortgages had already been created by Ameriquest, New Century, and other lenders. The *New York Times* described a meeting that had taken place sometime in 2004 or 2005 between Angelo Mozilo and Fannie's chief executive, Daniel Mudd. Fannie bought large volumes of Countrywide's plain-vanilla loans. Mozilo wanted Fannie to buy its riskier mortgages, too. He knew Fannie had lost much of its market share to Wall Street firms that were clamoring for loans made with little documentation and exotic features that, in the short term, masked the loans' true costs. "You're becoming irrelevant," Mozilo told Mudd. "You need us more than we need you, and if you don't take these loans you'll find you'll lose much more." Then Mozilo offered everyone in the room a breath mint.

After Obama took office in 2009, his administration moved to find money to help struggling borrowers stay in their homes. The federal government had, by some estimates, already committed more than $12 trillion to prop up failing banks and other firms that had helped create the economic crisis. Obama proposed to spend a fraction of that—$75 billion—on direct aid to home owners. This prompted complaints from some quarters that the government was rewarding irresponsible borrowers who'd bought houses they couldn't afford. On CNBC, reporter Rick Santelli unleashed an on-air rant about taxpayers being forced "to subsidize the losers' mortgages. . . . This is America! How many of you people want to pay for your neighbors' mortgage that has an extra bathroom and can't pay their bills?"

For those who had investigated the abuses in the mortgage market, the blame-the-borrower slogans didn't ring true. In Washington State, Chuck Cross had gone after FAMCO, Household, and Ameriquest. He thought there was truth in the idea that American culture had gotten out of whack. Many people had bought into the idea that credit cards were a way of life and that everyone should own as much house as possible. But Cross thought most people tried to be responsible; they just got caught by sophisticated, well-heeled companies that had laid clever traps for them. People who had little experience in the world of mortgage financing—some had never taken out a mortgage before, and many hadn't had more than two or three in their lifetimes—were matched against legions of loan officers who'd put together dozens, even hundreds of home-loan deals. Most borrowers had little hope of fathoming loan products that were so complex that even CPAs and lawyers scratched their heads over them. The professionals knew the ins and outs, and borrowers were often at their mercy. As Cross liked to say: "Borrowers shouldn't be required to outsmart their loan officers to get a fair deal."

* * *

After he left Ameriquest, Mark Glover went a little crazy. He started taking painkillers after he had dental surgery. After years of recreational drug use, he descended into full-scale alcohol and drug addiction. He had come into some money, too, as a result of his settlement with Ameriquest. The windfall only made things worse; he started becoming a bit like Tony Montana, Al Pacino's out-of-control, cocaine-snorting character in *Scarface*. "I was all messed up," he recalled. He wanted to parlay his money into even more money. He invested $622,500 with a financial adviser who worked in L.A.'s Century City for Citigroup's Smith Barney brokerage unit. The adviser, Glover later claimed in a lawsuit, was well aware of his drug and alcohol problems, and took advantage of his impaired condition, even bringing him contracts to sign while he was in rehab. Within a year, he said, his $622,500 portfolio fell to less than $40,000.

What happened to Glover's money? His lawsuit claimed that the Smith Barney adviser had persuaded him to invest in what turned out to be a Ponzi scheme that preyed on both investors with lots of cash and "unsophisticated, racial minorities and elderly victims" who wanted to buy homes in Las Vegas. The fraudsters, his lawsuit said, lured wannabe home owners with come-ons such as, "Stormy credit history? Own today. Move in today. No bank qualifying. Only a $5,000 deposit." The promise of home ownership was a subterfuge, the suit said; the con artists used inflated appraisals to take out multiple mortgages on the properties and siphon money away for themselves. When the scheme collapsed, the lawsuit alleged, it also ruined investors like Glover, who thought they were going to get rich off of the rising real-estate market.

Another former Ameriquest loan officer, Christopher Warren, got mixed up in a similar scam. In Warren's case, authorities said he was not a victim but a perpetrator. Warren, who'd started out at age nineteen at Ameriquest and then founded his own mortgage company, WTL, eventually moved on to work for a company called Nationwide Lending Group. He took over as Nationwide's general manager and built up its lending, he said, by securing financial backing from Lehman Brothers, IndyMac, Citigroup, and other big names.

Nationwide and its sister companies ran an elaborate swindle, using five hundred houses and condos in California, Arizona, Nevada, Colorado, Illinois, and Florida as their cover. In court documents, an IRS criminal investigator described a multilayered scheme involving bogus investment seminars, life insurance policies, sham home purchases, high-priced subprime mortgages, kickbacks, and falsified loan paperwork. Losses to investors and lenders totaled as much as $100 million. Citigroup said it had $6 million caught up in the scam.

Warren cooperated with the IRS agents, admitting his own role and describing how a top executive constantly warned him that he'd be fired if he didn't meet quotas for loan volume. "Do what it takes," the executive said. For his assistance in the investigation, he earned a chance to receive leniency from the government.

Instead, he got a passport in a false name—"Mark Andrew Seagrave"—and paid $156,000 to charter a private jet to fly him to Ireland and, after refueling, on to Lebanon. An armed escort met him at the airport and accompanied him to a luxury resort. He spent five days there, fleeing just before authorities burst into his room. Law officers found photos of his children and his fake ID. He flew to Toronto and was arrested as he tried to return to the United States. He had $70,000 in cash stuffed in his shoe, plus $5,800 worth of platinum.

Warren's wild actions—first cooperating with the government, then running—might be best explained by his desire to style himself as Frank Abagnale, whose life as a fraudster turned fraud prevention expert was dramatized by Leonardo DiCaprio in the movie *Catch Me If You Can*. Warren posted a seven-page essay on the Internet telling his story. Because of "the disparity between the talent of the regulators and the fraudsters," he said, only young, "agile" con artists like him had the expertise to stop mortgage abuses. "I helped ruin this nation's economy," he wrote. "Almost a billion dollars of toxic assets came from me, making others above me rich beyond my imagination. They asked for more and more, knowingly, and I gave it to them."

✳ ✳ ✳

In early September 2009, a reporter from Reuters, the British wire service, tracked down Dick Fuld alongside a river in Idaho. It was little more than a week before the first anniversary of Lehman Brothers' bankruptcy. The reporter had come to Fuld's vacation home, set among tree-covered slopes in the Rocky Mountains, in the hopes of getting the former CEO to talk about what had happened. Fuld stood in his gravel driveway dressed in a black fleece vest, dark gray shorts, and sandals. The first words out of his mouth were: "You don't have a gun. That's good." Fuld felt he had been slandered and mistreated by reporters, politicians, and others looking to blame someone for the economy's collapse. "You know what? The anniversary's coming up," Fuld told the reporter. "I've been pummeled, I've been dumped on, and it's all going to happen again. . . . They're looking for someone to dump on right now, and that's me." He said he wanted to tell his side of the story, but he didn't think much good would come of it. The next day, as he was catching a flight at the airport in Salt Lake City, Fuld continued his discourse. "I'm not a defeatist," he said. "I do believe at the end of the day that the good guys do win. I do believe that."

Back east, Fuld had started his own consulting firm, working out of an office on Third Avenue in Manhattan. Reuters said Fuld commuted three or four times a week from his mansion in Greenwich, Connecticut. "He's keeping a low profile but doing a lot of power lunches," one investment banker told Reuters. "He's keeping in touch with friends on Wall Street." By the fall of 2009, three grand juries had subpoenaed Fuld to testify. He had also been named in nearly forty lawsuits. Municipal governments and pension funds had accused him of securities fraud, blaming him for putting out misleading statements that encouraged them to make bad investments in Lehman's stock and bonds. In California, the San Mateo County Investment Pool claimed that the activities of Fuld and other top Lehman executives represented "the worst example of fraud committed by modern-day robber barons of Wall Street, who targeted public entities to finance their risky practices and then paid themselves hundreds of millions of dollars in compensation while their companies deteriorated."

As the legal assaults grew, Fuld and his wife, Kathy, tried to downsize their lives, in a manner of speaking. Kathy sold at least sixteen drawings by artists such as Arshile Gorky and Barnett Newman, netting some $13.5 million. The couple sold their Park Avenue apartment for more than $25 million. They hung on to four other homes: the house in Idaho, the Greenwich mansion, a house in Vermont, and a seaside mansion in Jupiter Island, Florida, that Fuld had "transferred" to Kathy for $100, raising questions about whether he was trying to put assets out of the reach of private plaintiffs and government officials. Reuters quoted a "source close to the couple" who said Kathy was no longer making shopping pilgrimages to Hermès and other New York luxury-goods stores, where in the past she had been spotted buying handbags, shawls, and other items that cost thousands of dollars each. "It could be that they're pulling back the spending," the source said. "Or it could be that she doesn't want to be seen spending, so she could be having someone else do the shopping for her."

* * *

As the financial crisis unfolded, the reputation of Alan Greenspan took a beating. The man once hailed as an icon was accused, by members of

Congress and the media, of doctrinaire mulishness that helped put millions of home owners at risk. One congressman compared him to Bill Buckner, the first baseman who let a ground ball go through his legs and cost the Boston Red Sox the 1986 World Series. "In the end," one commentator asked, "was he anything more than just a political operative and sideman?"

Greenspan defended himself in a number of forums. He went on *60 Minutes*. He published a memoir, *The Age of Turbulence: Adventures in a New World*. He said he couldn't have done anything to prevent the financial crisis, which he described as a "once-in-a-century credit tsunami." "I have said to many questions of this nature that I have no regrets on any of the Federal Reserve policies that we initiated back then, because I think they were very professionally done." He said there wasn't much he could have done about the fraud going on in the home lending market, despite the Fed's authority to regulate mortgages and financial institutions. "While I was aware a lot of these practices were going on, I had no notion of how significant they had become until very late. I really didn't get it until very late in 2005 and 2006," he said. The Fed took no action even when it became aware of the problems, he said, because "it's very difficult for banking regulators to deal with that."

Before a U.S. House committee, he admitted that he had been mistaken in presuming the self-interest of banks and other companies was all that was needed to protect their shareholders from disaster. Representative Henry Waxman, a California Democrat, was especially tough on the former Fed chairman.

> Waxman: The question I have for you is, you had an ideology, you had a belief that free, competitive—and this is your statement—"I do have an ideology. My judgment is that free, competitive markets are by far the unrivaled way to organize economies. We've tried regulation. None meaningfully worked." That was your quote. You had the authority to prevent irresponsible lending practices that led to the subprime mortgage crisis. You were advised to do so by many others. And now our whole economy is paying its

price. Do you feel that your ideology pushed you to make decisions that you wish you had not made?

Greenspan: Well, remember that what an ideology is, is a conceptual framework with the way people deal with reality. Everyone has one. You have to — to exist, you need an ideology. The question is whether it is accurate or not. And what I'm saying to you is, yes, I found a flaw. I don't know how significant or permanent it is, but I've been very distressed by that fact.

Waxman: You found a flaw in the reality—

Greenspan: Flaw in the model that I perceived is the critical functioning structure that defines how the world works, so to speak.

Waxman: In other words, you found that your view of the world, your ideology, was not right, it was not working?

Greenspan: That is—precisely. No, that's precisely the reason I was shocked, because I had been going for forty years or more with very considerable evidence that it was working exceptionally well.

Epilogue: Ashes

The boy from the village in France lived well in his later years. Roland Arnall became a billionaire by styling himself and his companies as advocates for home ownership. As his wealth grew, so did his own collection of homes. In 2002, he and Dawn spent more than $30 million on a ten-acre compound tucked between Sunset Boulevard and the Los Angeles Country Club in the Holmby Hills section of Los Angeles, not far from the Playboy Mansion. The estate included three houses that once were homes to the Hollywood elite. The largest was a forty-room, 12,000-square-foot mansion. Twentieth Century–Fox founder Joseph M. Schenck owned it in the 1950s. Schenck had allowed a young starlet-in-waiting, Marilyn Monroe, to live in his guest cottage. Tony Curtis owned the place in the early 1960s before giving way to Sonny and Cher, who owned it in the late '60s and '70s as their careers blossomed and their marriage disintegrated. Another house on the property was known as the Pink Palace. In the 1930s it had been home to song crooner Rudy Vallee, one of America's first pop stars. After Jayne Mansfield and her bodybuilder husband bought the place in the late '50s, she had the house and any other available surface painted soft pink and installed a heart-shaped bathtub and a fountain that burbled with pink champagne. The house eventually passed to singer Engelbert Humperdinck, who kept it until real-estate operatives packaged it into the deal that transferred the ten acres of Hollywood history to the Arnalls.

Months after the big purchase, motorists on Sunset Boulevard noticed that the Pink Palace had disappeared. The Arnalls had bull-dozed the Hollywood landmark into "pink rubble," as the *New York Post* put it.

Little more than a year later, the Arnalls added to their holdings by shelling out $46 million to buy Aspen's Mandalay Ranch from Holly-wood kingpin Peter Guber, the producer of *Flashdance* and *Batman*. At the time, it was the biggest home purchase ever in Colorado's Glitter Gulch, and one of the biggest in American history. The 650-acre spread was on a back road between Snowmass and Buttermilk ski areas. It included a 15,000-square-foot mansion and a 3,500-square-foot guesthouse with caretaker's quarters and two cabins. The deal sig-naled the beginning of an unprecedented boom in Aspen's high-end real-estate market. After the Arnalls bought Mandalay Ranch, "the market went nuts," one real-estate agent told the *Wall Street Journal*.

The Arnalls' homes became stopping-off points for the rich and powerful. Attendees at the couple's holiday soiree at the Holmby Hills estate in December 2004 included a who's who of California's top Democrats and Republicans. Among them were Gray Davis and his wife, Sharon, as well as the couple that had replaced them in the gov-ernor's mansion, Arnold Schwarzenegger and Maria Shriver. They also included California's attorney general, Bill Lockyer, a Democrat who, before his office joined the multistate investigation of Ameri-quest, enjoyed $250,000 in campaign support from Arnall and his companies.

✳ ✳ ✳

Gary Ozenne lived in less rarefied circumstances during the great mortgage boom. For one stretch of several months, his home was Room 301 at the Arizona Motel in Corona, California.

He had refinanced with Ameriquest in 1998, "at the beginning," he said, "of this gathering storm of loan securitization." He had been one of the early casualties, he thought, a guinea pig in the social experi-ment that Wall Street and the subprime industry had unleashed on America.

He had been in dire circumstances before he took out the loan, but the company's bait-and-switch tactics and nosebleed interest rates had ensured that he wouldn't be able to recover. He lost his four-bedroom house on Crestview Street. Roland Arnall's company had dumped the loan before Ozenne could challenge the way the lender had treated him. The mortgage had passed from Ameriquest to Lehman Brothers to Chase Manhattan, which in turn relied on yet another company, Ocwen, to act as the loan's servicer. Ocwen collected Ozenne's payments and, after he couldn't keep up, foreclosed on the home where he'd lived half his life.

He had to drive fifty miles to find a lawyer to file suit for him against Ameriquest and Chase. A judge threw out his lawsuit. He appealed. In arguing the case in the higher court, Ameriquest was represented by Roland Arnall's nephew and right-hand man, Adam Bass, who doubled as an attorney at Buchalter Nemer, a top corporate law firm that defended the company against borrowers' claims. The Fourth District California Court of Appeals upheld the judge's ruling against Ozenne on technical grounds. It said he hadn't raised his claims about Ameriquest's deceits soon enough and had failed to note them in the later bankruptcy petitions he'd filed to try and save his home.

Unable to keep paying his attorney, he became his own lawyer as he petitioned various judges, pleading for a day in court in which he would be allowed to lay out his claims against the big financial firms. On Presidents' Day 2003, Riverside County sheriff's deputies evicted him from his home. Over the next few years, he lived in at least seven different rented rooms in five different cities. His house on Crestview sat unoccupied. "I picked up the trash from my front lawn of my vacant home today," he wrote in a first-person, stream-of-consciousness pleading he filed in Riverside County Superior Court. "The lawn is over ten inches long." His "liquid assets" dwindled below $100. To make ends meet, he began spending his collection of Sacagawea $1 coins.

He could have given up. But he fought on. "No one is above the law," he wrote in another court document. "Bankers and their agents, like everyone else, are accountable to the law; our system demands it."

Weary of bouncing from place to place, Ozenne settled into a one-room apartment at the back of his nephew's home in Corona. His older brother, Dennis, had lived there until his death. Gary felt alone, a sixty-year-old man sleeping in his dead brother's room, fighting a legal battle he had little chance of winning. How could he keep going? "I listen to Winston Churchill's speeches," he said. "I drink too much. And I don't want these people to get away with this." Some nights he dreamed about the case. His unconscious mind churned over the words he'd written, trying to rephrase his story in a way that would persuade a judge to see simple justice and return his home to him.

✳   ✳   ✳

By 2007, Gary Ozenne had some company among the litigants asking judges to solve their problems. Roland Arnall had gone to court. This time he was not a defendant but a plaintiff. In a case filed in federal court in Tulsa, Oklahoma, Arnall claimed he'd been the victim of a multibillion-dollar scam. His lawyers bandied terms that were similar to ones that had been thrown at Arnall and his enterprises over decades of litigation: Breach of contract. Misrepresentation. Fraud. Arnall claimed he'd invested billions in oil and gas exploration and that he'd been ill-treated by a business partner who was savvier than he was about the industry.

It all started, Roland and Dawn Arnall said, in early 2002, when they met a man named Bippy Siegal. They were at a ski race in Sun Valley, Idaho. Bippy had torn his ACL and was hobbling around the lodge on crutches. Roland, Dawn said, felt sorry for him, and the couple went over and struck up a conversation. As they talked, Bippy mentioned that his father, Richard Siegal, was in oil and gas. He had a number of wealthy investors, the son said, and his ventures made a lot of money for them.

Roland had been a street peddler, a real-estate developer, an S&L operator, and the owner of subprime mortgage companies. Why not a Texas-style oilman? Richard Siegal told them, the Arnalls claimed, that he had a track record of providing his investors a $3.50 to $4 return on every dollar invested, and that the deal could be structured to allow them to take a $2 deduction for "intangible drilling costs" for every dollar put into the venture. The Arnalls were intrigued. With their subprime empire producing billions, the idea of putting their money to work, and getting a huge tax deduction in the bargain, was appealing.

Siegal came up with the name for the venture: RoDa Drilling Company, for Roland and Dawn. It was all done on a handshake. The key documents were left unsigned. "That was my husband," Dawn testified. "He did a lot of transactions on a handshake deal. He had visceral reactions to people and trusted them and proceeded to have business associations with them." By early 2005, Dawn said, they had plowed roughly $1 billion into the enterprise. She became concerned that they had yet to see much return on their investment. Even worse, the IRS had initiated an audit of RoDa's tax returns for 2003 and 2004. The IRS, she said, was threatening to disallow the Arnalls' "intangible drilling cost" deduction, suggesting they might have to pay as much as half a billion dollars in taxes, penalties, and interest. That, she claimed, would mean that she and her husband had lost no less than $1.5 billion on their investment.

Roland and Dawn Arnall sued Richard Siegal in July 2007. Siegal countersued, demanding that the Arnalls resume making the payments on hundreds of millions of dollars in promissory notes crucial to the structuring of the deal and the tax deductions. Siegal said Roland Arnall had never been promised any particular return; indeed, it was ludicrous to think anyone would guarantee results in a venture as speculative as drilling for oil and gas. The deal fell apart, Siegal said, only because Roland had quit paying his obligations. Roland, in other words, had refused to pay on his loans because he felt he had been a victim of fraud. Many Ameriquest borrowers had sued to try to renounce their mortgages on exactly those grounds.

* * *

Arnall resigned as ambassador to the Netherlands in early 2008. His family said he needed to come home to help care for his grown son, Daniel, who had been diagnosed with Hodgkin's disease. He returned to the United States and, on March 10, found himself in an Oklahoma courtroom. He was scheduled to testify during pretrial proceedings in the oil lawsuit. He never made it to the witness stand. He appeared noticeably ill from the first day, and seemed to get worse as the proceedings dragged on. At the end of the second day, Arnall's doctor advised him to return to Los Angeles and check into the hospital. The next day he was diagnosed with esophageal cancer. It had metastasized. Death was imminent. His lawyers asked the judge for permission to schedule an immediate deposition, from his hospital bed if necessary. The judge ordered that his testimony be taken on March 21.

He died March 17, 2008. He was sixty-eight years old. The obituaries and remembrances that followed noted his companies' legal problems. They also devoted space to the other side of his life story, recalling him as a generous benefactor to animal shelters and as a founder, in the '70s, of the Simon Wiesenthal Center for Holocaust remembrance. "One of the good guys died today," Jon Daurio, a former Arnall aide, said. Governor Schwarzenegger called Arnall "a wonderful and inspirational friend." Terry Rouch, who had worked for Arnall at Long Beach and Argent, attended the memorial service. To Rouch it felt almost like a political rally, with big-name officials dotting the crowd. He spotted Los Angeles mayor Antonio Villaraigosa, Gray Davis, and Schwarzenegger.

Seventeen months later, the Arnalls' lawsuit against Richard Siegal came to an end. In August 2009, on the eve of trial, the two sides cut a deal. The exact terms were secret. The parties noted that, under their agreement, Siegal would have to obey the judge's order that he transfer title to the oil and gas properties in question to the Roland and Dawn Arnall Trust. Roland Arnall, in death, had won at least a partial victory.

The late subprime mogul's legacy continued to be a matter of dispute, however, in other courts. His younger brother, Claude, filed court papers claiming that Roland and Dawn had stiffed him out of a fortune. The claim involved Olympus Mortgage, a wholesale mortgage lender the two brothers had founded in 2002. Each brother owned half of the company, according to Claude. In 2004, Roland asked Claude to sell him his half of Olympus. Roland, Claude said, offered him roughly $75 million to buy out his shares in the company. Over the next fifteen months, he received close to $30 million in payments from his brother. After that, he said, Roland began putting him off, coming up with excuses for not paying him the rest of what he owed. After Roland's death, Claude claimed, Dawn repudiated the agreement, telling him: "You have nothing in writing."

Claude demanded $47.6 million from Roland's estate. Dawn's lawyers said there were no facts to support the idea that there had been any "secret verbal agreement." It was unreasonable, they argued, to believe that Claude and Roland had entered into such a business deal "without a single document being created." It was an argument that seemed at odds with Dawn's testimony, in the oil case, that Roland had often put together big deals based only on a handshake.

In federal court in Chicago, the multidistrict litigation against Ameriquest and Argent neared its end. In early 2010, borrowers began receiving letters notifying them that the two sides had reached a tentative settlement. ACC Capital had agreed to dispose of twenty-nine class-action cases by coughing up $21 million to be distributed among the plaintiffs' attorneys and several hundred thousand customers. The average payout to borrowers was expected to be perhaps $100 each. Because Ameriquest and its sister companies had quickly offloaded its loans to Wall Street investors, and the profits were transferred into Roland Arnall's personal accounts, ACC Capital had few assets left over by the time the lenders closed shop. "Unfortunately, there isn't much left for borrowers," Ben Diehl, an assistant attorney general in California who had worked on the states' investigation of Ameriquest, told the *Los Angeles Times*.

As with the states' $325 million settlement, the agreement to resolve the private class actions didn't include any admission of wrongdoing. Roland Arnall's family members and business associates were consistent in maintaining that his lenders hadn't engaged in systematic fraud. During the oil lawsuit, Siegal's lawyers, unable to question Roland, pressed Dawn with questions about her service on the board of ACC Capital. They wanted to show that her husband's record for fair dealing and honest business practices was far from unblemished.

> Q. Did you learn about certain sales practices in your company?
> A. My understanding . . . is that the settlement included no admittance of guilt.

Q. But nonetheless, you voted to pay $325 million?

A. We had to.

Q. You say we had to. Why?

A. Because the attorney generals, if we hadn't paid it, would have suspended our licenses, and we couldn't have continued to operate in those states.

Q. As you sit here now, do you believe there was any conduct within Ameriquest which would have been what we call improper or unlawful sales practices?

A. There were some employees—as a matter of fact, we brought in the FBI ourselves to prosecute those employees.

Q. Were there ever any findings or determinations by the board made where you were present that it was the general business practices of Ameriquest which was being attacked as opposed to just particular rogue employees?

A. We agreed that it was not general business practice. It was rogue employees.

Q. How many rogue employees?

A. I can't answer that. I'm sorry.

* * *

In 2009, ACORN founder Wade Rathke published a book on community activism, *Citizen Wealth: Winning the Campaign to Save Working Families.* He devoted a passage to his organization's settlement nearly a decade before with Ameriquest. Rathke said the July 2000 agreement had ensured "fairer, more transparent lending operations" at the lender. While other companies, such as Household, had fought ACORN's efforts to clean up subprime, Rathke wrote, "Ameriquest benefited by being an early responder in this campaign, quickly realizing that it was smarter—and much cheaper—to settle and deal with the problems rather than endure a protracted war in public, in the courts, and in the marketplace." Rathke seemed unaware of the record of fraud and exploitation that had continued at Ameriquest. The company hadn't dealt with its problems as a result of its deal with ACORN. It hadn't become fairer and more transparent. The settlement with ACORN had helped the company wriggle free from an

FTC investigation and move forward with a seal of approval from one of the nation's biggest activist organizations. Ameriquest had used the deal as cover that allowed it to grow bigger and more predatory.

While some were laboring to rewrite the history of subprime's rise and fall, others were trying to put its lessons to work, or at least trying to put the ordeal behind them. For many, moving on wasn't easy.

Mark Glover, the former Ameriquest loan officer in Los Angeles, continued to pursue his legal claim against Citigroup and Smith Barney. He started a business that allowed struggling home owners to make money by renting out their homes as movie and TV film locations. He drafted a memoir of addiction and struggle. He began running marathons and became an advocate of long-distance running as a way to fight addiction.

Travis Paules, who rose from branch manager to vice president in his seven years at Ameriquest, wrote an autobiographical novel. Its main character is named "Trevor Palmer." He gave the book a working title of *Ameriquest: The Crack in the Liberty Bell*, then changed it to *Whiteout*, an allusion to the company's tradition of altering and fabricating borrowers' paperwork. After a decade of carousing and "wickedness," he said, he experienced a transformation. Not long after he left Ameriquest, he was sitting in a hotel room in Virginia. It was around midnight. He felt a presence in the room. Almost an electrical force. "God came down and conked me on the head," Paules recalled. "I had a vision of Jesus standing behind me for some reason." He went online and looked up the Ten Commandments. "I found I'd broken them all," he joked. He had broken some of them, anyway. After being lost for so many years, he said, he had found a new path. His second manuscript, *180*, is a memoir of that journey.

Carolyn Warren, who worked as a loan officer for Long Beach Mortgage and Ameriquest in the '90s, became so fed up with the slippery tactics that pervaded her industry that she, too, wrote a book, *Mortgage Rip-Offs and Money Savers*. She wanted to reveal some of the industry's secrets and arm consumers with information. The response from readers was so strong that she decided to start a consulting business. Now, mortgage shoppers can solicit her advice at www.askcarolynwarren.com. She reviews loan disclosures from various lenders, flagging junk fees that applicants should demand that their lenders delete. She's determined to root out fees that sound important (and even seem to hint at romantic bliss) but are in fact meaningless, such as "commitment fees" and "satisfaction fees." In 2009, she published a second book, *Homebuyers Beware: Who's Ripping You Off Now?*

Bob Ney, the Ohio Republican who had been the mortgage industry's go-to guy in Congress, resigned from the House of Representatives and was sentenced to thirty months in prison in the Jack Abramoff influence-peddling scandal. Another player in the subprime saga who spent time behind bars was Dickie Scruggs, the Mississippi plaintiffs' attorney who had jetted out to Orange County to take on FAMCO and Lehman. Four years after the big trial at the Reagan Courthouse, federal authorities charged him with trying to bribe a judge in Mississippi to influence how legal fees would be split in an insurance case. Scruggs was sentenced to seven years in prison.

Sheila Canavan, the lawyer who steered the attack on FAMCO and Lehman, continued working to defend home owners. She helped win a settlement in a case against Bank of America's former subprime unit. She also continued working on the Lehman Brothers case as it moved through the appeals process. The U.S. Ninth Circuit Court of Appeals upheld the jury's conclusion that Lehman had aided FAMCO's fraud. "Lehman admits that it knowingly provided 'significant assistance' to First Alliance's *business*, but distinguishes that from providing substantial assistance to *fraud*," the judges wrote. "In a situation where a company's whole business is built like a house of cards on a fraudulent enterprise, this is a distinction without a difference." The appeals panel ordered the trial judge, however, to recalculate the $5.1 million award. The two sides agreed to avoid a return to court. They were putting the final touches on a $3.5 million settlement when Lehman filed for bankruptcy in September 2008. The beneficiaries of the settlement took their place in line among Lehman's other creditors.

Prentiss Cox, the assistant attorney general in Minnesota who led the states' investigation of Ameriquest, took a job teaching law at the University of Minnesota. He drafted the Minnesota Subprime Borrower Relief Act, which would have allowed struggling borrowers to delay foreclosure sales for a year. Republican governor Tim Pawlenty vetoed the bill. Cox testified before Congress in favor of a new federal Consumer Financial Protection Agency, telling a House committee that predatory lending had been a disaster before it was a crisis—it had harmed millions of Americans long before it was recognized as the primary cause of the nation's financial meltdown.

Chuck Cross, the banking regulator who believed in hitting mortgage wrongdoers between the eyes, left Washington State for Washington, D.C. He took a job at the Conference of State Bank Supervisors, an association of state financial regulators. As he gave speeches around the country, he warned regulators to keep an eye out for dominant personalities—figures like FAMCO's Brian Chisick, Countrywide's Angelo Mozilo, or Ameriquest's Roland Arnall. When someone builds an empire from scratch, Cross thought, they begin to feel accountable to no one. They think they can get away with anything.

Brian Chisick looked back in anger, at Chuck Cross and at others who had brought FAMCO down. Cross, he said, was "a real villain"—a bureaucrat who joined a gang of class-action attorneys on a witch hunt against his company. Somehow, in their minds, he said, combining salesmanship and mortgages was deceptive and predatory. "The legal system, in a word, sucks," Chisick said. "We've got a terrible system going here. I wish I could phrase that in a nicer way." He was in his seventies, and he'd been out of the mortgage business for almost a decade. He had watched from the sidelines as Ameriquest and other lenders spun out of control and destroyed the subprime market. "Wall Street made so much money available and everyone was making so much money," he said, "they just threw all of underwriting criteria out the window and went for the numbers."

Roy Barnes, the Georgia governor who fought to hold Wall Street accountable for abusive lending, spent six months doing free legal work after he was voted out of office in 2003. He volunteered with Atlanta Legal Aid's Home Defense Program, working with Bill Brennan, the dean of home ownership protection attorneys in America. Barnes represented several Ameriquest borrowers, helping them save their homes. By the start of 2010, Barnes was preparing to try to recapture the governorship. Surveying the federal government's response to the financial crisis, he saw little real reform. "We're rebuilding the same system rather than trying to make changes," he said. The way he saw it, the only way to end the scourge of "dirty paper" in the mortgage market was to have tough "assignee liability" rules that forced everyone in the process to act responsibly. Bankers, he said, should be required to ask themselves: "Do I really want to make this loan? Because I may have to eat it."

Carolyn Pittman, the Ameriquest borrower in Atlantic Beach, Florida, continued to fight to hang on to her home. She prayed every day. "I'd like to keep it if I can," she told a newspaper reporter in 2007. "I thought I would live here the rest of my life. What little life I have left." Fearing the worst, she had many of her things in boxes, stacked in her dining room. Even as the company's Wall Street confederate, Deutsche Bank, pursued a foreclosure action against her, Ameriquest's sales machine continued to crank out mailings offering her yet another loan. The letters came twice a month. Boldface type proclaimed: Slash Your Monthly Payments.

Like Pittman, many of the borrowers in the loan pool that held her mortgage were struggling to stay afloat. Of the roughly three thousand loans that remained in her pool in the summer of 2009, 28 percent of the borrowers were delinquent, in bankruptcy, facing foreclosure, or had already had their homes repossessed.

Greg Walling did his best to put his time as a loan officer for FAMCO behind him. He once again worked in auto sales, as a used-car manager at a dealership in Minnesota's Twin Cities. He was glad, he said, to have a job that didn't require him to lie and manipulate the way he'd been taught at FAMCO. He had a fantasy, though, of winning the lottery and retiring, then devoting his time to giving lectures to schoolchildren on how to be smart consumers and protect themselves from rip-offs. He knew a thing or two about the subject.

He kept two boxes of documents from the FAMCO case stacked on a shelf in a downstairs closet in his home. One winter day—he thinks it was in 2005—he pulled the boxes off the shelf. It had been seven years since he had left FAMCO, and two years since he'd returned to Orange County and testified in the case against Lehman Brothers. He opened the boxes and read through the affidavits, the transcripts, and other documents. He thought: "I'm done. I never have to look at these things again." He felt lucky that he'd been shamed into doing the right thing. He'd been given a chance to play a part in exposing "The Monster" and all the other devices and deceptions that had fueled the rise of FAMCO and the rest of the subprime mortgage machine. He carried the boxes into the backyard to his fire pit. Snow and ice crunched under his boots. He started a fire and, one by one, dropped the documents into the flames. He made sure everything was burned to ash.

Notes

Introduction

PAGE

1. *Mark Glover looked up from his cubicle*: This account is based on a series of interviews with Mark Glover, as well as an interview with a confidential source, a former coworker, who confirmed many of the details provided by Glover. Some details came from Glover's lawsuit against the company, *Glover v. Ameriquest*, Orange County Superior Court, 2004, as well as Los Angeles Superior Court records, which document Glover's check-fraud case. (After Glover successfully completed probation, the case was dismissed and his record was expunged.) Also helpful was *Tamar Williams v. Ameriquest*, Orange County Superior Court, 2004. Williams, a coworker of Glover, alleged in her lawsuit that Ameriquest "forged income and asset documents, altered title reports, filed falsified grant deeds, fabricated and falsified credit histories, and sold non-beneficial loans." Williams, who worked as a loan processor, claimed loan files were taken away from her because she refused to falsify documents, and that a supervisor directed her to shred falsified paperwork to keep "dirty" loans from being turned up in an audit. When she complained, Williams said, the company fired her rather than investigate her allegations. More generally, Williams's and Glover's accounts of misbehavior at the company are remarkably similar to accounts provided in my interviews with dozens of former Ameriquest workers spread across the nation.

2. *Close to midnight Pacific time*: Interview with Wendell Raphael, a vice president who often made the calls.

2. *"He would just try to make you stretch"*: Interview with Travis Paules.

3. *"Every closing"*: The loan officer, Omar Khan, was quoted in a video produced by Angie Moreschi, a former TV journalist, for the Consumer Warning Network, an online site created by lawyers who represent borrowers suing Ameriquest and other subprime lenders. Consumer Warning Network, *Ameriquest: Anatomy of the Mortgage Meltdown*, Dec. 24, 2008.

3. *They buried the real documents*: This fixed-rate decoy was described to me by Travis Paules in an interview. See also Chris Arnold, "Former Ameriquest Workers Tell of Deception," *Morning Edition*, National Public Radio, May 14, 2007, in which a former Ameriquest employee from Florida, Tyson Russum, said: "Maybe the first couple of documents they saw in their package were fixed rate, and then they would slip in the adjustable rate docs at the end and then trash the fixed-rate docs."

4. *Carolyn Pittman*: Interviews with Carolyn Pittman and her attorney, Lynn Drysdale of Jacksonville Area Legal Aid. See also Caren Burmeister, "Beaches Woman Caught a Foreclosure Cycle," *Florida Times-Union*, Sept. 22, 2007; and "Defendant's Motion to Strike Count I, Answer, Amended Affirmative Defenses, Amended Counterclaims and Demand for Jury Trial," *Deutsche Bank v. Pittman*, Duval County (Fla.) Circuit Court, 2005.

6. *Ameriquest Mortgage Securities, Inc. Mortgage Pass-Through Certificates 2004-R7*: Details on this deal come from documents filed with the U.S. Securities and Exchange Commission, including the "Prospectus Supplement" dated June 30, 2004. UBS, J. P. Morgan, and Citigroup served as "Joint Lead Managers" and "Joint Book Runners," meaning they structured the deal and took the lead in peddling the resulting mortgage-backed securities to investors. Barclays Capital, BNP Paribas, and Deutsche Bank served as "Co-Managers"; they didn't take part in the "securitization" process but were allocated a portion of the securities to sell to their clients. Details on investors in the deal came from Bloomberg and *Mutual Fund Prospectus Express*.

7. *"We are all here to make as much fucking money"*: Quoted in testimony of Minnesota attorney general Lori Swanson before the Federal Reserve Board of Governors, "Regarding Predatory Mortgage Lending and Use of the Board's Authority Under the Home Ownership and Equity Protection Act of 1994 (HOEPA) to Curb Abusive Mortgage Lending," July 14, 2007.

7. *"It was like college"*: Interview with Travis Paules.

8. *At the branch where Mark Bomchill worked*: Interview with Mark Bomchill, who worked as a loan officer at Ameriquest from September 2002 to September 2003, as well as "Declaration of Mark Bomchill" in *Ricci v. Ameriquest*, U.S. District Court for Minnesota, 2005. In interviews, three others who worked in Bomchill's branch confirmed his version of how the office operated. See also Mike Hudson and E. Scott Reckard, "Workers Say Lender Ran 'Boiler Rooms,'" *Los Angeles Times*, Feb. 4, 2005.

8. *"People entrusting their entire home"*: Interview with a confidential source. When I interviewed this former loan officer in 2005, it was on the condition that his name not be used. He said the time working at Ameriquest was so disturbing that he didn't want to be publicly associated with the company.

9. *"The atmosphere was like this giant cocaine party"*: Interview with Sylvia Vega-Sutfin.

9. *"All roads lead to Lehman"*: Greg Griffin, "Risky Mortgages," *Denver Post*, Nov. 11, 2008.

10. *"the leading edge of a financial hurricane"*: Bernard Connolly, "Sub-prime Crisis Is the Edge of a Financial Hurricane," *Telegraph* (London), Aug. 20, 2007.

10. *"Lehman never saw a subprime lender"*: Interview with Sheila Canavan.

11. *"Roland could be the biggest bastard"*: Interview with a confidential source, a former Long Beach executive.

11. *"Roland was one of the most generous"*: A former business partner of Arnall, Jack Slomovic, quoted in "Roland Arnall, Philanthropist and Ameriquest Founder, Dies at 68," *Jewish Journal*, Mar. 20, 2008.

11. *"a trail of bodies"*. Interview with Bob Labrador, a banking executive who worked for Arnall in the 1980s and '90s.

11. *"I was screwed"*: Interview with Ray Mallel, a longtime friend of Arnall and a former top executive at Ameriquest

11. *"a good man"*: Interview with Mark Schuerman, a former executive at Long Beach Savings.

12. *"Keep your enemies close"*: Interview with Frank Curry, a former Long Beach Bank executive and Arnall confidant.

1. Godfather

13. *The regulators pushed Arnall to diversify*: Interview with Bob Labrador, former Long Beach Savings executive.

13. *"He hated the regulators"*: Ibid.

14. *"How soon can we get"*: This quote, as well as Mark Schuerman's account of his time working with Arnall, come from a series of interviews with Schuerman, a former Long Beach Savings executive.

16. *Arnall's parents and early history*: Ron Korver, "'Sometimes You Have to Make a Fist': U.S. Ambassador Roland Arnall Thinks Europe Talks Too Much," *De Telegraaf*, April 21, 2007; "Roland Arnall, Envoy for Bush and the U.S.," *Het Parool*, April 21, 2007. See also Arnall's official biography on the Web site of U.S. Diplomatic Mission to the Netherlands, "Ambassador Roland E. Arnall"; Arnall's speech to Rotary Club members in Dordrecht, "The Future of the U.S. as a Nation of Immigrants," May 31, 2007; and Stephen Miller, "Subprime Pioneer Turned to Diplomacy, Philanthropy," *Wall Street Journal*, Mar. 22, 2008.

16. *One story had Roland becoming an altar boy*: Miller, "Subprime Pioneer"; and interview with Frank Curry, former Long Beach Bank executive and Arnall confidant.

16. *"The next day I had my first major fight"*: "Roland Arnall, Envoy for Bush and the U.S."

16. *"My father returned"*: Korver, "'Sometimes You Have to Make a Fist.'"

16. *peddling flowers on street corners*: Arnall's biography at the U.S. Diplomatic Mission to the Netherlands.

16. *Arnall used the profits*: These passages draw heavily from E. Scott Reckard, "Ambassador Nominee's Company Is Scrutinized," *Los Angeles Times*, Aug. 7, 2005, the only true profile that has ever been written of Arnall, who did his best to keep his name and image out of the media after his missteps in the '60s.

17. *In the decades to come, Snyder*: Various news articles, including Bill Boyarsky, "Councilman Art Snyder Quits in Surprise Move," *Los Angeles Times*, Jan. 3, 1985; Rick Orlov, "Art Snyder's Conviction Upheld," *Los Angeles Daily News*, Feb. 25, 2000; Maura Dolan, "Justices' Ruling May Send Snyder to Jail," *Los Angeles Times*, Feb. 25, 2000.

17. *Arnall-Snyder land deal*: Los Angeles Times articles, including "Lincoln Heights Land Sale Gets Tentative OK," *Los Angeles Times*, Nov. 5, 1968; "Developer Explains Delinquency in Land Bid Payment," Mar. 13, 1969; "Snyder Asks Refund to Developer in Land Deal," Sept. 16, 1969; and "Council Upholds Controversial Land Sale," Oct. 2, 1969.

18. *"Real-estate development is a function"*: Martin Mayer, *Nightmare on Wall Street: Salomon Brothers and the Corruption of the Marketplace* (New York: Simon & Schuster, 1993), p. 163.

18. *"If there's money available"*: Interview with a confidential source, a former Long Beach Savings executive.

18. *For a time, Arnall teamed with Beverly Hills Bancorp*: Ibid.

18. *In 1974, the bank filed for bankruptcy*: "Bancorp on Coast Accused by S.E.C.," *New York Times*, Aug. 14, 1974; and *In the Matter of Beverly Hills Bancorp*, 649 F.2d 1329 (9th Circuit, 1981).

18. *One friend who provided last-ditch loans*: Interview with Ray Mallel, former Long Beach and Ameriquest executive.

19. *If S&Ls didn't have to pay high rates*: Much of the discussion of the S&L crisis is drawn from Stephen Pizzo, Mary Fricker, and Paul Muolo, *Inside Job: The Looting of America's Savings and Loans* (New York: McGraw-Hill, 1989); and Kathleen Day, *S&L Hell: The People and the Politics Behind the $1 Trillion Savings and Loan Scandal* (New York: W. W. Norton, 1993).

19. *"we hit the jackpot"*: Ronald Reagan, "Remarks on Signing the Garn–St. Germain Depository Institutions Act of 1982," Oct. 15, 1982.

20. *The new breed of S&L proprietors*: Pizzo, Fricker, and Muolo, *Inside Job*, p. 13.

20. *A car-wash operator shocked*: Interview with Bob Labrador.

20. *masquerading as an S&L*: This turn of phrase comes from Bob Labrador.

20. *Arnall and his staff agonized*: Interview with Bob Labrador, as well as with a confidential source.

21. *"It wasn't done in a very overt way"*: Interviews with Tom Tarter and Bob Labrador. Real-estate developer Bob Champion, who partnered with Arnall on strip-mall projects in the late 1980s, says he never experienced problems with Arnall.

21. *"intentional fraud"*: Romano v. Victory Square Ltd., filed Aug. 24, 1984, Los Angeles Superior Court.

21. *the case was settled on confidential terms*: In an e-mail correspondence, Kenneth Bley, the plaintiffs' attorney, said a check of his firm's files indicated the case had been dismissed after the parties settled. He said he couldn't disclose the terms.

22. *"Don't sit on your equity"*: These examples are taken from Louise Story, "Home Equity Frenzy Was a Bank Ad Come True," *New York Times*, Aug. 15, 2008, which includes an excellent compilation of advertisements urging home owners to borrow against their houses. See http://www.nytimes.com/interactive/2008/07/20/business/20debt-trap.html#.

22. *"Calling it a 'second mortgage'"*: Pei-Yuan Cha, a former vice president of Citicorp who ran the bank's consumer business in the 1980s, was quoted in Story, "Home Equity Frenzy."

23. *Hard-money and consumer-finance companies in the 1980s*: Some observers lump

consumer-finance companies into the term "hard-money lending." I prefer to make a distinction, defining hard-money lenders as those that focused purely on mortgages and charged the highest rates, often in the 20/20 range. Consumer-finance operations' rates were a bit lower, and their business models were different enough, that it's useful to distinguish between these strains of lending. Interviews with Kathleen Keest, a staff attorney at the Center for Responsible Lending and a former assistant attorney general in Iowa, and with Mark Schuerman. See also Robert J. Hobbs, Kathleen Keest, and Ian DeWall, "Consumer Problems with Home Equity Loans, Second Mortgages, and Home Equity Lines of Credit," National Consumer Law Center, July 1989; Kathleen Keest, "Second Mortgage Lending: Abuses and Regulation," National Consumer Law Center, Dec. 1991.

23. *"Miss Cash says 'Yes'"*: The definitive work on Landbank is Greg Raver-Lampman, "The Great White Loan Shark," *Regardie's Magazine,* Apr. 1991. See also coverage in the *Washington Post* and *Virginian-Pilot,* as well as Mike Hudson, "Little Relief for Consumers," *Roanoke Times,* Dec. 12, 1994.

24. *"Borrowers at finance companies"*: Quoted in Walt Bogdavich, "After Deregulation: Critics Charge Lenders Exploit Most Vulnerable," *Wall Street Journal,* Apr. 8, 1985.

24. *class-action settlements and Lennie Williams's case*: Larry Lopez, "Widow Battles Lending Giant for Home," Associated Press, Mar. 19, 1990; and Larry Lopez, "Transamerica Gives Up Fight for Widow's Home," Associated Press, Mar. 22, 1990. Transamerica said it had done nothing wrong. After a spate of bad publicity, it settled the case, allowing Williams to stay in her home.

25. *"To me, it's fun and challenging"*: Carla Lazzareschi, "Getting Ahead: Exploring Paths to Promotion," *Los Angeles Times,* Sept. 17, 1989.

27. *Mortgage-backed securities had first emerged*: Michael Lewis, *Liar's Poker* (New York: W. W. Norton & Company, 1989); Kurt Eggert, "The Great Collapse: How Securitization Caused the Subprime Meltdown," *Connecticut Law Review,* vol. 41, no. 4, 2009; and the testimony of Christopher L. Peterson in "Subprime Mortgage Market Turmoil: Examining the Role of Securitization," a hearing before the U.S. Senate Committee on Banking, Housing, and Urban Affairs, Subcommittee on Securities, Insurance, and Investment, Apr. 17, 2007.

2. Golden State

29. *Guardian Savings and the Jedinaks*: Interviews with Jude Lopez, a former Guardian executive, and with James Gartland, a mortgage broker who worked with the Jedinaks over the years. This discussion also draws upon extensive coverage in the *Orange County Register* and *Los Angeles Times.* Paul Muolo and Mathew Padilla, *Chain of Blame: How Wall Street Caused the Mortgage and Credit Crisis* (Hoboken, N.J.: John Wiley & Sons, 2008), pp. 61–63, includes much useful background on the Jedinaks, including the "frat boy" quote.

30. *"You're going to end up with forty REO"*: Interview with Jude Lopez.

30. *"if the owner has a pulse"*: Elliot Blair Smith and Jonathan Lansner, "Fortune Turns for Guardian Savings," *Orange County Register,* Jan. 13, 1991.

34. *"cowboy capitalists"*: See Lisa McGirr, *Suburban Warriors: The Origins of the New*

American Right (Princeton, N.J.: Princeton University Press, 2001), pp. 28–30, 37–38, and 52.

35. *history of North America Savings*: Stephen Pizzo, Mary Fricker, and Paul Muolo, *Inside Job: The Looting of America's Savings and Loans* (New York: McGraw-Hill, 1989), pp. 22 and 335, as well as copious accounts filed by the *Orange County Register*, *Los Angeles Times*, Associated Press, and other outlets.

36. *"full burn"*: Much of the description of boiler-room culture draws upon the definitive work, Robert J. Stevenson, *The Boiler Room and Other Telephone Sales Scams* (Urbana: University of Illinois Press, 1998).

36. *Orange County as a white-collar and S&L crime capital*: This discussion is drawn from numerous articles in the *Orange County Register*, *Los Angeles Times*, and other publications. See, for example, Henry N. Pontell and Kitty Calavita, "Orange County: Thrift Fraud Capital of the United States," *Journal of Orange County Studies* 5–6 (Fall 1990–Spring 1991); Andre Mouchard, "Criminal Culture," *Orange County Register*, Mar. 29, 2002 (a Q&A with Henry Pontell); and Jane Applegate, "Fraud Agents Seize Records in 5 Raids in Metals Cases," *Los Angeles Times*, Apr. 17, 1987. Especially helpful was Marc Beauchamp, "Côte De Fraud," *Forbes*, Nov. 2, 1987, which documents Orange County's rise as the boiler-room capital of the United States.

36. *"at a pace of just under one"*: Jonathan Lansner, "Shame: OC a White-Collar Crime Hotbed," *Orange County Register*, Dec. 30, 1990.

37. *"I've worked cases where the lender"*: Beauchamp, "Côte De Fraud."

37. *"Con men hate snow"*: Hal Lancaster, "Beware!—The Fraud Farm: In Newport Beach, Calif., Scam Artists Find a Place in the Sun," *Wall Street Journal*, Oct. 20, 1989.

37. *"a modern-day version of the California gold rush"*: McGirr, *Suburban Warriors*, p. 28.

38. *"Many of these people got too much"*: Beauchamp, "Côte De Fraud."

39. *front companies they controlled*: In addition to passages in *Inside Job* and coverage in the *Orange County Register* and the *Los Angeles Times*, two articles are especially rich in details about Christensen and McKinzie's frauds and their lifestyles: Kathleen Sharp, "The Dentist and the Junk Blonde," *San Francisco Chronicle*, June 30, 1991, and Richard W. Stevenson, "Untangling a Savings Failure," *New York Times*, June 30, 1988.

40. *During a congressional hearing*: Ricardo Sandoval, "Attack Launched on Fraud in OC," *Orange County Register*, July 27, 1990; Larry Liebert, "Probe of S&L Corruption Stepped Up," *San Francisco Chronicle*, Dec. 8, 1989.

40. *In Orange County alone*: Details of the S&L debacle in Orange County and beyond are drawn from *Orange County Register*, especially "S&Ls and the '80s: A Few Tales of Those Times," *Orange County Register*, Apr. 11, 1999; Jonathan Lansner and Ann Imse, "'This Is an Epidemic': Criminal Probes Creep Forward," *Orange County Register*, Nov. 8, 1987; Jonathan Lansner, "Report Blames Thrift Failures on Misconduct," *Orange County Register*, Oct. 20, 1988; Jonathan Lansner, "Actions on Irvine-Based Institutions Precipitated Troubles," *Orange County Register*, Dec. 5, 1989. Also helpful were Martin Mayer, *The Greatest-Ever Bank Robbery* (New York: C. Scribner's Sons, 1990); Pizzo, Fricker, and Muolo, *Inside Job*; and Kathleen Day, *S&L Hell: The People and the Politics Behind the $1 Trillion Savings and Loan Scandal* (New York: W. W. Norton & Co., 1993).

41. *Charles Keating and Lincoln Savings*: *Orange County Register* coverage, including Elliot Blair Smith, "Keating Ran S&L with Iron Hand, Ex-VP Says," *Orange County Register*, Sept. 19, 1991. Also invaluable were Pizzo, Fricker, and Muolo, *Inside Job*; Day, *S&L Hell*; L. J. Davis, "Will Charlie Keating Ride Again?" *Washington Monthly*, Mar. 1997; Richard W. Stevenson, "Independent Auditor Criticizes Lincoln Savings and Loan," *New York Times*, Aug. 4, 1989; Michael Binstein and Charles Bowden, *Trust Me: Charles Keating and the Missing Billions* (New York: Random House, 1993); L. William Seidman, *Full Faith and Credit: The Great S&L Debacle and Other Washington Sagas* (New York: Times Books, 1993).

41. *"captive" S&Ls*: William K. Black, *The Best Way to Rob a Bank Is to Own One: How Corporate Executives Looted the S&L Industry* (Austin: University of Texas Press, 2005), pp. 81, 255, 265, and 289–90, and George A. Akerloff and Paul M. Romer, "Looting: The Economic Underworld of Bankruptcy for Profit," *Brookings Papers on Economic Activity*, vol. 1993, no. 2, pp. 53–56. Akerloff and Romer provide lengthy excerpts of the FDIC's lawsuit against Milken, which alleged that Milken and his co-conspirators "cultivated a group of persons who controlled S&Ls" and were willing to "follow the bidding of the Milken Group." Milken, the FDIC alleged, used his "[r]eady, repeated, easy access" to the enormous pool of capital provided by the S&Ls' depositors as part of a scheme to create the illusion of heavy demand for Drexel-sponsored junk bonds and thus artificially inflate their values. Milken denied wrongdoing, attributing the government's allegations to "blame-it-all-on-Milken scapegoating." Milken, other former Drexel employees, and Drexel's insurance company later settled the FDIC lawsuit as part of a $1.3 billion global settlement that extinguished civil claims in the junk-bond scandal. Milken paid $900 million of the settlement.

41. *"sucking the blood"*: Benjamin J. Stein, *A License to Steal: The Untold Story of Michael Milken and the Conspiracy to Bilk the Nation* (New York: Simon & Schuster, 1992), pp. 97–109.

41. *"Auditors found the S&L"*: Stevenson, "Independent Auditor Criticizes."

42. *"the weak, meek and ignorant are always good targets"*: Many of the details of Lincoln's high-pressure salesmanship come from James Bates, "Bond-Sale Rallies: It Was Showtime," *Los Angeles Times*, Nov. 3, 1990. I am indebted to Associated Press reporter Scott McCartney's fine coverage, including "Lincoln Savings Memo: The Week, Meek and Ignorant Are Good Targets," Associated Press, Sept. 8, 1990; and "Elderly Victims of S&L Debacle Struggle to Pay Bills, Survive," Associated Press, Oct. 10, 1989. Other sources include "Former Lincoln Investor Commits Suicide," Associated Press, Nov. 28, 1990; Michael Connelly, "Victim of S&L Loss Kills Self," *Los Angeles Times*, Nov. 29, 1990; Jim Tranquada, "S&L Failure Took Emotional Toll," *Los Angeles Daily News*, Dec. 2, 1990; Michael Lev, "California Accuses Lincoln of Misleading Bond Buyers," *New York Times*, Mar. 3, 1990. In the *New York Times*, an attorney for Keating maintained: "The bond salesmen were scrupulous in advising people that these were subordinated debentures and were not insured by the federal government. There always may be a small group who honestly felt they were misled, but as to the vast majority I think it's a case of conveniently selective memory."

43. *"it is precisely the 'greed'"*: Quoted in Jonathan Weil, "Greenspan's '63 Essay Foretold Subprime Inaction," Bloomberg News, Dec. 19, 2007.

43. *As Keating's hired gun*: Mayer, *Greatest-Ever Bank Robbery*, pp. 140 and 324–26.

44. *"When I first met the people from Lincoln"*: Nathaniel C. Nash, "Greenspan's Lincoln Savings Regret," *New York Times*, Nov. 20, 1989.

44. *Greenspan had advised that S&Ls*: In explaining his views on so-called direct investments in big commercial deals for S&Ls, Greenspan told the *New York Times* in 1989: "If you give me two institutions, one that has a mix of short-term direct investments and long-term mortgages properly capitalized, or the same financing structure but invested only in long-term mortgages, I would say the first institution may well be safer."

45. *"He may have seen himself in Milken"*: Interview with Bob Labrador. Labrador told me he was grateful for Arnall's restraint in resisting the temptation to gamble Long Beach's future on Milken's junk. "Thank goodness he never let me do it," Labrador said. Columbia Savings, like other thrifts within Milken's orbit, failed. The government seized Columbia in 1991 at a cost to taxpayers of more than $1 billion.

3. Purge

46. *In the summer of 1990, Greenwich Capital*: John Gittelsohn, "How Subprime Lending All Started in O.C.," *Orange County Register*, Dec. 30, 2007.

46. *"It was a significant transitional moment"*: Interview with Bob Labrador.

46. *He eventually stopped driving*: Another account said Arnall hired the chauffeur to drive and maintain his car after he forgot to put oil in his Porsche and burned out the engine.

47. *"He was demanding"*: Interview with Frank Curry, a former Long Beach executive.

48. *"He was an idol worshipper"*: Interview with Ray Mallel.

48. *Long Beach fudged its books*: Interview with a confidential source.

48. *"What we're seeing is people"*: Allegations of questionable practices at Guardian were reported in the *Los Angeles Times* and the *Orange County Register*. See especially Elliot Blair Smith, "S&L Loan Practices Criticized," *Orange County Register*, Feb. 13, 1991; and Elliot Blair Smith, "S&Ls, Easy Lending Terms Hid Credit Exploitation, Regulators Say," *Orange County Register*, Nov. 29, 1992. See also *In the Matter of Russell M. Jedinak*, Before the Office of Thrift Supervision, Dec. 8, 1995, Order No. SF-95-023, and *In the Matter of Rebecca Manley Jedinak*, Before the Office of Thrift Supervision, Dec. 8, 1995, Order No. SF-95-024.

48. *delinquency rates of 23 to 51 percent*: Mary McGarity, "Hot Product or Hot Potato?" *Mortgage Banking*, Oct. 1, 1994. In early 1994 Standard & Poor's downgraded Guardian's credit ratings on a series of securities backed by six-month adjustable-rate mortgages made by the S&L from 1988 to 1991. S&P said its experience with Guardian prompted it to rethink its criteria on subprime mortgages. "We're trying to put in place some type of extra protection to prevent what happened with Guardian from happening again," an S&P executive said.

49. *"He's a high-powered salesman"*: Quoted in Elliot Blair Smith, "Regulators Seize Guardian," *Orange County Register*, June 22, 1991.

51. *"something that really wasn't broken"*: Interview with Jeanne Powers, a former Long Beach employee.
51. *"control thing"*: Interview with Mark Schuerman.
52. *He'd crossed out*: Paul Muolo and Mathew Padilla, *Chain of Blame: How Wall Street Caused the Mortgage and Credit Crisis* (Hoboken, N.J.: John Wiley & Sons, 2008), p. 63. Details of Quality's start-up phase come from *Chain of Blame* as well as from interviews with two executives who worked for the Jedinaks at Quality.
53. *"the first subprime/Wall Street joint venture"*: Frank J. Fabozzi, ed., and Robert Paul Molay, *Subprime Consumer Lending* (New Hope, Pa.: Frank J. Fabozzi Associates, 1999), p. 166.
54. *lion on a leash and the million-dollar pile of cash*: Interviews with Jude Lopez and James Gartland. Gartland worked as an outside broker feeding loans to Quality and later became an in-house branch manager for the company.
54. *"Anything aggressive"*: Interview with Adam Levine, a loan officer at Long Beach in the early 1990s.
55. *"signs of initiative and loyalty"*: Muolo and Padilla, *Chain of Blame*, p. 64.
55. *$2 million a year in lawyers' fees*: Interview with Jude Lopez. Lopez said that when the Jedinaks finally sold Quality Mortgage in 1996, the company still had more than thirty consumer lawsuits pending
55. *The lawsuits claimed Quality socked*: See, for example, *Ward v. Quality*, U.S. District Court for Northern District of California, 1995, which claimed Quality and mortgage brokers that fed it customers "failed to make proper disclosures under federal and state law . . . charged improper fees, made loans which failed to provide benefits allegedly promised, and made misrepresentations about the loans." This class action was settled in 1998. Quality and the brokers denied wrongdoing.
55. *"corrupted hundreds of small mortgage brokers"*: *Willis v. Quality*, U.S. District Court for the Middle District of Alabama, 1994.
55. *"manipulation and deception"*: See Hawaii Intermediate Court of Appeals' July 31, 2002, ruling in *Ocwen v. Russell*, on appeal from the Third Circuit Court of Hawaii.
56. *Fleet Finance*: I reported extensively on the company's practices in the early 1990s. See Michael Hudson, "Loan Scams," *APF Reporter*, a publication of the Alicia Patterson Foundation, 15:2, 1992; and Michael Hudson, "Stealing Home," *Washington Monthly*, June 1992. Much of my investigation built on the fine coverage of Fleet in the *Boston Globe*, including Peter S. Canellos and Gary Chafetz, "In 2 Regions, Fleet Under Fire for Buying High-Interest Loans," *Boston Globe*, May 22, 1991; and Peter S. Canellos, "Profitable Fleet Finance's Ethics Questioned," *Boston Globe*, June 9, 1991. The *Atlanta Journal-Constitution* also did excellent reporting on Fleet, including Jill Vejnoska, "Loan Trap," *Atlanta Journal-Constitution*, Oct. 11, 1992, which told Lillie Mae Starr's story in rich detail.
58. *"It's like finding a ten-dollar bill"*: This passage draws on many interviews with Brennan and those who know him as well as Tammy Joyner, "People in Business: Up Close/William J. Brennan Jr.," *Atlanta Constitution*, Jan. 22, 2008. A former colleague, Hugh O'Donnell, described Brennan's continual shock over injustice, in a letter dated May 10, 1993, nominating Brennan for an award from the state bar of Georgia.

60. *Brennan, Rothbloom, and Barnes used the power*: Interviews with Howard Rothbloom, Roy Barnes, and Barnes's aide Chris Carpenter, as well as news articles in
   the *Atlanta Journal-Constitution*; Robert Berner and Brian Grow, "They Warned Us
   About the Mortgage Crisis," *BusinessWeek*, Oct. 9, 2008; and CBS News, "A Matter
   of Interest" (transcript), *60 Minutes*, Nov. 15, 1992.
60. *Curry had to fire*: Interview with Frank Curry.
61. *One of the consumer-finance transplants*: Interviews with Terry Rouch, a loan officer
   at Long Beach from 1992 to 1995.
63. *"People taking shortcuts"*: Interview with Wendell Raphael, a manager in the mortgage unit at Long Beach in the 1990s.
64. *late-night loan closings*: In a 1993 lawsuit, a couple claimed a Long Beach salesman
   tricked them into signing an unfair mortgage by arranging the loan closing "at a
   dimly lit restaurant, late at night." See *Kellogg v. Long Beach Bank*, Riverside County
   (Calif.) Superior Court, Sept. 13, 1993.
64. *Even back in the mid-'90s*: Adam Levine, who worked at Long Beach during the
   same period as Rouch, doesn't recall seeing anyone forging borrowers' signatures.
   But he said it was common for workers to use bogus data when they drew up "profit
   and loss" statements analyzing borrowers' monthly income and spending.
66. *They worried that Long Beach*: See October 9, 1992, "Supervisory Agreement"
   between Long Beach and the Office of Thrift Supervision.
66. *"I'm done"*: Interview with Bob Labrador.
69. *When another aide left*: See Alyssa Katz, *Our Lot: How Real Estate Came to Own Us*
   (New York: Bloomsbury USA, 2009), pp. 54–63, as well as *Long Beach Mortgage Co.
   v. Manuel Palazzo*, Orange County Superior Court, 1996.
70. *Russ and Becky admitted no wrongdoing*: I tried to contact the Jedinaks through
   their former attorney as well as through Jude Lopez, their former aide at Guardian
   and Quality. Neither the attorney nor Lopez knew how to reach the couple. Lopez
   said he hadn't been in touch with Russ for several years; he'd heard that Russ might
   be living in the Caribbean. To get the Jedinaks' side of the story, I relied on Russ
   Jedinak's statements in news articles as well as interviews with Lopez, who defended
   the couple's business practices as reasonable and aboveboard.
70. *a 44 percent ownership stake*: Edmund Sanders, "BNC Mortgage Plans Stock Sale to
   Public," *Orange County Register*, Oct. 25, 1997.

4. Kill the Enemy

71. *"You can securitize virtually everything"*: Suzanne Woolley with Stan Crock, "'You
   Can Securitize Virtually Everything,'" *BusinessWeek*, July 20, 1992.
71. *"When everybody wants to securitize"*: Suzanne Woolley, "What's Next, Securitized
   Bridge Tolls?" *BusinessWeek*, Sept. 2, 1996.
72. *"one of the best Southern patriots"*: This history of Lehman Brothers from its founding through the 1980s is indebted to Ken Auletta, *Greed and Glory on Wall Street:
   The Fall of the House of Lehman* (New York: Random House, 1986).
73. *"narrowly focused pipsqueak"*: Andy Serwer, "Improbable Power Broker." *Fortune*,
   Apr. 17, 2006.

73. *The architect of Lehman's comeback*: Steve Fishman, "Burning Down His House," *New York Magazine*, Nov. 30, 2008, is a rich source of background on Dick Fuld.

73. *"bristling class resentment"*: Fishman, "Burning Down His House."

74. *"The major corporate names which Lehman Brothers desires"*: Auletta, *Greed and Glory*, p. 43.

75. *"He was extremely outgoing"*: Jeffrey Cohan and Jonathan D. Silver, "A Coal Town's Boom Turns to Bust," *Pittsburgh Post-Gazette*, Oct. 20, 1999.

76. *"Keystone knew nothing"*. This account draws heavily on the work of Bill Archer of the *Bluefield* (W.Va.) *Daily Telegraph* and Lawrence Messina of the *Charleston* (W.Va.) *Gazette*, as well as coverage by the Associated Press and the *American Banker*. See also John R. Engen, "The Collapse of Keystone," *Bank Director Magazine*, 2nd quarter 2001; Jeffrey Cohan and Jonathan D. Silver, "A Coal Town's Boom Turns to Bust"; Terence O'Hara, "Big Bank Scandal Unearthed in Tiny W.Va. Town," *Washington Post*, Oct. 19, 1999; Thomas Fields-Meyer and Susan Gray, "Dashed Hopes: A Devastating Bank Failure Leaves a Shocked Little Town to Pick Up the Pieces," *People*, 52 (21), Nov. 29, 1999; Timothy Roche, "Poor Town, Rich Bank," *Time*, Nov. 1, 1999. Useful government documents include Office of Inspector General, U.S. Department of Treasury, "Material Loss Review of the First National Bank of Keystone," OIG-00-067, Mar. 10, 2000; filings in various Keystone-related civil and criminal cases in the U.S. District Court for the Southern District of West Virginia, including *FDIC v. Mitchell et al.*, *Coast Partners et al. v. FDIC*, and *Grant Thornton LLP v. FDIC*; and the Fourth Circuit U.S. Court of Appeals' Oct. 25, 2007, ruling in *FDIC v. Sean Bakkebo et al.*

77. *"I thought the place sucked"*: Eric Hibbert's reaction to FAMCO is based on his March 11, 2003, testimony in *Austin et al. v. Chisick et al.*, U.S. District Court for the Central District of California, 2001.

77. *Brian Chisick was an immigrant*: Interviews with Brian Chisick as well as his 2001 testimony in *FTC v. First Alliance*, U.S. District Court for the Central District of California, 2000.

78. *"professional problem solver:"* Brian Tracy, *The 100 Absolutely Unbreakable Laws of Business Success* (San Francisco: Berrett-Koehler Publishers, Inc., 2002), pp. 191 and 202.

79. *In October 1987, Myrtle and Elmer Rogers*: Chris Woodyard, "Couple to Get $1 Million for Loan Damages," *Los Angeles Times*, Oct. 16, 1987.

79. *"We did nothing wrong"*: Interview with Brian Chisick.

80. *"In many cases, the victims do not even know"*: The state's investigation was covered in the *Los Angeles Times* and *Orange County Register*. See especially Al Delugach, "State Suit Alleges Mortgage Firm 'Redlined' Blacks," *Los Angeles Times*, Aug. 11, 1988; Al Delugach, "Ruling Postponed on Orange Loan Broker Accused by State of Racial Discrimination," *Los Angeles Times*, Aug. 12, 1988; Dan Weikel, "OC Lender Charged with Discrimination in Black Neighborhoods," *Orange County Register*, Aug. 11, 1988; United Press International, "Discrimination Denied by Lender," *The Record*, Aug. 14, 1988; and Jonathan Weber, "First Alliance Agrees to Pay $436,000 to Settle Bias Suit," *Los Angeles Times*, Oct. 6, 1989.

80. *"stage a Pearl Harbor attack"*: United Press International, "Discrimination Denied by Lender."

81. *Robert N. Kwong's battle with FAMCO*: Interview with Robert Kwong, a former staff attorney with the California Department of Corporations.

81. *"It was really insulting"*: Interview with Brian Chisick.

81. *John Dewey and FAMCO's early securitizations*: Interview with John Dewey, a former FAMCO executive.

82. *"I wouldn't give him the time of day"*: Interview with Brian Chisick.

84. Dunning *case and Robert Goldstein's allegations*: Both *Dunning v. First Alliance*, 1989, and *Goldstein v. McPhillips et al.*, 1994, which contained Goldstein's harassment and assault claims, were filed in Alameda County (Calif.) Superior Court.

85. *"It is a sweat shop"*: The quotations come from Eric Hibbert's undated four-page memo, "Review of First Alliance Mortgage Company," which was based on his July 25–26, 1995, visit to FAMCO's headquarters in Orange, California.

85. *"very capable and well informed"*: Undated memorandum from Lehman Brothers executives Martin Harding, Kurt Locher, and Stan Labanowski to the firm's Investment Banking Mortgage Securities Commitment Committee.

85. *"Lehman Brothers would enthusiastically welcome"*: Letter from Martin P. Harding, a Lehman Brothers managing director, to Mark Mason, chief financial officer of First Alliance Mortgage Co., Nov. 29, 1995.

85. *"Yeah, we had a beauty show"*: Testimony of Brian Chisick in *FTC v. First Alliance*.

5. The Big Spin

87. *Bill Clinton's attorney general, Janet Reno*: Interview with Alexander Ross, a lawyer in the U.S. Justice Department's Civil Rights Division during the Clinton administration. "Janet Reno was wonderful in this regard," Ross said. "There was no doubt in anybody's mind that she wanted these cases pushed."

88. *What, Arnall asked*: Ibid.

88. *The Justice Department's statistical analysis*: Complaint and settlement agreement in *USA v. Long Beach Mortgage Company*, U.S. District Court for the Central District of California, 1996.

88. *"When you've got an elderly black woman"*: Interview with Alexander Ross.

89. *salespeople's expectations about their customers*: See, for example, Ian Ayers, "Fair Driving: Gender and Race Discrimination in Retail Car Negotiations," *Harvard Law Review* 104(817) (1991). This study used paired testers who fit middle-class profiles and employed a uniform bargaining strategy. The testers visited ninety car dealers in the Chicago area and found salespeople's final offers favored white male customers by a large margin; the markups on sticker prices were 40 percent higher for white women, double for black men, and triple for black women.

89. *Betty Lacey*: Kathy Lynn Gray, "Woman Fell Prey to Lending Ploy," *Columbus Dispatch*, June 24, 2000.

91. *Long Beach had other allies*: Jaret Seiberg, "Regulators Asked to Spell Out Liability in the Event of Bias Violations by Mortgage Brokers," *American Banker*, July 11, 1996; Jaret Seiberg, "Settlement of Bias Case Against Calif. Lender Criticized for Vagueness," *American Banker*, Sept. 16, 1996; "Justice Delays Move on Lending Bias

Case," *Mortgage Marketplace*, July 8, 1996; Tim W. Ferguson, "Lender Beware (Home Loan Quotas)," *Forbes*, Dec. 2, 1996; and Kenneth Harney, "Minorities, Women, Elderly Often Pay More," *Chicago Sun-Times*, Sept. 13, 1996.

91. *"If you listened to Bill Clinton"*: Ferguson, "Lender Beware (Home Loan Quotas)."

92. *the investigation was led by Deval Patrick*: Patrick's biography is based on Scott Helman, "Beating Odds, a Uniter Rose from Chicago's Tough Side," *Boston Globe*, May 24, 2006.

93. *an extensive lineup of buck passers*. See Kurt Eggert, "Held Up In Due Course: Predatory Lending, Securitization, and the Holder in Due Course Doctrine," *Creighton Law Review* 35(503) (2002).

93. *Some industry insiders grumbled*: Heather Timmons, "Calif. Bias Settlement Brings Sighs of Relief from Industry," *American Banker*, Sept. 11, 1996; Seiberg, "Settlement of Bias Against Calif. Lender"; and "Fair Lending Settlement Does Not Affect Overages," *National Mortgage News*, Sept. 16, 1996.

93. *The leaders of these groups said Arnall impressed*: Those leaders were Ricardo Byrd of the National Association of Neighborhoods, Shanna Smith of the National Fair Housing Alliance, and Wade Henderson of the Leadership Conference on Civil Rights.

93. *Arnall renewed his support*: Mike Hudson, "Ameriquest's Ties to Watchdog Groups Are Tested," *Los Angeles Times*, May 22, 2005. In 2004, for example, Ameriquest gave a total of some $800,000 to seven watchdog groups, including $250,000 to the Leadership Conference on Civil Rights.

94. *"We sat around my conference table"*. Jonathan Peterson, "Ameriquest Exec Has Unexpected Backers," *Los Angeles Times*, Nov. 21, 2005. See also Tory Newmyer, "Arnall Secures Outside Help," *Roll Call*, Dec. 5, 2005.

94. *Arnall would suggest that Long Beach had won*: Paul Muolo and Mathew Padilla, *Chain of Blame: How Wall Street Caused the Mortgage and Credit Crisis* (Hoboken, N.J.: John Wiley & Sons, 2008), pp. 73–74. According to Muolo and Padilla, Countrywide Financial CEO Angelo R. Mozilo met with Arnall sometime in the early 2000s, with Mozilo coming away from the meeting believing Long Beach had come under the feds' scrutiny because of a single freelance mortgage broker. "He eventually won the case," Mozilo said.

95. *His timing was a bit off*: Barnaby Feder, "A Risky Business Gets Even Riskier," *New York Times*, Feb. 12, 1997; and Heather Timmons's coverage in *American Banker*, including "Winners and Losers from the Subprime Crunch," Feb. 21, 1997, and "Calif. Lender Plans IPO, But Timing Could Be Problem," Apr. 17, 1997.

95. *"the walking dead"*: See Aaron Elstein, "9 Subprime Lenders for Sale, May Die," *American Banker*, May 1, 1997; Heather Timmons, "Once Burnt, Big Investors Now Twice as Cautious About Finance Companies," *American Banker*, June 20, 1997, and Aaron Elstein, "The Cocaine Addiction of Our Industry," *American Banker*, July 1, 1997.

95. *"Even if you get sick"*: Documents in *In Re: Marriage of Arnall*, Los Angeles Superior Court, filed in 1996 and reopened in 2005. Much of this passage is drawn from Sally Arnall's account of the divorce negotiations, detailed in "Declaration of Miriam Sally Arnall," June 15, 2005. Also helpful was E. Scott Reckard's reporting in the *Los Angeles Times*, including "Ex-Wife of Loan Exec Asks for Probe," Aug. 22, 2005, and "Loan Exec Loses Ruling to Ex-Wife," Aug. 25, 2005.

96. *"in a shade of gold":* For this and other biographical details, see the profile of Angelo Mozilo in Gretchen Morgenson and Geraldine Fabrikant, "Countrywide's Chief Salesman and Defender," *New York Times*, Nov. 11, 2007.

97. *Carolyn Warren:* Interview with Carolyn Warren, a Long Beach/Ameriquest loan officer in the 1990s, as well her book, *Mortgage Rip-Offs and Money Savers: An Industry Insider Explains How to Save Thousands on Your Mortgage or Re-finance* (Hoboken, N.J.: John Wiley & Sons, 2007).

6. The Track

101. *Greg Walling:* Interviews with Greg Walling, a former loan officer for First Alliance Mortgage, as well as his testimony in court proceedings against FAMCO.

101. *Patty Sullivan, FAMCO's training director:* Patty Sullivan's background is drawn from her December 3, 5, and 6, 2001, testimony in *FTC v. First Alliance*, U.S. District Court for the Central District of California, 2000. Sullivan testified that at one point she owned 49 percent of an auto dealership in California.

103. *Walling's training and the "Track" sales pitch:* Interviews with Greg Walling, as well as testimony by Walling, Terence LaFrankie, and Matt Winston, and lawsuits filed by state authorities in Minnesota, Illinois, and other jurisdictions.

105. *"nothing misleading or deceptive":* Interview with Brian Chisick.

106. *"don't hide the ball":* Patty Sullivan's 2001 testimony in *FTC v. First Alliance*. The whole point of FAMCO's sales presentation was not to take advantage of people, Sullivan testified, but rather to find out how to meet their needs. "When you're speaking to people as a salesperson . . . you're always looking for . . . opportunities to sell benefits. For instance, if you see someone who had been working for thirty years was injured on the job and was off for two years, you would expect to see . . . that perhaps he was living on his credit cards until he could get back to work. So you would begin to get an idea of what benefits this person would be looking for in a loan."

107. *Chuck Cross:* Interviews with Chuck Cross, the former director of the Division of Consumer Services, Department of Financial Institutions, Washington State.

110. *He had gone after a preacher:* See *People v. Honeywood Development*, Cook County Circuit Court.

110. *Tom James and the Celeketics:* Interview with Tom James, a lawyer for the state of Illinois. Background on the Celeketics' loan also came from Alex Rodriguez and Bill Rumbler, "Loan Officers Told to Mislead, Ex-worker Says," *Chicago Sun-Times*, Apr. 4, 1999. "I went to therapy because of this," Gloria Celeketic told the *Sun-Times*. "I'm working very hard for my money. When this amount was stolen from me, you can just imagine how I felt."

7. Buried

119. *Gary Ozenne and Ameriquest Mortgage:* Interviews with Gary Ozenne, as well as documents in the numerous legal actions he filed in an effort to reclaim his home. They include *Ozenne v. Chase Manhattan et al.*, Riverside County Superior Court, 2002. Among the most helpful documents was "Declaration of Gary L. Ozenne in

Support of Petition for a Writ of Mandamus," filed Feb. 20, 2009, with the Ninth U.S. Circuit Court of Appeals.

121. *Paules picked up the phone:* Travis Paules's personal and professional history is drawn from interviews with Paules, who was forthcoming about Ameriquest's practices and his own behavior during his time as a branch manager, area manager, regional manager, and vice president at the company. He said he had experienced a religious awakening after he left the company, which freed him to talk frankly about those days. "I was a different person then," he told me.

126. *"Securitizations are all about guesswork":* Gary Silverman and Debra Sparks, "Asset-Backed Gambling? The Sector Is More Hazardous Than Many Investors Realize," *BusinessWeek*, Oct. 26, 1998.

127. *Lehman Brothers' stock price fell:* The passage on the effects of the Long-Term Capital Management debacle and currency crises on Lehman Brothers are based on Ianthe Jeanne Dugan, "Battling Rumors on Wall St.; Lehman Brothers Chairman Launches Aggressive Defense," *Washington Post*, Oct. 10, 1998.

128. *"They suck":* Testimony by Eric Hibbert, during the 2003 trial of *Michael Austin et al. v. Brian Chisick et al.*, part of the *In Re: First Alliance Mortgage Company* litigation in U.S. District Court in Santa Ana, California, which sorted out FAMCO's bankruptcy and the various allegations against FAMCO and Lehman Brothers.

129. *"absolutely amazing at ferreting":* Remarks from an eight-page memo, dated February 1, 1999, that Hibbert wrote during Lehman's "due diligence" review of the lender.

129. *The consensus among Lehman executives:* The review team's findings come from a confidential memo signed by a dozen executives in preparation for a February 11, 1999, meeting of Lehman's Investment Banking Commitment Committee. Among those receiving copies of the memo was Lehman chief executive Dick Fuld.

129. *"We are in the business of doing transactions":* Testimony of Steve Berkenfeld in *Austin v. Chisick.*

130. *Delta:* Coverage in *Newsday* and other New York–region media. Delta Financial agreed to pay $12 million to settle investigations by the New York State Department of Banking and New York State attorney general Eliot Spitzer. It also reached a settlement with the U.S. Justice Department, the Federal Trade Commission, and the U.S. Department of Housing and Urban Development. In an interview with *Newsday*, Delta's chief executive said: "The concept of us giving a loan to someone who is mentally challenged would make absolutely no business sense, never mind the ethics involved." See Ron Howell and Randi Feigenbaum, "Customers, Attorney General Say Mortgage Firm Uses Unfair Tactics," *Newsday*, Oct. 31, 1999.

131. *Lehman took an ownership interest:* Lehman started Finance America in 1999 and took its initial stake in BNC in 2000.

131. *"the only game":* Brian Chisick's testimony in *FTC v. First Alliance.* Lehman never exercised the stock warrants.

132. *First National Bank of Keystone:* See note on page 313, *"Keystone knew nothing,"* for citations on the history of Keystone's rise and fall.

134. *Under Lehman's guidance:* Lehman eventually backed away from Keystone, cutting back on the size of a later transaction and then not doing business with the bank for

roughly two years. However, according to *National Mortgage News*, Lehman eventually rekindled the relationship, putting together a $350 million securitization for the bank in December 1998. It canceled the securitization after it became clear that turmoil in the financial markets had made such deals "cost-prohibitive," the trade paper said. "Keystone was working on a deal with Lehman Brothers in December, but the pricing just got out of hand and they bagged it," an industry source told the paper. See "High-LTV Securitizations Tail Off," *National Mortgage News*, Jan. 29, 1999.

136. *The* New York Times *was working on a story:* Bill Ahearn's comments are drawn from a five-page memo dated March 6, 2000, under the subject line: "New York Times Predatory Lending Article."

137. *Henriques and Bergman's story:* Diana B. Henriques and Lowell Bergman, "Profiting from Fine Print with Wall Street's Help," *New York Times*, Mar. 15, 2000.

139. *"If an individual or class of victims":* Testimony of Christopher L. Peterson in "Subprime Mortgage Market Turmoil: Examining the Role of Securitization," Hearing Before the U.S. Senate Committee on Banking, Housing, and Urban Affairs, Subcommittee on Securities, Insurance, and Investment, Apr. 17, 2007. See also Erick Bergquist, "Preparing for a Bad-Loan Boom," *American Banker*, Oct. 6, 2000.

140. *"He's known some of the employees":* Edmund Sanders and Daryl Strickland, "Publicity, Pressure Force Decision," *Los Angeles Times*, Mar. 24, 2000.

140. *"If you're running a clean company":* Edmund Sanders, "Irvine Loan Firm Files for Bankruptcy," *Los Angeles Times*, Mar. 24, 2000.

140. *World Financial Center hearing:* Bruce Lambert, "Wall Street Shuns Invitation to Discuss Role in High-Rate Loans for Minorities," *New York Times*, May 13, 2000; Robert Julavits, "Warning on Predatory Lender Funding," *American Banker*, May 15, 2000; Mike Sorohan, "Predatory Lending Task Force Examines Wall Street's Role," *Real Estate Finance Today*, May 22, 2000; and Michael Gregory, "The Predatory Lending Fracas," *Investment Dealers Digest*, June 26, 2000.

141. *"some of the most abusive, anti-consumer overreaching":* Brian Collins, "FTC Catches Seven Abusive B&C Lenders," *National Mortgage News*, Aug. 2, 1999.

141. *"abusive lending practices":* Daryl Strickland, "Greenspan Joins Critics of Mortgage Fee Gouging," *Los Angeles Times*, Mar. 23, 2000.

141. *Lehman Brothers' relationship with Delta:* Brian Collins, "OTS Seeking Best Practices for Subprime," *Origination News*, Aug. 1, 1999.

141. *a surge of bank failures:* Mike Sorohan, "Bank Failures in Boom Times Draw Lawmakers' Attention," *Real Estate Finance Today*, Feb. 14, 2000.

142. *"To effectively combat predatory lending":* "FDIC Warns Banks on Predatory MBS," *National Mortgage News*, Oct. 30, 2000; and Rob Blackwell, "FDIC Chief Urges a Severing of Predators' Bank Funding," *American Banker*, Oct. 16, 2000.

142. *Citigroup and subprime:* See especially Michael Hudson, "Banking on Misery," *Southern Exposure*, Summer 2003. Citi claimed it bought Associates with the intention of cleaning up the lender's abuses by folding it into its existing subprime unit, CitiFinancial. But CitiFinancial had its own record of bad practices, and the newly combined subprime operations continued to gouge and exploit vulnerable consumers—targeting, one loan officer testified, anyone who "appeared uneducated, inarticulate, was a minority, or was particularly young or old." The

idea that Citigroup was interested in cleaning up a flawed company is also belied by this historical fact: Citi chief executive Sanford "Sandy" Weill had been involved in dicey subprime enterprises for nearly a decade and a half before the Associates acquisition. He had used a Baltimore-based subprime lender, Commercial Credit, as the platform for building the financial empire that provided him the cash and clout to take over Citi, and Commercial Credit had become the target of many lawsuits alleging lending abuses during the Weill era. In an interview for the *Southern Exposure* article, a former Commercial Credit manager in Mississippi recalled that, under Weill, employees were pressured to meet quotas for generating loans and selling costly insurance—and to use slick talk to prevent customers from understanding what they were getting. "Over a period of time," he said, "it went from a family, employee-oriented company—doing the right thing, trying to help its customers—to this cutthroat thing of anything that will get us more business."

143. *Ameriquest, ACORN, and the FTC:* See Mike Hudson, "Ameriquest's Ties to Watchdog Group Are Tested," *Los Angeles Times,* May 22, 2005; Marc Hochstein, "Activist Leader Defends Subprime Lender Whose Offices Were Picketed," *American Banker,* Dec. 1, 1999; Diana B. Henriques, "Taking on High-Cost Home Loans," *New York Times,* Mar. 19, 2000; "Community Activists to Protest Salomon Smith Barney," U.S. Newswire, Mar. 20, 2000; Dawn Kopecki, "Demonstrators Protest Salomon's Role in Subprime Lending," Dow Jones, Mar. 20, 2000; Daryl Strickland, "Greenspan Joins Critics of Mortgage Fee Gouging," *Los Angeles Times,* Mar. 23, 2000; Michael Gregory, "Subprime Reaps Bad Press of Predators," *Asset Sales Report,* Mar. 27, 2000; Brian Collins, "Ameriquest Mortgage Agrees to Meet with ACORN Protestors," *National Mortgage News,* Mar. 27, 2000; Edmund Sanders, "Ameriquest Defends Loan Practices," *Los Angeles Times,* Apr. 9, 2000; "Ameriquest, ACORN Partner on Pilot Lending Program," PR Newswire, July 26, 2000; Dawn Bailey, "Ameriquest/ACORN Conflict Ends in Collaboration," *National Mortgage News,* July 31, 2000; Lew Sichelman, "Mortgage Cautions—Let Buyer Beware: The Nation's Largest Subprime Lender Offers Borrowers Advice About the Tricky Loan Process," *Orlando Sentinel,* July 29, 2001; and Letter, from Joel Winston, the acting associate director of the FTC's financial practices division, to Thomas J. Noto, an attorney for Ameriquest, Feb. 15, 2001.

144. *ACORN-Ameriquest negotiations:* See Wade Rathke, *Citizen Wealth: Winning the Campaign to Save Working Families* (San Francisco: Berrett-Koehler Publishers, 2009), pp. 32–40; and Michael May, "The Legal Fleecing of Poor Minorities," Tom Paine.com, April 2002.

146. *case-by-case:* "FDIC Says Banks Undercapitalized for Subprime Lending," *National Mortgage News,* Feb. 14, 2000.

146. *"rigid approach":* Mike Sorohan, "Bank Failures in Boom Times," *Real Estate Finance Today,* Feb. 14, 2000.

146. *hammered from all directions:* Interview with Donna Tanoue, chairman of the FDIC from 1998 to 2001.

146. *"What the FDIC is proposing":* Gwendolyn Glenn, "FDIC's Capital Proposal Worries Lenders," *Real Estate Finance Today,* Feb. 7, 2000.

146. *feel the chill:* Interview with Alexander Ross.

8. Boil

147. *According to Kas: Kas v. The DDB Needham Worldwide Communications Group Inc et al.*, Los Angeles Superior Court, 2001. The suit was resolved on confidential terms in 2002.

149. *"two paychecks away"*: Seth Lubove, "Bust and Boom in the Subprime Market," *Forbes*, Dec. 27, 1999.

150. *Dawn Mansfield:* Details come from her June 9, 2008, testimony in *RoDa Drilling Company et al. v. Richard Siegal et al.*, U.S. District Court for the Northern District of Oklahoma, 2007.

150. *Eleven percent of subprime mortgages:* Joy C. Shaw, "Subprime Mortgages Still Appeal Despite Rising Delinquencies," Dow Jones Newswires, Sept. 10, 2001.

151. *"not enough to keep investors"*: Ibid.

151. *subprime defaults, investor interest, and CDOs:* Shaw, "Subprime Mortgages Still Appeal," Dow Jones Newswires; and Serena Ng and Michael Hudson, "Mortgage Shakeout May Roil CDO Market—Subprime Defaults Lead to Wavering at Big Street Firms," *Wall Street Journal*, Mar. 13, 2007.

152. *"It's not a math problem"*: Interview with Mark Adelson.

152. *"The issue isn't whether subprime"*: Robert Julavits, "Subprime Experts Downplay Risks of Delinquency," *American Banker*, Aug. 14, 2001.

153. *Kuhn was certainly motivated:* Extensive interviews with Stephen Kuhn, a former Ameriquest loan officer. See also *Kuhn v. Ameriquest*, U.S. District Court for the District of Kansas, 2004, a wrongful dismissal lawsuit that claimed Kuhn was fired after he complained about Ameriquest's unethical practices. Others who worked with Kuhn in Ameriquest's Leawood, Kansas, office, including Rob Hurtig and Brien Hanley, gave similar accounts of the practices in the branch. "The stuff you're asked to do, just to close files, was sick," Hurtig said. He said workers falsified documents and targeted vulnerable borrowers for "the shittiest deals possible." He said he quit after a few months because "it's really hard to sell people things when you know you're screwing them." Hanley said Ameriquest pressured would-be borrowers "to do it now, to do it right this second, so they couldn't shop around" and find better deals elsewhere. Falsification of documents, he said, "was just common practice. If you were trying to get a loan done, that's what you did."

155. *Armon Williams:* I interviewed Armon Williams, a former Ameriquest employee, for a story in the *Los Angeles Times*. See Mike Hudson and E. Scott Reckard, "Workers Say Lender Ran 'Boiler Rooms,' " *Los Angeles Times*, Feb. 4, 2005. Like many others at Ameriquest, Williams was a mortgage-industry neophyte who didn't fully understand until later how Ameriquest's tactics hurt consumers. He said he felt regret for some of the things he had done. When I contacted him again in 2009, he declined to discuss his experiences further. He said he didn't want to revisit that time in his life.

156. *"the worst case scenario"*: Interview with Jason DeBruler, a former Ameriquest employee.

156. *"dual purpose of both making sure the loan"*: Sept. 23, 2004, affidavit of Joseph Khaliq, who worked for Ameriquest in Santa Clara and Campbell, California, in

Landa v. Ameriquest, U.S. District Court for the Northern District of California, 2003.

156. *Loan officers pressured appraisers:* For our Feb. 4, 2005, *Los Angeles Times* article, Scott Reckard and I interviewed Michael Filip and appraisers in five other states, all of whom described Ameriquest's strong-arm tactics. Ameriquest told us it had "tight controls and policies to help ensure accurate property valuations."

159. *Christopher J. Warren:* Warren's personal written statement, which is attached to a Feb. 4, 2009, affidavit by an IRS criminal investigator in support of an arrest warrant for Warren in *USA v. Warren,* U.S. District Court for the Eastern District of California, Case # 2:09-mj-00046-KJM-1. The bank fraud charges in that case were later dropped in favor of charges of money laundering and other counts, Case # 2:09-cr-00121-FCD. None of these charges involved his work at Ameriquest.

160. *"Aryan Nation":* Interviews with Todd Strobel and Michael Bischoff, former Ameriquest employees, and documents in employment discrimination cases filed against Ameriquest, including Strobel's March 6, 2003, deposition in *In re: Tom Reed and Ameriquest Mortgage,* American Arbitration Association proceeding, and the complaint in *Theriot v. Ameriquest,* Orange County Superior Court, 2006. See also Kevin Lynch, "Fired Worker Says Employer Discriminated," *Detroit News,* Oct. 13, 2000.

163. *Wendell Raphael:* Interview with Wendell Raphael, a longtime mortgage executive. Raphael told me that he frequently fielded calls from appraisers who said they were being pressured by branch employees to inflate home values; in some cases, the appraisers told him, they were owed thousands of dollars for work they'd done for the company, but the money was being held hostage until they agreed to "hit the value" on a pending assignment. Raphael also heard from "pissed-off" borrowers. They claimed they'd been lied to, that documents had been forged, and that they'd been stuck with outlandish fees. He challenged them: "Do you have proof?" Most said: "What's your fax number?" The documentation they sent often satisfied him that they were telling the truth. I interviewed Raphael shortly before his death. In response to my questions about Raphael's statements to me, Ameriquest said: "Mr. Raphael was a longtime employee of the Company who passed away. We have no knowledge of Mr. Raphael ever making statements similar to the ones you have alleged. Nor are we aware of Mr. Raphael ever raising these issues with anyone at the Company. In fact, we are troubled that your only Company source is a deceased former executive who during his many years of employment had no prior history of making any statements similar to the ones you allege. Regardless, your assertions are simply not accurate."

163. *They were ordering appraisal after appraisal:* Barry Bates, who worked briefly as Ameriquest's chief appraiser in the early 2000s, confirmed that questionable appraisals were a problem at the lender. He told me he ran into problems with management when he tried to cull dishonest appraisers from Ameriquest's approved list. The sales force saw him as "the enemy," he said. "As soon as I removed one bad appraiser from the list, they put somebody new on" who was just as bad. When he tried to raise the issue with senior executives, he said, he got "a look that I'll never forget. It was calm, cool, and collected, but the look said: You are history." Soon

after, he said, he was called in by a human resources staffer and told he was being let go. The reason: "loss of confidence" in his work.

9. The Battle for Georgia

165. *"Our goal is to allow thrifts"*: Quoted in Binyamin Appelbaum and Ellen Nakashima, "Banking Regulator Played Advocate over Enforcer," *Washington Post*, Nov. 23, 2008. See also a policy brief prepared by the Center for Responsible Lending, "Neglect and Inaction: An Analysis of Federal Banking Regulators' Failure to Enforce Consumer Protections," July 13, 2009, http://www.responsiblelending .org/mortgage-lending/policy-legislation/regulators/regulators-failure-to-enforce -consumer-protections.html.

166. *involving small Texas banks:* Testimony of John C. Dugan, "Improving Federal Consumer Protection in Financial Services," Hearing Before the House Committee on Financial Services, June 13, 2007.

166. *"We cannot intercede"*: Greg Ip and Damian Paletta, "Lending Oversight: Regulators Scrutinized in Mortgage Meltdown; States, Federal Agencies Clashed on Subprimes as Market Ballooned," *Wall Street Journal*, Mar. 22, 2007.

166. *"regulatory capture"*: Federal banking regulators tended to accept the financial industry's argument that consumer protection rules are a drag on banks, cutting into their bottom line and thus endangering their "safety and soundness." Actually, the opposite has proven to be true. Consumer protection helps prevent reckless business practices that can end in disaster not only for the customers but also for banks and their shareholders. As FDIC chairman Sheila Bair has said, "Protecting the consumer from . . . perils is not simply a do-good public service. In fact, consumer protection and safe and sound lending practices are two sides of the same coin. Lenders who put their retail customers at risk also put themselves, their investors, and our entire financial system in danger." In particular, if borrowers can't afford their loans, the resulting foreclosures will cause losses for banks, threatening their safety. Sheila C. Bair, "The Future of Mortgage Finance," remarks at the 2008 annual meeting of the National Association for Business Economics, Washington, D.C., Oct. 6, 2008.

167. *"no evidence of predatory lending"*: See the OCC fact sheet, "Preemption Determination and Order Concerning the Georgia Fair Lending Act: Questions and Answers," July 31, 2003.

167. *National City Mortgage:* Eric Nalder, "Mortgage System Crumbled While Regulators Jousted," *Seattle Post-Intelligencer*, Oct. 11, 2008.

168. *"They let Citigroup off"*: Interview with Matthew Lee, director of Fair Finance Watch, a New York City–based watchdog group. For more on Citigroup and the FTC settlement, see Michael Hudson, "Banking on Misery," *Southern Exposure*, Summer 2003.

169. *Cross report on Household International:* Interview with Chuck Cross, former director of consumer services for the Department of Financial Institutions, Washington State, and various news articles. See in particular Brian Collins, "State Regulator Slams Household Practices," *National Mortgage News*, Sept. 2, 2002.

170. *"These guys are criminals"*: Interview with Chuck Cross.

170. *"There were a number of people who were kind of afraid"*: Interview with David Huey, assistant attorney general, Washington State.

171. *"We were ready to force the company"*: Richard Roesler, "Residents to Get Piece of Restitution Deal," *Spokesman-Review*, Aug. 20, 2003.

172. *"Investors appear to be betting"*: Paul Becket and Joseph T. Hallinan, "Household Settlement Boosts Stock," *Wall Street Journal*, Oct. 14, 2002.

172. *Lehman Brothers issued:* "Moody's Rates SASCO's 2002-HF2 Mortgage Pass-Through Deal Aaa," Moody's Investor Service press release, Nov. 26, 2002. See also Form 424B5, Structured Asset Securities Corporation, filed November 2002 with the Securities and Exchange Commission, and Wells Fargo Bank accounting of SASCO-HF2, dated July 25, 2006.

172. *"We see this as a fantastic opportunity"*: Quoted in Andrew Ross Sorkin, "HSBC to Buy a U.S. Lender for $14.2 Billion," *New York Times*, Nov. 15, 2002.

173. *After Los Angeles, Oakland, and Atlanta approved ordinances:* "Anti-Predatory Lending Ordinances," National League of Cities fact sheet, Feb. 2008.

173. *"keep our legislators focused"*: Bobbi Murray, "Hunting the Predators," *The Nation*, July 15, 2002.

174. *"render the business structure unusable"*: Christopher L. Peterson, Written Testimony to the U.S. Senate Banking Committee hearing on "Subprime Mortgage Market Turmoil: Examining the Role of Securitization," Apr. 17, 2007.

174. *"the legal laundering of bad loans"*: Barnini Chakraborty, "Republican Senators Offer Changes to Predatory Lending Bill," Associated Press, Jan. 27, 2003.

175. *"Consumers and advocacy groups need to understand"*: Kevin Donovan, "Mortgage Players Knock Legislation: New York, New Jersey Laws Will Be Georgia Fiasco All Over Again, They Claim," *Investment Dealers Digest*, Mar. 17, 2003.

175. *"fear-mongering"*: Eric Williamson, "Senator, Lobbyists Clash on Lending Bill," *Augusta Chronicle*, Dec. 12, 2000.

176. *Georgia's governor, Roy Barnes:* Interviews with Roy Barnes and his aide, Chris Carpenter, as well as reports in the *Atlanta Journal-Constitution*. See also Robert Berner and Brian Grow, "They Warned Us: The Watchdogs Who Saw the Subprime Disaster Coming—and How They Were Thwarted by the Banks and Washington," *BusinessWeek*, Oct. 20, 2008.

177. *Arnall and his associates sprinkled campaign contributions:* Glenn R. Simpson, "Lender Lobbying Blitz Abetted Mortgage Mess—Ameriquest Pressed for Changes in Laws," *Wall Street Journal*, Dec. 31, 2007. The *Journal*'s figures are for 2002 through 2006.

178. *"was a very candid conversation"*: Ibid. In a written reply to my questions about the meeting, Ameriquest said: "Mr. Bass did attend one brief (approximately 15 minute) meeting with Senator Fort and Chris Carpenter, a legislative aide from the Governor's office. . . . Senator Fort was present for less than half of the meeting and was clearly passionate about the issue. Thereafter, Mr. Carpenter apologized for Senator Fort's unwillingness to discuss the issues and his abrupt departure."

179. *OTS preempts Georgia Fair Lending Act:* Rob Blackwell and Erick Bergquist, "OTS Blocks Most of Georgia Predator Statute," *American Banker*, Jan. 23, 2003. The OCC followed suit six months later.

180. *"There's no way to quantify the punitive"*: The *Atlanta Journal-Constitution* and other news outlets covered the attacks on Georgia's fair-lending law. See especially Brad Finkelstein, Bonnie Sinnock, and Kyriaki Venetis, "GA Becomes a High-Cost Ghost Town," *National Mortgage News*, Oct. 7, 2002; "S&P Disallows Georgia High-Cost Loans as Collateral," Reuters, Jan. 17, 2003; and Jennifer Alban, "Georgia Law Sparks Mortgage 'Crisis,'" *Barron's*, Jan. 27, 2003.

10. The Trial

184. *Steinbock and Hofmann and the Durney case:* Sixth Appellate District, California Court of Appeal, 1999 ruling in *Durney v. First Alliance et al.*; Diana B. Henriques and Lowell Bergman, "Profiting from Fine Print with Wall Street's Help," *New York Times*, Mar. 15, 2000; and interviews with Sheila Canavan, David Hofmann, and Phillip Steinbock.
185. *Dickie Scruggs:* Susan Beck, "Mississippi Blues," *American Lawyer*, Mar. 1, 2008.
186. *Terry LaFrankie and Matt Winston accounts of FAMCO's sales practices:* Transcript of testimony in *Michael Austin et al. v. Brian Chisick et al.*, U.S. District Court for the Central District of California, Southern Division, 2001.
192. *An even bigger paper trail:* In addition to the court actions, reports by mortgage industry players—MBIA, the bond insurer, and Clayton Group, a mortgage analysis firm—also raised red flags about FAMCO's practices during this period. Clayton, for example, noted an "exorbitant number of loans made to borrowers in excess of 65 years of age" who were charged "unusually high points."
192. *"smoke and mirrors":* The fact that the lender gave borrowers the required federal lending disclosures, the judge said, "does not exonerate it when it purposely constructs a sales program to confuse and mislead the ordinary consumer."
193. *"It was a new industry, relatively":* Transcript of Eric Hibbert's testimony in *Austin et al. v. Chisick et al.* See especially day 14, vol. II, pp. 21–22, and day 16, vol. II.
198. *"This case should have made a difference":* Steven D. Jones, "Lehman Case Offers Slim Subprime Precedent," Dow Jones News Service, Jan. 31, 2008.
198. *to buy a larger stake in BNC:* Paul Muolo, "Lehman Buying More of BNC?" *National Mortgage News*, Aug. 11, 2003.

11. Feeding the Monster

200. *No. 1 subject of spam:* Based on surveys by Ipswitch, a software developer and marketer.
200. *"Guaranteed lowest rates on the planet":* These examples were drawn from spam e-mails that Robert Braver eventually traced to Ameriquest.
200. *He sued Ameriquest:* Interviews with Robert Braver and documents in *Braver v. Ameriquest et al.*, U.S. District Court for the Western District of Oklahoma, 2004, including the "Third Amended Complaint," and August 4, 2006, "Affidavit of Robert H. Braver." The case was settled in 2007 on undisclosed terms. For other confirmation of Ameriquest's links to spammers, see Scott Messina, "Quicken, Ameriquest, New Century, Others Rely on Spam," *Originator Times*, Jan. 24, 2005; "Attorney General Lockyer Goes to Court to Shut Down Major California-Based

Spam Operation," States News Service, Apr. 13, 2005; and Bob Sullivan, "Who Profits from Spam?" MSNBC.com, Aug. 8, 2003.

201. *the company was the fifth biggest U.S. advertiser:* "Kids Account for One Out of Five Internet Surfers in the U.S.," PR Newswire, Oct. 21, 2003. Nielsen defined the number of impressions as "the number of times an ad is rendered for viewing." Ameriquest was not far behind the No. 1 advertiser, online video merchant Netflix, which logged just under 2.5 billion ads in the month.

202. *Boiler Room training video:* Interviews with Brien Hanley, Lisa Taylor, Dave Johnson, and other former Ameriquest employees. Tyson Russum's comments appeared in Chris Arnold, "Former Ameriquest Workers Tell of Deception," *Morning Edition,* National Public Radio, May 14, 2007. See also Kenneth Kendall's August 15, 2002, sworn declaration in *Pierceall v. Ameriquest,* San Mateo (Calif.) Superior Court. Kendall worked as a salesman at Ameriquest's Carson, California, office, from September 2001 to March 2002. He said that "part of my job training was to watch the film *Boiler Room* . . . a movie depicting aggressive telephone sales tactics used to induce clients to purchase stock in non-existent companies." He said he also was shown videos of prizes, such as ski trips, Hawaiian vacations, and cars, that were available to salespeople who closed the most loans.

203. *"I wonder when the feds are coming?":* Interview with Dave Johnson, who worked as a loan officer and branch manager in Michigan.

203. *One longtime Arnall aide, Wayne Lee:* Lee's May 9, 2007, deposition in *In Re: Ameriquest Mortgage Co. Mortgage Lending Practices Litigation,* U.S. District Court for the Northern District of Illinois, MDL No. 1715, Lead Case No. 05-cv-07097.

203. *"Fans are essentially customers":* Based on a write-up in *Ameriquest Connection,* the company's in-house magazine, Dec. 2005.

204. *"minimally trained and minimally dressed":* Mara Der Hovanesian, "Sex, Lies, and Subprime Mortgages," *BusinessWeek,* Nov. 13, 2008.

205. *"disgusting, demeaning, and demoralizing conduct":* Lisa Taylor v. Ameriquest, Sacramento Superior Court, 2004, as well as an interview with Lisa Taylor prior to the settlement of the case. In her suit, Taylor alleged: "Ameriquest management condoned, encouraged and participated in extensive document alteration, manipulating and forging, in order to sell more loans. When there were impediments to loan funding, plaintiff and her coworkers were consistently asked by their superiors to just 'fix it' or 'book it.'" The suit said Taylor "continuously refused to alter documents at the request of her superiors and coworkers and would complain to her superiors about this conduct and that it should stop." The case was settled on a confidential basis.

205. *Nazik Santora: Santora v. Ameriquest,* Orange County Superior Court, 2005.

205. *a military vet who bragged: Nazaroff v. Ameriquest,* Sacramento Superior Court, 2005.

206. *"Omar did ten":* Interview with Omar Ross.

207. *in everyone's best interest if Kuhn and Ameriquest parted:* Stephen Kuhn decided to sue Ameriquest for wrongful dismissal. He went to half a dozen lawyers. Each of them, he said, told him they couldn't help him. Ameriquest, they said, was too rich

and too powerful. He sued anyway, representing himself and filing a handwritten legal complaint, alleging that he had been fired because "I stated . . . that Ameriquest's fees, rates & business ethics were terrible." See *Kuhn v. Ameriquest*, U.S. District Court for the District of Kansas, 2004. A judge ordered the case into arbitration. Kuhn didn't pursue his claims in arbitration, and his lawsuit was dismissed for good in 2006.

209. *Mark Glover's wrongful termination lawsuit: Glover v. Ameriquest*, Orange County Superior Court, 2004.

210. *Christopher J. Warren, the mortgage fraudster:* Warren's personal written statement attached to the February 4, 2009, affidavit in *USA v. Warren*, U.S. District Court for the Eastern District of California, Case # 2:09-mj-00046-KJM-1.

210. *New Century:* James R. Hagerty, Ruth Simon, Michael Corkery, and Gregory Zuckerman, "Home Stretch: At a Mortgage Lender, Rapid Rise, Faster Fall," *Wall Street Journal*, Mar. 12, 2007; and John Gittelsohn and Matthew Padilla, "Cutting-Edge Company to Cautionary Tale," *Orange County Register*, Apr. 19, 2007.

211. *"We were basically the black sheep":* David Heath, "At Top Subprime Mortgage Lender, Policies Were Invitation to Fraud," Huffington Post Investigative Fund, Dec. 12, 2009. The borrowers who went after Long Beach in court included Luis Mapula and Cristina Plata, a Latino couple from East San Jose, California, who claimed they had been saddled with a complex, unaffordable loan package after the lender approved an application that falsely claimed the family had an income of more than $100,000, as well as $19,700 in the bank, a $22,000 Acura, and $28,000 in furniture and personal property. The loan papers called for the family to initially pay over $3,500 a month, more than their actual take-home pay. Things would only get worse: the monthly payments were poised to adjust every six months and climb to $4,300 and beyond. Without admitting wrongdoing, Long Beach and the other firms involved in the deal settled the lawsuit for $250,000. See Pete Carey, "The Harsh Side of the Housing Boom," *Mercury News*, Mar. 11, 2007.

211. *"They were just nasty products":* Drew DeSilver, "Reckless Strategies Doomed WaMu," *Seattle Times*, Oct. 25, 2009.

212. *The two moguls met:* Paul Muolo and Mathew Padilla, *Chain of Blame: How Wall Street Caused the Mortgage and Credit Crisis* (Hoboken, N.J.: John Wiley & Sons, 2008), pp. 73–74, 87, and 95. See also E. Scott Reckard and Jim Puzzanghera, "SEC Suit Accuses Mozilo of Fraud," *Los Angeles Times*, June 5, 2009.

212. *When Countrywide sold prime loans:* Gretchen Morgenson, "Inside the Countrywide Lending Spree," *New York Times*, Aug. 26, 2007. Figures are for 2004.

213. *"It was Roland's baby":* Interview with Terry Rouch, a former wholesale loan officer at Argent Mortgage.

214. *Elizabeth Redrick's complaint:* Mark Gillespie, "Argent Lender Found Biased Against Blacks," *Cleveland Plain Dealer*, Mar. 19, 2008.

214. *Kramer charged that Argent had colluded:* Wells Fargo's relationship with Argent in Cleveland was not an anomaly. Government lawsuits alleged that Wells Fargo's mortgage operations were driven by a sales culture where profiteering and discrimination went hand in hand. In court papers, one former employee recalled

coworkers calling minority customers "mud people," describing mortgages in minority neighborhoods as "ghetto loans," and justifying putting minorities into high-priced mortgages by saying, "Those people don't pay their bills." Wells Fargo aggressively sold subprime loans to black home owners by building alliances with influential figures in the black community. Its Affinity Group Marketing unit targeted black churches, trying to use pastors' sway over their flocks to help the company sell loans. The bank also teamed with Tavis Smiley, one of the nation's most influential African American authors and talk show hosts. Smiley was the keynote speaker at "Wealth Building" seminars that the banking giant held in predominantly black neighborhoods in Baltimore, Chicago, and other cities. Wells Fargo had representatives on-site to meet with audience members afterward, using the events to lure them into subprime mortgages, according to a lawsuit filed by Illinois's attorney general. (In a written statement, Smiley acknowledged that he had partnered with Wells Fargo on wealth-building initiatives. He said, though, that he had not been a "spokesperson or representative" for Wells Fargo and pointed out that many African American and Latino national civil rights organizations had had similar relationships with the bank. "In this economic climate we continue to be reminded every day that there is no perfect company," he wrote, adding that he supported "any official and credible investigation of allegations of any company accused of disrespecting communities of color with discriminatory practices.")

See affidavits by Elizabeth M. Jacobson and Tony Paschal in *Mayor and City Council of Baltimore v. Wells Fargo Bank*, U.S. District Court for the District of Maryland, 2008, documents 74-16 and 74-17; *People of the State of Illinois v. Wells Fargo and Company*, Cook County (Ill.) Circuit Court, 2009; and Mary Kane, "Suit Alleges Trusted Blacks Drew Minorities to High-Rate Loans," *Washington Independent*, Sept. 17, 2009.

215. *He had received roughly $500,000:* Figures based on author's analysis of data at OpenSecrets.org, a service of the Center for Responsive Politics that tracks federal campaign data.

215. *Responsible Lending Act:* Background on this bill comes from Richard Lord, *American Nightmare: Predatory Lending and the Foreclosure of the American Dream* (Monroe, Me.: Common Courage Press, 2004), pp. 194–97.

215. *"I think that everyone in this room agrees":* Ney's words and other remarks from the hearing come from a Federal Document Clearing House transcript of House Committee on Financial Services, Subcommittees on Financial Institutions and Consumer Credit and on Housing and Community Opportunity, Hearing on "Protecting Homeowners: Preventing Abusive Lending While Preserving Access to Credit," Nov. 5, 2003.

217. *New Century had finished a distant second:* Citigroup and Household ranked third and fourth, both recording just over $20 billion in subprime loan volume.

217. *The industry's overall loan volume topped $330 billion:* Bernard Condon, "Till Debt Do Us Part," *Forbes*, Feb. 16, 2004.

217. *"They're on fire right now":* Paul Muolo, "Did Ameriquest Earn $1B Last Year?" *National Mortgage News*, Apr. 5, 2004.

12. Chimera

219. *Cedric Washington:* This account is based on Washington's complaint in *Washington v. Finance America*, Sacramento County Superior Court, 2005. Lehman Brothers said Washington's lawsuit "had no merit" and was "not brought in good faith." The lawsuit was settled in 2006 on undisclosed terms.

220. *BNC and Finance America employees:* I investigated BNC and Finance America as a reporter for the *Wall Street Journal*. See Michael Hudson, "Lending a Hand: How Wall Street Stoked the Mortgage Meltdown," *Wall Street Journal*, June 27, 2007. I collected accounts from twenty-five former BNC and Finance America employees who stated that questionable loans and falsified paperwork were a problem. Most were on the record and specified in detail the bad practices they witnessed. It should be noted that five other former employees told me that the companies had run a tight ship, at least in the offices where they worked. They said the lenders had good fraud controls in place and worked to screen out dicey loans. "We didn't just push things through," Barbara Webb, who worked for Finance America and BNC in Texas in 2004 and 2005, told me. "Everything we did was by the guidelines." Lehman was vehement that everything was on the up-and-up at its subprime origination platforms. It questioned the credibility of the former employees who criticized the lenders' practices, noting that many of them had never said anything about fraud while they worked for the companies. Lehman said its employees were committed to "the highest standards of governance and ethical behavior." The weight of the evidence from former employees' statements and from borrowers' lawsuits, however, led me to conclude that fraud and reckless sales policies were serious problems at BNC and Finance America. Kendra Eckhart worked as an underwriter in BNC's Roseville, Minnesota, branch. Employees who tried to stop questionable loans, she said, got verbal lashings from salespeople and managers: "Are you going to blow the deal over this?" Little else mattered but selling loans. "You sacrifice everything, really, to get volume," Eckhart said. Upper management rarely backed the underwriters, she said; usually sales won and the loans were eventually pushed through. The accounts collected from employees were supported by those provided in court records by borrowers who alleged their loans had been pushed through via falsified paperwork and other unseemly tactics.

220. *BNC's Sacramento branch:* The lawsuit, filed by Coleen Colombo and five other women who worked at the branch, claimed that managers punished employees for reporting fraud and allowed sexual harassment to flourish at the branch. For a 2007 article in the *Wall Street Journal*, I interviewed eight women who had worked in the office, including five of the six plaintiffs in the suit against BNC. The details of their allegations are also described in Mara Der Hovanesian, "Sex, Lies, and Subprime Mortgages," *BusinessWeek*, Nov. 13, 2008, as well as in the television report "Mortgage Company Employees Claim Harassment," KCRA, Sept. 7, 2005, http://www.ksbw.com/news/4946507/detail.html, and *Colombo et al. v. BNC Mortgage Inc.*, Sacramento Superior Court, 2005. The *Colombo* case was put on hold due to Lehman's bankruptcy filing in late 2008. In a statement in 2007, Lehman said: "The factual context for the events in Sacramento reflects the seriousness with which we take allegations of fraud. . . . With regard to the allegations made by six

former employees in the pending lawsuit, we also have reviewed them thoroughly and are confident that they are baseless and without merit."

222. *"contributed to the highest homeownership"*: Testimony of Stephen W. Prough, chairman, Ameriquest Mortgage Company, before the U.S. Senate Committee on Banking, Housing, and Urban Affairs, Washington, D.C., July 26, 2001.

222. *In 2004, just one-quarter of 1 percent of its mortgages*: Home Mortgage Disclosure Act data for 2004 show that Ameriquest made 177,806 refinancing loans, 17,303 home improvement loans and 492 home purchase loans.

223. *Best estimates were that less than 10 percent*: Center for Responsible Lending, "Subprime Lending: A Net Drain on Homeownership," Mar. 27, 2007. This groundbreaking study found that 62 percent of subprime mortgages during the period from 1998 to 2006 were refinancings. Of the remainder, the study found, roughly 9 percent were for first-time home purchases and another 29 percent went to current home owners who were buying another house (either to replace their current home, as a second home, or as an investment). The study estimated that subprime loans made in 2005 produced fewer than 225,000 new home owners, but would result in more than half a million foreclosures, mostly from unaffordable refinance loans.

224. *"foundation of healthy communities"*: Quoted in an Ameriquest press release.

225. *Duane and Gertrude O'Connor*: Documents in *Duane and Gertrude Connor v. Ameriquest et al*, U.S. District Court for the District of Minnesota, 2007, including the August 10, 2007, complaint and the January 16, 2007, affidavits from Gertrude and Duane O'Connor.

227. *In addition to Deutsche Bank*: As of 2005, Deutsche Bank and Morgan Stanley had the biggest lines of credit in place for Arnall's companies, at $3 billion apiece. JPMorgan Chase and Merrill were close behind, at roughly $2.8 billion each. Citigroup maintained a $1.85 billion line of credit for Arnall's lenders. These figures are based on ACC Capital Holdings' "Consolidated Financial Statements" for the three years ending December 31, 2005. Lehman Brothers didn't provide a line of credit to ACC; it provided funding to Ameriquest by buying the lender's loans and then wrapping them into Lehman's own securitizations.

227. *The O'Connors' mortgage was one of more than eighty-five hundred*: Documents filed with securities regulators regarding Ameriquest Mortgage Securities Inc. Asset-Backed Pass-Through Certificates, Series 2004-R11, including the November 2004 Prospectus Supplement and Form 8K, Dec. 30, 2004, Exhibit 99.2, "Characteristics of the Mortgage Pool."

228. *2004-R11 securitization techniques*: "Moody's Rates Ameriquest's 2004-R11 Deal Aaa," Moody's Investors Service press release, Nov. 29, 2004.

228. *Moody's, S&P, and Fitch*: Elliot Blair Smith, "Bringing Down Wall Street as Ratings Let Loose Subprime Scourge," Bloomberg News, Sept. 24, 2008.

228. *2004-R11 investors*: Information from Bloomberg and *Mutual Fund Prospectus Express*. The firms purchased the mortgage-backed securities through various investment funds they sponsored, such as the JPMorgan Global Strategic Income Fund and Citigroup's Smith Barney Diversified Strategic Income Fund. Fidelity appeared to be one of the most active buyers of securities from the deal. Investments

in the deal ended up in the Fidelity Investment Grade Bond Fund, Fidelity Inflation Protected Bond Fund, Fidelity Tactical Income Central Fund, Fidelity VIP Investment Grade Central Investment Portfolio, and so on.

229. *"Eager to scrape the X-rated mud":* Bruce Horovitz, "Ameriquest Places Super Bet," *USA Today,* Oct. 7, 2004.

229. *Progress for America Voter Fund:* Jeanne Cummings, "Republicans Tap Rich Donors to Form Group Targeting Kerry," *Wall Street Journal,* Aug. 25, 2004.

230. *National Mortgage News floated a story:* Paul Muolo, "Ameriquest Looks at IPO," *National Mortgage News,* Dec. 20, 2004.

230. *the third-largest IPO:* "The Biggest U.S. IPOs Ever," *BusinessWeek* online, http://images.businessweek.com/ss/06/10/us_ipos/index_01.htm.

13. The Investigators

231. *Ed Parker:* Multiple interviews with Ed Parker, former fraud investigation manager at Ameriquest; testimony by Parker and Ameriquest executives in *Parker v. Ameriquest,* American Arbitration Association, 2007; and Parker's June 9, 2008, deposition in *Ricci v. Ameriquest,* Hennepin County (Minn.) District Court, 2005.

In a written response to my questions, the company said, "Mr. Parker is not a credible source, according to an independent arbitrator who evaluated Mr. Parker's allegations against the Company." Parker did lose his wrongful dismissal claim against the company. The arbitrator wrote that Parker didn't prove the elements of his claim: "Virtually the only evidence pointing to discrimination by Ameriquest against him is his own unsubstantiated conclusory opinion." It should be noted, however, that the arbitrator didn't hear from other former Ameriquest employees who shared Parker's view that the company didn't aggressively move to stamp out fraud, and encouraged employees to do whatever it took to book loans. It should be noted, too, that the arbitrator also wrote: "One can agree that Mr. Parker was not treated as well by Ameriquest as he might have been, or should have been. He had been a good and trusted employee, and there is no criticism of his performance as a fraud investigator."

Besides, whether he was wrongfully fired or demoted didn't go to the heart of the issue that Parker's account in this book raises; it was hard for him to find a legal hook on which to hang claims that he was marginalized and that various personnel moves and reorganizations helped discourage aggressive investigation of fraud. Because California is an "at will" employment state, the arbitrator added, employees such as Parker could be "terminated at any given time for any ordinary reason." Parker's dismissal came in 2006 as Ameriquest was closing its branch offices across the nation and he was among the thousands of employees who were laid off. That made it hard to determine whether he had been fired in retaliation for his investigative work or simply as part of the bigger staff purge.

235. *"You're like a dog on a leash":* Interview with Kelly J. Dragna, who worked at Ameriquest from 2002 to 2006 as an internal auditor and fraud analyst, joining Ed Parker's team in 2005. For the fraudsters inside the company, Dragna said, it was a bit like driving seventy-five miles per hour in a sixty-five-mile-per-hour zone. Some might get pulled over and penalized, but most zoomed by without a care.

Managers preferred to look the other way. "There was never an attempt to send a message that they wouldn't tolerate this," Dragna said. "It was just: 'You get caught, you're on your own.' The company wasn't really totally opposed to the fraud. They were willing to tolerate it as long as you didn't get caught."

236. *Ameriquest's new and improved standards:* In a September 25, 2003, Ameriquest press release, several leaders in politics and community organizing praised the companies' updated "best practices." Sheila Bair, a former assistant secretary of the Treasury (and later head of the FDIC), called Ameriquest's revised list "the most progressive set of lender best practices I have ever seen. Three cheers for Ameriquest for leading the industry."

237. *"You can either make the sale or you can make the disclosure":* Interview with David Huey, assistant attorney general, Washington State.

239. *The two sides mingled before dinner:* The account of the dinner is based on interviews with David Huey, Chuck Cross, Prentiss Cox, Tom James, and Ben Diehl, an assistant attorney general of California. See also the transcript of the May 9, 2007, deposition of former ACC Capital chief executive Wayne Lee in *In Re: Ameriquest Mortgage Co. Mortgage Lending Practices Litigation,* U.S. District Court for the Northern District of Illinois, MDL No. 1715, Lead Case No. 05-cv-07097, pp. 95–96.

14. The Big Game

242. American Nightmare: Rich's book was published in the fall of 2004. It reflected his deep reporting—sifting through court records and knocking on doors in and around Pittsburgh—as well as his prescient analysis of how Wall Street was fueling abusive lending. See Rich Lord, *American Nightmare: Predatory Lending and the Foreclosure of the American Dream* (Monroe, Me.: Common Courage Press, 2004).

243. *dozens of lawsuits:* Following up on one of the cases in PACER, I talked to Nate McKitterick, the attorney for a woman from East Palo Alto, California, who was suing the company. She claimed that Ameriquest employees tricked her into signing a mortgage that required her to pay $2,494 a month, more than she was earning cleaning houses. All the negotiations were in Spanish, McKitterick said, but all the loan documents were in English—a language she could not speak or read. "The only thing she ever got from Ameriquest that was in Spanish was a foreclosure notice," he said. See Mike Hudson and E. Scott Reckard, "Workers Say Lender Ran 'Boiler Rooms,'" *Los Angeles Times,* Feb. 4, 2005, and *Landa v. Ameriquest,* U.S. District Court for the Northern District of California, 2003.

243. *"I couldn't live with myself":* Interview with Gilbert Stansell, who worked for just two months—May and June 2004—at Ameriquest's Grand Rapids branch. He said he was fired for lack of production.

243. *"We just couldn't take it":* Interview with Caleb Conklin, who worked for Ameriquest from October 2003 to August 2004 at its Grand Rapids branch. Conklin was part of the group that helped reopen the Grand Rapids office after Ed Parker had helped clean house there. "It just felt like it just wasn't right," Conklin said. "They're making us sell and sell, but we're not pitching good deals." The fees on Ameriquest's loans were twice what borrowers could have gotten at other lenders, Conklin said.

One of Conklin's coworkers at the branch was Jason DeBruler. During his eleven months at Ameriquest, DeBruler said, he realized that borrowers were "lied to all the way up to the day of closing as to what the closing costs were." He said management told loan officers to reveal only $1,500 of the closing costs, and to not mention the $3,000 to $5,000 most borrowers were charged in up-front points. He said inflated appraisals continued to be a problem at the Grand Rapids branch, long after the branch was shut down and reopened with a fresh staff. The branch would pay appraisers a bonus on top of their regular fee so long as they would "come in with the value that we need."

244. *Lawsuits in St. Louis and Alabama: Rednour et al. v. Ameriquest,* U.S. District Court for Eastern District of Missouri, 2004; *Powell et al. v. Ameriquest,* U.S. District Court for the Southern District of Alabama, 2004.

246. *"a couple may come out bad":* Rodrigo J. Alba, Ameriquest's vice president for federal and regulatory affairs, was quoted in David Feldheim, "Subprime Lenders Ameriquest Eyes Prime Mortgage Market," Dow Jones Newswires, Mar. 11, 2005.

246. *three women in Tampa:* E. Scott Reckard and Mike Hudson, "Doubt Is Cast on Loan Papers," *Los Angeles Times,* Mar. 28, 2005.

246. *more than $2.7 billion:* ACC Capital Holdings' "Consolidated Financial Statements" for the three years ending December 31, 2005.

247. *"As we reflect on the evolution of consumer credit":* Alan Greenspan, "Consumer Finance," remarks at the Fourth Annual Community Affairs Research Conference, Federal Reserve System, Washington, D.C., Apr. 8, 2005.

247. *"the impression that there were a lot":* Edmund L. Andrews, "Fed Shrugged as Subprime Crisis Spread," *New York Times,* Dec. 18, 2007.

248. *"He just wasn't interested":* Ibid.

249. *Other watchdog groups that had benefited:* Mike Hudson, "Ameriquest's Ties to Watchdog Groups Are Tested," *Los Angeles Times,* May 22, 2005.

250. *"six to eight times oversubscribed":* Grant Catton, "Ameriquest Unscathed by Legal Woes," *Asset Securitization Report,* Feb. 28, 2005.

250. *"replete with questionable loans":* Kathleen C. Engel and Patricia A. McCoy, "Turning a Blind Eye: Wall Street Finance of Predatory Lending," *Fordham Law Review* 75 (2007), p. 2041.

251. *"your heads are buried in cash":* Interview with Prentiss Cox. Subprime had become "more or less a pirate industry," he said. "It was just plunder and take everything you can today."

251. *the real culprits:* There was little doubt that professional fraudsters were targeting the mortgage industry, taking advantage of lenders' lax underwriting standards and the go-go exuberance of the housing boom. In Dayton, Ohio, for example, ABN Amro Mortgage Group Inc. reported that it lost $2 million after a convicted felon and other conspirators arranged as many as twenty-three mortgages in the names of dead people. Chip Burrus, assistant director of the FBI's criminal investigative division, noted that criminal gangs involved in drug dealing and other street crimes had branched into mortgage fraud. "It's more profitable and less risky," he said. See James R. Hagerty and Michael Hudson, "Town's Residents Say They Were Targets of Big Mortgage Fraud," *Wall Street Journal,* Sept. 28, 2006.

251. *"It is a serious, and sometimes criminal"*: Letter from Jonathan L. Kempner, president and CEO of the Mortgage Bankers Association, dated Apr. 1, 2005.

251. *Many borrowers had no idea:* Many of the mortgage professionals I interviewed said borrowers were, more often than not, unaware that information had been falsified to push their loans through. Scott Montilla, a former IndyMac mortgage underwriter in Arizona, confirmed to me that many borrowers were not aware that their stated incomes were being inflated during the application process: "A lot of times you talked to the customer and the customer said: 'I never told them I made that much.'" The case of Ben Butler, an eighty-year-old retiree in Savannah, Georgia, is instructive on this point. Butler secured a loan from IndyMac in 2005 to build a modular house. IndyMac approved the mortgage based on an application that said Butler made $3,825 a month in Social Security income. The only problem: the maximum Social Security benefit at the time was barely half that. Butler had no idea his income had been inflated by IndyMac or the mortgage broker who arranged the deal, his attorney maintained. Even if IndyMac wasn't the one that puffed up the dollar figure, the attorney said, it should have caught such an obvious lie. In a letter to IndyMac, the attorney argued that the income listed in his client's application paperwork "was not provided by Mr. Butler and was a complete fabrication by someone 'in the loop' so to speak. The mortgage broker and IndyMac are two of the persons/entities in that loop. . . . There is no amount of income filled in on the original application. Mr. Butler was never asked to state his income. Any prudent underwriter should have questioned the income considering the amount/source and required proof." See Mike Hudson, "IndyMac: What Went Wrong? How an 'Alt-A' Leader Fueled Its Growth with Unsound and Abusive Mortgage Lending," Center for Responsible Lending, June 30, 2008.

252. *"if the housing bubble burst"*: This is not an exercise in hindsight. Prentiss Cox said exactly that in telephone discussions with me in the second half of 2005, after he was free to talk generally about his concerns about the subprime market: "Ultimately, these pools are much more risky than the people who are investing in them think they are. These pools have been created almost completely in the context of an unprecedented rise in home values. Imagine what happens if the housing bubble bursts."

253. *It was far less than what Household:* For Roland Arnall, it was a relief to attach a dollar figure to his company's exposure. After spending years in a single-minded effort to build his fortune, Arnall was now spending more and more time trying to protect his wealth from those who wanted a piece of it. To reduce the tax bite from the IRS, he had poured much of his money—more than $1 billion—into oil and gas exploration, a venture that he hoped would be both a tax shelter and a new profit center. In the summer of 2005, Arnall also found himself fighting a battle closer to home. His first wife, Sally, had filed to reopen their divorce case, suggesting that he had cheated her out of tens of millions or even hundreds of millions of dollars. "I believe I was misled and that I received substantially less than my share of the financial empire we amassed during our marriage," she said in a court filing. For all his secrecy, he had been unable to hide his newfound wealth from his ex-wife. Sally said she had first learned how big Roland's business operations were when she

saw the November 2004 issue of *Forbes*, which placed his fortune at $2 billion. The case was settled on undisclosed terms. *In Re: Marriage of Arnall*, Los Angeles Superior Court, filed in 1996 and reopened in 2005; and Scott Reckard, "Ex-Wife of Loan Exec Asks for Probe," *Los Angeles Times*, Aug. 22, 2005.

254. *"Their words were not so much heard as acclaimed"*: Lawrence G. McDonald with Patrick Robinson, *A Colossal Failure of Common Sense: The Inside Story of the Collapse of Lehman Brothers* (New York: Crown Business, 2009). See especially pp. 106–13 and 125–38.

254. *McCarthy believed Dick Fuld:* Larry McCarthy told Reuters he quit Lehman after repeatedly warning that the firm was too leveraged on borrowed money and the real-estate market couldn't keep going up forever. For his part, Fuld denied that he had isolated himself from those who tried to warn him of the risks the company was taking on: "I left my office, I left my office plenty." Clare Baldwin, Jui Chakrovorty, and Jonathan Spicer, "Fuld Says Being 'Dumped On' for Lehman Failure," Reuters, Sept. 7, 2009.

255. *The firm that had barely survived:* Note that Lehman's fiscal year ran from December 1 through November 30.

255. *"I don't want you to tell me why we can't"*: McDonald's account of Gelband's unsuccessful efforts to get Lehman to pull back on its real-estate exposure is corroborated by reports in *New York* magazine and the *Observer* (London). *New York* reported that Gelband had pointedly told Fuld, "The world is changing. We have to rethink our business model." Fuld retorted that Gelband was too conservative. Steve Fishman, "Burning Down His House," *New York*, Dec. 8, 2008. The *Observer* quoted "Lehman insiders" who said Gelband railed against Lehman's investment in subprime lenders as well as the huge stake that Lehman bought in the United States's largest apartment company. Nick Mathiason, Heather Connon, and Richard Wachman, "Risky Business: Banking's Big Question, Why Didn't Anyone Stop Them?" *Observer*, Feb. 15, 2009. I tried to arrange an interview with Fuld through his attorney, Patricia Hynes. In an e-mail reply in 2009, she told me, "Mr. Fuld is not doing any interviews."

256. *"It was quite hard to stand in the way"*: Former Lehman executive Andrew Gowers was quoted in Mathiason, Connon, and Wachman, "Risky Business." Another former top Lehman executive told the *New York Times* that it was unrealistic to have expected Lehman and other Wall Street firms to exercise self-restraint: "From a policy perspective, the regulators have to step in. It would be an awful lot to ask the Street to not look for revenue opportunities where their competitors are finding revenue." Louise Story and Landon Thomas Jr., "Tales from Lehman's Crypt," *New York Times*, Sept. 12, 2009.

257. *"the SOBs knew how to get to me"*: E-mail interview with Irv Ackelsberg.

257. *Arnall's nomination process:* Transcript, "Hearing of the Senate Foreign Relations Committee," Federal News Service, Oct. 20, 2005. See also coverage by the Associated Press, *Washington Post*, *Los Angeles Times*, *Roll Call*, and other news outlets.

258. *By the time the committee held its first hearing:* Despite his conversion into one of the GOP's key money men, Arnall also enjoyed support from Democrats he had cultivated over the years. These included New Mexico governor Bill Richardson, a

2008 presidential hopeful. Richardson wrote that he could "attest to the strength of [Arnall's] personal convictions, his commitment to community and his deep love for our country." A spokesman said Richardson considered Arnall a friend and that Richardson "respects him for being a leader of a very large company." Tory Newmyer, "Arnall Secures Outside Help," *Roll Call*, Dec. 5, 2005; and Steve Terrell, "Roundhouse Roundup: Governor's Ameriquest Contacts in Question," *Santa Fe New Mexican*, May 18, 2006.

261. *the vote was deadlocked:* Connecticut senator Chris Dodd reluctantly joined his fellow Democrats in voting against Arnall. He considered Arnall a friend. "He did a fundraiser for me," Dodd explained. "I don't like voting against the man." Tory Newmyer, "Floor Fight Looms over Arnall Vote," *Roll Call*, Nov. 9, 2005.

263. *"We take great pride":* One critic of the nomination, consumer attorney Ira Rheingold, went on ABC's *Nightline* and denounced the Senate's vote as an insult to the borrowers who'd been defrauded by Arnall's company. "The notion that the person who owns that company would become a U.S. representative to a foreign country, really, is absolutely appalling to anybody who's watched Ameriquest's practices over the years." Rheinhold suspected he understood, though, why Arnall might want to seek the job: "I think he's got all the money in the world he could possibly want. And I think what he's looking for . . . is legitimacy. He's looking for recognition. And I think it's sort of the icing. You know, money can buy you an awful lot. And, you know . . . being called Mr. Ambassador is a pretty cool thing, I guess. And when you own everything else, why not?"

A *Nightline* correspondent also talked to Wade Henderson, the director of the Leadership Conference on Civil Rights and one of Arnall's biggest supporters. "Have you ever seen any of Ameriquest's paperwork?" she asked. "'Cause I have some here to show you if you haven't."

"I've seen some of it," Henderson answered. "I'm disappointed, I'm profoundly disappointed, that some of these practices that have now come to light would be associated with Ameriquest. Because the company that I know, the company that I had thought achieved a pretty substantial status, as a company engaged in fair practices, had somehow slipped and fallen and run afoul of existing practices. And I think that's terrible. And, yes, I do believe it should be addressed. But at the end of the day, I'll stand by the fact that I think Roland Arnall is a man of integrity." ABC News, "Dutch Treat? Just Dessert?" *Nightline*, Jan. 24, 2006.

263. *In Massachusetts, Deval Patrick was fighting:* Coverage in the *Boston Globe* and *Boston Herald*, especially Frank Phillips, "Patrick Tied to Company Under Fire," *Boston Globe*, Apr. 20, 2005; and Dave Wedge and Kimberly Atkins, "Deval Denies Lobbying Obama for Envoy," *Boston Herald*, Oct. 21, 2006.

15. Collapse

264. *George and Evelyn Lee:* Interviews with Evelyn Lee and with her attorney, Sharon Withers, as well as the Lees' loan documents and filings in *Lee v. Wolverine Builder LLC et al.*, Tenth Circuit Court of Michigan, 2007. The case was settled on undisclosed terms.

265. *the subject of twenty-five complaints:* Michigan regulators dismissed some of the

complaints, but as of mid-2007 the state had upheld eight of them and referred others for investigation. Real Financial's attorney said the allegations stemmed from an unfavorable economy that had sparked rising foreclosures as well as unjustified complaints against lenders and brokers. Lehman said it only checked to see whether brokers were licensed in their states, not whether the licensing agencies had received complaints about them. Lehman said it removed Real Financial from its broker list after Evelyn Lee filed her lawsuit. See Michael Hudson, "Lending a Hand: How Wall Street Stoked the Mortgage Meltdown; Lehman and Others Transformed the Market for Riskiest Borrowers," *Wall Street Journal*, June 27, 2007.

266. *"stormed out of a meeting"*: Operative Plasterers and Cement Masons International Association Local 262 Annuity Fund v. Richard S. Fuld et al., U.S. District Court for the Southern District of New York, 2008, pp. 57–58 and 72–73.

267. *First Magnus*: Local coverage, including Christie Smythe, "Gov't Report Slams 1st Magnus," *Arizona Daily Star*, Aug. 9, 2008; Gabriela Rico and Josh Brodesky, "First Magnus Executives Are Sued for $1 Billion," *Arizona Daily Star*, Feb. 27, 2009; Josh Brodesky, "Suit Says First Magnus Officers Fueled Crisis," *Arizona Daily Star*, Feb. 28, 2009; and Joe Pangburn, "$1 Billion Lawsuit: First Magnus Wasn't a Victim: It Caused Credit Crisis," *Inside Tucson Business*, Mar. 6, 2009. See also *Romero v. First Magnus*, U.S. District Court for the Northern District of California, 2007.

268. *"I'm standing in the middle of a cornfield"*: Interviews with Steven Jernigan, who worked as a senior fraud analyst at Argent from May 2005 to December 2006.

269. *a con man named Robert Andrew Penn*: See James R. Hagerty and Michael Hudson, "Town's Residents Say They Were Targets of Big Mortgage Fraud," *Wall Street Journal*, Sept. 28, 2006; and Erika D. Smith, Madhusmita Bora, and J. K. Wall, "Red Flags Preceded Home-Fraud Lawsuit," *Indianapolis Star*, Oct. 1, 2006. Penn pleaded guilty to three felonies and was sentenced to seven years in prison. Details of his scheme are described in an October 7, 2009, document, "Stipulated Factual Basis," signed by Penn, his attorney, and the prosecutor. See *USA v. Penn*, U.S. District Court for the Southern District of Indiana, 2009, Case No. 1:09-CR-114-01-DFH-KPF.

269. *"You've got to stop"*: In a written response, an ACC Capital spokesman did not specifically respond to my questions about whether Steve Jernigan had been instructed to back off on investigating higher-ups within Argent who turned a "blind eye" to fraud. The spokesman said: "The company terminated Steve Jernigan for cause, and we also do not believe he is a credible source for your book." As for the Robert Penn case, the spokesman said that "Argent aggressively pursued its criminal and civil options against the individuals and corporations who perpetrated this fraud. . . . Argent repurchased every loan that was identified as problematic—more than two hundred loans in all." In the wake of the Penn case, the spokesman said, Argent significantly increased its fraud detection efforts.

270. *"It's just like somebody flipped a switch"*: James R. Hagerty and Michael Corkery, "After the Boom: Housing Slump Proves Painful for Some Owners and Builders," *Wall Street Journal*, Aug. 23, 2006.

272. *"a call by a rich man"*: David A. Mittell, "Anatomy of a Telephone Call, from One Rich Guy to Another," *Patriot Ledger*, Mar. 17, 2007.

273. *"the alter ego"*: Borrowers' First Amended Consolidated Class Action Complaint, filed June 18, 2007, in *In Re: Ameriquest Mortgage Co. Mortgage Lending Practices Litigation*, U.S. District Court for the Northern District of Illinois, MDL No. 1715, Lead Case No. 05-cv-07097.

274. *Wayne Lee: Lee v. Ameriquest*, Orange County Superior Court, 2007, as well as Lee's May 9, 2007, deposition in *In Re: Ameriquest Mortgage Co. Mortgage Practices Litigation*.

278. *"We all saw the mortgage stars"*: Andrew Galvin, "Is There a Backlash Against Former Mortgage Workers?" *Orange County Register*, Feb. 12, 2008.

278. *Other communities in California*: "Priest Aims to Save Flock from Foreclosure," Associated Press, Aug. 5, 2009.

279. *Ameriquest and Argent accounted for*: Based on data compiled by the U.S. Office of the Comptroller of the Currency; letter from John C. Dugan, Comptroller of the Currency, to Elizabeth Warren, chair, Congressional Oversight Panel, Feb. 12, 2009.

In the letter, the OCC reported that as of early 2009 the ten worst foreclosure zones in the United States were (1) Detroit (with 22.9 percent of subprime and Alt-A loans made between 2005 and 2007 in foreclosure); (2) Cleveland (21.6 percent); (3) Stockton, California (21.5 percent), (4) Sacramento (18 percent); (5) Riverside–San Bernardino, California (16.1 percent); (6) Memphis (15.6 percent); (7) Miami–Fort Lauderdale (14.3 percent); (8) Bakersfield, California (14.3 percent); (9) Denver (14 percent); and (10) Las Vegas (13.9 percent).

In those ten zones, the following ten lenders had the highest foreclosure totals for loans made between 2005 and 2007: (1) Ameriquest/Argent (with 14,854 subprime and Alt-A loan foreclosures); (2) New Century (14,120); (3) Long Beach (11,736); (4) WMC (10,283); (5) Fremont (8,635); (6) Option One (8,334); (7) First Franklin (8,037); (8) Countrywide (4,736); (9) Resmae (3,558); and (10) American Home (2,954). In looking at the lenders with the most foreclosures in the ten zones, the OCC ranked Argent and Ameriquest separately, which would plant Argent third on its list (with 10,728 foreclosures) and Ameriquest ninth (with 4,126). But because these companies were owned by the same man and run under the same corporate flag, ACC Capital, I recalculated the rankings by combining Argent's and Ameriquest's numbers. Of the top six companies on the list, the only one not based in Orange County was WMC Mortgage, which was headquartered just down the highway in San Diego. No. 9, Resmae, also an Orange County company, was founded by former executives who had worked under Roland Arnall at Long Beach Mortgage. Other Orange County lenders that landed farther down the list included No. 16, People's Choice (with 1,783 foreclosures), and No. 17, BNC (1,769), Lehman's subprime mortgage lending unit.

These figures are a snapshot of the toll of subprime lending, but they don't show the full force of its devastation; they don't include foreclosures on loans made in the earlier boom years (2002–2004) and they don't reflect foreclosures that have been filed since early 2009 on any 2005–2007 loans. Using data only for loans made from 2005 to 2007, in particular, understates the foreclosure rates among Ameriquest borrowers since the lender drastically reduced its loan volume in 2006 and 2007 as a result of the limitations put on it by its settlement with state authorities.

279. *Implode-O-Meter:* By the start of 2010, the number of imploded lenders listed on the site had reached 374. See http://ml-implode.com/.

279. *Mozilo's home-loan giant had been done in:* Defending the company's practices, a Countrywide spokesman, Rick Simon, said, "No one . . . could have foreseen the unprecedented combination of events that led to the problems borrowers, lenders and investors face with many of these loans today." Gretchen Morgenson and Geraldine Fabrikant, "Countrywide's Chief Salesman and Defender," *New York Times,* Nov. 11, 2007.

280. *Countrywide did little to pull back:* See especially Paul Muolo and Mathew Padilla, *Chain of Blame: How Wall Street Caused the Mortgage and Credit Crisis* (Hoboken, N.J.: John Wiley & Sons, 2008), p. 303; E. Scott Reckard, "Is Angelo Mozilo a Villain or Just Vilified?" *Los Angeles Times,* Aug. 30, 2009; and E. Scott Reckard and Jim Puzzanghera, "Countrywide's Angelo Mozilo Is Target of Federal Lawsuit," *Los Angeles Times,* June 5, 2009.

281. *Lehman wasn't as secure as it claimed:* This account of Lehman's failure and the global meltdown is based on coverage by Bloomberg News, the *Guardian* (London), the *Times* (London), the *New York Times,* and the *Wall Street Journal,* and in particular Carrick Mollenkamp, Susanne Craig, Jeffrey McCracken, and Jon Hilsenrath, "The Two Faces of Lehman's Fall: Private Talks of Raising Capital Belied the Firm's Public Optimism," *Wall Street Journal,* Oct. 6, 2008.

282. *"There is no way a person like me":* Mark Pittman and Bob Ivry, "London Suicide Connects Lehman Lesson Missed by Hong Kong Woman," Bloomberg News, Sept. 10, 2009.

282. *"Everything was refocused on loan volume":* Pierre Thomas and Lauren Pearle, "WaMu Insiders Claim Execs Ignored Warnings, Encouraged Reckless Lending," ABC News, Oct. 13, 2008.

282. *The mortgage meltdown was a ticklish subject:* John R. Emshwiller, "A Top Obama Fund-Raiser Had Ties to Failed Bank," *Wall Street Journal,* July 21, 2008; and David Saltonstall, "Key McCain Advisors Were Lobbyists for Shady Lender," New York *Daily News,* Mar. 31, 2008.

283. *Community Reinvestment Act, Fannie Mae, and Freddie Mac:* Ronald Campbell, "Most Subprime Lenders Weren't Subject to Federal Lending Law," *Orange County Register,* Nov. 16, 2008; and Zachary A. Goldfarb, "Fannie, Freddie Become Hot Topic in Campaign," *Washington Post,* Oct. 9, 2008.

283. *"You're becoming irrelevant":* Charles Duhigg, "Pressured to Take More Risks, Fannie Reached Tipping Point," *New York Times,* Oct. 4, 2008. In late 2008, in the wake of Lehman Brothers' bankruptcy, Republicans on the U.S. House Committee on Oversight and Government Reform issued a report that managed to get Fannie Mae and Freddie Mac's role exactly backward. "Lehman Brothers didn't cause this mess but it certainly jumped head first into trying to make money on securitizing mortgage-backed instruments. They followed on the heels of Fannie Mae and

Freddie Mac and for precisely the same reasons. If we understand the initial cause of the cancer at Fannie and Freddie, then we can understand how it metastasized to Lehman Brothers, Wachovia, Countrywide and beyond." Lehman had been a leader in the market for subprime loans long before Fannie and Freddie followed Wall Street into subprime. From 1996 to 2006, in every year except 2001, Lehman ranked first or second on the list of top underwriters of subprime mortgage–backed securities, according to *Inside Mortgage Finance*.

As CNBC correspondent David Faber has written: "Wall Street rushed into the vacuum created by the *absence* of Fannie and Freddie in 2003–2005." Under pressure from Congress and federal regulators in the wake of accounting scandals, "Fannie and Freddie retreated from the market they had dominated for the past twenty years. They began to buy fewer mortgages in a period where people were buying and refinancing more homes than ever before." As a result, Fannie and Freddie's share of the secondary mortgage market dropped from 70 percent in 2003 to just 30 percent in 2006. See David Faber, *And Then the Roof Caved In* (Hoboken, N.J.: John Wiley & Sons, 2009), pp. 63–66.

285. *Mark Glover: Glover v. Citibank et al.*, Los Angeles Superior Court, 2007. Glover could not say how much he reaped from the settlement of his lawsuit against Ameriquest, but court papers noted that he had won "a sizable settlement from a legal suit." His case against Citibank was later transferred out of court to arbitration.

285. *Christopher Warren:* "Affidavit of Christopher S. Fitzpatrick in Support of Arrest Warrant and Criminal Complaint," Feb. 4, 2004, filed in *USA v. Warren*, U.S. District Court for the Eastern District of California, Case # 2:09-mj-00046-KJM-1. Warren's personal statement, "Restoring International Confidence in American MBS/CMBS/ABS Investment System," is attached to the affidavit. See also Denny Walsh and Sam Stanton, "Jet-setter Fugitive Seized at Border," *Sacramento Bee*, Feb. 12, 2009; Joe Friesen, "How a Mortgage Fraudster's Jet-set Life Proved to Be His Downfall," *Globe and Mail* (Toronto), Feb. 13, 2009.

287. *a reporter from Reuters:* Clare Baldwin, Jui Chakrovorty, and Jonathan Spicer, "Fuld Says Being 'Dumped On' for Lehman Failure," Reuters, Sept. 7, 2009.

288. *"the worst example of fraud":* San Mateo County Investment Pool v. Fuld et al., San Francisco Superior Court, 2008.

289. *Alan Greenspan:* Leon Gettler, "Greenspan Lifts Lid on Case of Mistaken Identity," *The Age*, Feb. 11, 2008, and Allan Sloan, "Why the Fed Has Lost Its Mojo," *Fortune*, Jan. 21, 2008.

Epilogue: Ashes

292. *Pink Palace compound:* See, for example, Ruth Ryon, "Hot Property" column, *Los Angeles Times*, Sept. 29, 2002, and Dec. 29, 2002.

292. *Mandalay Ranch:* Adam Preskill, "Aspen Ranch Sells for $46 Million," *Rocky Mountain News*, Feb. 4, 2004.

293. *upheld the judge's ruling: Ozenne v. Chase et al.*, Fourth District California Court of Appeals. No. E033043, Nov. 14, 2003.

294. *Arnall claimed he'd been the victim:* Details of the Arnalls' dispute with Richard Siegal come from various documents filed in *RoDa Drilling Company et al. v. Richard*

Siegal et al., U.S. District Court for the Northern District of Oklahoma, 2007, including the July 19, 2007, complaint and Dawn Arnall's June 9, 2008, testimony.

296. *Roland Arnall's death:* Obituaries in various news outlets, in particular Stephen Miller, "Roland Arnall (1939–2008): Subprime Pioneer Turned to Diplomacy, Philanthropy," *Wall Street Journal*, Mar. 22, 2008.

296. *memorial service:* E-mail exchange with Terry Rouch, as well as Paul Muolo and Mathew Padilla, *Chain of Blame: How Wall Street Caused the Mortgage and Credit Crisis* (Hoboken, N.J.: John Wiley & Sons, 2008), p. 308.

297. *Claude Arnall:* "Safe Harbor Application" filed by Claude Arnall, Sept. 18, 2008, in *In Re: The Roland and Dawn Arnall Living Trust*, Los Angeles Superior Court; and John Gittelsohn, "Brother: Ameriquest Founder Stiffed Me on $47 Million," *Orange County Register*, Jan. 16, 2009.

299. *In 2009, ACORN founder:* Wade Rathke, *Citizen Wealth: Winning the Campaign to Save Working Families* (San Francisco: Berrett-Koehler Publishers, 2009), pp. 32–40.

299. *he experienced a transformation:* Travis Paules wasn't the only former Ameriquest salesman who made a change in his life. Mark Bomchill had turned whistle-blower in our February 2005 exposé in the *Los Angeles Times*, condemning the company's boiler-room tactics and recalling the manager who stalked between the loan officers' cubicles like "a little Hitler." After the story ran, he provided testimony in court cases and continued to speak to the media about the company's practices. "I feel bad that I was part of this. I feel like I was one of the Enron people who ripped off the little guy," Bomchill told National Public Radio. "A lot of Ameriquest customers were not educated. They were vulnerable to this kind of deception. They were trusting. And because of that, they lost a lot." See Chris Arnold, "Former Ameriquest Workers Tell of Deception," *Morning Edition*, National Public Radio, May 14, 2007.

300. *Bank of America case: Pope v. Bank of America*, U.S. District Court for the Southern District of Mississippi, 2004. The lawsuit called EquiCredit, Bank of America's former subprime lending subsidiary, "a notorious lender" that had used "a network of corrupt contractors, real estate brokers, mortgage loan brokers, appraisers and settlement agents" to fund home loans "that were shockingly unfair and abusive." The lawsuit alleged that Clara Pope, a sixty-seven-year-old widow who suffered from diabetes and other serious health problems, had been stuck with an EquiCredit mortgage she'd had no hope of repaying. The suit also raised the question of whether her signature had been forged on the paperwork. The case was settled in late 2004 on undisclosed terms. Don Barrett, another one of the Mississippi litigators on the Lehman case, served as Canavan's cocounsel in the case.

300. *"built like a house of cards":* In Re: First Alliance Mortgage Co., 471 F.3d 977 (9th Cir. 2006).

301. *Prentiss Cox:* Prentiss Cox, "The Proposed Consumer Financial Protection Agency: Implications for Consumers and the FTC," testimony before the U.S. House Committee on Energy and Commerce, July 8, 2009. The main problem, Cox said during his testimony, was that the nation's regulatory system was "thoroughly dominated" by the thinking and needs of lenders and their allies rather than the needs of average consumers and home owners.

301. *"The legal system, in a word, sucks"*: Interview with Brian Chisick.
302. *"We're rebuilding the same system"*: Interview with Roy Barnes.
302. *Carolyn Pittman:* Interviews with Carolyn Pittman and her attorney, Lynn Drysdale of Jacksonville Area Legal Aid; Caren Burmeister, "Beaches Woman Caught in a Foreclosure Cycle," *Florida Times-Union*, Sept. 22, 2007; and "Defendants Motion to Strike Count I, Answer, Amended Affirmative Defenses, Amended Counterclaims and Demand for Jury Trial," *Deutsche Bank v. Pittman*, Duval County (Fla.) Circuit Court, 2007. Unlike many beleaguered home owners, Pittman was fortunate to find attorneys to help her fight to save her home. Jacksonville Area Legal Aid, a not-for-profit legal clinic that has gained a national reputation as an anti-foreclosure campaigner, took up her cause and stuck with her for years. A report from New York University Law School's Brennan Center for Justice found that many home owners were losing their homes because they lacked legal representation. Nonprofit legal aid clinics had been "besieged with requests for foreclosure assistance." In Connecticut, more than 60 percent of home owners facing foreclosure in 2007–2008 did not have counsel. In Staten Island, New York, 91 percent of foreclosures on subprime or "non-traditional" mortgages "proceeded without full legal representation" for the home owners. See Melanca Clark with Maggie Barron, "Foreclosures: A Crisis in Legal Representation," Brennan Center for Justice, Nov. 6, 2009; and Alex Ulam, "Stacked Deck Against Homeowners," *The Nation*, Dec. 22, 2009.

Author's Note and Acknowledgments

This is a book of investigative reporting. I brought no special skills in financial analysis to this project. What I brought mainly was a willingness to read reports and court documents and pick up the phone and ask people to talk to me about things that, for many, were painful or incriminating. I read hundreds of lawsuits, read thousands of pages of court transcripts, and interviewed hundreds of people over the past five years. Virtually all of the key sources for this book spoke to me on the record. Their names are indicated in the text or in the source notes. The accounts of some come from court transcripts or other official documents. A few spoke to me on a not-for-attribution basis. I've tried to identify them by indicating where they worked and what kind of job they were doing during the time they described.

I was heartened by the number of former industry insiders who felt compelled to tell what they knew about the bad practices in the mortgage business. A few merit special notice. They include Mark Glover, Stephen Kuhn, Travis Paules, and Greg Walling. They were willing to talk frankly about their years in the industry and about things they'd done that they regretted, in large part because they wanted to set things right.

Other folks who provided substantial help in my reporting include Terry Rouch, Angie Moreschi, Melissa Huelsman, Bill Brennan, Howard Rothbloom, Mark Adelson, John Dewey, Kathleen Engel, Gregory Burke, Patricia McCoy, Kevin Stein, Larry Gabriel, Dan Immergluck,

Lynn Drysdale, David Humphreys, Sheila Canavan, Josh Zinner, Jude Lopez, Chris Peterson, Dennis Rivelli, Ira Rheingold, Prentiss Cox, Tom James, Chuck Cross, and Chris Carpenter. One person who deserves special thanks is Bob Labrador, the former treasurer at Long Beach Savings and Loan. When I first called Bob, he was skeptical. He asked lots of questions about who I was and what I was doing. After he was satisfied I had done my homework, he became a supporter of my work. He put me in touch with former colleagues and drove me around Orange County, giving me a tour of the landscape of the county's subprime lending industry. His help was crucial to my understanding of Roland Arnall's early years as a developer and lender. Another former Long Beach executive who was a big help was Mark Schuerman. He, too, talked to me for hours, answering question after question without complaint. I should add, though, that neither Bob nor Mark necessarily agrees with all of the conclusions that I reach in this book and shouldn't be held responsible for what I've written. The same holds for all the other people who helped me piece together this story.

I drew on many publications in weaving together this narrative. Two deserve special mention: *Mortgage Lender Implode-O-Meter* and *Inside Mortgage Finance. IMF* is a rich and definitive source of data on the mortgage industry. Unless otherwise noted, mortgage volume data quoted in this book for the subprime industry or specific lenders come from *IMF*'s reports.

✳ ✳ ✳

I've spent the better part of two decades investigating predatory lending. I began reporting on the subject in 1992, thanks to a fellowship from the Alicia Patterson Foundation, an organization that supports in-depth journalism. APF's director, Margaret Engel, provided advice and encouragement. Katherine Boo, then an editor at *Washington Monthly*, helped me develop my first piece on lending abuses, "Stealing Home," which appeared in the magazine's June 1992 issue. *Southern Exposure* was a home for my reporting on the subject over a period of ten years; Eric Bates, Bob Hall, and Chris Kromm and others at *SE* were willing to edit and publish long cover packages about businesses that market to disadvantaged consumers. I was project editor and coauthor of a package of stories in the magazine's Summer 2003 issue titled, "Poverty, Inc." A decade later, I called Gary Ashwill, the magazine's managing editor, and pitched him a story about Citigroup's role in the subprime market. I'd struck out with other publications, because they weren't interested in the story or because they didn't want to invest the space to tell the story with the depth that I believe the story required. Gary said they would take it as a cover story. When I asked, "How much space can we have?," he gave an answer that is rarely heard in modern American journalism: "How much space do we need?" The magazine devoted forty-eight pages in its Fall 2003 issue to "Banking on Misery," a package of articles about Citigroup and other businesses that target poor and minority consumers.

Greg Bates of Common Courage Press encouraged me to put together my first book on the subject, *Merchants of Misery: How Corporate America Profits from Poverty* (Monroe, Me.: Common Courage Press, 1996). The book was a collection of my writings as well as pieces by Penny Loeb, Eric Rorer, Bill Minutaglio, Rita Jensen, Alix Freedman, Kim Nauer, Martha Brannigan, Adam Feuerstein, and others.

At the *Los Angeles Times*, I had the pleasure of working with a group of top-notch editors. Deborah Nelson and Rick Wartzman saw the potential in my reporting on Ameriquest, and John Corrigan oversaw the investigation and edited the stories with tough love. *Times* staff writer Scott Reckard was a great reporting partner. He's a tireless worker, a fine reporter, and an all-round good guy. Many passages in this book are built on the reporting that Scott and I did together.

At the *Wall Street Journal*, where I worked in 2006 and 2007, a number of colleagues supported my efforts to report on abuses in the subprime market, including Sue Craig, Susan Pulliam, Mike Siconolfi, Bob Hagerty, Alix Freedman, and Nik Deogan. Others at the *Journal* provided support as I tried to learn the ins and outs of Wall Street, including Serena Ng, Greg Zuckerman, Karen Richardson, Shefali Anand, Kate Kelly, Jesse Drucker, and Joanna Slater.

This book was independent of my work at the Center for Responsible Lending, where I earned my paycheck as a researcher from late 2007 through the spring of 2010. Nothing in it should be automatically deemed to reflect the views and policies of CRL, and it was not vetted or approved by anyone in a position of authority at the center. That said, my work with the smart and dedicated people at CRL greatly benefited my understanding of how mortgage markets work and of the problems of average consumers. CRL is a nonprofit policy and research outfit headquartered in Durham, North Carolina. I went to work for CRL because I needed a job and because CRL was an organization that had gotten it right. While industry groups touted the benefits of subprime and news organizations for the most part downplayed the problems in the industry, CRL was doing well-documented research that exposed the dicey practices in the subprime business and accurately predicted a coming wave of foreclosures. Once I got to CRL, Jim Overton and I worked together on research projects focusing on Countrywide Financial, IndyMac Bank, and the Office of Thrift Supervision. Jim proved to be a dogged, kind, and perceptive collaborator. Eric Stein, a superb editor, thoughtful colleague, and first-rate boss, oversaw much of my work. Many others provided encouragement and enlightenment: Martin Eakes, Keith Corbett, Mary Moore, Kathleen Day, Mike Calhoun, Aracely Panameño, Keith Ernst, Wei Li, Sam Rogers, Ellen Schloemer, Eric Halperin, Caryn Becker, Lisa Pittman, Daniel Mosteller, Sharon Reuss, Sara Weed, Evan Fuguet, Paul Leonard, Chris Kukla, Ellen Harnick, Nina Simon, Romy Parzik, Toni van Rijssen, and many more.

I also want to thank the folks at the Center for Public Integrity, where I now work as a staff writer. They include Bill Buzenberg, Gordon Witkin, Julie Vorman, Brian Grow, and many others. The Center is one of the oldest and most respected of the nonprofit journalism operations, and I'm honored to be part of that tradition.

I also want to thank friends and colleagues who have supported me. They include Barry Yeoman, Mary Kane, Jeff Bailey, Richard Ziglar, Dean Starkman, James Scurlock, Bob Manning, Stephanie Mencimer, Ron Nixon, Jim Campen, Christine Richard, Roland Lazenby, Jim Morris, Taylor Loyal, Rex Bowman, Brian O'Neill, Dan Casey, Neal Thompson, Beth Macy, Doug Pardue, and Mary Bishop.

I especially want to express gratitude to the folks who read all or parts of my manuscript and offered insightful comments: Biz Mitchell,

Alyssa Katz, Kurt Eggert, Kevin Byers, Kathleen Keest, and Ellis Levine. Their help was immeasurable. They are not, however, responsible for errors, faulty logic, or grammatical transgressions that turn up in the text. Those are all owned by me. I also thank Grace O. Smith for her research assistance.

✦ ✦ ✦

Many thanks should go to my agent, Sam Stoloff, who believed in this project and found it a home at Times Books. Credit must go also to the many fine folks at Times Books. They include Robin Dennis, who shaped and polished the narrative in ways big and small, and Emi Ikkanda and Paul Golob, who shepherded it across the finish line.

Finally, I want to send thanks and love to my family, which supported me—and put up with me—as I worked on this book. My son, Ben Hudson, my mom, Gail Hudson, my wife, Darcey Steinke, and Darcey's daughter, Abbie Hornburg, all helped me and inspired me to keep working and finish this book. I couldn't have done it without them.

INDEX

Los Angeles Business Journal, 221
Los Angeles Times, 140, 243, 251, 279–80, 296
   exposé on Ameriquest, 243–48
Lugar, Richard, 258, 259, 261

Madonna, Frederick, 194
mail fraud, 36
Maloney, Carolyn, 146
marijuana, 161
Maryland, 159, 162
Massachusetts, 263, 271, 272
MassMutual, 6
Maxed Out (documentary), 242
Mayer, Martin, 18
McCain, John, 43, 282–83
McCarthy, Larry, 254, 255
McCartney, Paul, 245
McConnell, J. Knox, 75–76, 132–35
McDonald, Lawrence G., 253–55
McKinzie, Janet Faye, 35, 38–39
media, 59–60, 107, 143, 180, 200, 229, 230, 235, 242–43, 253, 283, 286
   on Lehman/FAMCO relationship, 136–38, 185, 192
   Los Angeles Times exposé on Ameriquest, 243–48
   on Starr case, 59–60, 67
   on Wall Street links to subprime industry, 136–38, 202
   See also specific publications and televisions shows
Melgar, Daniel, 75–76, 134–36
Memphis, 278
Mercury Finance, 94–95
Merrill Lynch, 140, 226, 227
Miami, 83, 278
Michigan, 8, 9, 206, 232, 243, 264
Milken, Michael, 28, 30, 41, 44–45, 53, 90
   junk bond scheme, 41, 44–45
Miller, Brad, 215

Miller, Tom, 172–73
Minneapolis, 8, 102
Minnesota, 99–102, 112, 115, 127, 168, 170, 185, 192, 224–25, 236, 299, 301
Minnesota Subprime Borrower Relief Act, 299–300
Missouri, 153, 154, 244
money laundering, 132
Money Store, The, 74, 81, 193
Monster, the, 104–5, 106, 112, 117, 191, 195, 206, 302
Moody's Investors Service, 150, 151, 180, 181, 227–28
Morgan Stanley, 6, 215
mortgage-backed securities, 6–7, 9, 26–28, 46, 86, 92, 125–26, 227–28
   of early 2000s, 136–46, 150–52, 169–75, 179–81, 182–98, 209–11, 214–17
   FAMCO, 81–84, 128–41, 182–98
   FAMCO fraud trial and, 182–98
   of mid-2000s, 218–21, 226–28, 247, 249–56, 264–76
   of 1990s, 46, 56, 71–86, 120–36, 216
Mortgage Bankers Association, 52, 90, 91, 251
Mortgage Lender Implode-O-Meter, 279
Mozilo, Angelo, 11, 96, 211–12, 270, 279–80, 283, 300
Mudd, Daniel, 283
Muolo, Paul, 212, 280

NASCAR, 221
National Association of Mortgage Brokers, 215
National Association of Neighborhoods, 93, 258
National City Bank, 167
National City Mortgage, 167
National Fair Housing Alliance, 93, 248, 258
National Home Equity Mortgage Association, 173

Scurlock, James, 242
Seattle, 83
second mortgages, 15, 21–25, 68, 83, 279
 Long Beach Savings, 15, 25–28, 31
 "piggyback," 279
Securities and Exchange Commission
   (SEC), 40–41, 46
securitization, 26–28, 313, 45, 56, 75–76,
   92, 125–26, 227–28, 249–50
 CDOs, 151–52
 of early 2000s, 136–46, 150–52, 169–75,
   179–81, 182–98, 209–11, 214–17
 FAMCO, 81–84, 128–41, 182–98
 FAMCO fraud trial and, 182–98
 Keystone Bank, 75–76, 133–36
 of mid-2000s, 218–21, 226–28, 247,
   249–56, 264–76
 of 1990s, 46, 56, 71–86, 120–36, 216
 ratings, 179–82, 227–28
"Seven Dwarfs," 56–60
sex, 158
 Ameriquest politics and, 204–6
 for loans, 204
sexism, 160, 202, 204–6, 220–21
sexual harassment, 202, 205, 209, 220
 lawsuits, 220
Seymour, Michelle, 8–9
Shea, Mike, 249
Shearson Lehman Mortgage, 128
shopping malls, 13, 19, 20, 37
Shriver, Maria, 291
Siegal, Richard, 293–95
Simmons, Pamela, 90
60 Minutes, 60, 137, 176, 288
Smith, Dorothy, 166
Smith, Jeff, 128
Smith, Shanna, 248, 258
Smith Barney, 284, 298
Snyder, Art, 16–17
Social Security, 6, 8, 62, 89, 90, 223, 225,
   268
spam, mortgage, 199–201

Spitzer, Eliot, 212
sports marketing, 203, 213, 221–22, 224,
   228–29, 245
Standard and Poor's, 179, 180, 181, 228
Standard Pacific, 118
Starr, Lillie Mae, 58–60
"stated income" loans, 53
Stein, Ben, 41
Steinbock, Phillip, 184, 194–95
Steinbock and Hofmann, 183, 184, 192
"straw buyers," 268
strippers, 123–24
"subordinated debentures," 41–42
subprime mortgage loans, 1–12, 32
 Ameriquest, 1–12, 94–98, 118–25,
   142–45, 147–64, 177–78, 181,
   199–209, 212, 213, 217, 221–30,
   231–36, 242–63, 264–76
 Argent, 213–14, 267–69
 Bush administration and, 146, 150,
   165–81, 257–58, 282
 CDOs, 151–52
 collapse of industry, 270–89
 Countrywide, 211–12
 delinquencies, 150–51
 of early 2000s, 136–46, 147–64, 165–81,
   182–98, 199–217
 escrow accounts, 5
 falsified paperwork, 3–4, 6, 8–9, 49,
   646, 97, 108–12, 119, 122–23, 126,
   134, 135, 157, 158–59, 163, 184,
   188–89, 207–8, 218–21, 223, 232–39,
   246–49, 251, 267–68, 285, 298
 FAMCO, 81–86, 101–17, 128–41,
   182–98
 FAMCO fraud trial, 192–98
 Fleet Finance, 56–60
 forerunners of, 22–25
 House Financial Services Committee
   hearings on, 214–17
 IPOs, 94–95
 Keystone, 133–36

About the Author

MICHAEL W. HUDSON is a staff writer at the Center for Public Integrity, a nonprofit journalism organization. He previously worked as a reporter for the *Wall Street Journal* and as an investigator for the Center for Responsible Lending. The winner of a George Polk Award, Hudson has also written for *Forbes*, *The Big Money*, the *New York Times*, the *Los Angeles Times*, and *Mother Jones*. He edited the award-winning book *Merchants of Misery* and appeared in the documentary film *Maxed Out*. He lives in Brooklyn, New York.